NORMANDY
CRUCIBLE

The Decisive Battle That Shaped
World War II in Europe

JOHN PRADOS

AMBERLEY

This edition first published 2019

Amberley Publishing
The Hill, Stroud
Gloucestershire, GL5 4EP

www.amberley-books.com

British Library Cataloguing in Publication Data.
A catalogue record for this book is available from the British Library.

ISBN 978 1 4456 7883 2 (print)
ISBN 978 1 4456 7884 9 (ebook)

Maps by Jason Petho
Set in Electra
Designed by Ginger Legato
Printed in the UK

To World War II veterans everywhere

CONTENTS

MAPS

INTRODUCTION

S ome years ago I published a book, *Combined Fleet Decoded*, that reexamined the Pacific theater of World War II through the lens of U.S. intelligence, reanimating the story of how Japan had gone down to defeat. While researching that project I had the occasion to read the *New York Times* and *Herald Tribune* for the summer of 1944, because a key naval battle, plus the campaign for the Mariana Islands, had taken place at that time. The newspapers of those days were full of reporting on the D-Day invasion and Normandy campaign. D-Day inspired; the long, slow, inching battle through the Norman countryside infuriated; but then the sudden Allied breakout and liberation of France thrilled readers everywhere, except perhaps in Germany. In any case, my visit to the news of the time struck a chord because I had been raised on histories of World War II, including those of the Normandy campaign, and there was an oddity here.

In the histories I had read, including official histories, memoirs of the Allied field commanders, personal narratives, and campaign accounts, there were certain figures for the number of German soldiers taken prisoner in the "Falaise Pocket," the encirclement of Nazi armies that took place as the Allies broke out of Normandy. Many of these studies, in particular the official histories and the campaign narratives, had been written years after the fact, in some cases decades, when the evidence was presumably all in. There were some new wrinkles later, most importantly the evidence of Allied code-breaking successes that emerged in the 1970s and 1980s, but nothing that changed the basic casualty reporting. What seemed odd to me in the 1990s was that the numbers for German prisoners and losses in the Falaise Pocket published by war correspondents within *days* of that August 1944 battle were the same as those that appeared in the later histories. How could Allied commanders have known that number at the time? Surely once prisoners were actually processed, and the dead buried, the count had to be more accurate. If confusion was such that deriving a solid figure never proved possible, what does that say about other Allied claims for the results of the campaign?

This project began as an effort to explore that question, and another. The second was to investigate an enduring mystery: Without doubt the outcome of the Normandy campaign was decisive—a huge military disaster for Nazi Germany. Yet within a very short time the enemy army was back up and actively contesting the Allied advance toward the German frontier. How was it that amid catastrophe German combat power could regenerate with such rapidity? Somehow the foundations for the new forces had to have been preserved even within the calamity. These questions seemed related and susceptible to inquiry.

But as my work progressed, something else about the Normandy campaign became increasingly evident. I had not realized when simply reading the histories the extent to which this campaign affected the remainder of World War II. Let me put that differently—the impact of German and Allied losses and changes in territorial control were real enough, and had been appreciated well enough, but the campaign had had other effects that are less well appreciated. Suddenly Normandy appeared to be a crucible for combat tactics and logistics techniques, and raised questions that drove subsequent strategic planning on both sides. Reframing the Normandy story to highlight those aspects seemed desirable. *Normandy Crucible* is the story of how and why that experience proved so formative, and it reconstructs the climactic Allied Normandy breakout from both sides of the hill.

It has been popular recently to frame history as memory and focus narratives at the level of individuals and their personal experiences. While there are, in fact, many individual stories in this book, my intent is not to focus primarily on memory. I have chosen instead to keep the lens on the Big Picture, because it is at that level that answers to the dilemmas of strategic plans and maneuvers must be sought. Individual stories are recorded not for their own sake but to illuminate larger aspects of the inquiry. It might have been possible to incorporate both levels of analysis into a longer book, but from the beginning the goal here was to create a short work that could still explore in depth. Let me hasten to add that the hardships, experiences, and achievements of all the men who fought in Normandy are important and worth recording.

Finally, one other aim of this book is to attempt a synthesis of intelligence history with combat narrative. In effect—and some readers familiar with my work in that area may be surprised at this—at one level it is time to *stop* writing intelligence history. By that I mean that the moment has come, by dint of diligent research and reconstruction, that our knowledge of World War II intelligence matters has attained a level sufficient to retell the battle story while filling in the blanks. It is not that nothing is left to discover about intelligence, rather that studies in that area are attaining the level of minute detail without our having paused to reinterpret the overall history. For example, after multiple explorations of code breaking, historians are turning to deception activities, while still ignoring—with the exception of D-Day—the battles they influenced. The purpose of intelligence operations was to inform war strategy, and without examining their impact, larger questions remain unanswered.

Normandy Crucible attempts to do this for a critical passage of the war in Europe, just as *Combined Fleet Decoded* tried to achieve a similar synthesis for the war in the Pacific. Since the latter work appeared, the task of integration has progressed unevenly. In general, naval histories are more advanced than those of ground warfare. Some studies on the Pacific Theater, on North Africa, and on D-Day have integrated intelligence in some detail. For Northwest Europe in 1944–1945, however, despite the existence of a detailed British official history and a more popular study, the several dozen Normandy battle histories published since the mid-1990s have made little progress in providing a full picture. Reframing our previous understanding of the conflict, save for the exceptions, has hardly begun. This I believe is the next great challenge for World War II historians.

Normandy Crucible is a narrative history. Along with official studies, documents, memoirs, personal and campaign accounts, journalistic works, and military press releases, it benefits from official records, including the postwar official reports of the First U.S. Army, the Third U.S. Army, the 12th Army Group, and the war diary of the German High Command. Participants from both sides have produced valuable recollections, and in some cases able translators have helped bring them to foreign audiences. The labors of other historians should also be recognized. They have mined the archives to produce secondary accounts as well as additional primary source material—accounts by German officers who, in captivity, recorded their own reflections on these events. I consulted a number of these combat narratives at repositories of the National Archives and Records Administration, but the published versions are more accessible to readers and are buttressed by the editors' contextual and explanatory material. I have confined my references to the published versions whenever possible. For their energy and dedication to this task of making official records available, I would like to commend David C. Isby, Samuel W. Mitcham, Jr., Frederick P. Steinhardt, P. A. Spayd, Helmut Heiber, and David M. Glantz. Special recognition should also be accorded to Niklas Zetterling for his exhaustive records-based statistical analysis of the German army in Normandy, which should provide much data to future students of these events. In addition, let me extend heartfelt thanks to Ellen Pinzur, who read and edited every successive version of this manuscript and caught numerous errors and awkward formulations. Many persons contributed to the good elements of this book, but the responsibility for its omissions, oversights, and OMGs is mine alone.

The Normandy campaign was one of the most important of World War II. It set the stage for the battles for the German frontier and the final assault into the Nazi heartland. The brave men who crouched behind cover, and rushed from one hedgerow to another, knew they were participating in great events but had no idea their fight was a crucible for what followed. Theirs was the ultimate sacrifice and *Normandy Crucible* is a testament to their achievements.

John Prados
Washington, D.C.
June 2010

PREFACE

ccounts of the Normandy campaign that appeared in the newspapers of the summer of 1944, I wrote in my original introduction to this book, first infuriated, then enthralled readers everywhere, except, perhaps, Germany. This book tells the story of Allied armies inching their way forward after the spectacular D-Day invasion, their sudden breakthrough and breakout, leading to a huge pocket of German troops trapped in the West. A long-disguised or minimized part of the story—the contributions intelligence made to the military campaign, also concerned me. The synthesis of combat narrative and intelligence history continues to loom as the area of inquiry that will add the most to our understanding of these momentous events. Plus I was anxious to show both sides of the front, detailing the history from both the Allied and German points of view. *Normandy Crucible* has stood the test of time. In the decade elapsed since I first put pen to paper on this book, there has not been a Normandy history which covers this array of material in a more felicitous way.

What happened in France starting on June 6, 1944, truly a mammoth undertaking, could not have succeeded without much more than cooperation between the soldiers and the spies. On the first day, D-Day, more than 5,000 ships carried 83,115 British and Canadians, 70,500 American, and a smattering of French troops across the formidable obstacle of the English Channel in the face of an approaching storm. Of those troops,

23,000 were delivered by air, parachuting or glidering to their objectives. Tens of thousands more sailors and airmen crewed those ships and planes. More than 11,000 aircraft flights on D-Day carried troops or supported the landings by strafing and bombing German defenders. Eight different nations supplied the planes and ships. Beyond the invasion beaches partisan fighters of the French, Belgian, and Dutch Resistance helped isolate the combat zone, preventing German defenders from reacting to the landings before the Allies had gotten solidly ashore. Cornelius Ryan calls his D-Day account the story of a people, not a military history. Anthony Beevor writes of Allied commanders awed by what they were attempting. Carlo d'Este called D-Day the most complex and daring undertaking in modern warfare. Cooperation made it happen.

These were intricate—and carefully plotted—maneuvers. The Day of Liberation did not happen by chance. It was the product of a carefully designed and structured apparatus that assigned citizens of different countries to fulfill a range of functions from supplying the necessary food and fuel, to arranging that all the aircraft flights and ship sailings would not conflict, to commanding the troops on the ground. Even on the German side, where there were soldiers of Russian and other ethnic minorities, or units grouped by such commonalities as medical conditions, among an ostensibly homogeneous whole, cooperation was the keystone of success.

In a real sense the events of D-Day were aspirational. Great Britain and its allies dreamed of toppling Hitler. Peoples in the Occupied Countries dreamed of overcoming Nazi overlords. The codebreakers, pilots of photo reconnaissance planes, interpreters of pictures and texts, even meterologists, aspired to help their comrades win. Germans hoped to defeat the invasion. The lessons of D-Day and the Normandy campaign after it, were that cooperation maximizes possibility, persistence wins through, and that the difference between grinding disappointment and exhilarating advance can be a matter of days, sometimes mere hours. For all the heat generated by the personality and strategy differences among the high commands, Anglo-American cleavages prominent among them, the aim of Liberation kept shoulders to the wheel, and trucks moving onwards. In fact, a secondary, but real, lesson of Normandy is that command differences were points of friction—difficulties that could slow progress but not stall it.

The friend who recounted to me his frustration as a boy, sticking pins into a map to mark the progress of the Allied armies, who found no movement day after day as he listened to the radio and read the papers, learned those lessons. So did the veterans of World War II. The leaders of that time and those who followed them—my friend's generation—attempted a series of aspirational endeavors. The General Agreement on Tariffs and Trade followed by the World Trade Organization. The Brussels Pact, then the North Atlantic Treaty Organization. The United Nations. On the European scene, the Coal and Steel Community, European Economic Community, European Free Trade Association, the Common Market, now the European Union. Indeed the project for European integration became one of the most important areas of international development for decades.

As we approach the 75th anniversary of D-Day, it is worth reflecting on that mighty endeavor. Today aspirational achievements seem to be under challenge. The rise of populism, fueled by immigration and national economic miseries that require international responses, argue for abandoning cooperation, replacing it with insularity. Certainly this is one impetus for Brexit. This year is also the 30th anniversary of the fall of the Berlin Wall. It is worth recalling that the Soviet Bloc's attempt at autarky—insularity—became an important factor in generating the political, social, and economic rigidities that first stripped the Soviet Union of its buffer zone in Eastern Europe, and then helped bring down the USSR itself.

Forging a fairer, safer, healthier, better-off, better-adjusted community of nations is an endeavor as mighty as D-Day in Normandy. Avoiding the consequences of human-induced climate change is a prime example. Whether Great Britain's role is to stand off to the side or be an active associate of an integrated Europe has become the question of the day. With populism gathering strength in the United States, across Europe, and elsewhere, the future seems bleak for international cooperation. But that does not make coalition and communion any less important. Problems that face the world today are no less critical than those of the Western democracies facing fascism.

Normandy Crucible shows that friction, the minute variance in the application of Allied firepower to the trapped Germans in the Falaise Pocket, made a huge difference in the enemy's ability to escape and fight another day. But the issues at stake, then and now, are too important to sit back and wait for the tides of history to take us back to a moment when cooperation beckons.

John Prados
Washington, DC, January 2019

PROLOGUE:
THE DECISION

M any passages in war prove momentous, recognized for what they are at the time. Others are apparent only in the light of later events. In the massive Operation Overlord, the Allied invasion of France in World War II, the huge undertaking for the final Anglo-American campaign against Nazi Germany, the choice to go ahead with the D-Day landings in Normandy on June 6, 1944, was among those events whose importance was widely appreciated in the moment. In Normandy the Anglo-American armies would be tested. Another set of decisions took place for an air-ground offensive. The American commanders who conceived and carried out this attack, separated from D-Day by barely a month, knew it would be important, but even they had no idea how crucial the consequences would prove to be. That understanding dawned only after the fact. In a very real way the decisions made here determined the final result in Normandy. And the campaign would itself become the crucible for the Battle for France and the last stages of the war in Europe. The personal relationships among the men at the top, which evolved in ways that made them a key factor in the outcome, are also visible this early, in the generals' deliberations on the military plans. These encounters— fleeting episodes that set the stage for understanding much, much more— illuminate the dynamics that made Normandy the crucible it became.

Normandy, July 1944: by many lights the most essential military campaign of World War II. Beyond any doubt Normandy—the sequel to the Allied invasion of northwest Europe on D-Day—represented the Allies' first direct opportunity to fight their way into Nazi Germany, capture Berlin, and end the war. This was the German nightmare. But a month after D-Day, the outlook for Allied commanders remained decidedly mixed. Though their positions were solid—and stronger than those of the adversary—the campaign seemed to have bogged down. As of July 7—D+31 in the argot of the staff planners (D-Day plus thirty-one days)—the millionth man of the expeditionary forces had stepped ashore. So too had an American idol, General George S. Patton, arrived by air the previous day. Patton was the acknowledged master of mobile warfare, and until then his presence at the head of a notional Allied army group had been at the heart of a clever Allied deception. Some tactical air units had begun relocating to Norman airfields. There were more divisions—thirteen American, eleven British, and a Canadian—and more supplies. General Omar Bradley, the American field commander, felt comfortable enough to celebrate the July 4th holiday with a bombardment in which every U.S. Army artillery gun simultaneously opened fire. It was spectacular. The Americans had sent an armored division into the Normandy battlefield for the first time. General Bradley with the First U.S. Army had slugged his way into the Cotentin Peninsula, the heart of Normandy.

On the other hand, the Allies had nowhere broken into the clear. The British had yet even to capture their D-Day objective, Caen. After many efforts they remained on that city's outskirts. In their sector the Americans were grinding away, but the fight remained a punching match. On the neat planning maps at Supreme Headquarters Allied Expeditionary Forces (SHAEF) before the invasion, a yellow line had indicated the positions Allied troops were supposed to attain by D+25. Phase Line Yellow included the entire Normandy peninsula and anticipated that Bradley's army would have advanced into the adjacent Brittany peninsula in search of critical ports, while the British would be in the interior of France, one-third of the way to Paris. Neither had happened. The day had already passed, with the armies far from planned positions. There was no way the D+35 phase line would be achieved, either. This anticipated that Bradley would have reached the Loire River, with some Breton ports in American hands. In fact, on D+35 the Allies were still penned up in Normandy, their liberated zone less than a quarter of the area expected to have been cleared ten days earlier. The grinding advance seemed like World War I, not modern warfare.

General Bradley had just completed a round of attacks with two of his corps. He had hoped this offensive would finally break the stalemate, but it had not. Another of Bradley's corps had begun a fresh assault, south and southwest, to capture or outflank the centrally situated Norman town of Saint-Lô. That, too, made only gradual gains. George Patton observed that "Brad," as Bradley was nicknamed, in his frustration at the slow progress, was "too prone to cut off heads," replacing division commanders he found wanting. The same seemed true, by Patton's lights, of Major General J. Lawton Collins, leading Bradley's important VII Corps.[1]

The day after George Patton's arrival, Omar Bradley took him to the command post of the Allied ground forces commander, General Bernard Law Montgomery. Their British host had them to lunch, followed by an extended meeting. Montgomery had sent a letter that day to the SHAEF supreme commander, General Dwight D. Eisenhower, which expressed uncertainty as to where the Allied field armies should put their main effort. At the meeting Montgomery ranged over the same subject. Seconding him was his chief of staff, Major General Francis de Guingand. At the briefing, Patton noted in his diary, "Montgomery went to great length explaining why the British have done nothing. Caen was their D-Day objective, and they have not taken it."[2] (The next day, however, British troops began a ground assault that finally cleared a portion of that city.) Discussion of the American sector, to infer from Patton's notes, centered on Montgomery asking when the U.S. forces might reach Avranches, at the foot of the Cotentin, and when Bradley might activate the Third U.S. Army, which Patton had been chosen to lead.

American soldiers on Bradley's front made little progress that day. General Bradley reconsidered his operations. Chafing at the slog through the Cotentin, more than two weeks earlier Bradley had told General Eisenhower that the plans for getting out of Normandy needed revision. The First Army chief set about this early in July. Bradley sat in his command truck poring over the terrain maps, looking for a path of attack that avoided swamps and minimized encounters with river barriers. Following the luncheon with Montgomery, Bradley consulted his top operations staffer, Colonel Truman C. "Tubby" Thorson, concluding that an attack from around Saint-Lô offered the best possibility. Bradley spent two nights pacing in the map tent next to his truck, concocting a plan. He liked to use colored crayons on an acetate overlay to outline the movements his plans might require. Such sketches helped Bradley visualize what the maneuvers entailed. Once he was satisfied, Brad summoned top staff—Lieutenant General Courtney Hodges, deputy commander; Brigadier General William J. Kean, the chief of staff; Thorson and his deputy, Colonel Robert A. Hewitt; and Colonel Benjamin A. Dickson, the intelligence officer—for a first look. Tubby Thorson christened the plan Operation Cobra. It was based on a mass heavy bombing of a type the British had just demonstrated in the assault that had finally reached Caen. Bombing would shock the defenders, then strong assaults against the shattered enemy would smash a hole through their line, and finally exploitation forces could break through. The date was July 10, D+34. This version of the origins of Cobra is Bradley's own, but there is no reason not to take him at his word.

General Bradley worried about a World War I–style stalemate. With the tough German defenses, that seemed a real possibility. SHAEF commander Eisenhower worried, too. He sent a strong missive to Montgomery—who, as ground forces commander, held the responsibility—demanding that the British general aggressively take the offensive in his own sector. In the midst of his latest Caen attack, Montgomery responded that he saw no stalemate. Then, also on July 10, Montgomery held another command conference. Here General Bradley first revealed his Cobra plan. Bradley anticipated loosing the blow once ammunition had been stockpiled and his troops had attained a proper starting position. The two generals were outwardly cordial but, to Bradley's mind, "political undercurrents were causing a strain in our relationship."[3] Those undercurrents flowed precisely from the feeling the British were marking time at Caen while U.S. armies did most of the fighting. This thread will be taken up later, but it had everything to do with Normandy's final result.

General Bradley selected J. Lawton Collins and his VII Corps for the main role in Cobra. To back Collins he placed U.S. armor in reserve positions, assembling units eventually intended for Patton's Third U.S. Army. They would exploit the initial penetration. General Collins and other First Army corps commanders learned the details at a two-hour briefing at Bradley's headquarters on July 12. Bradley's deputy, Lieutenant General Courtney Hodges, also sat in. General Bradley told his line commanders of the saturation bombing he intended on a narrow front. Brad considered this vital. "I've been wanting to do this now since we landed," the general declared. "When we pull it off I want it to be the biggest show in the world. We want to smash right on through."[4] Bradley wished his commanders to be bold, prepared to accept substantial losses, but above all committed to rapid advance.

"Lightning Joe" Collins, as he was known, understood the danger that air attacks might hit friendly troops. "The number of times we've actually bombed our people has been small," Collins remarked. "I've said more than once I'm willing to take that risk."[5] He recommended a target zone west of Saint-Lô, which all the corps commanders agreed was a good point of departure. Collins asked for more troops, and Bradley assigned him two extra divisions, plus armor. That night, imagining his First Army divisions coiled like a snake ready to strike, Bradley accepted Thorson's suggestion for a code name. The next day, the outline plan was printed on a mimeograph duplicator. Collins tinkered a bit with Bradley's scheme, providing for more tanks with the spearheads. To avoid giving anything away the armor would move to its assembly areas by night just prior to the attack. Artillery would assume new positions and, to the extent possible, stay inactive to avoid revealing itself. The lineup gave VII Corps four infantry and two armored divisions, more than any U.S. corps had ever had. Weather forced a postponement, but the final plan, in VII Corps Field Orders 6, would be issued on July 20. Omar Bradley called Cobra "the most decisive battle of our war in western Europe."[6]

Shortly after the July 10 command conference the British came up with a new plan for Caen, one for the biggest attack yet, to capture the rest of the city and clear away the Germans south of it, with armored divisions leading the way, plus another strategic bomber strike. Efforts have been made to assert that its intent was entirely to divert the Germans and keep their panzers tied down in front of the British while Americans broke through with Cobra. The essential argument is that the British operation was subordinated to *Allied* strategy and had no other motive than to clear Bradley's path. But several days ahead of Operation Goodwood, as this offensive would be called, Montgomery issued a directive clearly anticipating an independent breakout from Normandy. Other aspects of Goodwood also hint at this. Montgomery later revised his instructions to restrict the operation's scope, but those orders went only to his immediate subordinates. Eisenhower and SHAEF were told only of the ambitious version. On July 12 "Monty," as he was familiarly called, enthused to Eisenhower that "the operation may have far-reaching consequences," and predicted "my whole eastern flank will burst into flames." Montgomery followed this on July 14 with a message to the SHAEF deputy commander, British air chief marshal Sir Arthur Tedder, envisioning that his planned offensive at Caen, "if successful, promises to be decisive." General Bradley speculates that Goodwood had the hidden agenda of inflicting that extra dollop of attrition that might break the German will and enable the British to be the ones to "win" the battle of Normandy.[7]

This is important because, behind the scenes, tempers were rising and rivalries burgeoning among the Allies' senior commanders. The discomfort centered on the role of General Montgomery, and Monty was perfectly aware of the facts through his back channel with the top British military leader, Field Marshal Lord Alanbrooke, chief of the Imperial General Staff. Montgomery and Alanbrooke denigrated Eisenhower and SHAEF, while the latter kept Monty apprised of plots to fire him. Air Marshal Tedder was a prime mover in the effort to get rid of Montgomery, which reached its climax at precisely this time. Eisenhower had repeatedly urged action on Montgomery, and Tedder needled the SHAEF supremo with each bit of evidence that Monty had not performed. Tedder encouraged General Eisenhower to relieve Montgomery for not fighting hard enough. British prime minister Sir Winston Churchill had given Eisenhower authority to relieve *any* British officer under his command— including Montgomery—but SHAEF's leader, aware of the political and diplomatic aspects of his role, hesitated to take any such action. A powerful

British offensive at Caen was exactly what General Montgomery needed to get out of hot water with Eisenhower.

Monty had another motive, also. His post as overall ground forces commander under SHAEF was to be abolished. This position had been created especially for the D-Day invasion. Once the Americans put Patton's Third Army in play, the intention was to elevate Bradley to lead an army group of American forces. Montgomery himself would activate a Canadian army in addition to his British one and take charge of a Commonwealth army group. SHAEF headquarters would move to the Continent, where General Eisenhower would assume direct command. But General Montgomery wanted to keep the job of overall ground boss.

Meanwhile a mere look at the map showed the apparent stalemate in Normandy, and journalists could read maps as well as anyone. The prevailing factors were simple to understand and could not be kept secret. Negative commentary on Allied operations began appearing in the press, growing steadily louder. Montgomery, Eisenhower, and Bradley all comment in their memoirs on the rise of press criticism, specifically at this time, and Bradley guesses the Goodwood plan had the public relations aspect of enabling Montgomery to show a victory. This might still quavering voices and it could also have contributed to Montgomery's effort to retain his post as SHAEF ground forces commander.

The historian Nigel Hamilton, Montgomery's most vociferous defender, has attempted to demonstrate that *Montgomery*, not Bradley, invented the idea of Cobra as an encirclement of the Germans. Hamilton points to a June 30 conference and an accompanying directive in which Montgomery spoke of a broad intention to have the American forces move south, then eastward in a wide sweep "so as to threaten the line of withdrawal of such enemy divisions [as may be] to the south of Paris."[8] There are several problems with this construction. Most important, the language suggesting encirclement clearly refers to German forces in southern France, not Normandy. There is nothing in the material indicating Montgomery aimed at trapping the Germans *in* Normandy. Second, Overlord had always envisioned a turning movement to the east out of the invasion zone, combined with an effort to capture French ports in Brittany—and the Montgomery directive of June 30 did nothing to alter that. Third, General Montgomery did nothing at his conference or in this directive—or his meetings with Bradley on July 7 and 10—to pursue the idea of a trap. Rather, his exchanges all conformed to SHAEF's conventional concept. After the July 10 meeting Monty issued another directive—at a point where he had become aware of Bradley's plan—and his instructions for an American sweep beyond the Normandy position was silent about closing a trap on the enemy. Bradley's actual Cobra plan accorded with Montgomery's strategic directive, also without departing from the Overlord strategy. French ports remained the goal. Arguments otherwise are too clever by half.

The centerpiece of Omar Bradley's great offensive was to be a massive concentrated aerial bombardment on a hapless segment of the German front line. The particulars of arrangements for this show the Allied High Command at work as well as illustrating some of the difficulties of this kind of effort. The record is especially important because General Bradley himself would later dispute what had or had not been decided.

The first point is that the massive bombing idea was not a complete novelty, nor was it an innovation confined to the British at Caen, where they used such attacks several times. When Bradley's army had pushed off the D-Day invasion beaches it aimed tentacles toward the port of Cherbourg, at the northern tip of the Cotentin Peninsula. A big strike by the strategic bombers of the U.S. Eighth Air Force under Lieutenant General James A. Doolittle had been laid in late June to help the First Army get past German defenses. It is not coincidental that the troops Bradley chose to execute the ground attack in his Cobra offensive—General Collins's VII Corps—were the same soldiers who had fought their way into Cherbourg behind Jimmy Doolittle's B-17 and B-24 bombers. The specific idea of plastering a segment of the German line was also something that had been floating around. Omar Bradley writes that he had been searching for an appropriate place for an attack like this. Observing the Cherbourg operation, Brad had told staff of his desire to replicate the achievement on the main front, and, of course, he had been quick to adopt the bombardment idea for his Cobra plan. The wrinkle that made the plan exceptional was to couple the strike with an immediately following ground offensive.

Even air bombardment of a narrow section of front was not new. Omar

Bradley's army had an army air force component specifically dedicated to support it, Major General Elwood R. "Pete" Quesada's IX Tactical Air Command. On July 9 Quesada had laid plans for half a dozen of his fighter and bomber groups to pummel a small 2,250-by-800-yard German sector along the Périers-Carentan road, only a few miles from where the actual Cobra air strike would take place. Quesada had had to cancel his operation due to bad weather, but the interesting part is that he devised this idea at the exact moment General Bradley was brainstorming the Cobra plan itself. Bradley quickly incorporated Pete Quesada's design into his own offensive.

The British had used a big bombardment as part of the attack that finally got them into Caen. Sir Solly Zuckerman, Churchill's scientific adviser, had surveyed the results immediately afterward. A zoologist by trade, Zuckerman was an innovator not wedded to tradition, and his application of mathematical analysis to military data had created the powerful analytical tool of operations research. By 1944 these techniques had become well established—particularly in regard to bombing strategy—and Zuckerman had observed bombing effects at Caen. Only a few days later he was asked to attend a meeting at Bradley's headquarters. Aware that the mix of ordnance used in Monty's Caen attack had impeded the ground operation, Bradley and Quesada asked for Zuckerman's help. They were especially concerned about the placement of a "keep-out" zone, the distance that U.S. troops should maintain to avoid danger from the aircraft bombs, and about the size of the bombs that should be used.

General Bradley gradually worked his way up to a scheme he could present to air force commanders. He did that on July 19, just after American troops reached the agreed launch position at Saint-Lô. Bradley flew to England with Lawton Collins and Pete Quesada to see the air leaders at Stanmore, the estate that served as headquarters of the Allied Expeditionary Air Force, which comprised units serving both American and British Commonwealth armies. Bradley's staffers thought Stanmore dreadful, in poor repair, painted in horrible colors, filled with rickety Victorian furniture. One aide, told that Queen Adelaide, consort of William IV (1830–1837), had died there, quipped the house ought to have been embalmed with her. But General Bradley seemed in high spirits as he asked for heavy bombers to prime his assault. His host, Air Chief Marshal Sir Trafford Leigh-Mallory, a believer in air support for armies, posed no objections.

Attending were a host of top brass, including Lieutenant General Lewis H. Brereton of the 9th Air Force, Quesada's direct superior; Air Chief Marshal Tedder, representing Eisenhower; Leigh-Mallory's deputy, the American air general Hoyt Vandenberg; the British tactical air commander Air Marshal Arthur M. Coningham, nicknamed "Maori" because he was actually Australian (but inaccurately since the Maori are inhabitants of New Zealand); and Lieutenant General Carl A. "Tooey" Spaatz, the leader of the United States Strategic Air Force, the final authority over Jimmy Doolittle's big bombers. The science guru Solly Zuckerman was also there. These men were the best and the brightest of the air war.

Acting for SHAEF, Tedder approved the heavy bombardment. Brereton was put in charge of planning the air operation. That only began the heavy bargaining. Strategic air force commanders like Tooey Spaatz—and his British counterpart, Sir Arthur Harris of Bomber Command—considered these operations a diversion from their task of plastering German cities and industry. Efficacy of mass air attacks remained obscure—Pete Quesada himself had come to doubt that the big attack during the Cherbourg advance had actually killed even a dozen German soldiers. And the heavy bombers were not trained or equipped for air-ground cooperation—for example, their radio nets could not communicate with those of army units. Indeed, Brereton's technical mavens were only now creating a mechanism for this among the tactical air commands themselves (by equipping forward observers' tanks with army air force radio sets). At D-Day there had been compelling reasons for strategic air participation. Now, not so much—and Bradley wanted fifteen hundred heavy bombers. Leigh-Mallory's deputy, the American Hoyt Vandenberg, was inclined to side with the strategic bomber generals. But none could deny SHAEF—Tedder prevailed.

The air generals stood fast on execution, however. Bradley wanted carefully orchestrated strikes to hit a bomb zone seven thousand yards wide and twenty-five hundred deep. He believed the best way to effect that would be for the aircraft to approach from the west of Normandy, prepare to drop when they passed over the town of Périers, and then make a straight final approach parallel to the Saint-Lô–Périers road. The bomb zone itself would be located between the towns of Marigny and Saint-Gilles. Bradley reasoned that if the aircraft never flew over American troops there was little danger GIs would be hit by friendly planes. The west-east flight path also seemed ideal for navigation, but the sky captains argued it would disrupt the concentration of their bombardment and expose aircrews to excessive losses from German flak. They viewed the route as trying to pour almost two thousand large warplanes down a funnel in an hour's time. The bomber barons demanded a north-south approach. It was also true that the sky captains' preferred route afforded aircrews minimal time to release their loads on target, and maximized the difficulty of recognizing the markers and colored smoke used to denote the U.S. front. Leigh-Mallory supported Bradley. The army commander believed he had won that argument, but both he and Leigh-Mallory left before the end of the meeting. In his memoirs, General Collins differs with Bradley in retrospect, unwilling to go so far as to insist there had been a clear understanding at Stanmore.[9] The bomber barons would follow their own lights.

Another key dispute centered around the safety zone, demarcated by a line behind which no bombs were to be loosed, the implementation of which required Bradley's troops to pull back before the attack. The air generals wanted a safety zone three thousand yards wide. Withdrawing that far meant abandoning several days' worth of hard-bought U.S. ground gains. Bradley would have none of it. He opted for pullbacks no greater than eight hundred yards. One of Spaatz's staffers countered that even three thousand yards would not guarantee safety, but the air officers halved their bid to a fifteen-hundred-yard zone. Bradley rejected any withdrawal deeper than a thousand yards, but in the end compromised at twelve hundred fifty. An additional buffer of two hundred yards beyond the bomb line would be hit only by fighter-bomber attacks in order to minimize danger to the ground troops.

There was also talk of bomb size. General Bradley wanted to avoid the kind of damage that created ruins or toppled stone buildings into the street, things that would complicate the ground advance. The heavier the ordnance the more its explosive potential—but also the greater the danger of creating obstacles to the American advance by collapsing buildings into roads or cratering the land. The British had had problems with heavier bombs around Caen. Bradley favored munitions up to a thousand pounds. General Collins agreed, opting for these bombs to inflict heavier but not crippling damage. Bradley relied on Solly Zuckerman's findings from the Caen area to assert these larger bombs would not be detrimental to Allied purposes. Collins based his position on conversations with his own division commanders. On the other hand, the "lighter" ordnance automatically ruled out participation by Bomber Command because Sir Arthur Harris's heavies were only equipped to carry larger munitions.

Omar Bradley left Stanmore aboard one of Leigh-Mallory's C-47 transports. He thought he had complete agreement on his Cobra air plan—in fact, promises for an even bigger strike than he had asked for: more than two thousand aircraft all told. Only part of what Bradley imagined was true. The failures in communication were partly rooted in military services' standard procedures, but also in rivalries among the Allied generals. The situation was pregnant with dangers of which Bradley remained ignorant. Operation Cobra could become a nightmare. It was perhaps a small consolation, but it was one nonetheless, that the Allies' headaches were far less onerous than the nightmare that had afflicted their German adversaries since long before the Normandy invasion.

CHAPTER 1

GERMAN NIGHTMARES

The Allied invasion of France on D-Day, June 6, 1944, at once crystallized German fears and created the problems that Omar Bradley sought to solve. D-Day had been an enormous undertaking, befitting the huge military campaign now under way in Normandy. As the Allies marshaled their armada for the invasion there could be no doubt of their aims. The impending invasion could be perfectly anticipated. As early as November 1943, the German leader, or führer, Adolf Hitler, had issued his order designed to defeat this enterprise, Führer Directive 51. Hitler depended on what the Germans called the Atlantic Wall, the set of defenses along the European coast from Norway to Spain. The strength of the Atlantic Wall and of the German garrisons in Western Europe would be challenged on D-Day. Late at night, when fear played at the mind, the German nightmare was that their defenses would fail that test.

Adolf Hitler, more than a national leader, was also the commander in chief (C in C) of the German armed forces, or Wehrmacht. Detail-oriented to a fault, Hitler delved into every aspect of Wehrmacht activity and insisted on making every significant decision personally—plus many unimportant ones, too. The führer could not have been ignorant of the realities of the Atlantic Wall, which had begun life two years earlier as part of a propaganda initiative to extol the invincibility of German-occupied Europe. Works had indeed been built, artillery guns emplaced, and millions of tons of concrete poured through 1943, but real questions remained as to its actual potential. There had been one dry run of sorts, at the French Channel port of Dieppe, where in August 1942 a Canadian-British force had attempted a landing and been roundly defeated. But at Dieppe the Allies had unaccountably chosen one of the best-defended German targets and had executed a flawed plan. They were unlikely to do that again, and during the interval the meat grinder of the German-Soviet war had greatly weakened the Wehrmacht. Looking ahead, Hitler foresaw that if he could crush a real invasion Germany would gain considerable advantage. He determined to do so. The quest for that victory had to begin with a realistic assessment of the Wehrmacht in the West. For this task Hitler called on one of his favorite officers, Field Marshal Erwin Rommel.

At the time Rommel was commanding German forces in northern Italy. Hitler's assignment to survey defenses in the West was at first to be just that, a survey, though on both sides there may have been some expectation of a greater role. His inspection showed Rommel there were numerous chinks in the Wehrmacht's armor. The vaunted Atlantic Wall was mostly a fiction. The army, navy, and the Todt Organization construction service did not even have a coordinated plan for how to improve it. Meanwhile, a high proportion of the troops in the West comprised units rebuilding after having been broken on the Eastern Front, or else were poor-quality formations made up of older soldiers or auxiliaries not even of German nationality. While a few places—like Dieppe—had real fortifications, many more were protected only by entrenchments or occasional strongpoints at great intervals. The Oberbefehlshaber West (OB West), the high command for this theater, under Field Marshal Gerd von Rundstedt, had been laboring to improve conditions, but was hampered by a lack of equipment, limited construction materials, and Hitler's practice of sending reconditioned units elsewhere, mostly back to Russia, as soon as they were ready. Rommel presented Hitler with an unvarnished view of this picture. The führer asked him to make it right, and Hitler's directive for defeating the invasion gave the West priority it had lacked, as well as a general scheme for the conduct of operations. Field Marshal Rommel would take charge of Army Group B, a major component of von Rundstedt's force, responsible for German troops along the Atlantic and Channel coasts.

Erwin Rommel had many qualities that suited him to his new assignment, which he took over in January 1944. Most important, the fifty-two-year-old officer enjoyed Adolf Hitler's trust. Rommel had once led the führer's guard battalion. He had been responsible for Hitler's personal security for eighteen months before assuming command of a panzer division. And he was technically adept. As a boy Rommel had wanted to fly and to study aeronautical engineering. When his father forbade him a career with zeppelins, young Erwin joined the infantry instead. He had fought in World War I on several fronts, earning Imperial Germany's highest decoration. Rommel was also an innovator, creating novel infantry infiltration tactics, which he later put into a book. During the interwar period he served as an infantry commander, an instructor, and a military school director. He had actually had no prewar mechanized experience.

But that was not Rommel's reputation. He was a natural. Rommel was known as a master of mobile warfare, the "Desert Fox," for his leadership of Italo-German motorized armies in North Africa from 1941 through 1943. Defeating the invasion was expected to be a set-piece battle. Yet in North Africa, before the battle of El Alamein, Rommel had been responsible for creating the most sophisticated fortified position built during that campaign, and a repeat performance was exactly what was needed to solidify the Atlantic Wall. He was also incredibly brave. Once, trapped behind British lines in Egypt, Rommel had driven right up to a British field hospital, proceeded to tour it as if he were *honoring* British *prisoners*, and tarried long enough to connect with a passing German mobile unit, with which he had escaped. He was always at the front, always with the units. That tremendous energy Rommel now poured into goading German garrisons into improving the Atlantic Wall. The same North African experience had endowed him with a respect for technical innovation that would be important in France. Rommel encouraged the development of new kinds of beach obstacles that threatened to tear the hulls of landing craft. "Rommel's Asparagus" became the slang expression for another kind of obstacle designed to obstruct glider landings or paratroops. Rommel's emphasis on forward defense also led to more line infantry divisions being stationed near the coast.

Another aspect of Rommel's North African experience proved valuable—he had learned about warfare against Anglo-American matériel and aerial superiority. Not Field Marshal von Rundstedt, not other German commanders, indeed, only Rommel's erstwhile subordinates with Panzerarmee Afrika—most of whom had trudged into Allied POW camps in May 1943—knew the cyclone of Allied airpower. This understanding lay at the heart of Rommel's differences with von Rundstedt over the strategy for meeting D-Day. Rommel believed that fortifications could provide a modicum of protection from Allied airpower, and that closing immediately with the Allied invaders would make it difficult for the enemy to fully apply his forces. Fighting from fortified belts of the Atlantic Wall and using nearby panzer reinforcements, the best chance to defeat the invasion would come right on the beaches.

Field Marshal von Rundstedt believed in holding back the panzer forces as a mobile reserve, committing them only once the center of gravity of the invasion became evident. This was a classic German approach worthy of "the Old Gentleman," as the sixty-eight-year-old von Rundstedt was known. Rundstedt had commanded German armies from the beginning of the war right through the Russian campaign, and he had already gone into retirement once, brought back to lead OB West. Born into a traditional Prussian military family, Karl Rudolf Gerd von Rundstedt was used to German technical superiority. He had never encountered Anglo-American tactical airpower. Though he had witnessed the Allied strategic bombings before D-Day, their depredations gave von Rundstedt little inkling of the conditions that would obtain once the full panoply of Allied power was brought to bear. For von Rundstedt the function of the Atlantic Wall was to oblige the British and Americans to deploy their whole force, after which German reserves could mop up the enemy. Rommel countered that airpower would delay and weaken the reserves and that only troops right behind the coast, who could launch immediate counterattacks against the invasion, would be able to break it up.

As a proper supreme commander, Adolf Hitler should have adjudicated this dispute. Instead he wavered, siding with Rommel at times and with von Rundstedt at others. As a practical matter this dispute governed how the Germans would employ their reserves, and here the führer split the difference, allocating several panzer divisions as close backup for Army Group B, with eight more of these units in OB West's strategic reserve.

Because Hitler insisted on personally approving any use of the panzers, he probably felt he was simply satisfying both of his subordinates. But on D-Day only Rommel's reserves stationed near the coast would have any capability for intervention.

Hitler similarly blew with the wind on the other key strategic question—where the Allies would invade. Von Rundstedt held to the view that the Allies' D-Day would come where the water crossing was at its narrowest—the English Channel at the Pas de Calais. Hitler sometimes agreed, and sometimes foresaw the invasion happening at Normandy. To be fair, Rommel wavered, too, but in the last weeks before D-Day, Hitler and Rommel tended to fear that Normandy would be the cockpit of conflict. Rommel's emphasis on forward defense led to more line infantry divisions being stationed in Normandy. His changes included moving the 91st Air Landing Division to the Cotentin and the 6th Parachute Regiment to Carentan, both of which challenged U.S. airborne forces, and redeploying the 352nd Infantry Division to a sector that became Omaha Beach. The fierce battle at Omaha on D-Day owed much to these changes, which Allied intelligence detected only in part, so late that operational planning was modified only for the airborne drop. In Normandy there would be roughly fifty-five thousand German troops on D-Day. Nevertheless, German indecision meant that the panzer formations were distributed widely, not focused on what became the actual battle area.

Another source of the German nightmare would be their intelligence, exploited both by German officers and by the Allies to falsify the true state of affairs. The staff called Foreign Armies West, an army unit, was responsible for tracking the Allied forces available for D-Day. For some time this staff had schemed to keep Hitler from denuding the West of good troops for other fronts by inflating its estimates. Any Allied unit that seemed the least able to participate in operations was included. Over time Foreign Armies West began carrying on its books units that had been sent elsewhere, as well as entirely fictional ones. At a certain point it became impossible for German intelligence to present a true appreciation without admitting its manipulation. Foreign Armies West played into Allied hands when the British and Americans concocted their own deception plan, Operation Fortitude, creating whole fictional combat divisions—and even the "First U.S.

Army Group," a high-level headquarters—deliberately misleading the enemy regarding Allied strength. In a brilliant maneuver, the British counterintelligence services captured and took control of German spies in England and elsewhere, using them to feed the Nazis information that lent even more credence to the fictive combat forces. When D-Day actually came, the German command continued to believe another Allied invasion was possible.

Beyond questions of strategy, intelligence, and fortifying the Atlantic Wall, another massive German headache lay in actually preparing the troops. Under the old rubric, the West had really served as a holding area. In the fall of 1943 the Germans were drawing an average of twenty thousand troops a month from there, shifting them to the Eastern Front. Hitler's November diktat stopped that: Over the half year through D-Day only five German divisions would be sent to Russia from the West. In a supplementary directive later in November, the führer had demanded a million men for the forces. By combing out staffs and service units, slicing the rear elements of divisions, recalling disabled soldiers (there would be an infantry battalion composed entirely of the deaf, and a division on special rations because all its men had stomach ailments), and employing Russian and Eastern European auxiliaries, the Replacement Army actually fielded over 968,000 men in the last six months of 1943. Many went to von Rundstedt, who cooperated with the Replacement Army, which had primary responsibility to fill out existing units and form new ones.

By means of extraordinary measures, the unit strength of OB West increased almost 50 percent during these months. Mechanized forces almost doubled (from six divisions to eleven), and good-quality infantry increased more than that (from seven divisions to sixteen). A tremendous buildup took place. Rommel pitched in to this task, too, with his usual energy. His constant inspections, exhortations, and demands spurred greater efforts. Depending on what occupied countries' garrisons are counted, by D-Day OB West could draw upon between fifty-five and sixty combat divisions. Not that things were perfect. The combing out of equipment had resulted in the assembly of a hodgepodge of guns, trucks, and tanks, some of German, Czech, or Russian ancestry, for which there were doubtful supplies of ammunition and spare parts. Though there were German weaknesses, the army in the West on D-Day would be stronger than at any time since the moment in 1940 when Germany completed its conquest of France.

The forces in the West on D-Day included many new units, so only a few examples must suffice. Take the 116th Panzer Division, for one. This formation had a long heritage as an infantry unit, then a motorized and *Panzergrenadier* one. In early 1944 in Russia, the 16th Division, as it was then known, had been almost destroyed fighting along the Dnepr River. General Count Gerhard von Schwerin-Krosigk led the remnants briefly to Germany and received a few replacements and more convalescents. For months the German army had been considering converting the 16th to a panzer unit, and now it did so. In March 1944 von Schwerin took his division to Laval, in France, where it absorbed parts of a panzer reserve formation and was reconstituted as the 116th Panzer Division. Lacking full complements of artillery pieces, flak, mobile kitchens, and trucks—the 116th had just 67 percent of required vehicles as late as July—its short existence also limited the time available for retraining. The goal of preparing the division for battle by May had to be abandoned, but by July 10 it would be combat ready. As of D-Day General von Schwerin had over 13,600 soldiers and nearly a hundred tanks and assault guns. A few days later the 116th Panzer was ordered to positions behind the Pas de Calais.

The German unit perhaps best known to Americans would be the Panzer Lehr Division. An unusual formation—"Panzer Lehr" meant "armor demonstration" or "teaching"—the unit also carried the number 130th Panzer, but would forever be notorious simply as the Panzer Lehr. Both at Normandy and in the Battle of the Bulge, the Panzer Lehr proved a hard-hitting, determined foe that belied its deceptive name. Created from training units at the German army's main mechanized center, the Panzer Lehr Division moved to the Verdun area of France around Christmas of 1943. Its leader, Major General Fritz Bayerlein, a Rommel intimate, had served with the field marshal in North Africa, and was among those few who knew the Allies' operational methods. Wounded in Tunisia, Bayerlein, flown home for medical treatment, escaped capture. His division was first-rate, with 14,700 men on June 1, 1944, along with double the usual complement of half-tracks, and more than 220 tanks and assault guns. Bayerlein's division was one of those affected by the German debate over use of the panzer reserves and was reassigned to Rommel's control. In consequence, Bayerlein moved Panzer Lehr to the Le Mans–Orléans area, near the headquarters of the Seventh Army, the force responsible for the defense of Normandy. Allied planners worried that Panzer Lehr could directly contest the D-Day landings.

In addition to the German army, the Nazi Party possessed its own uniformed military force, the Waffen-SS. Five Waffen-SS divisions and several smaller formations would eventually fight in Normandy, but a good example of the genus is the 12th SS Panzer Division, called the Hitlerjugend— the Hitler Youth, a sort of Nazi version of the Boy Scouts. The idea of raising a combat unit from very young Nazis was suggested to the führer by a party official in early 1943. Hitler liked the idea of relying on the devotion and enthusiasm of youth, and approved. Orders for the creation of the Hitlerjugend Division followed that February, and the first batch of eight thousand recruits arrived at camp in Belgium in May. The 12th SS marked its official activation on June 24, 1943. The average age of its recruits was seventeen. Under SS Brigadier General Fritz Witt, the 12th SS Panzer Division moved to France two months before D-Day to be positioned between Paris and Normandy. On June 1, 1944, it had eighteen thousand troops with 160 tanks and assault guns. The Hitlerjugend would quickly acquire a reputation as fanatical fighters.

By no means were all of the German divisions of the caliber of the Panzer Lehr or the 12th SS. In particular, the units garrisoning the Atlantic Wall were so debilitated they were commonly referred to as static divisions. And the weaknesses in equipment have been noted. But with 880,000 frontline troops, plus their fortifications and panzer reserves, the Germans would be formidable. Yet Rommel and von Rundstedt feared the invasion. Despite their preparations, D-Day hung over them like the sword of Damocles.

THE LONGEST DAY

General Dwight David Eisenhower, the Allied C in C, knew long before D-Day that all the careful preparations would come down to weather.

Eisenhower, a four-star U.S. Army general, was the supreme commander of the Allied Expeditionary Forces. He had led multinational contingents in the Mediterranean and during previous invasions of North Africa, Sicily, and Italy.

At the head of the combined command, the Supreme Headquarters Allied Expeditionary Forces (SHAEF), Eisenhower also saw the grating effect of inaction on his subordinates, not only on their eagerness to get on with the job, but on their individual insecurities. Combat could be an outlet.

More than anyone, Eisenhower appreciated how weather could disrupt plans, knowing that the invasion rested on a very precise combination of the elements. The Anglo-American armies needed to land when there would be two low tides, both in daylight, the first early enough to complete the initial assault. There were only a certain number of days in the month when those conditions existed. In addition, for the major paratroop drops that would support the landings, the planners wanted moonlit night, with moonrise occurring late, so airborne troops could land in darkness but approach their objectives with greater visibility. As with dual tides, there were only a few days that featured this combination. Both conditions would exist on June 5, 6, and 7. The next potential dates for tidal aspect began after June 19, then slipped into July. Tide and moon would not both coincide again until August. If Operation Overlord did not happen in early June, its future would be affected by more than technical military issues.

Beyond that, ephemeral weather conditions were also vitally important. Too much wind and the airdrops would be affected—transport planes would find it difficult to keep formation, schedules could be delayed, gliders bearing heavy equipment might be blown off course, and the landing of the troops and their supplies could be scattered even more widely than they were. Heavy seas were an obstacle for landing craft, the smallest of which could be swamped by high waves. Cloud cover and ceilings, if excessive, could make air support impossible; thus, storms had obvious implications. These were cases of meteorological science having a direct bearing on military strategy. The final execution order depended on weather, not strategy. Eisenhower's "go" order for the invasion, made in the face of uncertain but promising predictions, unleashed the German nightmare.

General Bernard Law Montgomery was the overall Allied tactical commander for D-Day. He had been instrumental in insisting the invasion area be widened and include more forces. Six divisions would land from the sea in Operation Overlord: three British and Canadian above Caen, on the Calvados coast, and three American to the west, at the corner where the Calvados met the Cotentin Peninsula. Beyond the beaches the Allied aerial juggernaut would land a British and two U.S. airborne divisions for a vertical envelopment to complete the destruction of the Atlantic Wall. The amphibious invaders would surge inland, link up with the paratroopers and with each other, and seize key territorial objectives.

At the rehearsal of the D-Day plan and again at the final briefing of Operation Overlord, both of which took place at London's St. Paul's School—where Monty was at home, since he had attended it as a boy—the general declared that his British-Canadian forces would take Caen on D-Day. This needs to be mentioned because it is central to the Normandy crucible. General Bradley attended both presentations and saw a phase-line map that put Caen within British lines on the first day, and heard Montgomery say that he would break free with his armor and thrust it forward to "knock about a bit" around Falaise, thirty-two miles beyond Caen.[1] One of Bradley's corps commanders, Major General J. Lawton Collins, witnessed a scene between Bradley and Monty over the phase-line map where the American expressed irritation with Monty for the first time, in Collins's experience, because Bradley did not want such artificiality. He demanded the phase lines be removed, at least for Americans. Brad himself writes that the maps did show Caen taken on D-Day. In 1946 General Bradley also remarked that he believed, though he was not sure, that talk of using Caen as the hinge for a breakout did not begin until July.

In his own memoir Montgomery writes, "It is important to understand that, *once we had secured a good footing* in Normandy, my plan was to *threaten* to break out on the eastern flank, that is in the Caen sector," suggesting capture of the city was not a priority.[2] The historian Carlo D'Este has traced the recollections of participants and made the most detailed analysis of the planning documents. He concludes, "Contrary to most later interpretations of Montgomery's master plan, his remarks then and later did not reflect a defensive posture around Caen or a ploy to use the city as a hinge."[3] Monty's notes for his own briefings spoke of the offensive use of armor right off the beaches, as well as an intention to accept losses, even of complete tank brigades, as an acceptable price for freedom of action, to be used to maneuver beyond Caen. A variety of colleagues, including Monty's senior intelligence officer, confirm his determination to capture the city on the first day. He even spoke of the importance of securing airfields near Lisieux, miles past Falaise. To the degree that General Montgomery, before the fact, expected to divert Germans from the American front, his purpose was to cover Bradley's army while it accomplished the vital task of freeing the port of Cherbourg.[4]

The American role under the Overlord plan was different. The First U.S. Army under Omar Bradley was to storm ashore at the eastern corner of the Cotentin Peninsula. The Americans were to link up with General Miles Dempsey's British army while attacking westward to reach the Cotentin's other coast, cutting the peninsula in two. Holding that line, Bradley's troops would then work their way north to capture the port of Cherbourg, important for supplying the Allied armies. Then Bradley and Dempsey would each attack south on the main front in order to break out of Normandy. During this phase of the campaign the armies would have to fight their way past the "hedgerows," dense thickets of bushes and trees that enclosed Normandy's farm fields and the towns that dotted the land.

Late in the night of June 5–6 American airborne troops began dropping along the eastern side of the Cotentin Peninsula, while British troops were dropped to the east of the Orne River and Caen Canal. The drops were more disorganized than expected, not only due to weather but to pilot error, darkness, and German flak. Planeloads of paratroops were scattered widely over the Cotentin. But the confusion was in some ways an advantage: Those little bands of wanderers, desperate to find their buddies, created massive confusion in the German rear. Though up to three-quarters of the thirteen thousand American airborne men were scattered near and far, the 82nd and 101st Airborne Divisions, the formations involved, managed to gather enough troops to reach toward their goals. General Maxwell Taylor of the 101st initially had just a thousand men, but these were sufficient to secure the landward exits from the invasion beach code-named Utah. In the 82nd Division area, the fight for the town of Sainte-Mère-Église became a classic in the annals of airborne warfare. It was captured by early morning. On the British sector, the airdrop of forty-eight hundred troops was also scattered, but less widely—partly due to more use of gliders, partly because the larger part of the 6th Airborne Division arrived after daylight. Glider-borne troops captured the Ranville bridge across the Caen Canal. A British attempt to destroy the German shore battery at Merville succeeded even though only a few men of the 9th Airborne Battalion reached that target. D-Day had begun.

One of the Germans' few intelligence achievements was their success in learning one part of the language (lines from a Paul Verlaine poem) the Allies used to alert the French Resistance. Those words were heard in a BBC radio broadcast on the evening of June 5. Not long afterward came reports of paratroop landings. The German armies in Normandy and Calais called local alerts, but nothing was then done about the reserves. Hitler had gone to bed and staff refused to disturb him. Theater commanders were reluctant to accept that the "real" invasion was at hand, and von Rundstedt lacked the authority to commit the panzer reserves on his own. The benefit of German intelligence knowledge was thus largely lost.

With dawn came the amphibious landings. On the American sector, Utah Beach became the big success story. Craft bearing the 4th Infantry Division lost their heading and mistakenly landed in a different place than intended, which happened to be less heavily defended. Some twenty-three thousand troops stormed ashore at Utah on D-Day. A raid by the 2nd Ranger Battalion at Pointe du Hoc, between the invasion beaches, aimed at neutralizing a key German artillery battery. The rangers scaled a sheer cliff at great cost, only to discover the Germans had moved the guns. The other American beach, Omaha, became an epic battle against strong defenses. High waves swamped all but a handful of the tanks that had been specially adapted to "swim" ashore with the riflemen—the clearest effect of weather on D-Day. On Omaha troops of the 1st and 29th Infantry Divisions were pinned down and only gradually inched forward, infiltrating past German strongpoints, finally overwhelming them. Although General Bradley's First Army at Omaha landed the most men on D-Day—thirty-four thousand, even more than planned—the Americans ended that day far short of their intended objectives.

Americans' image of D-Day, June 6, the proverbial Longest Day, is really conditioned by just three of its myriad events: the fierce fight of the paratroops for the town of Sainte-Mère-Église, the brave Ranger attack on the battery that was not there, and the desperate struggle of soldiers to cross the sand and scale the bluffs at Omaha Beach. These were hard-fought battles, and there were other key firefights, too, but on the whole Bradley's D-Day went rather well. The soldiers, known as GIs (for Government Issue), fought only very briefly before moving smartly inland, and quickly connected with the paratroops. Even had the Omaha Beach assault failed completely—which it did not—General Bradley's army would have been solidly ashore because of the success at Utah. Darkness found Bradley with a sound foothold on the Cotentin around Utah, and a narrower but still stable beachhead at Omaha.

Even the Americans' mistakes ended up helping them. The scattered airdrop on the Cotentin created such confusion that German commanders had difficulty appreciating what was actually happening. Meanwhile, all those little bands of lost paratroopers functioned to harass and delay German troop movements. At Utah Beach, where currents and ocean waves pushed the invasion flotilla off its course, the final landing took place at a point less strongly defended than the planned invasion site.

On the British sector there were three beaches, Gold, Juno, and Sword. Here Monty landed three full infantry divisions, the 50th, 3rd Canadian, and 3rd British, reinforced by three armored brigades, including tanks designed especially to fight pillboxes, bridge ditches, and clear minefields. Busy with his task as overall commander, Montgomery delegated conduct of this engagement to Dempsey's Second British Army. The British landed over seventy-five thousand troops on D-Day. General Montgomery's plan provided that Commonwealth troops should move quickly south to capture Caen. The only real city in the invasion zone, Caen lay astride the Orne River. It was a transport hub that German reserves must pass. The nearby airfield at Carpiquet would provide a base immediately behind the lines that could quickly be used to maximize the effectiveness and range of British tactical air forces led by Air Marshal Coningham.

Less than 50 miles from the Seine River and 120 from Paris, the Germans ignored an Allied army at Caen at their peril.

General Montgomery's real intentions were borne out not just by the Overlord preinvasion planning but by the fighting. Wading ashore at Sword Beach, closest to Caen, Major General T. G. Rennie of the 3rd Infantry Division actually had instructions to capture or mask Caen on the first day. Rennie assigned one of his brigades to take the city, supported by tanks of the 27th Armored Brigade. Most of his infantry were ready from late morning, but the armor failed to appear. Some of the tanks were stuck in traffic on the beach, while others were late getting ashore, as was Rennie's own reserve brigade. General Rennie was further distracted by the need to reach the newly dropped British 6th Airborne Division, whose light equipment made its relief a priority. "Tommies," as the British called their soldiers, finally began to move toward Caen at midafternoon. German counterattacks soon stopped their progress.

Field Marshal Rommel's hopes to defeat the invasion on the beaches would be dashed. Rommel himself happened to be away—relying on weather predictions that seemed to preclude an invasion, he had returned to Germany to celebrate his wife's birthday. But Army Group B quickly asked for release of the panzer reserves, and Field Marshal von Rundstedt, though he remained uncertain this was the actual invasion, lost no time telephoning to request the führer's approval. Von Rundstedt was not going to be caught flat-footed. But at Rastenburg Hitler still slept. His minions refused to wake him. When the führer did finally rouse himself around ten a.m., the very moment GIs were beginning to break the deadlock at Omaha Beach, he shared von Rundstedt's doubts and decided not to release the panzers. By midafternoon, following a staff conference, he finally gave permission to employ some of the reserves, the divisions under Rommel's control.

It would be General Erich Marcks who reacted most quickly to the invasion. Marcks led the LXXXIV Corps, the command directly responsible for Normandy. Though the armor had not been released, one formation, the 21st Panzer Division, was stationed in the immediate vicinity of Caen, some of its units so close to the coast that they fought British paratroopers during the night. The panzer division's response was initially hampered because its own leader, General Edgar Feuchtinger, looking at the same weather forecasts as Rommel, had decided there could be no invasion and had gone to Paris for the weekend. Major Vierzig's tank battalion had been on a maneuver the night before the assault. Recalled, he awaited instructions for hours. About nine a.m., the battalion was dispatched—against the paratroops. Feuchtinger's units started to move off without him. General Marcks saw the 21st Panzer as already embroiled. He ordered attacks against the British landings to restore the situation. Vierzig's panzers were recalled before they ever encountered the British airborne troops. By midafternoon the tanks, plus some of the division's *Panzergrenadiers*, were poised to attack into the gap separating the British beaches called Sword and Juno, between the 3rd Canadian and 3rd British Divisions. Marcks came from his headquarters to observe, standing on a little hill. He turned to the panzer regiment's commander. "If you don't succeed in throwing the British into the sea," the general commented, "we shall have lost the war."[5]

The German units moved off. Their assault put a wedge between the Allied spearheads. Before dark some of the Germans actually reached the coast, but without knocking back the invaders. There was no real chance to drive them into the sea. Nevertheless, the British commander General Miles Dempsey cautiously ordered a halt to the advance on Caen. Rennie's 185th Brigade, the main strike force, ended the day only halfway to its goal.

Actually, the most successful invaders on D-Day were the Canadians of Major General R. F. L. "Rod" Keller's 3rd Infantry Division, who stormed ashore on Juno Beach. By ten a.m., vehicles of the attached 2nd Canadian Armored Brigade were arriving, helping overcome the last coastal defenses. Challenged to interpret confusing dispatches from the beach when making his decision to land the reserve, Brigadier Cunningham's 9th Infantry Brigade, Rod Keller chose the sector from which he had the most favorable reports—which turned out wrong. But Cunningham's brigade moved out smartly nonetheless. Artillery caught one German company in the open, searching for nonexistent Allied paratroops. Some strongpoints put up a stiff fight, such as at the château of Tailleville, the fortified headquarters of a battalion of the 21st Panzer Division. Keller's plan featured two phase lines, the second of which, Oak, anticipated his Canadians would reach the Caen-Bayeux road—that is, *passing* Caen to the west. Keller's objectives included the Carpiquet airfield. Cunningham's rifle battalions were ready to move on Carpiquet when Dempsey's halt order reached them. Canadian tanks were nearby, too. Keller's Canadians had advanced farther than any of their British comrades. At that time Canadian spearheads were within sight of Caen. The Canadian performance at Juno Beach makes perplexing the British tendency to regard their Commonwealth allies as second-class troops.

Whatever Montgomery's intentions, the German reaction would be one reason he faltered. There is an odd disconnect here, in that Allied appreciations always assumed a certain scale of German reinforcement, as well as that the bulk of early arrivals would be panzer troops. That is exactly what happened. Yet Monty, in formulating his intentions, and Dempsey, in laying down plans and objectives, assumed their own troops would be able to maneuver with impunity. The British were fortunate in that Hitler hesitated to commit the reserves, but the forces of the 21st Panzer Division and the Atlantic Wall defenders had by themselves impeded a triumphal Allied procession into Caen. The bridgehead became a "lodgment," a platform the Allies would expand into France, starting with Normandy.

THE CRUX AT CAEN

The days after June 6 brought a race to build up. The Allies scrambled to put troops ashore, the Germans to bring up reinforcements. Monty's repeated efforts to break into Caen belie his claim to be simply acting as a hinge. On D+1, Rennie's and Keller's troops tried again to break into the city and failed once more. Monty told London that he had decided to avoid "butting" against the city and had instructed Dempsey to bypass it by attacking across the Odon River toward the towns of Villers-Bocage and Evrecy, and thence southeast toward Falaise. This strategy sounds better than it was: West of Caen the Orne River bends away, but its tributary the Odon branches out to obstruct easy movement southward. The difficulty of the terrain west of the river bend was comparable to that of the hedgerows that bedeviled the Americans, and the Orne itself was a highly defensible river line that would still have lain between Monty and Falaise. The first British attacks failed.

Regardless of Monty's intentions, German countermeasures had now begun. The Oberkommando der Wehrmacht (OKW), the German armed forces high command that served Hitler directly, might not have released the panzer reserves, but it prepared for that eventuality. General Walter Warlimont, a senior OKW staff planner, telephoned General Fritz Bayerlein with an alert order for the Panzer Lehr Division at two thirty a.m. on D-Day. The 12th SS Panzer Division assembled on its own initiative and received official orders—misguided, but orders nonetheless—at seven a.m. Both were sent to Normandy later that day. Bayerlein was told to be on the road by five in the afternoon. Remembering the power of Allied aircraft from North Africa, Bayerlein protested the demand to move in daylight. The Seventh Army rejected his pleas. On the road, Panzer Lehr would be attacked around the clock by Allied aircraft, suffering significant losses. The 12th SS sustained losses, too. Soldiers soon dreaded the appearance of jabos, as they came to call the Allied fighter-bombers. Fighting here would be nothing like the Eastern Front.

Rommel and von Rundstedt understood the danger of the Allies breaking out into the good tank country south of Caen. If only to preserve their ability to move, the German commanders were obliged to intervene. After the failure of the counterpunch on D-Day, the next idea was to hit the British with Feuchtinger's 21st Panzer and SS Brigadier General Witt's 12th SS Panzer. That attack on June 7 ran headlong into Dempsey's renewed effort to capture Caen. The Canadians were driven back from their positions close to Carpiquet, but a different Canadian spearhead slammed into the German flank and Witt's SS troopers had to halt. The Allies held on tight. Next would be a concentrated blow by the three mobile divisions that had arrived by June 8. The 21st Panzer, Panzer Lehr, and 12th SS Panzer Divisions together represented a formidable force. Colonel General Freiherr Geyr von Schweppenberg, the senior armor commander in the West, arrived to supervise personally. But then the town of Bayeux fell to British of the 50th Infantry Division, which was at the point of linking up with the Americans. Field Marshal Rommel abandoned the big attack in favor of a Panzer Lehr attempt to retake Bayeux, which was just as well because the Germans had their hands full near Caen. A Canadian spearhead threatened to split Bayerlein's division apart from the Hitlerjugend in line next to it. The Bayeux plan was scrapped. As the hours passed, the Germans found themselves completely on the defensive.

General Montgomery now ordained a pincer move on and past Caen, passing the 51st Highland Division through the British airborne bridgehead east of the Orne, while the 7th Armored Division maneuvered through Villers-Bocage to the west. Monty acknowledged the problem of the Orne, intending to drop his 1st Airborne Division behind it to compromise the river line. This gambit disintegrated when the ground troops proved unable to generate any real momentum. The 51st Division attack on June 10 faded within hours in the face of fierce German resistance. Along the Odon the 7th Armored, famously known as "Desert Rats" from their time in North Africa, fared no better on June 13—here the German tank commander Michael Wittmann stopped the attack virtually singlehandedly by ambushing the British armor and destroying a great number of its tanks. Meanwhile, the RAF objected to diverting tactical aircraft to protect another airdrop on the Continent.

What the British did accomplish was to foil German plans for counterattacks on their beachhead and fend off those that took place. Rommel's idea of driving the British into the sea with an offensive by three panzer divisions collapsed, partly due to piecemeal arrival of the reinforcements, partly to attrition inflicted as they moved up to the front, partly to the weight of Allied naval gunfire and air support, but also due to the determination of British and Canadian soldiers. The Germans suffered a further setback at the same moment the British pincer attack failed, when Allied warplanes plastered the command post of Panzer Group West, responsible for the putative offensive. The Allies had a vital window into German activity, intelligence Source ULTRA (see chapter 2), and that plus radio direction finding identified its headquarters. Commanding general von Schweppenberg suffered slight wounds, but his staff chief and a number of senior officers died. Similarly, a few days later, a British naval bombardment targeted the Hitlerjugend Division command post and killed its leader, General Witt. SS Colonel Kurt Meyer, nicknamed "Panzer" for his dynamism, took over the 12th SS. German leaders still dreamed of driving the invaders into the sea. First they needed to stabilize the front. Battles continued before Caen. The Germans' nightmare had materialized.

A month after D-Day, Monty's troops had attained a line ten miles from their nearest invasion beach. In that time Dempsey had suffered 24,500 losses. The British had their gripes, believing U.S. generals too aggressive, lacking strategic vision; regarding American staff work to be sloppy; and decrying the poor quality of some U.S.-produced equipment furnished them under Lend-Lease. But General Bradley's First Army had linked up Omaha and Utah beaches, thrust west to cut the Cotentin, isolated and then captured Cherbourg, and made a start at advancing in the peninsula, scratching their way through the hedgerows. Their casualties had totaled 43,500. Perceptions grew that Montgomery, intent on conserving British strength, had left the United States to do the real fighting. That was when the generals met to plan their breakout.

FÜHRER AND GENERALS

General Walter Warlimont stood among the most skillful German planners. For five years he had been a leading strategist on the OKW operations staff, reporting directly to Hitler in his capacity as commander in chief. The OKW controlled all German fighting fronts—with the exception of Russia, where Hitler's orders were executed by the army high command—and thus was Hitler's right arm in fighting the invasion. A forty-eight-year-old Rhinelander, Warlimont had had vital roles in many operations. He supplied the brainpower that enabled his chief, Colonel General Alfred Jodl, to give the führer sound advice. By June 1944, Warlimont was frustrated, increasingly concerned at Hitler's penchant for dominating the daily conferences, where he consumed endless hours with minutiae while procrastinating on major strategic decisions. Warlimont had just made an extensive survey trip to the Italian front. While presenting his results at one of Hitler's conferences, the führer cut him off, ordering his displays and data sheets taken away. Instead, Hitler focused on his new anxiety, the Battle for France.

Despite this preoccupation, Warlimont recalls, "search the pages of Jodl's diary of this period as you will, no mention will be found of any strategic thoughts or decisions on the situation in the West."[6] Warlimont makes an example of Hitler's order to recall the II SS Panzer Corps from Russia, for which no staff work was demanded or done, yet the diktat went out on June 11. General Jodl left his staff in ignorance while providing his views directly to the führer. On June 12, Jodl told the naval commander in chief, Grand Admiral Karl Doenitz, that if the Allies broke out of Normandy all of France would be lost, and that the next defensive position would be the German frontier. Warlimont only learned of this from Doenitz after the war. Field Marshal Rommel and the OKW operations staff—Jodl's staff—independently reached the conclusion that all efforts must be bent to make a concentrated push against the Allies before they consolidated their strength. Yet Jodl never expressed agreement. In Warlimont's view the chance had passed by June 9 at the latest: "all strategy for defense against the invasion was becoming lost in a morass of indecision on major matters and interminable discussions of detail."[7]

The führer and OKW went through three stages in their thinking on countering the Allied invasion, none at their own initiative. All started from the preconception, powerfully impelled by the Fortitude deception, that the Allies intended a second invasion. The first approach was to deter D-Day, primarily by erecting the Atlantic Wall and making it seem impregnable. The second concept, a chance lost on the beaches, was to defeat the invasion by means of immediate counterattacks. There remained the possibility of a strategic stroke, either a major offensive or some novel effort. "I was unable to understand Hitler's attitude," wrote his Luftwaffe adjutant, Colonel Nicolaus von Below. "He still seemed convinced the invasion force could be thrown back into the sea despite the enemy's air superiority and the huge amounts of matériel coming ashore unchecked. The situation was that the Army stood alone."[8]

Through most of this final period of the war Hitler fixated on the novel response, the notion that his "secret weapons" would reverse the tide. The most concrete of those possibilities—and the only one that could be applied in the short term—was the use of the V-1 "flying bomb." This was a cruise missile, powered by a pulse-jet engine, guided by a gyroscope-stabilized automatic pilot, carrying an explosive warhead of nearly one ton to a distance of 150 (later 250) miles. The V-1s took off from long rail catapults that came to be known as ski ramps, and a typical installation at peak effort could launch fifteen of them in a day. The V-1 campaign began on June 14, 1944, aimed at London from sites in the Pas de Calais and Belgium. At the time of Normandy it was early days, and Hitler's confidence, if not ultimately justified, seems at least potentially reasonable.[9]

The more prosaic and conventional, but also far more reliable, response to Overlord would have been a large-scale counteroffensive. Here the initiative again came from the front, not OKW. Field Marshal von Rundstedt proposed a multi-corps attack on a sector to be determined, using all forces, including the reinforcements en route. That was on June 15. Rommel's chief of staff, Lieutenant General Hans Speidel, takes up the story: "an unexpected telephone call on the evening of June 16 ordered both field marshals and their chiefs of staff to be at Battle Headquarters 'W-II,' north of Soissons, at nine a.m. on June 17 to make a report to Hitler."[10]

The command center had been built by the Todt Organization, near the town of Margival, for the specific purpose of housing Hitler. First planned during the French campaign, the idea for W-II had been dropped, then revived in anticipation of the inevitable invasion. Construction started in October 1942. Führer headquarters architect Siegfried Schmelcher designed a complex consisting of a number of bunkers, with bombproof quarters and work spaces, plus aboveground barracks. It could be accessed by rail, with trains protected by a tunnel, and was defended along a perimeter set more than four miles out from the central bunkers. With this part of rural France served poorly by telephone services, the Paris net had to be extended to include W-II. The underground headquarters was located not far from where the führer, as a corporal in the distant days of the Great War, had won his Iron Cross. Hitler's visit in June 1944 would be only his second trip to France during the war, and the one time he ever made use of W-II.

Like several of President Lyndon Johnson's summit conferences during the Vietnam War, this meeting would be called on a "flash" basis.

No advance work was possible. OKW had done nothing to prepare the führer or the participants. Field Marshal Rommel had to drive 140 miles to attend. The Margival conference has been slighted in accounts of the Normandy campaign, yet the proceedings underline its centrality. Several elements were at play here. Had Margival truly been the equivalent of one of President Johnson's photo opportunities, questioning its importance would be appropriate. But in reality, Margival is a key event for at least two reasons: because it lay at the heart of the German strategic response, such as it was; and because it perfectly reflected Hitler's disintegrating relationship with his generals.

On the evening of the sixteenth, even as Rommel and von Rundstedt were being summoned so peremptorily, four Focke-Wulf Fw 200 Condors flew Hitler and his party to Metz. The air force cleared a corridor for the flight, grounded all fighters in the West, and stood down its flak crews to ensure Hitler would be in no danger. The führer and General Jodl motored to W-II in the morning. Among Hitler's party was Luftwaffe aide von Below, who recalled Margival as a "singularly unfruitful" and "thoroughly unpleasant reunion."[11] For his part Rommel had been in Normandy that day, a twenty-one-hour trip to visit the commands of the II Parachute and LXXXIV Corps, the latter of which had just lost General Marcks, its D-Day leader. He had to leave at three a.m. to arrive on time. Because Hitler had forbidden commanders in the West to travel by air, Field Marshal von Rundstedt also drove to Margival.

In General Speidel's view, Hitler appeared nervous, greeting his field marshals gruffly, in a loud voice, expressing anger the Allies had invaded successfully, demanding that Cherbourg be held. Von Rundstedt made introductory remarks, then turned to Rommel, whose presentation he supported. The field marshals stood. Hitler sat on a stool and played with colored pencils. Rommel rejected charges that the army had been caught napping or was responsible for the looming defeat. He had warned often of the hopelessness of struggling against an adversary with such power in the air and on the sea, not to say the land itself. The coast defenses had been inadequate, but Army Group B troops had fought to the last bullet, "like young tigers," Rommel said.[12] In many cases losses were such that one could no longer speak of divisions, merely combat groups. Infantry formations were melting away like ice exposed to blazing heat.

The field marshal predicted the fall of Cherbourg within a week and estimated that Eisenhower's armies intended to break out first to the south, then toward Paris, with a secondary thrust into Brittany to seize the ports there. Rommel demanded freedom to maneuver all his forces, panzers especially. He recommended a withdrawal to the Seine, defending Paris. Hitler demanded the army hold at all costs. Rommel then countered that he needed orders for what to do once the Allies broke out. Alfred Jodl, the führer's minion, later testified at the Nuremberg trials that Rommel had been especially forthright and had laid out the situation in an unmistakable fashion. Speidel thought Rommel's exposition mercilessly frank.

Hitler did not recognize the troops' weakness and stood fast on defending the ports, starting with Cherbourg. He insisted Allied power could not possibly be so destructive as the generals were saying. Field Marshal Rommel shot back that neither Hitler nor any senior OKW officer had ever come to see for themselves—though judging from Warlimont's recent experience with his Italian survey, one might wonder whether that would have been worth the effort. The sole concession came when Hitler said that eliminating the Allied battleships that provided gunfire support off the Norman coast would ease the lot of the *Landser*; the führer's naval aide immediately left the meeting to inform Admiral Doenitz that Hitler wanted the Kriegsmarine to sink the Allied fleet.

Field Marshal von Rundstedt requested permission to withdraw into the Cherbourg fortress. Hitler acceded, but demanded the troops pull back slowly to extract the greatest toll of GIs. After the first hour General Speidel left briefly to telephone these instructions.

To the degree there was a real, if sterile, exchange of views at Margival, it hinged on the whole question of "fortresses," in this case the ports. Defending localities as fortresses had become Hitler's mantra and had led to many setbacks in Russia, where irreplaceable formations were frittered away in useless positions. In the West the ports tied down mountains of equipment, particularly heavy artillery, plus a quarter of the strength of the armies. The field marshals had a point. But so did Hitler—the ports were the hard kernels of the Atlantic Wall; if any place could be defended, they could. And—as will become apparent in our discussion of Allied supplies—without ports Eisenhower could hardly hope to reach the German frontier, much less capture Berlin and end the war.

A second point went unexamined. This was Jodl's sense that if Normandy was lost there could be no stopping the Allies short of the frontier. Here, too, yawned a gulf between field marshals and the führer. Von Rundstedt believed a delaying action fought across France could cost the Allies tremendously and buy time to perfect the Westwall, the fortified line along the German border, which had been stripped to benefit the Atlantic Wall. The Germans knew little of the Allied manpower shortages, but an expensive campaign might conceivably have brought Eisenhower close to the end of SHAEF's tether, with unforeseen political and diplomatic consequences. If the German armies were frittered away in Normandy, there could be no possibilities for delaying action. So much for the field commanders. From Hitler's perspective the picture looked radically different. The Normandy front was only about eighty miles long. Abandon that and the combat area immediately widened, at a minimum to the distance between the Swiss border and the Dutch coast, more than five hundred miles. If the Germans were outgunned on the short Norman front there was no reason to suppose they could defend a much wider battlefield. And of course there was the führer's penchant for holding every inch of ground.

Were it not for Hitler's proclivities, a frank airing of these matters might have led to the view that von Rundstedt held—that Germany ought to sue for peace. But Hitler would not go there. Instead, he replied with an extended monologue—Speidel called it "a strange mixture of cynicism and false intuition"—extolling the virtues of the V-weapons.[13] In fact, Hitler interrupted this disquisition to call in propaganda officials and dictate wording for a press communiqué announcing the Nazi use of flying bombs.

During three nights, five hundred of the weapons had been launched toward London. Military commanders questioned the efficacy of the so-called wonder weapons, whereupon Hitler summoned General Heinemann, the leader of the field rocket unit, who had to admit their margin of error was as much as nine to twelve miles. The führer insisted on using them to bombard London rather than the British ports supplying the forces in Normandy. This led to the field commanders denouncing the ineffectiveness of the Luftwaffe—and in turn Hitler admitted his own disappointment, attributing Luftwaffe weakness to delayed, misguided, and disorganized aircraft development programs.

All this left only the option already on the table, von Rundstedt's proposal for a large-scale offensive. At some point, in discussions that lasted late into the afternoon, the führer approved. According to Warlimont, Jodl's record indicates no examination of the specifics of the concept, yet that same afternoon OKW sent out an order to concentrate four SS panzer divisions in the Caen sector for use in a counterstroke at Hitler's discretion.[14] General Jodl briefed the group on the stream of reinforcements making their way to the front. Finally, Hitler accepted a minor adjustment of the line below Caen.

"You demand our confidence," Rommel exclaimed, "but you do not trust us yourself."[15]

Hitler made no reply.

Suddenly the entire proceeding was interrupted by an Allied bomber raid and all the senior officers repaired to a W-II bomb shelter. There Field Marshal Rommel took advantage of the close quarters and absence of scribes to broach even larger questions. Noting that German defenses must collapse and the Allies would certainly break out, Rommel nudged the führer to reach appropriate "political" conclusions. Hitler blanched. With a tight face he ordered Rommel to confine himself to military duties.

Before the group broke up, the führer's adjutant, General Schmundt, informed the visitors they should expect to see Hitler at Army Group B, or possibly OB West, on June 19. Returning to his headquarters at La Roche-Guyon, Rommel walked with his naval aide, Vice Admiral Friedrich Ruge, and revealed that the führer had plans for a big counteroffensive. Ruge felt Rommel had been somewhat influenced by Hitler, whom, he noted, "must have an uncanny magnetism."[16] In fact, the field marshal wrote his wife the next day, telling her he had seen the führer and now viewed the future with greater optimism. Speidel phoned that day to arrange Hitler's inspection, only to learn the führer had already left for Germany. Rommel's staff chief was told Hitler had been shaken when a V-1, off course, exploded near Margival.

In fact, Hitler had left for Berchtesgaden immediately after the generals departed.

The battle for Cherbourg held meaning for Hitler far beyond its limited port capacity or objective military importance. It was the day after Margival, June 18, that the Americans split the Cotentin Peninsula and isolated Cherbourg from the main front. Some Germans of the 77th Infantry Division broke out to the south rather than be trapped in the resulting pocket. That very night Hitler pressed Jodl on whether this escape had been sanctioned by higher authority, and the OKW operations chief allowed that it seemed so. The division commander was killed in the breakout. Otherwise, he would have been court-martialed. Hitler, of course, had ordered that *more* rather than fewer soldiers be sent to defend Cherbourg. A demand to inform OKW of exactly what troops held the fortress resulted in a radio message that was intercepted—and furnished Allied intelligence with precise knowledge of the available German forces. Later the führer wanted the Luftwaffe to airlift a parachute regiment into the port to supplement its garrison, an illusory option given Allied aerial superiority. The Luftwaffe did manage at least one aerial supply drop into the city. But when Cherbourg's commander reported diminished supplies and requested an airlift of additional matériel, Hitler groused that in two years the army had done nothing to provision the fortress. Cherbourg would fall on June 27 without any extended siege. The führer demanded that OKW investigate the facts surrounding loss of the port, and he later used Cherbourg as a proof of the Wehrmacht's inadequacies.

One reason for German concerns about Cherbourg is that they knew a certain amount about Allied supply difficulties as a consequence of their radio intelligence. Under Colonel Baron Maximilian von Oer, the higher commander for communications reconnaissance, there were two radio regiments focused on intercepting Allied messages and tracking the emitters. A base at Euskirchen, Germany, covered British radio traffic. Communications Reconnaissance Battalion 12 followed American broadcasts with listening posts at several places in France. Late in June the Germans succeeded in breaking into a logistics code used by the ferry control authority for the British beaches, which gave daily totals for supplies landed. Radio monitoring had also identified a U.S. Army headquarters ashore, four corps commands, and fifteen combat divisions. German field intelligence confirmed these and identified other units. Staff officers could calculate how near the Allies were to their limits. That did not make Cherbourg's defenses any more powerful, but it does help explain Hitler's desperation to hold the port.

In the meantime, the German offensive plan was real, no fantasy. Von Rundstedt originally lacked specific objectives, but there were people ready to weigh in on that. "Up to the end of June," Warlimont notes, "Supreme Headquarters was continuously occupied over the use to which Hitler intended to put [his panzer divisions] and with the issue of orders for the purpose."[17] On June 19 Rommel sent a pair of sketch maps to panzer commander von Schweppenberg, back in the saddle after the Allied air attack on his headquarters. One of Rommel's concepts coincided with thinking at both OB West and OKW: Seek the junction between the U.S. and British armies. On June 20 OKW issued a directive to that effect. Panzer Group West would lead the operation, and von Schweppenberg plunged into detailed planning. The assembly of forces moved ahead. There were arguments over whether the blow ought to be based on three panzer corps or four—basically a dispute over what weight to give the U.S. front. Warlimont's planners argued in a June 25 memorandum that Germany should accept risks everywhere else in order to maximize the punch. Since the first response to Overlord, when the Germans had sent 130,000 *Landser* to Normandy in a week, there had never been such an effort. Between June 25 and July 5 the OKW deployed 90,000 troops to the battlefront, including the 1st, 2nd, 9th, and 10th SS Panzer Divisions, a corps headquarters, and massive amounts of artillery, along with infantry to relieve panzers already on the front.

Two factors ultimately put paid to the grand plan. One would be the German difficulty concentrating forces, the other the führer's own wavering. As far as the troops were concerned, Allied transportation bombing largely accomplished its goal of isolating Normandy. The OB West war diary on June 25 noted that the earliest date the offensive could be attempted would be July 5 because of the assembly problem—the Germans already knew that the last required formation, the 1st SS Panzer Division, would not be complete until that date. Warlimont's OKW planners recommended the same date for the same reason. Field Marshal von Rundstedt would tell Allied interrogators after the war that his biggest troubles in the West had been the incredible Allied air superiority, which made daytime movement impossible; his fuel problems, which also related to Allied bombing of German fuel resources, storage, and transport; and the crippling of the railroads, a collaboration between the bombers and the Resistance. Von Rundstedt complained he could not get a loaded train across the Rhine. The Allies knew it, too—by June 24 ULTRA decrypts showed that the II SS Panzer Corps (9th and 10th SS Panzer Divisions) had begun arriving from Russia six days earlier—but 80 percent of the trains bearing its troops and equipment had been obliged to unload as far east as the Saarbrücken-Nancy region and complete the move by road, imposing wear on the tanks and trucks and exhaustion on the men. Only a small percentage could rail as far as Paris and drive from there. The road marches added ten days to the time necessary to deploy the corps. And no one reached Normandy without running the gauntlet of Allied air.

Though Field Marshal von Rundstedt had backed an offensive, he also had some doubts. While Allied intelligence knew nothing of the plan itself, Source ULTRA did report on OB West's weekly appreciation for the period of June 19 to 26, during which the preparations were under way. Von Rundstedt expected Allied forces to pivot on Caen and attack toward the Seine, a justification for employing the bulk of panzer troops on the British sector. Rundstedt indicated that he continued to fear a second Allied invasion in the area of the Pas de Calais and was holding back some mobile forces to counter such an eventuality. This attitude also hindered any concentration for a major offensive.

Hitler's distraction put another nail in the coffin of the attack plan. At Margival he had acquiesced. Focused on the West, Hitler had been startled when the Russians began a huge offensive on June 22, quickly resulting in a German disaster. So far Hitler had acceded to Rommel and OKW planners on the objective in the West. But by June 25, with Lawton Collins's U.S. VII Corps closing in on Cherbourg, the führer conceived the new idea of attacking into the "rear" of the American forces grasping for the port—*in addition to* the original concept—another deleterious effect of the führer's fixation on Cherbourg.

Rommel and von Rundstedt were apoplectic. OB West immediately responded that it lacked forces for simultaneous attacks and could not assemble supplies for an offensive toward Cherbourg. It also worried about Caen. The same day, Hitler agreed that troops need not wait to concentrate fully and should counter Allied advances, which amounted to an acknowledgment of the threat to Caen. On June 26, von Rundstedt, after visiting Rommel—unusual for him—sent OKW a further paper noting that both field marshals agreed the Cotentin option was just not feasible, and that it could become necessary to commit the assembling forces to stop the British. At this point Hitler reverted to his idea that the blow be made against the Americans. But the troops were already being deployed against the British, especially south of the Odon. Source ULTRA told the Allies of these troop movements. In fact, the British decided to hold off certain operations pending commitment of II SS Panzer Corps.

All this peripatetic maundering sparked a fresh confrontation between the führer and his generals. On one of their evening walks, Admiral Ruge found Rommel very upset: "He had been ordered to launch relief attacks for Cherbourg when he felt fortunate that he had established some sort of defensive line at all." They mulled over the disaster, Ruge recalls, debating whether in the event of catastrophe one should shoot oneself. The admiral saw making peace with the Allies as the only possibility, and since the Allies refused to deal with Hitler, "he would have to commit suicide in order to open the way."

"Aren't you the tough warrior," Rommel chided.[18]

The two men were feeling delicately around the edges of the plot against Hitler, which Rommel knew of but with which he had yet to associate himself. Suddenly, on June 28, Hitler called both Rommel and von Rundstedt to his mountain retreat at Berchtesgaden for a meeting the next day. Again the long drive, now to the Bavarian Alps. As the field marshals made their way, General Eugen Dollmann of the Seventh Army, humiliated by his inability to stop the invasion or defeat it afterward, poisoned himself. This gave concrete illustration to the exchange Rommel had had with Ruge a few days earlier. Without reference to the field marshals or indeed the German army, Hitler named SS General Paul Hausser of the II SS Panzer Corps to replace Dollmann, whose death was presented as the result of a heart attack. Not only did Hitler put a Waffen-SS officer at the head of the troops fighting the Americans, he began an initiative to assign National Socialist Political Officers, in effect Nazi political commissars, to all top army commands. Army Group B was informed the commissar expected to have at least an hour alone with its commander every day.

The meeting of Field Marshals von Rundstedt and Rommel with the führer on June 29 can only be interpreted as a calculated snub. Von Rundstedt arrived late in the morning, Rommel early in the afternoon. Both were left to cool their heels until evening, when they were admitted into Hitler's presence. Von Rundstedt had asked for a private session—he was denied. A broad swath of acolytes surrounded the führer—the field marshals were alone. They faced Hitler across a long table surfaced in red marble.

According to Heinz Guderian, the inspector general of armored troops, Rommel no longer believed a mobile defense was possible. General Jodl recorded a conversation that recognized the situation now drove events—the priority had to be stopping the British. Perhaps there could be an offensive later on. If so, Jodl's notes specified, it would be against the Americans. But mostly there was another Hitler monologue on miracle weapons, punctuated with a display of aerial photographs of damage from V-weapons. Hitler cut Rommel off when he again raised the matter of appropriate conclusions. The field marshal mistakenly thought he had recruited Goebbels and Himmler to his side during the long hours waiting to be admitted to the führer's presence, but in the event they stood mute when Rommel spoke up. Hitler then dismissed his marshals. In a final, petulant act, he sent his western commanders off without any dinner.

Much of the substantive discussion at Berchtesgaden concerned the Luftwaffe and took place after Rommel left. Hitler directed that a thousand fighter planes be sent to the West. Guderian reports that Goering offered eight hundred fighters if the Third Air Fleet could furnish the pilots and crews. Field Marshal Sperrle ignited Hitler by reporting that no more than five hundred crews were available. The führer also demanded redoubled efforts to block Allied supplies with aerial mines, cruise missile bombings—any means that could be brought to bear.

The führer's childish behavior at the meeting did not deter Rommel.

The field marshal had told Admiral Ruge he could probably endure efforts of the higher-ups to saddle him with the blame for failing to defeat the invasion. Now Rommel took aside Jodl's direct superior, Field Marshal Wilhelm Keitel, the OKW chief of staff, to say what Hitler had forbidden. "A total victory, to which Hitler is still referring even today, is absurd in our rapidly worsening situation, and a total defeat can be expected," Rommel declared, according to Hans Speidel. "Our aim should be to use every means to end the war in the West immediately." Rommel hoped that by giving up Germany's conquests and "wishful dreams," the Soviets might be defeated. "We must save Germany from chaos and especially from complete destruction by enemy bombing." Speidel writes that Keitel expressed agreement and promised to relay these arguments to Hitler.[19] It is highly doubtful that he did so, unless as one more element in the bill of particulars against the "defeatist" generals. Unknown to them, waiting in the wings was Field Marshal Günther Hans von Kluge, whom the führer had decided to appoint to one of the top posts in the West.

Rommel reached his headquarters shortly before midnight on June 30. While he was in transit OKW issued a new directive shelving the grand offensive pending arrival of additional reinforcements and neutralization of Allied naval and air support, while ordering counterattacks against the British. The directive continued to foresee the offensive as aimed at the Americans. The true importance of the latest round of fighting was to Führer Headquarters, where it convinced Hitler to purge his commanders. Premeditation is apparent in that for several days the führer had already hosted Field Marshal von Kluge, grooming him to take the reins.

At OB West, Field Marshal von Rundstedt now received a memorandum from General Geyr von Schweppenberg that advocated withdrawal from Caen to a line beyond the range of the Allied naval guns. Its core argument read:

It is no longer possible (a) to achieve a breakthrough to the coast . . . (b) to hold lines with panzer divisions without their dwindling or already depleted units . . . being consumed in a very short time; (c) to expect a change in the situation by badly equipped or mediocre infantry divisions, which have indeed been allocated but cannot get here within the predictable future. . . . A clear choice must be made between the inevitable patchwork of a rigid defense, which leaves the initiative to the enemy, and flexible tactics which give us the initiative sometimes at least. . . . An elastic conduct of operations is the better course.[20]

Von Rundstedt also obtained a report from General Paul Hausser, who might have been SS but was a very competent soldier, summarizing his preliminary observations on taking over the Seventh Army. Hausser agreed with many of von Schweppenberg's points. Field Marshal von Rundstedt forwarded both papers to OKW, using the opportunity to ask in writing for freedom of action. That afternoon OKW replied, rejecting retreat, demanding that every inch of ground be held by tenacious defense or regained by local counterattacks. On July 1 von Rundstedt had to telephone OKW and report the SS panzers' inability to make any headway against the British, which confirmed what he and others had been saying. Field Marshal Keitel took the call.

"What shall we do?" Keitel wondered, then repeated, "What shall we do?"

"Make peace, you idiots. What else can you do?" von Rundstedt shot back.

That brought an immediate reaction. The next day one of Hitler's aides arrived at OB West with a letter relieving von Rundstedt. The cashiered commander left a final testament: he told Rommel he was happy not to have to preside over the coming disaster. Why Hitler kept Rommel himself can probably be attributed to Goebbels, always conscious of political aspects, who would have warned that the dismissal of the popular Rommel would cripple the morale of the German people.

Field Marshal Günther Hans von Kluge turned up soon after to assume command. The sixty-one-year-old Prussian field marshal had had prominent roles in the campaigns in Poland, France, and Russia, where he had been constantly employed until he was badly injured in a road accident the previous fall. Von Kluge was known to compare himself to the Napoleonic marshal Michel Ney, but had acquired the nickname "Clever Hans," a play on the meaning of the German word klug. An artilleryman, von Kluge had nevertheless gone out of his way in the interwar German army to learn to fly, and all his major field commands had included important panzer forces. But there are doubts as to how well the field marshal understood mobile warfare. In fact, von Kluge's disputes with Germany's renowned panzer leader, Heinz Guderian, were legendary, and by 1943 had become so bitter the field marshal challenged Guderian to a duel, nominating Adolf Hitler for his second. Hitler had managed to get the two men to stand down, but von Kluge remained a favorite. Hitler recalled him from convalescing after his car crash. Now he turned to Field Marshal von Kluge to save the situation in the West.

On July 3, von Kluge staged a scene with Rommel, accusing him in an insulting fashion, and in front of his chief of staff and operations officer, of failure to obey orders. The newly minted OB West had certainly never fought in an operational environment where the adversary possessed such complete aerial superiority, and Rommel argued that he had done everything humanly possible in the face of adverse conditions. Rommel's salvation may have been that he disagreed with von Rundstedt and von Schweppenberg over the need to evacuate Caen. The next day Hitler dismissed General von Schweppenberg, whose replacement at the head of Panzer Group West would be General Heinrich Eberbach. The inspector general of armored troops, Eberbach had previously led tanks in Russia, had held administrative responsibility for SS armored units in the West, and—possibly significant—as a young officer in 1917 had fought in Flanders, as had then Corporal Adolf Hitler. A couple of weeks later the führer also fired his military commander for Belgium and northern France.

Hitler's intransigence and his purge were the last straw for Rommel. One of the conspirators planning to move against the führer passed through Paris, where he saw the field marshal on July 9. Rommel expressed the view that there would be an Allied breakthrough within a matter of weeks. There are varying accounts of what passed between the field marshal and this Luftwaffe lieutenant colonel. One version is that the Army Group B commander merely declared himself willing to help make peace in the West, which put him among the conspirators to a degree. Another has it that Rommel said, more explicitly, that he would support action against Hitler in France once it had begun in Germany. Rommel only asked that Hitler be put on trial. The field marshal was not told the plotters intended to assassinate the führer.[21] With varying degrees of involvement, those who aligned with the plotters included the chiefs of staff of OB West and Army Group B, two commanders of panzer divisions, and other key officers. Field Marshal von Kluge, once he saw the reality at the front, also backed the plot, albeit more timorously.

HILL 112

General Montgomery's Operation Epsom aimed at breaching the Odon River, with a right hook to outflank Caen from the west. New troops off the beach added to Monty's punch, though storms in the English Channel delayed landings and forced Epsom's postponement until June 25. The Odon was not very wide, but it had a strong current, swollen by the endless rains, with banks that rose straight from the water, often topped by trees. German defenders gave ground, fighting stubbornly all the way. ULTRA afforded excellent insight into German countermeasures. On the third day the British captured a bridge across the Odon and poured their fresh 11th Armored Division across the river to take a little rise that became notorious as Hill 112. An immediate German counterpunch failed, but the Seventh Army ordered another. The 11th Armored Division and other units, originally intent on reaching the Orne and outflanking Caen's defenses, instead faced spoiling attacks.

On June 28 the British ended up holding a portion of Hill 112, roughly halfway between the Odon and the Orne. The 11th Armored Division had lost forty tanks to gain it. A few *Landser*, cut off, still held out in bunkers on the hill, and the Germans' local counterattacks and shelling were unnerving. The worst were the *Nebelwerfers*. Recalled Norman Habertin, a Tommy with the 8th Battalion of the Rifle Brigade, "Before a single trench had been dug, down came those dreaded 'moaning minnies.' There was nothing to do but lie down and bite the earth."[22]

Alerted by ULTRA to the approach of II SS Panzer Corps, Dempsey called a halt while the situation clarified. The projected German counterstroke had now shrunk to a mere attack on the British around Hill 112.

Though the offensive would be overtaken by events, it says something about *Allied* strategy in Normandy. For decades arguments have raged over Montgomery's asserted intention to draw German forces away from the Americans with his attacks around Caen. The OKW's abortive plan substantiates *one* instance of the success of Montgomery's scheme: His Epsom had coincided with Hitler's fresh reinforcements—and the führer was tempted into using them. Two SS panzer divisions and parts of another participated. But on another level, the realities of the road net ensured the German troops arrived on Montgomery's sector because Caen was the nexus it was. It did not matter what attacks Monty made, the bulk of the panzers would move against his Tommies.

The German follow-up had to be delayed, partly due to British air strikes on the gathering forces, but also because Paul Hausser left to take charge of the Seventh Army, handing the corps command to SS Lieutenant General Wilhelm Bittrich. The delay helped the British consolidate their positions below and around Hill 112. General Bittrich concentrated his 9th and 10th SS Panzer Divisions, a battle group of the 12th SS, and other units for the maneuver. The German sally on July 3 and 4 was stopped at the crest of Hill 112 and beaten back on the other bank of the Odon. The British held off the SS panzers. Desperately contending for a rise that formed barely a pimple in the Norman countryside, one pock-marked by shells at that, *Landser* began to call Hill 112 "Calvary Mountain." The ordeal indeed suggested the tribulations of Christ. The British benefited from strong artillery, fighter-bombers, and naval gunfire support. The Germans threw in as many Luftwaffe sorties as they could manage. Forces continued to arrive, with the 1st SS Panzer fully assembled only after the initial attacks.

General Sir Richard O'Connor, the VIII Corps commander, expected the Germans to strike again. O'Connor ordered a partial withdrawal of the 11th Armored Division, abandoning Hill 112 but retaining a bridgehead across the Odon River. General Dempsey concurred. He felt the troops were overexposed, and feared the next German attack would come with even greater power. The British finished with a narrow bridgehead across the river.

The Germans reoccupied Hill 112. The 10th SS Panzer held the line, the 9th pulled into reserve. After a few days Dempsey began to nibble at the defenses. Instead of knocking directly on Hill 112, the British jabbed at nearby supporting positions. Every day there were losses. The inferno of shell and bomb and bullet went on for almost three weeks. Positions changed hands repeatedly. Dempsey came back with Operation Jupiter, an assault by the reinforced 43rd Wessex Infantry Division on July 10. A full brigade of the Wessex advanced up Calvary Mountain. It was close-in fighting, with grenades and submachine guns often deciding the issue. German riflemen sometimes let the British pass their trenches unopposed, then fired on them from the rear. The British seized important works on Hill 112.

Bittrich sent in the 9th SS, then Tiger tanks. But the German artillery had only seven hundred shells available to support them. Corporal Will Fey, a tank commander with the just arrived 102nd SS Heavy Tank Battalion, was in the thick of the fighting, and his calvary began with the appearance of British aircraft. "They came at us like a swarm of hostile hornets," Fey recorded, "and covered us with a hail of medium-heavy bombs. At the same time smoke shells landed among us and covered everything around with an impenetrable white fog." The Tigers had to halt. "This was a new way of fighting to us, something we had not encountered on any battleground before."[23]

The adversaries fought to a standstill on Hill 112. Not daring to try for its north slope, the Germans now placed their front line behind the crest. Operation Jupiter petered out after two days. Casualties were horrific throughout this succession of battles. One British officer who took charge of his platoon toward the end of the month discovered he had less than half the standard complement for that unit, with three-quarters of the men recent replacements. Only five of his thirty-six men had survived the Orne battles.

Meanwhile, Montgomery recalled General O'Connor and his headquarters to prepare an attack on Caen itself, inserting the XII Corps in the Hill 112 sector. Another high point in the fighting came on July 15–16, when this corps launched a fresh attack with the 15th Scottish and 43rd divisions. They made minor gains but lost some to German counterattacks. Nazi units in the field continued to be pulverized. That day the 9th

SS Panzer Division mustered the equivalent of only a regiment of infantry with thirty-eight battleworthy tanks and fifteen assault guns. Its sister division, with only about twenty-three hundred effective troops, was in no better condition. Panzer Group West nevertheless refined its plans for a major offensive in this area, and sent a revised proposal to OKW on July 17. At this point Army Group B feared a breakout to the southeast from the Hill 112 sector. By now Dempsey's attacks were actually a diversion to draw German eyes away from Caen and Operation Goodwood, but Field Marshal Rommel expected assaults there as well. Nothing ever happened with the offensive plan, for at this moment General Montgomery unleashed powerful forces in his Goodwood gambit.

The Wessex Division tried once more with Operation Express on July 22. This brigade-size attack, not powerful enough to make a breakthrough, again aimed at distracting the German command. But SHAEF continued to pressure Montgomery to mount offensive actions, particularly as Cobra got under way, and the British leader contrived to do so. A new British probe came south of Hill 112 on July 28, followed by Operation Bluecoat, farther to the west, beginning on July 30. Grandly, Monty wrote Ike, "I have ordered Dempsey to throw all caution to the wind."[24]

CHAPTER 2

ALLIED ANXIETIES

T he Americans who met to decide on the Cobra plan gathered at a moment when Allied chieftains, far from triumphant, felt increasingly afflicted. The interplay of interest and fear atop the Allied command is at the root of what happened at Normandy. General Dwight D. Eisenhower was a man with pernicious problems. As SHAEF commander in chief it was his job not only to set strategy but to oversee the combat, organize the supply flow to his forces, manage their training and the deployment of fresh formations, supervise the media's coverage, be the focal point between the field armies and the American and British high commands, respond to the concerns of U.S. and United Kingdom political leaders, *and* adjudicate among his unruly commanders. Of the myriad tasks of a military institution, virtually the only one not in SHAEF's purview was that of providing replacement soldiers to make good on losses—and even there Eisenhower had a watching brief. His job required many skills—military diplomat, strategist, psychologist, logistician, and, not least, leader. The Normandy campaign tested Ike to the utmost, for Hitler's armies did not fold their tents and flee, but instead stood for battle against Allied forces superior to them in nearly every respect. In Normandy's broken terrain the Allies had bogged down.

Unlike today's war of individuals, patrols, and platoons, this was a war of battalions and regiments, scraping ahead to take the next farm or village, even divisions and corps executing grand maneuvers. Six weeks after

D-Day, the Allied armies stood on positions SHAEF had planned to hold five days after the invasion. Not that the armies were stalled—every day brought reports of new gains—but advances could often be measured in the hundreds of yards. The Normandy lodgment, the Allied liberated zone, filled up with about as many troops as it could hold. Supplying those forces over the invasion beaches strained SHAEF's logistics, both its landing capacity and its means to move matériel from storage dumps to the field.

Solving every problem required combat. Restoring the ability to conduct a war of movement entailed getting past the difficult Norman terrain, with its small fields bounded by high hedgerows that formed natural defenses. Landing supplies in bulk meant ports, and Normandy had only one, the relatively small one at Cherbourg. Its capture at the end of June illustrated a further difficulty: Destruction of dock and warehouse facilities could require lengthy rehabilitation before harbors could unload at capacity. When British prime minister Sir Winston Churchill visited Cherbourg in late July, he would be astonished at the amount of rubble, even after several weeks of clearing, and the scale of what remained to be accomplished. Deploying the Allied divisions still in the British Isles also required ports. Developing new air bases close to the front entailed pushing the lines out beyond the range of German heavy artillery. By July only ten Allied fighter groups (nine of them American) had relocated to the Continent. The vast majority of Allied air assets were still in Britain.

General Eisenhower exhorted his commanders, encouraging their schemes to move the armies forward, but the grinding pace tested everyone's patience. In that climate, with a multinational SHAEF force, every little difference provoked. The Allied Expeditionary Force that Eisenhower led was more than a combined British-American armada, and in itself that became a source of concern. The United Kingdom was its first beneficiary, and the British Isles, the indispensable rear base for Northwest Europe. The British had a major stake in the outcome and committed the bulk of their combat troops to SHAEF. But Great Britain, majestic as ever, no longer possessed the power it had had in 1914, or even 1941, though Churchill bent herculean efforts to preserving the image of British power and as much of its substance as he could. Nevertheless, by 1944 the dominions and colonies, in the form of the Commonwealth, furnished the majority of British forces. This would not be so evident in Normandy, partly due to the fact the British concentrated many of their metropolitan formations here, and—at least during this period—because they front-loaded their deployment, matching the Americans during the early weeks. In the middle of July the British commander informed the chief of Imperial General Staff, Lord Alanbrooke, that his contingent had reached its full potential strength.

Meanwhile, even within the existing dispositions, Commonwealth troops (the Canadian army would provide about a quarter of the available divisions) made up a substantial fraction of the force. When Montgomery activated another field army, it would be Canadian. There were small units of Dutch, Belgians, and Czechs, plus a larger contingent of Polish troops, counted as parts of the British force, creating sensitivity in London and at headquarters that a significant portion of the "British" army really consisted of other allies' soldiers—over 100,000 Canadians and perhaps 30,000 more from the captive nations of Europe. Even so, when the British reached their full stretch, dozens of American divisions were still to be sent to the Continent.

Acutely aware of this, matters of command were supremely delicate for the British. When SHAEF was created, months before D-Day, the British had been equal partners and it made sense to establish a headquarters where American and British officers were paired at every level. Recognizing the importance of the United States, Prime Minister Churchill acceded to President Franklin D. Roosevelt's desire to have an American head the command, and General Eisenhower had been selected. But he had a British deputy. That pattern existed throughout. General Bernard Law Montgomery became Eisenhower's top subordinate by virtue of the creation of the temporary post of ground forces commander, with authority over the forces that landed at D-Day and fought in Normandy. But as American numbers surpassed the British, Montgomery's position became increasingly tenuous. Indeed, Monty complicated matters through his decisions, his disregard for colleagues, and his conduct of the campaign on the British front.

THE MAN AT THE TOP

By this point in the war Dwight David Eisenhower had become the consensus commander in chief. He had held a similar post in the Mediterranean. Eisenhower had been top boss when the Allies invaded French North Africa in late 1942, ejected the Germans from Tunisia in 1943, and leaped across to Sicily, and then during the invasion of Italy that knocked that Axis power out of the war. On his watch Eisenhower had encountered many of the same kinds of political-military problems that now surfaced in Normandy. But he had also earned the enmity of Field Marshal Lord Alanbrooke, the British chief of staff, for alleged hesitancy and a preoccupation with political matters. True, Eisenhower had been slow and had failed to take advantage of certain opportunities in Tunisia. But, as the product of an American military system that emphasized aggressiveness, he was far abler than Alanbrooke advertised.

United States chief of staff General George C. Marshall regarded Eisenhower as the foremost strategist of his generation. Marshall's mentor, the redoubtable General Fox Conner, had also been impressed with Eisenhower, familiarly known as "Ike," who had worked for him in the early 1920s. Shortly before Pearl Harbor, Marshall had insisted upon Ike's assignment to the War Plans Division, the center of U.S. strategy. Marshall had supported Eisenhower in every post since, and he had been Ike's key promoter for the SHAEF command. Eisenhower had also earned the respect of America's acknowledged military supremo, General Douglas MacArthur, who relied on him when the army acted against bonus marchers during the Great Depression and who engineered Ike's last prewar post, assisting MacArthur in creating a Philippine army.

When he arrived at SHAEF, General Eisenhower was fifty-four years old, a graduate of West Point, of the class of 1915, which World War II made famous as the "class the stars fell on." Born in Texas, Ike was reared on the Plains with five brothers in a small white wood frame house in Abilene, Kansas. Eisenhower knew how to be self-effacing and worked his purposes with subtlety and patience rather than bombast and guile. Upon first meeting General Montgomery, then his senior in rank, Ike had complied meekly when the Britisher peremptorily ordered him to extinguish the cigarette he'd been smoking. Fox Conner, who had been operations chief for the U.S. armies in France in World War I, had educated Ike in the niceties of coalition warfare, the tools needed for his role after 1942. This proved important with Montgomery in particular, since, beginning with the Tunisian campaign, the British general would come under Ike as supreme commander. Eisenhower had helped create the army's first tank brigade, served in Panama and the Philippines, led the staff that managed a very successful large-scale maneuver before the U.S. entry into the war, and worked at high levels in the War Department. Not least, he got on very well with Churchill, whom Ike had first met while planning the North Africa invasion. Churchill often lunched with Eisenhower at Downing Street or invited him to Chequers, the prime minister's country estate.

SENIOR AMERICANS

General Omar N. Bradley was also among the class the stars fell on. Known as the "soldier's general," it was typical of Omar Bradley that he gave away his fleece-lined jacket to a soldier on the D-Day beaches, remarking that he could easily get another. Like Ike, Bradley was a man of the Plains, born in Clark and raised in Moberly, two Missouri towns, where he hunted and fished. Years later, as an instructor at Fort Benning, Bradley used to harvest berries on training hikes and take them home to can. Benning became the key assignment for Bradley, who, again like Eisenhower, had missed out on the Great War, for the fort was then commanded by the young George Marshall, who kept a little black book in which he listed officers he deemed of high caliber. Omar's name was near the top. Not from any service family, though his grandfathers had fought on opposite sides in the Civil War, Bradley nevertheless absorbed military science like a sponge. Even before Fort Benning he had served as an instructor at a state college and at West Point. He returned to West Point to head the tactics department there. Later he commanded Fort Benning in his own right. Bradley would be the first in his cohort, ahead of Dwight Eisenhower, to attain the rank of brigadier general. Omar, who pronounced his name "Ohmer," and perhaps for that reason was known in the army as Brad, commanded one of the new divisions raised after Pearl Harbor, trained up another division mobilized from the National Guard, served briefly on Eisenhower's staff in North Africa, then led the II Corps in Tunisia and Sicily. Bradley was assigned early to lead the U.S. Army slotted for D-Day. When Eisenhower took over SHAEF, he marked Bradley to command the American army group that would form on the Continent.

Another key American general, in some ways the most famous of all, would be central to the events of Normandy, Lieutenant General George S. Patton, Jr. Unlike his colleagues, George Patton *was* the scion of a military family; his father and grandfather, the latter a brigadier general, were both graduates of the Virginia Military Institute (VMI). The flamboyant Patton, whose behavior occasionally verged on the irrational, and who fancied himself the reincarnation of warriors of antiquity—infantryman under Alexander the Great, Roman legionnaire, horseman for Napoleon, Civil War soldier, pirate or Viking—was undoubtedly brilliant. Though dyslexic, Patton still managed to transfer to West Point after a year at VMI. He did not fare so well as a plebe cadet, flunking math and being held back, but he graduated West Point in 1909 with a respectable class standing (46 of 103). Patton entered the cavalry and actually attended the prestigious French cavalry school at Saumur. Equally remarkable, Patton represented the United States at the 1912 Stockholm Olympics and placed fifth in the pentathlon. While stationed at Fort Riley, Kansas, he wrote the army field manual on the use of the saber.

When the United States sent a punitive expedition into Mexico to fight the revolutionary Pancho Villa, Patton went along as an aide to its commander, General John J. Pershing, and led a raid during which he personally killed Villa's ally General Julio Cárdenas. He accompanied "Black Jack" Pershing again, to France with the headquarters of the American forces in World War I, which he left to head the army's first tank training center and later a tank brigade in combat. His battles included Saint-Mihiel and the Meuse-Argonne, where Patton was badly wounded in the thigh and earned a Distinguished Service Cross and the Purple Heart.

Soon after that war Patton led an experimental U.S. Army tank unit, where he was Eisenhower's boss. Subsequent assignments were divided among army staffs, the higher service schools, and repeated tours with the 3rd Cavalry, which Patton finally commanded for a year and a half. He then led a novel U.S. armored brigade, expanded to a division, in the Louisiana-Texas maneuvers in the summer of 1940. Patton's methods, including ordering tank parts from Sears, Roebuck he could not get from army supply sources, added to his reputation as a determined, dynamic commander. When the Allies invaded North Africa in November 1942, anticipating the need for mobile warfare, it was almost a given that Patton would lead a task force. He then took over the II Corps in Tunisia after the battle of Kasserine. Quickly promoted to head the Seventh Army in the invasion of Sicily, Patton there commanded Omar Bradley.

Not merely dynamic but controversial, too, in Tunisia Patton became embroiled in spats with British counterparts, first over air support, then whether his corps should fight under British command. In Sicily he encountered General Montgomery, leading the other army in that invasion, whose ideas struck Patton as impractical. Though they did not then cross swords, Patton triggered a different controversy when he slapped two of his own soldiers, whom he saw as cowards, although they were afflicted with post-traumatic stress disorder. Ike reprimanded Patton. Though particulars were suppressed, once the press got hold of it, the "slapping incident" threatened Patton's career. His selection marked a reprieve.

Just before receiving orders to go to England, early in 1944 Patton wrote his wife, Beatrice, to denounce Omar Bradley as a decidedly mediocre general, a view no doubt colored by Brad's promotion past him on the army list, only somewhat ameliorated when Patton learned that he would again command an army himself. Ike, in Patton's view, was sometimes thoughtful, sometimes mean and condescending, and no military genius. George Patton *was*, in his own mind, and he had a passion for war. As one of his staff characterized the relationship among the higher-ups, "Very few of Patton's superiors liked him. All respected him professionally. But most of them feared him and were jealous of him. They had good reasons for that."[1] Patton returned the sentiment in spades.

For the invasion Patton would be held back as the publicized leader of a fictional army group, its pretend mission to invade Europe, constituting the heart of the Fortitude deception. Even then he embarrassed U.S.

leaders when the press got wind of remarks he had made that anticipated a future Anglo-American condominium over the world. Bradley had misgivings over Patton's prospective appointment to an army command on the Continent, and would have advised against it, but he was not asked, and in retrospect decided the choice had been a good one. Meanwhile, Eisenhower took the supreme command and Bradley the U.S. field command. When "Old Blood and Guts," as Patton was nicknamed, returned to battle, his bosses were both former subordinates. That had to rankle.

One more American general would have a role in the personality wars, not so much for his ego but perhaps the lack of it. This may have flowed from Courtney H. Hodges's dislike of the attention that fell on him as the army's reigning pistol-shooting champion, a title he held for many years. The unassuming Hodges, who turned fifty-three a week after D-Day, went out of his way to avoid controversy. "Hodges was left behind in the European headline sweepstakes," Bradley would say of the soft-voiced Georgian. "He was essentially a military technician whose faultless techniques and tactical knowledge made him one of the most skilled craftsmen of my entire command."[2]

A small-town boy, Hodges had entered West Point with Patton and, like him, flunked math. Unlike Patton, Hodges was sent home—a fact that George used to flay Hodges when he wanted to. Determined to join the army, Hodges enlisted anyway and proved so good at soldiering he was commissioned directly from the ranks in 1910, only a year behind what would have been his West Point class, virtually unheard of in the army of that day. Hodges, too, chased Pancho Villa with Pershing and Patton, and went to World War I in the infantry, rising to command a rifle battalion, fighting at Saint-Mihiel and the Meuse-Argonne. Hodges won the Distinguished Service Cross for a scouting mission across the Meuse River, where, trapped for almost two days, he fought on and secured a U.S. bridgehead across it. Bradley met Hodges in 1924 as the latter finished a tour instructing at West Point, and caught up with him at Fort Benning in 1940, when he relieved Hodges as commandant. Bradley thought Hodges the quintessential Southern gentleman and admired him greatly. George C. Marshall believed the two officers were equal as masters of military practice. Hodges commanded a corps in the United States, became a lieutenant general early in 1943, and took the Third Army headquarters to England when it deployed for the invasion. He became assistant commander to Bradley at First Army, from an early date designated to succeed him when Bradley moved up to lead the U.S. Army group.

WILL AND EGO

Despite his own reticence, Courtney Hicks Hodges became embroiled in the ego wars as a foil for the ire of Bernard Montgomery. This was not a question of suffering fools. Monty picked feuds all around. As ground forces commander it was not politic for him to bare knuckles with General Bradley—though bad blood arose there soon enough—and Patton stayed behind for weeks, but Hodges provided a ready target. Monty also complained to Lord Alanbrooke about his direct boss, Eisenhower. These differences, occasionally muted, reemerged, and Monty's circle of perceived incompetents widened. The Americans' predilection for constant attack across the entire front, Monty thought, was mindless.

Some call the British-American differences the War Between the Generals, but they were more than that, and not simply between the two Allies. General Montgomery waged a back-alley dogfight with the RAF, and Air Chief Marshal Sir Arthur Tedder, Ike's deputy commander, reciprocated by plotting Monty's demise. Montgomery also despised the British tactical air boss, Air Vice-Marshal Sir Arthur Coningham, with whom he had been at odds since Tunisia. Among Commonwealth forces, Montgomery distrusted the top Canadian commander, General Henry D. G. Crerar, and would have replaced him if he could. Crerar, safe due to the realities of imperial politics, was a former chief of the Canadian general staff who had taken voluntary demotion to get into the shooting war and had worked his way up to the top field command.

Efforts to plumb the depths of Montgomery's heart continue to this day. The historian Nigel Hamilton tries to explain away each circumstance and prove Monty's primacy as a battlefield leader. Certainly the general had brilliant achievements to his credit. He had preserved his 3rd

Infantry Division in the 1940 Dunkirk debacle. In fact, Monty's troops came away possibly in the best condition of any British unit saved there. Alanbrooke, then his corps commander, whom Monty replaced at the height of the danger, had been duly appreciative. And by his own and some other accounts, Montgomery's role proved crucial to the evacuation's success. The two men remained close—important to Monty since Alanbrooke rose to chief of staff in December 1941 and held that post throughout the war. In Egypt in 1942, General Montgomery took over the Eighth Army at a moment when the British had barely halted the German advance on Cairo, and he defeated Field Marshal Erwin Rommel's forces at the battle of El Alamein. Monty had pursued the retreating Italo-German panzers to Tunisia, joined Eisenhower coming from Algeria, and completed the conquest of North Africa. He then had fought under Ike in Sicily and Italy until recalled to participate in the invasion. His insistence on a larger initial force at D-Day undoubtedly became a factor in the invasion's triumph. In all these posts General Montgomery had preserved the troops' morale and their combat edge.

Bernard Montgomery's career was not blemished or blighted. Instead his prickly personality seemed to seed the cloud that hung over him. Bradley found Montgomery cool and aloof. Eisenhower felt Monty "deliberately pursued certain eccentricities of behavior,"[3] among them not only isolating himself from staff but refusing to interact with staffers other than his own. He also argued like a bulldog, not backing down until a decision had been made—sometimes not then, either. Aside from Monty's feuding, disturbing enough as it was, he had a propensity for bombast. Whatever happened, the general would claim he had foreseen it, and all was according to plan. Instances had occurred in North Africa and Sicily, but the European campaign would bring more, starting in Normandy. Monty's addiction to claims of this sort sparked some knotty disputes, especially with American colleagues. Conversely, Montgomery remained suspicious of the quality of American staff work and planning. The fact that Monty, having served under Eisenhower's supreme command for half of 1943 and now again for the French campaign, had yet to forge a workable relationship with the supremo speaks poorly for the British general.

A maverick in the British army, with service in India before the First

World War, and Palestine before the second, Montgomery had seen the empire. He was also a veteran of the Western Front in the Great War, fighting with the British Expeditionary Force at the early battle of Le Cateau, was badly wounded in Flanders, and spent the rest of that conflict in staff positions. The carnage of 1914–1918 weighed on him. The son of an Anglican bishop and the fourth of nine children, the fifty-eight-year-old general's socialization also inclined him to conservatism. A reluctance to take risks was a feature of this. That could be a negative—commanding forces in southern England in 1942, when the British conceived the disastrous "raid" at Dieppe, Monty had had a chance to cancel it but held his tongue at a key meeting before Churchill. He had also refused to insist on bombing support that had been canceled for spurious reasons. The risks in those things had been merely bureaucratic. Monty's dislike of General Crerar, who had had a major role securing Canadian participation at Dieppe, may be traced there. That attitude had consequences in Normandy. At El Alamein, Montgomery had held back the British armored reserves until very late in the battle. On Sicily, his buildup for the attack on Messina had been slow. Cautious to a fault, Monty favored the set-piece battle and moved only with every element in place. These traits lay at the heart of his difficulties in Normandy.

The sixty-year-old Lord Alanbrooke was also a key player for the British. The Chief of the Imperial General Staff (CIGS), Alanbrooke watched Montgomery's back and functioned as a circuit breaker to deflect Churchill's ire. Extremely close to Monty, Alanbrooke quietly warned the field commander of threats to his primacy and, in the manner of some U.S. chiefs of staff, advised him on what to say to preserve his position. Commissioned in the Royal Artillery around the turn of the century, Alanbrooke had served in Ireland and India even before the Great War, in which he gained renown as a technical innovator. By the Second World War he had become a very senior officer with a reputation as a brilliant planner and briefer. Born and raised in France, he had commanded an army corps in the disastrous 1940 campaign. Alanbrooke had some sympathy for the Overlord enterprise, but he remained a proponent of the Mediterranean strategy, and forever regretted that he had had to turn down the top post in the Med in 1943 in order to remain CIGS. Throughout this period he engaged in a protracted debate with the Americans over whether an Allied invasion of southern France was necessary or could be useful.

He regarded Churchill as his greatest challenge—an obstreperous, cantankerous leader who needed to be coddled and endured. Nor was Lord Alanbrooke much enamored of the Americans. Both hostilities came together when Prime Minister Churchill agreed that an American should lead Overlord, for Alanbrooke himself had been promised that command several times. This combination of views made Lord Alanbrooke Montgomery's natural ally. In his official capacity Lord Alanbrooke was automatically informed of all pertinent information from the British armed services, from SHAEF, and from intelligence. As a matter of fact, when the Cobra offensive began on July 25, Alanbrooke was huddled with the British chiefs of staff to review the latest appreciation from the Joint Intelligence Committee, London's senior interpreters of the tea leaves. Their view was that the Germans were on the ropes.

ULTRA AND INTELLIGENCE

Until the mid-1970s, one major advantage the Allies enjoyed—also a headache—remained a closely guarded secret. This was the communications intelligence source known as ULTRA.[4]

By then many histories of Normandy—and most of those specifically on the breakout—had already been written. As a result, the impact of ULTRA has remained poorly integrated into our overall understanding. Once its existence became known, writers tended to endow it with omniscient powers. Here an effort will be made to correct that. A more balanced view requires treatment of the advantages and limitations of ULTRA and the place of that material within overall Allied intelligence efforts.

First, ULTRA was a "source"—a channel for a category of information comprising the results of efforts to break encrypted German communications. The generic term "signals intelligence" (SIGINT) applies to this type of information. A multiplicity of specifically targeted efforts contributed to source ULTRA, each with its own code name and story. All the projects were run by a dedicated corps of SIGINT specialists who broke the ciphers, decrypted messages, decoded them into their "plain" text, then either summarized the content or translated the entire communication. These Allied codebreakers were headquartered at Bletchley Park, England, the location of the Government Code and Cypher School (GC&CS), the euphemistically named British codebreaking operation. Americans worked shoulder to shoulder with their British counterparts at Bletchley. In the spring of 1944 this unit employed fifty-six hundred persons. The work evolved organically from the original effort to recover the cipher keys Germans used for their Enigma code machine (and changed daily), eventually encompassing a series of "huts," initially literal shacks outside the estate house, later larger barracks-style buildings, in each of which experts focused on particular tasks, from technical aspects of codes and ciphers, to translation, to huts that related the messages to what was known about the German army, navy (Kriegsmarine), and air force (Luftwaffe). From early 1944 through the end of the war ULTRA decrypted an average of ninety thousand Enigma messages each month. Ralph Bennett, one of Britain's most experienced translators, estimates that roughly twenty-five thousand of the Enigma decrypts over this period concerned the war in the West. He has supplied the best summary account of ULTRA's contributions, and along with the British official history his work establishes a basis for incorporating intelligence into the Normandy narrative.[5]

All German services used the Enigma machine, but army message traffic, Kriegsmarine, and Luftwaffe communications all had their own peculiarities of coding and encryption. Messages traveled on "circuits"—each a channel between specific pairs of communication centers—such as between the German Seventh Army in Normandy and its corps commands, or the Luftwaffe circuit that connected to its liaison officers with the army. Every type of traffic used different Enigma settings, requiring distinct decryption solutions. Each circuit was a code-named target.

The Germans also operated a high-speed, automated teleprinter device (the *Geheimschreiber*), only vulnerable to interception where its transmissions (source "Fish") were not sent on landlines. It is vital to understanding the SIGINT question to point out that all communications among top headquarters—Army Group B, OB West, and OKW—went by teleprinter.

Accessing these targets was a matter of many steps and decrypting the traffic had numerous facets. Messages first had to be intercepted, the responsibility of radio listening posts with the U.S. Secret Intelligence Service or the British Y Service. Enemy circuits could be off the air due to movement, power failures, Allied bombing, or the like. Interception could falter because of atmospheric conditions, combat, or for other reasons. The German teleprinter traffic, when it went by radio, was focused in a narrow beam, not broadcast, and traveled at high speed and information density. The Allies coped by relying on a great number of receivers listening in on many German circuits, which tended to ensure that at any given moment some slice of German traffic was being intercepted. The British alone operated more than a thousand interception posts in the European theater at the time of D-Day.

Organizations responsible for interception also worked the German communications by locating and identifying the emitters and tracking the volume of their messages, providing a type of intelligence called radio traffic analysis. The form, length, and number of messages, regardless of the ability to decrypt them, could reveal the hierarchy of the German command structure, the movement of units or appearance of new ones, changes in command, and other characteristics of the enemy forces.

It is important to note that many German communications were impervious to interception. Directives from Hitler's headquarters, or OB West to subordinate commands, were often written on paper and carried by hand of officer. Impromptu planning changes could occur at face-to-face meetings, or in the field among officers responding to an immediate situation. Others took place on the telephone, such as the D-Day exchanges between OB West and OKW over release of the panzer reserves. Of Margival and the führer's intentions for a big offensive, to take another example, the Allies knew nothing until after the war. Their intelligence was not omniscient after all.

Experts observe that all was not lost—though important orders might remain secret, they eventually led to messages on circuits that *could* be intercepted. But the fact remains that in those cases the meaning behind pieces of the puzzle the Allies could see had to be inferred, not observed directly. The term "high-grade SIGINT" is often bandied about indiscriminately in reference to ULTRA, but it is very misleading. Enigma was used only within German armies and sometimes from one army to another. The higher-level traffic went by teleprinter. True high-grade SIGINT would have been the directives themselves, not mere corollary orders. Yet this term has most often been applied to the circuit or source, not the data content. This is a misappreciation. What ULTRA produced most frequently actually amounted to tactical intelligence, not high grade at all—details of unit transfers, sectors, reinforcements, strength, immediate intentions, objections from unit commanders and the responses of senior leaders—perishable information that was immediately relevant but ultimately ephemeral. This was "high grade"—as the term is misapplied—because it came from the adversary's own mouth, but its substance was inherently limited. On numerous occasions in Normandy the take from Enigma proved invaluable in tactical situations without attaining the level of true high-grade SIGINT.

During the entire European campaign, the instances in which ULTRA directly produced truly strategic intelligence can probably be counted on the fingers of one hand. Fortunately, a couple of those occurred at Normandy.

Without getting too technical, a special word is in order about the German teleprinter traffic, "Fish" and its derivatives, because that represented the most sensitive material with the best potential for "high-grade SIGINT." The OKW command variant would be known as "Tunny." In the vernacular of intelligence history these systems are usually grouped together and called the *Geheimschreiber* (secret writer), although, strictly speaking, the *Geheimschreiber* was one particular machine produced by the Lorenz company, while Siemens machines (SR-40 and -42) were actually more numerous. Thus, the Germans employed several makes and models of these online encryption devices. Dispatches on the system went in a format that often condensed several messages into one.

Allied codebreakers first intercepted transmissions of this sort in late 1940, encountered them regularly beginning in 1941, understood the workings of the system by early 1942, and first broke into it that spring. Early breaks in the encryption were made by hand calculation, though a prototype decryption machine (Colossus) for use against Fish was delivered in early 1943 and substantially perfected by the end of the year, entering service in February 1944. A combination of machine and hand decryption had worked previously, but the Germans repeatedly improved their communications security. By now Allied codebreakers knew the system would soon become impervious to all but machine solutions, and they needed more Colossus machines. Prime Minister Churchill personally approved a crash production effort. A second machine was delivered soon after D-Day, and two more that summer. Eventually the machines were added at a rate of about one a month, to finish the war with ten Colossi, but during the Normandy campaign capabilities remained more modest. Fish messages typically required several days to turn around but were nevertheless considered invaluable because of their nature.

At that point the Germans had twenty-six circuits using the *Geheimschreiber.* The Allies had great success against the OKW-Rome circuit ("Bream"), links to the Balkans and the Eastern Front, and they also penetrated the OKW–OB West circuit, "Jellyfish." A particular difficulty with Jellyfish was that interception was much less extensive than the Y Service's effort with Enigma as a whole. Interception was concentrated at the Knockholt station, with fewer than three dozen receivers. Intercepts might not compare to capacity. For example, in August 1944 Knockholt receivers averaged 250,000 characters daily against a Colossus codebreaking capacity assessed at 320,000 characters. With the additional Colossus machines, for the period of July to September the number of characters of German transmissions decrypted increased by nearly a third, but the number of messages broken each day averaged 12.6—not much different from the 11.6 average for April–June—and that was for all varieties of Fish. Codebreaking experts projecting Fish output had estimated that once four Colossi were online they would be reading 70 messages each day. The take never quite matched expectations.

German security measures temporarily protected Fish in February 1944—a month later, only Bream was being read regularly. Then, a few days after the invasion, the Allies virtually lost Jellyfish. The Germans, as they did with Enigma, began changing their key settings every day instead of once a month. More than a week passed until the codebreakers realized exactly what had happened, and they immediately understood that a much greater machine capacity had become necessary. It took almost four months until the number of Colossi again sufficed. Though some solutions were achieved nonetheless, the stream of data was much reduced. Before D-Day Jellyfish had yielded field strength data and general appreciations, a great deal of intelligence, yet at this critical moment the German circuits became less productive. There were some vital decrypts, but by and large Jellyfish remained dark. The near blackout included nearly the entire Normandy campaign. Once the Allies regained access to Jellyfish they would not again lose it.

The heart of decryption activity overall was at Bletchley Park's Hut 6, and that for Tunny (and Fish) at the newer Hut H. There analysts attacked the mysteries of the daily keys Germans used in their encryption devices and teleprinters. Success was obtained by dint of brilliant mathematical analysis and the Allied "bombe"—an early specialized computer—but also related directly to the volume of messages, the codebreakers' raw material. Despite the loss of Fish/Tunny/Jellyfish, by June 17 the codebreakers had penetrated the system used by OB West to subordinates ("Bantam") and that of the German Seventh Army in Normandy ("Duck"). Bletchley maintained this penetration for almost ten days, then repeated the achievement sporadically through July. "Penguin," Bletchley's code name for the 12th SS Panzer Division key, was broken on June 15 and read intermittently through August. On the other hand, the Panzer Group West (by then Fifth Panzer Army) key, called "Dodo," was not broken until August 10. Of course, that would be a key moment in the campaign.

The codebreakers generally had their best results with Luftwaffe keys, several of which yielded vital information during Normandy. Ground liaison officers who arranged air support for German units used a key the Allies called "Ocelot" and read regularly. Assigned to corps and to panzer divisions, the officers unwittingly supplied the Allies with a steady stream of data. "Firefly," the key used by the First Parachute Army, revealed much about the German parachute troops in the Cotentin and the units on their flanks. The III Flak Corps had detachments interspersed with the Wehrmacht all over Normandy and its key, "Platypus," first read on June 16, yielded intermittent but valuable data on many aspects of German activity. Most of the Luftwaffe's aircraft operational command circuits were also penetrated, yet another reason—beyond sheer disparity in strength—why the Luftwaffe failed in Normandy.

If the volume of traffic was too high, the Allied intercept stations might not be able to capture all of it. If the Germans did not use their circuits, the Y Service failed to intercept them, or weather hampered communications, that reduced success. Weather could also help the attack on the codes when German radiomen, repeating transmissions in an effort to get through, made mistakes. But traffic volume continued to be the primary limitation. On January 31, 1945, the only date for which we have data (because the German chief of operations staff noted this in his diary), OKW headquarters transmitted or received 33,000 *Geheimschreiber* dispatches and 120,000 telephone calls but only 1,200 radio messages. (Between January 1 and May 8, 1945, the Allies intercepted slightly fewer than 12,500 Fish messages, an average of about 100 a day; for July through September of 1944, that figure had been 5,200. At best only a fraction of the traffic was being recorded.) This was the period of the GC&CS's most successful penetration of the teleprinter traffic—yet calculations from data on Fish decrypts indicate that at peak the Allies read no more than 35 percent of the high-level German dispatches *that had successfully been intercepted.* The number of actual Fish decrypts *over the entire war* amounted to about two-thirds of the Enigma take for a single month of the 1944–1945 period. However lucrative Allied reading of lower-level traffic might be, the German High Command remained an elusive target.

The decrypted messages went to Group Captain Sir Eric Jones's Hut 3, where linguists rendered them into English; the translations were carefully checked and garbles noted, and analysts added value by supplying occasional "comments" that related the content to other known intelligence. While the codebreakers have garnered most of the attention history has lavished on ULTRA, the Hut 3 work was crucial to how Allied commanders understood this intelligence and what they drew from it. Hut 3 proved able to turn out some completed Enigma messages in as little as three hours from the moment the intercepts arrived at Bletchley. As recounted, Fish took much longer.

The German information was then converted into Source ULTRA cables and transmitted, using Allied codes, to what the Americans called

Special Communications Units/Special Liaison Units attached to the key commands. A typical unit—the one with Patton's army—comprised two U.S. officers, two British ones, and two enlisted men. Every liaison unit was led by an individual—a "special security officer"—responsible for conveying ULTRA material personally to his assigned leader. The liaisons extended down to army level. Thus, Eisenhower, Montgomery, and Bradley were all recipients, and their tactical air commanders, plus Generals Hodges and Patton, would also benefit from Source ULTRA. Tens of thousands of Allied communications personnel, codebreakers, and intelligence analysts all came down to the twenty-eight men who served as ULTRA liaison officers. They had had an orientation on the source material at Hut 3, but only two were professional soldiers. In civilian life most of the rest were lawyers.[6] Everything depended on their relationships with their principals.

General Montgomery took his ULTRA very seriously. Alistair Horne, one of Monty's staff, learned from a comrade of how a young officer had come to Montgomery's Normandy headquarters late one night, long after the general had gone to bed. He insisted on waking Montgomery to give him crucial information (how to convey urgency to the uninitiated remained an insoluble problem with Source ULTRA). Knowing Monty hated such intrusions, staffers told the man it was out of the question. The officer insisted. Montgomery was awakened, heard the report, and later told staff to summon him anytime, day or night, if an officer arrived from that unit.[7] Montgomery thereafter met directly with communications officers bearing critical messages, but normally his top intelligence officer, Brigadier Bill Williams, received ULTRA reports sent through British channels. Williams made the exchange a two-way street by circulating a daily summary, which showed Montgomery's intentions as well as his command's appreciation of the enemy, thus alerting Bletchley Park of specifics to look out for in the SIGINT as well as what data from its reports was being accepted at the front.

General Bradley handled ULTRA differently. His liaison at First Army was a captain named Adolph G. Rosengarten, a Philadelphia lawyer. A different team liaised with Bradley in his capacity as army group commander, headed by the New York lawyer William H. Jackson. Bradley had Rosengarten collaborate with his intelligence chief, Colonel Benjamin A.

Dickson, "to distill the output from the Park." Dickson, not Rosengarten, briefed Bradley twice a day. The ULTRA data was displayed on Bradley's German order of battle maps in the command trailer only he used. Dickson personally updated the maps. Underlining the value of ULTRA as a source of tactical intelligence, Rosengarten later wrote that its key contribution after the invasion was to give Bradley advance notice of arriving German reinforcements.[8] Bill Jackson functioned in a similar fashion with the army group intelligence boss Brigadier General Edwin L. Sibert, who had known Bradley since both taught at West Point. At George Patton's headquarters messages were given to intelligence officer Colonel Oscar W. Koch, who prepared a single daily briefing.

The ULTRA apparatus represented a major advantage to the Allies. But it could fall short in different ways at each stage of the effort. Most important, the Germans might not entrust crucial information to the airwaves. The intercept posts could miss the message. The codebreakers might not be able to solve the encryption key or be late in doing so. Translators could make mistakes. Analysts might neglect to notice some key feature in the intelligence. *Allied* radio nets might blunder in retransmission of the ULTRA decrypts, and there could be decoding errors at the special liaison units. Finally, the generals might be too busy or untrusting to entertain their ULTRA briefers. Enormous efforts were made to avoid each possibility, but there is no escaping the equal danger—that data could be overtaken by events. Delays in the process could rob the intelligence of its immediate value. Some measures designed to prevent mistakes themselves contributed to the possibilities for delay.

Another major intelligence source was aerial reconnaissance, including overhead photography. By 1944 this had become well developed—in much the same fashion as ULTRA—with an articulated structure of specialized air units, laboratories, and photographic analysts. Photo "covers" were typically requested at each level, compiled at corps headquarters, then coordinated and approved by army commands, which solicited them from either the assigned tactical air force or an appropriate strategic reconnaissance unit. Covers could be operational, aimed at parts of Normandy where battle raged, or strategic, photographing areas where the army expected to fight later. In the fortnight before D-Day, for example, the 10th Photographic Reconnaissance Group of the U.S. 9th Air Force flew 400 missions to update intelligence on the American beaches. During the campaign in June, the 9th would fly more than 3,000 recce flights, completing 2,700 of them. In the first week of Bradley's Cobra operation there would be 655 photo sorties. On Montgomery's side of the fence, the labs that made prints of the aerial photos processed nearly 1.5 *million* pictures during the Normandy fighting. Photographic intelligence was vital for revealing the characteristics of German defenses and identifying troop concentrations. Photos were especially useful in planning artillery shoots. Strategic reconnaissance often spotted German movements far behind the front not mentioned in ULTRA intercepts. Aerial reconnaissance also played a key role in confirming that troop movements known from ULTRA were actually taking place.

The Resistance, like air reconnaissance, was a frequent contributor to the strategic picture. Resistance networks reported railroad traffic and troop concentrations beyond the battlefield, alerting the Allies to look for evidence of redeployments. With their sabotage and bombings, the Resistance also played a direct role in tying down German garrisons and in retarding the movement of reinforcements, while inflicting some losses and causing many disruptions. And the Resistance was crucial in running an escape net for Allied pilots shot down on combat missions. The Allies considered the Resistance so valuable they took action to strengthen it, inserting dozens of teams of commandos to strengthen Resistance groups in a combined Anglo-American covert operation known as Jedburgh. The best-known Resistance intervention against a Nazi formation was the action by partisans, *maquisards*, against the 2nd SS Panzer Division at Oradour in south-central France. Though the uprising led to a German massacre of a thousand civilians, the Resistance delayed the German division's arrival in Normandy by about a week.[9] But the Resistance did not depend on mass actions to affect the Nazis. In the case of the 2nd SS, it is reported, significant results were achieved by three little girls who got into the rail yards at Toulouse, where the SS vehicles were being loaded on flatcars, and poured a mixture of grease and grit into their axle boxes. There would always be a tension between relying on the Resistance as intelligence gatherers or as action teams.

Finally, there is the very much overlooked role of combat intelligence. The Allied armies themselves contributed a great deal to the picture with scout patrols infiltrating German lines, their harvesting of samples of German equipment, the capture of documents in the course of fighting, and interrogations of prisoners. By early July the Allies had captured Panther and Tiger tanks to examine at leisure. Knocked-out German tanks and vehicles were towed to Montgomery's headquarters, which soon had a pasture dotted with samples. Information from prisoners alerted the Allies to many German local counterattacks and provided a window into enemy morale. Documents captured by various units included operational orders, field reports, strength returns, notes on telephone conversations with higher commanders that furnished insight into the Nazi state of mind, and much else besides. This bread-and-butter intelligence effort receives very little attention but was among the Allies' most useful information sources. Lyman D. Kirkpatrick, later a senior Central Intelligence Agency officer, who spent this part of the war as an intelligence officer on an army staff, later estimated that up to 70 percent of the useful data came from the combat intelligence effort.

Intelligence, so valuable, was also a headache for Eisenhower and his cohorts. The security of ULTRA and relations with the Resistance were the biggest concerns. Source ULTRA was a security problem because anything that betrayed the fact that the Allies were reading German codes, or which ones, could lead to enemy communications changes that denied this vital intelligence. Sometimes the Allies had to *not* act on things they knew in order to preserve the source of that knowledge. Conversely, there were doubts from moment to moment as to whether or how much of this gold mine of information to believe.

With the Resistance, aside from the dilemma of intelligence versus action, there were thorny problems due to the fact that groups and networks were drawn from different political tendencies, including a strong communist element that some did not trust. In addition, there was concern with the fighting capabilities of the networks and the extent to which the Allies could depend on them. With the French provisional government soon to establish itself in France, SHAEF had also to worry that Allied orders, especially if they led to massacres like Oradour, might sour relations with a political entity with which the generals would soon have to deal. The Allies' huge intelligence advantage came with a price.

SINEWS OF WAR

French ports were critical to the Allied buildup and the supply of the armies. Even before D-Day, Eisenhower writes, "we knew that . . . after we captured Cherbourg its port capacity and the lines of communication leading out of it could not meet all our needs."[10] Yet only by landing troops and equipment on the French coast could the Allies increase their strength. The immediate solution was to invent ports—right on the invasion beaches—contrived from block ships for artificial breakwaters; caissons cast in concrete, ingeniously raised and lowered by tides; steel blocks, piers, and dockways extended out from the shore with bridging material; even specialized components with antiaircraft positions. This solution, Ike recounts, proved so radical "as to be classed by many scoffers as completely fantastic." The artificial port, called a Mulberry, was an innovation of Combined Arms Headquarters, the British special operations command, and Eisenhower first learned of it from Admiral Lord Mountbatten as early as the spring of 1942. By D-Day the concept was not only fleshed out but the equipment designed and two complete sets produced, one for the Americans, another for the British. Less ambitious installations called Gooseberries, primarily composed of block-ship breakwaters, would calm the sea inside and permit over-the-beach unloading in most weather. The same facilities that handled troops and equipment would offload supplies.

The difficulties of activating the Mulberries were legion, not least of them the Germans. Until June 11 the defenders could bombard the invasion beaches at will, and only on the twelfth did the Germans lose the ability to observe the fall of their shells. Residual resistance along the coast also retarded supply discharge. Rear Admiral John Hall, leading U.S.

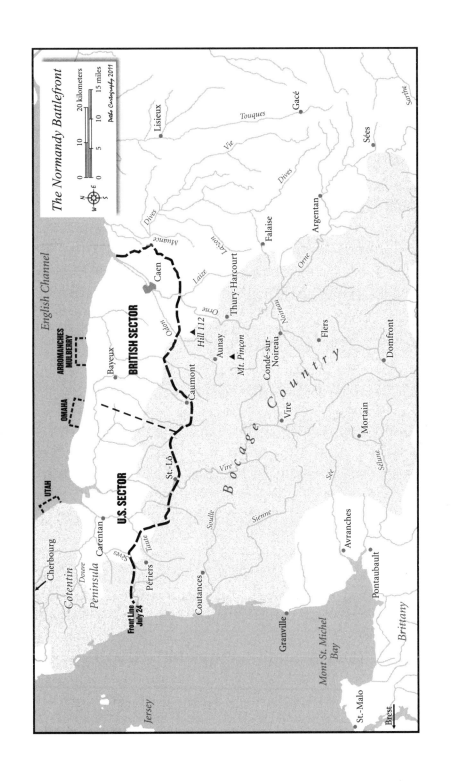

The Normandy Battlefront

N
W E
S

0   10   20 kilometers
0   5   10   15 miles

Pete Cartography 2011

English Channel

Cherbourg

Cotentin
Peninsula

Jersey

Douve

Carentan

UTAH

U.S. SECTOR

Périers

Sèves

Taute

Coutances

Soulle

Sienne

Front Line
July 24

Granville

Mont St. Michel
Bay

St.-Malo

Brest

Brittany

Pontaubault

Avranches

Sée

Sélune

Mortain

OMAHA

Bayeux

ARROMANCHES
MULBERRY

BRITISH SECTOR

Caumont

St.-Lô

Vire

Vire

Condé-sur-
Noireau

Noireau

Vire

Flers

Domfront

Caen

Odon

Orne

Hill 112

Aunay

Mt. Pinçon

Bocage Country

Thury-Harcourt

Orne

Laize

Laçon

Falaise

Argentan

Sées

Gacé

Dives

Muance

Dives

Dives

Vie

Touques

Lisieux

Sarthe

naval forces off Omaha Beach, worried that unloading just would not keep up. On D+2, when supply landings amounted to less than a quarter of that planned, he made his concerns known up the chain of command. From that day the Allies adopted new methods—rather than transshipping loads from the relatively large Landing Ship Tanks (LSTs), these were grounded at low tide and unloaded directly onto the beach. D-Day planners had previously rejected that technique for fear of breaking the hulls of the LSTs. The new practice quickly became routine. Supply deliveries immediately surged, from fifty-eight hundred long tons landed in the American sector on June 8 to ninety-eight hundred on the twelfth, to an average of about thirteen thousand tons starting on June 14.

Calculated from standard planning factors of pounds of supplies per man per day, on D+2 the Americans ashore needed virtually every ounce unloaded. By June 10 deliveries were a little ahead of consumption, but that very day the U.S. had to make a special delivery by air of 200,000 rounds of small-arms ammunition to alleviate growing scarcity. The situation improved, but spot shortages in assorted categories developed repeatedly, plaguing both Americans and British.

Volume increase in deliveries was due not just to new over-the-beach techniques but also to the arrival of equipment for the Gooseberries and Mulberries. The U.S. Mulberry would be installed off Omaha, the British one around the small port of Arromanches. Emplacement began immediately, the first convoys sailing on D-Day, starting with block ships and progressing to caissons, "Phoenixes" (blocks raised and lowered by the tide), "Bombardons" (floating steel blocks), and antiaircraft positions. The American port, "Mulberry A," opened for business on June 16. The British Mulberry, more extensive, would be delayed. By June 18 the situation looked very good on paper. By then the Americans and British had each deployed over 314,000 troops; the Americans had landed 41,000 vehicles (over 1,000 of them tanks), the British 54,000 (including more than 2,200 armored vehicles); supply deliveries amounted to 116,000 tons for the United States, 102,000 tons for Monty's forces.

But the very next day came a fierce storm in the English Channel, one that swamped or sank several hundred landing craft, drove hundreds more ashore, and came close to wrecking the Mulberries. Had the Overlord invasion been pushed back to June 19, this storm would again have forced its cancellation. The British Mulberry, its completion delayed by the storm and components lost in the Channel, was actually advantaged because it was not there to be wrecked by the gale. Estimates of supplies lost or ruined on the beaches and in depots range up to 20,000 vehicles and 140,000 tons of matériel. Worse, the American Mulberry emerged from the three-day storm so badly damaged that it was never reconstituted. American supply deliveries fell off quickly—to less than 1,000 tons on June 20 (against consumption of more than 10,000). For days afterward General Bradley had to ration artillery shells. Monty followed suit just as the British kicked off Epsom. Troop arrivals were also curtailed. The pace of unloading recovered by June 23, when the United States landed 16,000 tons, and American deliveries peaked at 23,000 tons on June 29, averaging a little over 18,000 tons daily for the part of the month after the storm. But on June 30 the Americans still landed only 80 percent of the preinvasion plan—the highest degree of fulfillment yet achieved. And despite the huge numbers of soldiers who stepped ashore, troop arrivals were behind schedule by 247,000 men.

It was on June 29 that the British Mulberry opened at Arromanches. Several minor Normandy ports were pressed into service for the thousand or two thousand tons they could land each day. Other innovations included offshore pipeheads for tankers to pump gasoline ashore, and "Pluto," a gas pipeline laid across the Channel. The pipeheads came into service on June 25, after the plan for locating them had to be completely scrapped and the site moved. Meanwhile, major efforts were made to construct oil tanks to store fluids. Bayeux became a depot for the American armies, Arromanches for the British. The tight packing of warehouses, fuel tanks, new airstrips, and troop and equipment receiving centers strained the Norman towns and particularly the rural road net. By June 30, 452,000 Americans plus 398,000 British, Canadian, and minor allied soldiers were ashore. Among the vehicles there were more than seventeen hundred American tanks and twenty-four hundred British ones. At that point the Allies had landed a cumulative 589,000 tons of supplies according to SHAEF summaries. Calculations of consumption by that point yield a figure of roughly 440,000 tons for the armies. If losses from the storm were as high as evidenced, SHAEF's stockpiles were meager indeed—only the equivalent of about three days' consumption.[11]

Cherbourg figured as indispensable in Allied plans, the port that would raise deliveries to tolerable levels. Overlord planners wanted to capture Cherbourg by June 20 and anticipated using it within days, initially at a capacity of only sixteen hundred tons, but quickly reaching about seventy-five hundred tons daily. This was not to be. Tough German resistance slowed the Americans. Berlin trumpeted that it had not forgotten the lessons of Singapore, referring to the ignominious collapse of that "fortress" in early 1942. The attacking corps commander, J. Lawton Collins, asked for and got an intervention by U.S. strategic bombers along the approaches. There could be only one result. The military commentator J. F. C. Fuller wondered at how strange it was that the vital port "is crumbling like a sand castle." He added, "Put Cherbourg in Allied hands and the whole picture changes. Instead of fighting for or against room and communications, we may expect fighting for a tactical decision." Cherbourg held a week longer than anticipated, though a fortnight less than Hitler demanded. Fuller argued Cherbourg's fall made two things clear: "The first is that the time is long past when an Allied army can be ejected from the continent and the second is that with Cherbourg in [Allied] hands, [they] will be able to concentrate such superiority of force . . . [that the] offensive is not likely to be stayed until the Seine is reached." A little breathlessly he compared the fall of Cherbourg with the Battle of Waterloo.[12]

Yet the liberation of Cherbourg had no immediate tactical impact. At SHAEF headquarters on June 29, Eisenhower's naval aide, Captain Harry Butcher, noted that the C in C "didn't even seem to get a kick out of the fall of Cherbourg."[13] The defeated Germans had sowed large numbers of mines in the harbor and done extensive demolition at the docks. Von Rundstedt had issued orders for the destruction of Cherbourg's port facilities as early as June 10. Though clearing and reconstruction began immediately, and Allied experts discovered the Germans had been more enthusiastic than skilled, it was July 16 before the first Liberty ship unloaded at Cherbourg, and then the cargo had to be lightered to shore on amphibious tractors (DUKWs). Minesweepers swept the ship channel daily for nearly three months. By late July the piers could finally be used.

Cherbourg reached its planned capacity in early August. At that point there was another big storm, again closing the Arromanches Mulberry for days. One of the offshore gasoline terminals was badly damaged and another put out of action for a week. This came at the height of combat, when gas had become critically important.

The Overlord plan provided for capacity augmentation after a Normandy breakout by means of capturing the Brittany peninsula. That region contained the major ports of Brest, Lorient, and Saint-Nazaire, plus several smaller ones. Lock gates and other features of those ports were vulnerable to demolition, so the Allies wanted to create an instant port at Quiberon Bay not quite like the Mulberries, but using some of that technology.[14] With the armies stuck in Normandy this seemed remote. Eisenhower's gossipy aide Harry Butcher overheard the boss tell Prime Minister Churchill early in July that he needed another big port into which to funnel the divisions that were stacked up and awaiting transport.[15] The immediate problem was to prevail within the available supply flow.[16]

To layer in one more complication, getting matériel ashore was only an intermediate step. The wherewithal for battle had still to reach the troops. Preference for bulk shipment went to railroads, but these were in very poor condition after fighting across Normandy. The worst devastation lay near Cherbourg. Rail construction began on D+7, sometimes so close to the front the repairmen came under fire. The 1077th Engineer Port Construction and Repair Group began refurbishing the rail yard at Carentan on June 17. Four key bridges were restored in July. By then there were 126 miles of track connecting Cherbourg with Carentan and extending into the Cotentin to Saint-Sauveur-le-Vicomte. Scheduled rail service began on July 11 on the Cherbourg-Carentan line. The lines were operated by the 729th Railway Operating Battalion, whose personnel in civilian life had run the New York, New Haven & Hartford Railroad (today New York's Metro North line).

The poor state of the railroads put motor transport in the lead, and here the Allies were hampered by Normandy's primitive route net. There were just no multilane, high-capacity highways, and the roads were often country lanes hemmed in by the hedgerows. Equally problematical, much of the net ran east to west, connecting the region's coasts, making high-volume throughput into the interior that much more difficult. Americans created a provisional motor transport brigade almost immediately. On June 13 the logistics apparatus of the First U.S. Army took control, and as troops drove into the interior the Advanced Section of SHAEF established a Communications Zone behind the armies. By the end of June there were fourteen truck companies directly assigned to the engineers, divisions or corps, and twenty-nine for the army pool, with forty-five trucks in each unit. The last crossed the beach on July 1.

Fuel was especially critical. At that time the Americans had only a five-day gasoline reserve. Until June 26, when the first company of tanker trucks arrived, all of it had to be decanted from bulk storage into fifty-five-gallon drums, moved forward, then poured into five-gallon cans. The delivery network itself consumed fuel, too—fifty thousand gallons in June, but six times that much in July. By the end of that month the system was running 94 truck companies (short of 130 planned) and moving thirty thousand tons of matériel from depots to the army supply dumps each day. The British had a similar setup, but a shorter distance from Arromanches to Monty's front at the Odon River and Caen.

There would be a contest between supply delivery and consumption in Northwest Europe that endured for months, beyond the Normandy campaign itself. Units consumed supplies even when doing nothing—standard U.S. allotments for an infantry division in reserve mode, for example, were over 120 tons a day. In an offensive role the same unit consumed more than 560 tons. The requirement for an armored division on the offense totaled over 650 tons. Even an airborne division was expected to need 360 tons daily under those conditions. For pursuit—highly relevant for the U.S. forces in this story—American requirements were just under 300 tons for an infantry division and 330 tons for an armored one.[17] Bradley would write that each division needed 700 tons a day, no doubt adding extra to account for corps- and army-level support units. Add consumption by the service forces plus the need to stock up for future operations, and the scale of the challenge becomes evident.

General Bradley had to maintain restrictions on consumption of artillery shells—only the preprogrammed standard (termed a "unit of fire") per division on the first day of a major attack, half that amount on subsequent days, and only a third of a unit of fire for a "normal" day. Despite this, ammunition expenditure between July 4 and 15 would be at its highest for the campaign. In addition, in mid-July an accidental explosion at the huge munitions depot at Formigny consumed two thousand of the fifty thousand tons stored there. To permit stockpiling, for the ten days before Cobra Bradley limited expenditure to light covering fire in cases of dire necessity. By means of herculean efforts, at the end of July the First Army had a seventeen-day reserve of food and a ten-day supply of fuel.[18] Nevertheless, this Allied headache played havoc with combat operations right into the winter of 1944.

American soldiers were increasingly frustrated with the British, who repaid the compliment. Though the British did not lack for supplies, they also seemed to have a certain envy at the Americans' plenitude of everything from cannon to cocoa. One of the most serious difficulties would be replacing losses. British Commonwealth commanders specifically cited fear of casualties as justification for their brand of combat tactics. By June 30 Montgomery's forces had sustained nearly 25,000 casualties. The number of soldiers available to replace infantry losses then stood at 7,300. By the time of Operation Cobra losses had doubled while infantry replacements became scarce, numbering only 2,800. Planners' misestimates of the need for various kinds of troops formed part of the problem—contrary to estimates, up to 70 percent of losses occurred among the infantry. At the point where the infantry pool had declined to this low level there were actually 19,300 total replacements available. In addition, British losses in June had been *fewer* than anticipated, though July casualties would be greater than expected. The problem British generals faced in squaring this circle was a real one.

But the Americans had the identical problem, complicated by the fact that the U.S. Army training system had shortchanged the European theater in its replacement pipeline. And the proportion of American infantry casualties was even higher—85 percent. Where army planners had agreed that 64 percent of those sent to Europe would be infantrymen, between May and July actual percentages never attained that level, averaging less than half, in fact. In July 1944 the army in Europe lacked sufficient infantry replacements but had an excess of 20,000 men available in other military specialties. Yet two weeks before Cobra SHAEF asked that replacement shipments scheduled a couple of months later be reduced to permit the landing of more of the big units awaiting shipment to the Continent. American commanders woke up to the infantry shortage within days, asking that 25,000 infantry replacements be sent by the fastest possible means so as to arrive before the end of the month. For August, requests in all categories *except* infantry replacements were canceled. The army also adopted the obvious solution—retraining GIs with other branches as infantry, an effort that began to yield results in August. Nevertheless, at the end of September, with a replacement pool of 119,000 GIs—more than the authorized number—the army was short 7,000 infantrymen but over its requirement in other combat arms by 34,000 men.

In short, the British did have a manpower problem, but the Americans did, too. That left unanswered the question of whether it was okay for British troops to fight "less" than Americans. The war of the generals festered with such suspicions. Magnifying them were real, practical problems affecting combat strength. In truth questions of supply and replacements bedeviled everyone. Physical realities and the sinews of war had everything to do with the Allied attacks and, once the opportunity arose, the pursuit of the German foe.

THE WEIGHT OF MATÉRIEL

For all their supply difficulties the Allies brought a tremendous weight of arms to bear on the enemy in Normandy. German campaign accounts commonly marvel at the sumptuous scale of Allied support, particularly on the U.S. sector. Observations that thousands of shells were expended ahead of inconsequential ground attacks are typical. From the British side it was possible for Montgomery to throw three armored divisions into the first wave of one Caen attack simply because he had hundreds of tanks he could afford to lose but lacked the riflemen to make an infantry-centered attack. For all that, the Allies had important qualms about their equipment and its capabilities versus the Germans.

The U.S.-designed Sherman tanks that equipped the American armies as well as two-thirds of Monty's were contemptuously known to the British as Ronsons, after a brand of cigarette lighter, for their propensity to catch fire when hit. Everyone understood the technical inferiority of Allied armor, and a major shortcoming of both the United States and Great Britain lay in the failure to introduce tank designs beyond those of 1942–43. The Allies had been aware of the power of the German 88mm gun early on—even the Americans had actual exemplars of these weapons captured from 1942 on. The German Tiger tank, the notorious PzKw VI, armed with that weapon, had first been encountered in Tunisia. The Panther, PzKw V, with a high-velocity 75mm weapon and the then revolutionary innovation of sloped armor, had been met in Italy. Even the German PzKw IV, the workhorse tank that typically furnished about half the strength of the panzer divisions, now featured a 75mm gun with sufficient power to penetrate Allied tank armor at intermediate range. British officers worried their troops were developing a Tiger and Panther "complex."

Without getting too technical, the standard M4 Sherman's gun, a low-velocity 75mm, could achieve reasonable results against the PzKw IV, but was useless against the bigger German tanks except at short range *and* firing at their less-well-armored surfaces. During the Normandy campaign the press would report approvingly when the U.S. command revealed that a Sherman had managed to destroy a Tiger tank by *ramming* it and then shooting at a vulnerable part from point-blank range. An improved Sherman (M4A1) with a 76mm gun materialized early in 1944, but even that tank, relatively good against the Panther, could barely fight the Tiger. General Bradley remarked that its gun often "scuffed" German armor rather than penetrating it.

Eisenhower was unhappy when he learned this. "You mean our 76 won't knock these Panthers out?" he began. "Why, I thought it was going to be the wonder gun of the war."

"Oh, it's better than the 75," Bradley responded, "but the new charge is much too small. She just hasn't the kick to carry her through the German armor."

"Why is it that I am always the last to hear about this stuff?" Ike complained.[19]

The British matched the 76mm gun of the M4A1 with their Firefly, a Sherman modified with a seventeen-pounder cannon (76.2mm), with better penetrative power. An older weapon, the seventeen-pounder was well liked and highly reliable. One of his division commanders urged General Bradley to get the British gun for U.S. tanks. Brad approached Monty on the matter. He asked for enough cannon to equip one tank in every U.S. armored platoon. Montgomery replied that British industry was already behind producing the weapons. Bradley then inquired about getting some towed seventeen-pounders, which Monty rejected for the same reason. The general had described the state of affairs accurately: The British themselves could not field more than one Firefly squadron in each of their armored regiments.

The most capable U.S. weapon against German tanks would be the 90mm antiaircraft gun, very much akin to the German 88. Eight antiaircraft battalions landed in Normandy during the first weeks and General Bradley used them to set up antitank screens. Bradley's expedient was one the Germans themselves had long relied on. He employed his antiaircraft battalions this way often, typically disposing several of them a mile or two behind the front to guard against armored breakthroughs. Louis Sarris, a young GI with the 125th Field Artillery Antiaircraft Battalion with the First U.S. Army, recalls his unit deploying in antitank mode almost more often than on their conventional mission. In fact, Sarris's battalion was still in antitank mode when it arrived at Bastogne to take part in the Battle of the Bulge.

Both the up-gunned Sherman and British Firefly tanks existed in only limited numbers before D-Day. Most M4A1s would enter combat as replacements for destroyed Shermans. In the meantime, field expedients, like strapping more armor on the Shermans' key surfaces, provided marginal survivability improvements. The British had virtually halted tank development in 1942 except for the specialized adaptations used at D-Day. Instead they focused on manufacturing existing models. Only the Americans had a more advanced tank design, the M26 Pershing, mounting the 90mm gun, capable of engaging both the Tiger and Panther. A project begun in mid-1942, the M26 could have entered mass production in early 1944 except for George Patton. The U.S. War Production Board had given the M26 the highest priority and the Tank Automotive Center in Detroit awaited only SHAEF's final approval. It happens that a few days after Patton's arrival in England—in fact, on the same trip during which he first met his future Third Army staff—the general attended a demonstration at Tidworth Downs, SHAEF's main ordnance depot. Various weapons were shown or illustrated, including movies of the prototype M26, which also had armor far superior to the Sherman and soft-terrain maneuverability comparable to the Germans' advanced tanks. Officers waxed enthusiastic, but General Patton insisted the Sherman was faster and needed less fuel. Brigadier General Maurice Rose of the 2nd Armored Division argued vociferously for the Pershing, but, relying on U.S. armor doctrine (which held that heavy tanks should go to independent battalions), Patton rejected that. SHAEF upheld his recommendation.

Not long into the European campaign SHAEF reversed itself and Pershing production began. The first tanks arrived in February 1945 and, in contravention of doctrine, were allotted to the 2nd and 3rd Armored Divisions. Ironically General Rose—by that time commanding the 3rd Armored—would die from wounds inflicted on March 30, 1945, when he was trapped by four Tiger tanks and German soldiers misinterpreted his attempt to surrender.

Among other types of equipment there was little clear advantage between the sides when it came to armored personnel carriers. The American M3A1 half-track had an advantage with its front-wheel drive and ease of use, but it was difficult to steer and had a high silhouette that made the M3 a looming target. The British bren carrier was low-slung and fully tracked, but hampered by a small carrying capacity. The German half-track represented an intermediate solution, with longer tracks than its American equivalent that gave it better soft-terrain mobility, which, in the rains that made Normandy so miserable, represented an advantage. On the other hand, both Allied armies were light-years ahead of the Germans in numbers of trucks and vehicular mobility in general. This did not count for much during the weeks of hedgerow fighting on the Cotentin, but if the Allies broke out it would make a huge difference.

In guns, the Americans had the biggest, a massive 240mm howitzer, firing a shell half again as large as anything in Monty's artillery park.

Those howitzers and the more recent model of the U.S. 155mm howitzer also outranged both the British and the German. The heaviest British guns had a lesser but still considerable range. Allied heavy artillery was markedly superior to German. In field artillery, on the other hand, the advantage went to the Germans, whose guns either fired a greater weight of shell (than the British) or outranged their opponents (Americans). The Germans had the single best light artillery piece, a 100mm gun with a heavier shell than anything on the Allied side with a range greater than anything but the biggest Allied guns. With their *Nebelwerfer* artillery rockets, in several brigades, the Germans also had an indirect-fire weapon the Allies could not match, with a considerable shock value. The Germans, again, had the heaviest mortars, and used excellent fire tactics with these weapons. As with armor, Allied advantages stemmed from their great quantities of guns and the number of shells they could expend.

Both allies worried about the quality of German forces, and the British had their anxieties about their American comrades. Inevitable disparities between U.S. and British Commonwealth military capabilities, the diplomatic niceties of a combined Allied headquarters, and simple personal differences among the officers atop the chain of command dictated this should be so. By late July, amid unrelenting fighting, alliance relations had assumed a delicate shape. Differences were exacerbated by press reports that noted emerging doubts over whether the two allies were carrying their weight in the Normandy battle. It was less apparent—especially to the media—that on the German side a different set of factors was about to blow the situation wide open. Once that happened the Anglo-American differences would have a huge impact on the final outcome in Normandy, as well as the war for the West.

THE TYRANNY OF TERRAIN

Omar Bradley selected the axis of advance for his planned offensive after an extensive map study. Bradley's own account is that he chose carefully to avoid rivers. The hedgerows of the bocage country usually garner the most attention in campaign histories, but the general's point opens the door to discussion of the Normandy battlefield. Bradley was quite right to see rivers as a problematical feature. A multiplicity of them, most small but a few large, plus a number of canals (France had an extensive canal system), intersect the terrain. Even minor rivers could pose significant problems if they had high or wooded banks, which several of those in Normandy did. Even those that did not could offer the Germans strong positions on the far banks to prevent crossing. In a number of cases the combination of minor rivers, low hills, and forests created potential lines difficult to assail. For this exact reason Monty's fight proved so difficult along the Odon River, at Evrecy, and the elevation known as Hill 112, where the Orne constricted the battlefield. Other rivers channeled movement, limiting flanking maneuvers.

Two important rivers that ran north to south, the Orne in the British sector and the Vire in the American, created natural battle corridors. Bisected by the Orne, the city of Caen and the Caen-Falaise road defined the easternmost corridor, on the Allied left flank, bounded to the west by the river. The obstacle of Bourguébus Ridge, which lay south of the city, was only the first to surmount once Montgomery captured Caen and sought Falaise. Beyond that ridge the Laize and Loison rivers—and the Dives east of that—created a land bridge to Falaise that would narrow as the British approached. Nevertheless, the Caen-Falaise corridor offered the most suitable tank country, least obstructed by hedgerows, plus the potential for a breakout toward Paris using the Orne to shield the Allied flank.

Between the Orne and the Vire, in the Allied center, where the Anglo-American armies made their junction, tough battles had already occurred at Carpiquet, Tilly-sur-Seulles, Caumont, Villers-Bocage, and elsewhere. Until the Americans captured Saint-Lô the road net hampered operations to the south. This sector also represented the heart of the bocage. The British side of the zone offered a different possibility, using the Orne to protect the flank for a push south past Aunay and Mount Pinçon and then a thrust at Falaise from the west, getting behind and past the Caen position. The German generals were very sensitive about this sector and also saw it as the place for a counterstroke to split apart the Allied armies and perhaps reach the sea.

West of the Vire lay the corridor Bradley actually selected. Here the rivers were smaller but created natural defensive barriers. Though nowhere near the stature of the Orne, the Vire River remained an important feature because it bounded the battle zone. The town of Vire, like Saint-Lô a junction astride three major Norman roads, accessed the best-developed lateral route behind the German front. Except for troops arriving from Brittany or southern France, Germans sent to the Cotentin were likely to show up first at Vire. The town of Coutances, near the west coast, lay on routes out of the peninsula. In fact, the original Overlord strategic plan had envisioned the American breakout being launched from a Saint-Lô–Coutances baseline. The good roads out of Normandy converged at Avranches, at the foot of the peninsula, and the bocage country came to an end a little above there, making this the obvious objective, also foreseen in Overlord. The natural corridor for action was therefore to gain the coast by attacking southwest and south. But between Bradley's army and Avranches lay several potential river defense lines, the Soulle, Sienne, and Sée, streams some of them but all water barriers, with the Sée River a critical one. Slightly south of Avranches stood Pontaubault and the Sélune River, the final obstacle before exiting Normandy. General Bradley could not really avoid rivers in his attacks. Rather, he needed to minimize their potential for the adversary by moving so quickly the Germans would not be able to organize themselves.

Before they could reach tank country, the Americans had still to negotiate the hedgerows, which had bedeviled progress from the beginning. The thick hedges, deeply rooted in the embankments that lined many Norman roads, not only separated fields, they created a patchwork quilt of virtual fortifications. A couple of machine guns at two corners of a field, an antitank gun to dominate the lane, a few mortars for fire support, and you had an instant strongpoint. Mass assaults were practically impossible since infantrymen could only squeeze through the hedges, where they could, one by one, come under fire. Tanks, half-tracks, and other vehicles could not get off the sunken lanes. Demolition teams could blow holes in the hedgerows for troops and tanks, but that gave away the point of attack, and anyway was exactly like assaulting fortifications. Combat engineers studying the problem for the 29th Infantry Division calculated that hedgerows would block a tank company thirty-four times in moving a mile and a half cross-country. With the preferred demolition formula consisting of two fifty-pound charges placed eight feet apart, that added up to more than a ton and a half of explosives. This method needed to be kept for special cases. Bulldozers could smash through hedgerows, but their operators were very vulnerable doing it and the machines were in short supply—officers of the 2nd Armored Division planning to enter the battle suddenly realized they had just four bulldozers.

Bocage country did reveal the Sherman tank's one advantage over the Panther—its shorter gun barrel could actually traverse within the confines of a hedgerow-lined road where the Panther, with its long 75mm cannon, usually could not. The Allied tanks could thus change targets much more easily.

In any case the Allies needed a way to deal with hedgerows and American ingenuity went to work. The problem was solved shortly before Cobra. In early July the 79th Infantry Division introduced a hedgecutter attached to the front of a tank, but that did not work very well. At V Corps soldiers innovated a "brush cutter" and a "greendozer." Then the XIX Corps came up with a "salad fork," designed to poke holes for demolition charges, but which GIs discovered could work like a pitchfork to lift sections of the hedges. But the ingenious solution would be the "rhinoceros," the adaptation by Sergeant Curtis G. Culin, Jr., of the 102nd Armored Cavalry Regiment, who mounted the fork on a tank.[20] Major General Leonard T. Gerow set up a demonstration and invited Bradley, advising him to bring his ordnance staff officer.

"We've got something that will knock your eyes out," Gerow told Bradley.[21]

On July 14 Gerow's V Corps people demonstrated the rhinoceros on both a light M5 Stuart tank and an M4 Sherman. The tanks drove at a hedgerow at ten miles an hour. The light tank could sort of tunnel through; the Sherman simply carried away the section of bushes. Tanks with these devices were soon called Rhinos. First Army ordnance officer Colonel John B. Medaris rushed to initiate manufacture of the pronged devices out of metal from German beach obstacles. Medaris also went to England to arrange for tank depots and factories to install the devices on vehicles yet to be shipped. The device was demonstrated for General Patton at the 2nd Armored Division on July 22 with the same effect—Patton, too, ordered conversion of Third Army tanks into Rhinos. When Operation Cobra began, three out of every five U.S. tanks would have the equipment. They would need it. The Germans considered Sherman units with Rhino equipment, extra armor, and improved guns virtually invincible. They called those tanks Jumbos. But all across Normandy the Germans seemed primed for vicious battle. No one knew that better than the lowly GIs facing the enemy.

CHAPTER 3

THE BEGINNING OF DISASTER

As Omar Bradley finalized his Cobra plan, German panzers were assembling to attack in the American sector. The Panzer Lehr Division, among the Wehrmacht's best, had previously been arrayed against the British on the left bank of the Orne. Now it moved to the Cotentin. Two corps, LXXXIV and II Parachute, were fighting the Americans desperately. LXXXIV Corps had used up all its assets. A key division in II Parachute Corps admitted to losing troops at a rate of a hundred a day. The German command had but one reserve, the 2nd SS Panzer Division, and that now went to the Cotentin, as Allied codebreakers soon learned. The only possibility for more troops was to free them from the British front—thus, the move of Fritz Bayerlein's Panzer Lehr.

This came as no surprise to the Allies, who intercepted messages detailing Panzer Lehr's efforts against the British as well as, on June 29, news of its reassignment, and then its relief by the 276th Infantry. Americans in the units that were assailed recorded hearing "rumors" days before the battle that the panzers were coming. And minor counterattacks the Germans carried out during that time were interpreted as precursors to the real operation. The Germans could hope for surprise, but the best they would be able to achieve would be that American troops, preoccupied with their own offensive, might fail to notice the final warning signs.

On July 1 Bayerlein's division had had sixty-eight battleworthy tanks and twenty-eight assault guns, with eighty-three more of these types under repair. Panzer Lehr received orders to detach a combat group with some infantry and perhaps a third of the armor. Troopers groused that it made no sense to leave a large fraction of Lehr's strength behind, and the Allies learned that, too—from a Luftwaffe forward observer's report, which ULTRA forwarded on July 5. Traveling by night to minimize aerial interference, Bayerlein's shift, expected to take a day, consumed three. One night Allied planes indeed obstructed the roads in front of the panzers, which arrived on July 7. Major General Bayerlein went ahead of his division. Panzer Lehr was slated for army group reserve, but U.S. troops slugging toward Saint-Lô pushed across the Vire canal, muscling aside German infantry. General Paul Hausser of the Seventh Army worried the Americans were about to capture Saint-Lô by means of a pincer attack. Hausser wanted Panzer Lehr to intervene.

General Bayerlein conferred with his new boss, Lieutenant General Dietrich von Choltitz of the LXXXIV Corps. Von Choltitz was demanding and not very well informed, but it is also true that his headquarters had recently been hit by fighter-bombers, a strike in which von Choltitz had suffered a slight head concussion. Von Choltitz told Bayerlein the Americans north of them were still weak and could be ejected. But intelligence was poor—the corps commander could not even name the American units that would oppose the attack. And General Hausser knew nothing more—he had taken over the Seventh Army just a week earlier. Bayerlein went to see for himself, driving a tracked motorcycle, stopping at the command post of the 275th Division to consult its leader, Lieutenant General Hans Schmidt. Besides Schmidt's battle group, the sector contained a detachment of parachutist reconnaissance troops, some Seventh Army engineers, and a battle group of the 17th SS Panzer Grenadier Division, in all about two thousand men with a dozen assault guns. Bayerlein found the Waffen-SS demoralized but insisted they remain. Later a battle group from the 2nd SS Panzer Division joined, too. Panzer Lehr itself had perhaps twenty-five hundred combat troops available. When Bayerlein warned von Choltitz of their marginal chances in an attack, the latter repeated his order. Von Choltitz did give Bayerlein forty-eight hours to complete his arrangements.

Source ULTRA perfected its warning even as the Germans completed their preparations. One decrypted message gave notice that the panzer formation was assigned to von Choltitz; another told of its new sector. Before dawn of July 10 General Bradley had been sent news of Panzer Lehr's intention to attack from one of its own messages. This was confirmed in a different message from the German division's Luftwaffe forward observer, which ULTRA decrypted later that day. A third message, again from Bayerlein, reported reaching assembly position and affirmed his aim of attacking at dusk.

After some last-minute delay, the panzer leader flung four reinforced battalions at the junction between the U.S. VII and XIX Corps shortly before dawn on July 11. There was artillery support from several battalions of 105mm and 150mm guns, and Hausser's Seventh Army command had some 210mm cannon as well. The attackers made good progress in the darkness, but after dawn the action became heated. The spearheads initially struck the recently arrived U.S. 9th Infantry Division. Its GIs reacted sluggishly at first because the division redirected one of its regiments to strike the German flank. Another, Colonel Harry A. "Paddy" Flint's 39th Infantry, attacked right down the German line of advance. One German prong, Lieutenant Colonel Philipps's 1st Battalion, 901st Panzergrenadier Regiment (I/901), nevertheless made it far into the U.S. rear. The *Landser*, as Germans called their soldiers, much as Americans knew theirs as GIs or the British as Tommies, overran a couple of U.S. command posts and captured part of a 9th Division battalion. Phillips's regimental commander, Colonel Scholze, with another Panzer Lehr column, was very satisfied.

The American general J. Lawton Collins of the VII Corps concedes that "some confusion and slight withdrawals occurred before veteran subordinate commanders rallied their men and began to check the German armor."[1] Part of this confusion resulted from tense relations among American commanders. The German attack crossed into the sector of Major General Leland Hobbs's 30th Infantry Division, "Old Hickory." To help him capture certain towns, Hobbs had recently been given control of Combat Command B (CCB) of the 3rd Armored Division, newly arrived and inexperienced. The tankers and infantry had gotten in each other's way and messed up the supply lines. Tankers monopolized an important bridge and their vehicles kept cutting 30th Division telephone wires. Believing the armor insufficiently aggressive, Hobbs had fired CCB's leader. Communications difficulties and crowding hindered the GIs switching from their offensive stance to a defensive one, but once the Americans recognized the seriousness of Panzer Lehr's counterattack they buckled down and fought hard. A CCB armored column led by Colonel Dorrance S. Roysden held out in the village of Hauts Vents for several days until being relieved by Old Hickory infantrymen.

Meanwhile, Colonel Philipps continued toward his goal and by noon had reached the outskirts of a village that was the German objective, according to artillery observers, but I/901 was never heard from again. Only fourteen *Landser* got away. GIs of the U.S. 9th Division and the 113th Armored Cavalry Group cut the Germans off and wiped them out. Philipps had been moving up a road lined with trees when Americans knocked out his first and last tanks, and then artillery and tank destroyers smashed the rest at leisure. These tactics were partly born of desperation. "Wolverine" tank destroyers of the division's 899th Battalion saw their shells bounce off the faceplates of the Nazi tanks and then sought better firing angles from the flanks and rear. "Lightning Joe" Collins visited the battlefield the next day and recoiled at the sight of the charred bodies of panzer crews unable to escape their burning tanks, now mute hulks.

Colonel Scholze's 901st and Colonel Gutmann's 902nd Grenadiers captured some other villages but were pinned down by the U.S. 30th Division. A series of nasty little firefights stymied the attackers. Below Hauts Vents a battalion of Colonel Hammond D. Birks's 120th Infantry GIs duked it out with Bayerlein's spearheads and fought them to a standstill. German tanks and assault guns bogged down in soft ground. One column had to break off to meet a U.S. counterpunch. Small parties of GIs and antitank teams with bazookas stalked the panzers. Near the command post of Birks's 3rd Battalion, officers lobbed grenades into the open turret hatches of passing German tanks. An American ammunition resupply party was captured, then the Germans who had taken them were overwhelmed. The battalion ended up with sixty German prisoners and a tally of five tanks and four armored cars. Despite Bayerlein's attacks, the U.S. regiment gained ground that day.

On the sector of the neighboring 119th Infantry, the story proved much the same. An engineer lieutenant working to clear the road behind U.S. lines discovered Germans in his area and recruited a tank and some riflemen to knock out a panzer and flush out German infantry sheltering at a farmhouse. A flight of P-47 fighter-bombers swooped down on another of Bayerlein's columns and left panzers burning. The 1st Battalion, 119th Infantry actually seized Pont-Hébert that afternoon.

Hauts Vents dominated the terrain in the area. From its crest Roysden's tankers could shoot at or call in artillery on anything that moved among the bocage. That made Panzer Lehr's maneuvers exceedingly difficult. When General Bayerlein tried to divert troops to save the I/901 they were pinned down by tank fire. The panzer leader found that his own Panthers, with their very long gun barrels, could not maneuver among the hedgerows. A number were destroyed. Bayerlein finally withdrew to his starting position, less twenty tanks or assault guns and five hundred to seven hundred men, about a quarter of his strength. The 30th Division also incurred losses—the left flank battalion of the 119th Infantry lost half its men that week, climaxing in the fight with Bayerlein. Old Hickory as a whole sustained thirty-two hundred casualties in attacks along the Vire and then the German counterthrust.

General von Choltitz upbraided Bayerlein for the failure. If infantry like the weak 275th could hold on, von Choltitz thundered, he expected more of a panzer division. Furious at the slight, Bayerlein nevertheless had to deal with emergencies on the front—the demoralized 17th SS Panzergrenadiers were relieved on July 12. The SS troopers had crumpled under the pressure and had come unhinged. The front had to be stabilized before Bayerlein could renew the attack. With General Hausser, whom he considered sensible, the panzer commander protested his reprimand. Panzer Lehr had fought hard for a month around Caen, its efforts acknowledged in the OKW daily communiqués. Given the weakness of the front, Bayerlein predicted, Panzer Lehr would be crushed no matter who led it. Hausser spoke to von Choltitz. The next day the corps commander apologized to Bayerlein.

Panzer Lehr made more counterattacks, but they succeeded no better than on July 11.[2] The division continued defending, its opponents including three U.S. infantry divisions and the 3rd Armored. Each day the front hovered nearer Saint-Lô, though that town was the responsibility of General Eugen Meindl's II Parachute Corps, not von Choltitz. Rommel's July 16 weekly report records that fierce fighting continued around Saint-Lô, with his formations forced to yield up to three miles in some places. Units were hopelessly thin on the ground. The 3rd Parachute Division, holding a sector west of Bayerlein, was down to 35 percent strength. One battle group of the 353rd Infantry had just 180 soldiers. The very next day, Army Group B noted, the Americans launched a concerted attack. Saint-Lô had to be abandoned during the night of July 18–19.

As German troops reluctantly pulled out of Saint-Lô, the front below Caen remained in extremis. In late June, OB West had been expecting Montgomery to push on the right bank of the Orne. Thus, the deployment of II SS Panzer Corps against Monty's Operation Epsom. Many other arriving units were fed in there, too, the notable exception being the 16th Luftwaffe Field Division, which replaced the 21st Panzer near Caen.[3] The Germans worried that British attacks south from Tilly could hook east or southeast toward the Seine and Paris. In the second week of July the battle for Hill 112 seemed to confirm that. To cite just one indication of the German focus, during the period when Panzer Lehr shifted for its jab at the Americans, Field Marshal Rommel visited the Cotentin front just once (Meindl's parachutists on July 7), but saw generals and units opposite the British almost every day.

The Wehrmacht continued bleeding. Allied codebreakers read new installments of the story daily. On July 13 Panzer Lehr reported heavy casualties. The next day, von Choltitz noted such high losses that defending his positions appeared questionable. Officer casualties were especially troubling. On July 20 General Meindl told his Luftwaffe superiors that 90 percent of the few paratroop replacements he had received became casualties themselves, within days, because the emergency obliged him to put them into the fight without any preparation. The chief of staff at Hausser's Seventh Army later evaluated the combined strength of its thirteen divisions as the equivalent of three infantry and two panzer. The Americans had thirteen divisions in the line at nearly full strength, three more assembled for Cobra, and two fresh divisions deploying into Normandy.

Beyond bleeding, the Germans were starved for supplies of all kinds.

The limited availability of gasoline retarded troop movements. Ammunition was in extremely short supply. Army Group B staff estimated its requirement in early July at thirty-five hundred tons daily against receipts of just a tenth of that amount. Even procuring food became a headache—and foraging was badly affected by the inability of French farmers to work their fields with the war raging around them. This type of information had become less accessible to Source ULTRA because of the problems decrypting Fish, but that situation began improving toward the end of July, on the eve of Cobra. The stage was set for Omar Bradley's big power play.

CAEN

On the British front the fight for Caen continued. General Montgomery tried again in the first week of July when he ordered Operation Charnwood, an offensive with more newly landed troops plus veteran formations, accented by a major air strike—467 heavy bombers of the strategic air forces, which dropped 2,560 tons of munitions on a narrow box behind the German positions. Though the bombing stiffened the morale of Monty's troops, it also killed several hundred French civilians. Officers of the 12th SS Panzer Division maintain their units incurred few losses. Naval gunfire pounded the line, after which four British and Canadian divisions advanced. The fighting was terrible. Private Jim Wisewell of the 223rd Field Ambulance Unit was assigned to the hospital treating wounded of the 3rd British Infantry Division. The casualties began coming in at five a.m. For thirteen hours—only relieved by other medics for lunch—Wisewell faced a flood of ghastly emergencies, from crushed skulls and mangled arms to perforated abdomens and buttocks. For him the worst were the fractured bones extruding from men's leg wounds. The medics would barely be getting a handle on one batch of wounded when the cry went up that more casualties were arriving. More than five hundred wounded soldiers—nine-tenths of them Tommies—were treated in that hospital alone on Wisewell's shift.

British determination seemed evident—General Hans Speidel, Rommel's chief of staff, noted that the SS panzers knocked out 103 British tanks without causing Montgomery to hesitate. Repulsed in an initial attempt to capture Carpiquet airfield, General Keller's 3rd Canadian Infantry Division succeeded the next day, driving back the 12th SS. But Kurt Meyer remained puzzled. Instead of flinging armored spearheads into Caen ahead of the rifle units, the SS commander saw Montgomery using his tanks only to support the infantry. Aided by the bombardment, British troops progressed smartly in some zones—the 3rd British in the Hérouville suburb was one example—but the assault encountered repeated obstacles.

The Germans fought desperately, hoping for nightfall, for only then would they be able to maneuver. During this battle, by dint of bending all efforts and starving other sectors, the Wehrmacht loosed forty-five hundred artillery shells against the attackers. The British fired many times that number. Kurt Meyer, visiting his troops, found them at the end of their tether, men with "emaciated faces whose eyes had, all too often, looked into another world."[4] His request for permission to withdraw having been rejected—Hitler had directed that Caen be held to the last man—Meyer ordered the retreat anyway. But Monty's overall plan miscarried. Slowed by the devastation from bombing and shelling, the Commonwealth forces were unable to negotiate Caen's streets quickly enough to leap the Orne before the Germans re-formed their defenses on the other bank. Ruined buildings were enough to stall the advance.

Keller's Highland Light Infantry and Inns of Court battalions drove right into the city. "We advanced into Caen behind a bulldozer," wrote Neal Hamilton, one of the Canadian soldiers. "That was the only way as the streets were blocked with rubble from the bombing. I remember seeing a church complete with steeple, which was the only place I recall standing."[5] Soldiers of the 3rd British, paired with the Canadians, passed huge craters dug by fifteen-inch naval guns. One estimated that more than three-quarters of the city was destroyed by shells or bombs. Frenchmen huddled in terror as the fighting raged all around them. More than a thousand took refuge in one cloister alone. A nun at Bon Sauveur abbey recorded the climax on July 9: "*Date of the liberation of Caen. But liberation in part only, for we passed another month before tranquility was restored.*"[6] Designed for twelve hundred patients, the related Le Bon

Sauveur hospital was crammed with seventeen hundred wounded and more than that many townspeople. A smaller hospital across the street was treating five hundred wounded and held thousands more citizens. Caen had been a beautiful city of sixty thousand in 1940. Now two-thirds of those people had left. More than ten thousand French men, women, and children hid in nearby limestone quarries, and many others took to the road as refugees. Once the war had moved away and civilians returned to Caen, authorities discovered over 80 percent of the city's dwelling spaces in ruins. Across Normandy it has been estimated that some 20,000 Frenchmen perished during the fighting.

Meanwhile, the Canadians moving through the city linked up with Tommies of the 3rd British Infantry. As the guns fell silent Montgomery had finally secured the part of Caen that lay on the north bank of the Orne. The 3rd British handed over their last positions there to Keller's Canadians. One battalion marched out in parade formation—with pipers playing—in full view of the enemy. By now Rommel's staff viewed the fighting west of the Orne (Hill 112) as a prelude to renewed battle below Caen. The army group assumed the British would persist: "After taking the whole of the Caen area and throwing adequate bridgeheads across the Orne the enemy intends to commence the main thrust on Paris." Army Group B warned of the impending invasion of the Pas de Calais, expected in conjunction with the anticipated British thrust, evidence of the effect of Allied deception in Operation Fortitude.[7]

Operation Charnwood ended as the Germans reached these conclusions. The Third Air Fleet, the Luftwaffe command for the West, issued a directive on the sixteenth terming the fight at Hill 112 "a battle crucial for the future of the war."[8] Although Rommel believed the British would strike Caen, a fight west of the Orne remained likely. Leaving Wilhelm Bittrich's SS Panzer Corps there, Rommel pulled back the Hitlerjugend, which had been split between both battlefields, regrouped it, and put it in the line at Caen. Soon the young troopers were relieved to rest, though Hitler then demanded Meyer's panzers to move to another area to meet a possible new invasion or a British attack eastward. Field Marshal von Kluge managed to reduce the force that departed to just a combat group of the division. This had a big payoff when Monty renewed his assault, for the 12th SS played a key role in halting it.

Montgomery's next Caen offensive, Goodwood, would be the largest British tank attack of the war. Three armored divisions packed so tightly into the British airborne bridgehead left over from D-Day, they had to follow in each other's tracks. The armor would fan out and head south. In subsidiary assaults Canadian troops would cross the Orne at Caen itself and seize the city's suburb, Vaucelles. British infantry would support the maneuver by pushing out to the east of the front, toward Troarn, but they were to avoid losses. General Richard O'Connor of the VIII Corps would lead the armored fist. Monty's tactics were controversial even at the time. One of O'Connor's division commanders, Major General Philip "Pip" Roberts of the 11th Armored, one of Britain's most experienced tankers, wondered why they could not have more infantry in company—there were two whole divisions in the area, after all. When Roberts complained, O'Connor threatened to lead with another formation. The offensive went ahead as ordained. As a result of the peculiar dispositions, Roberts had no infantry to augment his mechanized brigade, and no time—because the mechanized troops had temporarily been assigned elsewhere—to organize combined arms groups of tanks and infantry.

Oddly enough, given the extreme sensitivity of the question of British ground strength and losses, none of the dozens of accounts of Operation Goodwood, including book-length studies and official histories, contain figures for British Commonwealth combat strength. The seven divisions engaged, assuming they were up to strength, would have totaled almost 120,000 troops. Together with artillery units and tank brigades attached to the infantry divisions the overall figure may have been nearer 140,000. At best the Germans numbered a fraction of that.

Careful dissections of the origins of Goodwood attribute the concept to General Dempsey of the Second British Army. First discussions took place at the same July 10 meeting among senior commanders where Omar Bradley tabled his idea for Cobra. Two days later Monty gave preliminary approval. Dempsey issued an operations order on July 13. Montgomery visited Second Army headquarters for a private meeting with Dempsey and O'Connor. There he modified his instructions in a personal note, significantly reducing the scope of the attack, no longer demanding a full-blooded maneuver to Falaise. Afterward the British and Canadian corps commanders finalized plans. SHAEF was not informed of the change—and troops of the participating British and Canadian divisions were told the more ambitious version only. German officers recount capturing Canadian prisoners who revealed that Monty had sent them off with the shout, "To Falaise, boys, we're going to march on Paris!"[9]

Miles Dempsey had been impressed by the mass bombing that led off the earlier Charnwood operation, and he wanted a similar grand-slam bombing now. Montgomery backed him up, asking the high command for the strategic bombers. The British took an extra day to complete preparations. Dempsey launched Goodwood on July 18. In several waves beginning at five thirty a.m., more than 1,850 aircraft bombed almost a dozen strike zones with over seven thousand tons of ordnance. The artillery then began a creeping barrage, behind which O'Connor's lead unit, Pip Roberts's 11th Armored Division, thrust ahead. In all the British fired eighty thousand shells in support of the attack, from both warships in the Bay of the Seine and land-based artillery. In Caen itself the 2nd Canadian Division began extending tentacles across the Orne, while the 3rd cleared its south bank.

The Canadians' fight can be dealt with briefly. General Guy Simonds's II Canadian Corps was to bridge the Orne in a part of the operation known as Atlantic. Simonds led with Rod Keller's 3rd Division, and Keller put two brigades into his effort. He would take Vaucelles on the south side and seize key points. The 2nd Canadian Infantry Division of Major General Charles Foulkes would clear the north bank, bridge the river, and prevent any possible interference from the Germans around Hill 112. If they could, the Canadians were to fan out below Caen. But within hours their advance bogged down. Keller's division needed a full day to capture a steelworks the bombers had turned into a ruin—and made an even stronger position. Bitter resistance there and elsewhere slowed efforts to bridge the Orne River and canal. There were also problems with Canadian artillery shelling their own side. The Canadians managed to reach their initial objectives only at the end of the second day. By then German resistance in forward positions had bought time for the bulk of the 1st SS

Panzer Division, after participating in counterattacks on the British sector, to concentrate opposite them.

Meanwhile, Goodwood's main thrust struck Colonel Hans von Luck's battle group of the 21st Panzer Division. Luck had defended this sector since D-Day, when his *Landser* had hit at the British paratroops. By now he had suffered many losses, been augmented by bits and pieces of other formations, and led a mixed bag of units in well-prepared defenses. Colonel von Luck had been in Paris the night before, delivering some papers for the corps commander and taking advantage of the trip to see his girl-friend. He returned just as British tanks rolled forward.

Stiffened by assault guns, a battalion of Luftwaffe infantry held the immediate front. Behind it the two battalions of Luck's own 125th Pan-zergrenadier Regiment, backed by panzers, were stationed in a pair of villages from which they could either intervene or create a blocking position. Von Luck also had the Tigers of the 503rd Panzer Battalion, and a unit of *Nebelwerfer* rocket launchers. Interspersed through the area, especially on Bourguébus Ridge, were 88mm flak batteries. With the aerial bombardment there was no radio contact with either the Luftwaffe infantry or one of von Luck's grenadier battalions. He climbed into a Panzer IV and dashed forward. The colonel encountered an 88mm flak battery in the village of Cagny. At pistol point von Luck convinced its officer to forget about airplanes and use his guns to shoot tanks. Later the colonel threw his headquarters guard platoon into the village to protect the 88s. Von Luck's last grenadiers plus some assault guns went into action there. In the center, Cagny blocked the advance of the Guards Armored Division.

The Germans benefited from the narrow front on which the British advanced, which forced General O'Connor to commit his armored divisions one behind another rather than in a broad swath. With two squadrons abreast the 3rd Battalion, the Royal Tank Regiment formed the lead echelon. Thus, the entire offensive effectively came down to two companies of tanks. Because Pip Roberts had lacked combined arms strength, he had been instructed to mask Cagny and leave it to the Guards. Major William Close, leading 3rd RTR's A Squadron, had orders to ignore opposition and press on. The result was that 88s in Cagny village had a turkey shoot, while those on Bourguébus Ridge blunted the British spearhead.

The officer commanding B Squadron, the other vanguard unit, was killed by an errant friendly shell. The 3rd RTR lost its link to air support when the forward observer's tank was knocked out early in the battle. After advancing just over half a mile, recounted Sergeant Jim Caswell of B Squadron, "We . . . found the railway embankment steeper than expected. This slowed us down considerably . . . and gave the enemy time to recover." Minor setbacks multiplied into major ones as German fire intensified.

Lance Corporal Harry Secretan of the 2nd Battalion, King's Royal Rifles, described the scene this way: "As the tanks got near the ridge, all hell broke loose. Tanks were going up in flames all over the place. These tank formations were supposed to go between . . . two villages . . . because both were supposed to be outside the German defense line but both were in fact strongpoints, well equipped with antitank weapons. In fact all the villages on the Bourguébus ridge . . . were likewise heavily occupied."[10] Bourguébus Ridge was a virtual sea of fire. The Germans blasted away with almost a hundred 88s or heavy antiaircraft guns, almost two hundred artillery pieces, and nearly three hundred *Nebelwerfers*.

Most of the British artillery was beyond the Orne, unable to reach the Bourguébus area. This was a clear flaw in British preparations. Source ULTRA had provided an accurate troop list for the Germans, noting the presence of the Tiger battalion in reserve. ULTRA decrypts on July 10 and 14 had specified the German flak units in the exact attack sectors. Aerial photography had supplied detailed layouts of the defenses. The officer commanding Royal Artillery for the offensive had an accurate account of the German guns, though perhaps not of their rocket launchers. In any case, there was no lack of intelligence, while planning failures abounded.

With minimal infantry support—a consequence of concern to husband rifle strength—Montgomery's tanks proved the aptness of the "Ronson" sobriquet for their Shermans. Pip Roberts's division lost 126 tanks on the first day. By nightfall the 3rd RTR had just 17 tanks in working order. Twenty-four hours later it had 2. Except for its commander—and one officer killed—every officer in the unit had been wounded.

On the German side, units of the 1st SS Panzer Division shored up the ridgeline and made other key interventions. In expectation of the British attack, General Eberbach had delayed departure of the 12th SS except for one battle group, and by midafternoon he had secured permission to send Meyer back into the fray. Toward evening the lead battalion of the Hitlerjugend came up and reached around the British flank. Panzer Meyer's troops supported von Luck's *Landsers*. The moment of crisis passed. O'Connor committed his two remaining divisions, but German defenses plus the units reaching the front fought the British to a standstill. When the Guards did come up Cagny finally fell, but only toward the end of the action.

On the evening of July 18, General Montgomery appeared before journalists and read a press release that implied, again, that his attack aimed at a breakthrough. He had to have known that the advance had already stalled—before noon. His army had cleared the remainder of Caen (Vaucelles), reached the vicinity of Troarn, and fought for Cagny, nearly seven miles from the starting position. Over the following days it would advance little farther.

Soaking rain began with a violent thunderstorm the night of the nineteenth and continued into the next day. Lord Alanbrooke, visiting Monty, departed shortly before the storm erupted. The weather forced Monty to halt the battle. More than four hundred British tanks were destroyed—without counting those lost by the tank brigades supporting cooperating forces on the flanks. A tremendous calamity. Montgomery's reliance on armor had also proved that there was no way to shield Commonwealth forces from losses—the battle resulted in more than fifty-five hundred British or Canadian casualties. Dempsey ordered the Canadians to take over some of O'Connor's positions and pulled the armor back to refit. Tank replacements were so plentiful the divisions were quickly made whole, but momentum had completely dissipated. Guy Simonds's Canadians could do little more than man the front while O'Connor's armor was temporarily out of action. Any chance Goodwood had had to divert the Germans, by starting a couple of days before Cobra, was obviated when bad weather and other factors forced Bradley into repeated postponements. In the end any relationship between the two offensives would be canceled once Dempsey called off the operation, still days ahead of the American kickoff.

THE JULY 20 PLOT

It came to pass that with fierce fighting taking place all along the front—the British in the midst of a fresh offensive against Caen and the Americans positioning themselves for the Cobra attack—German officers attempted to kill Adolf Hitler and overthrow the Third Reich. These events bore great consequence for the war in the West. The July 20 Plot affected relations between Hitler and his generals, disrupted the high command at a critical moment, and impacted the führer's strategic outlook. In addition, the plotters' means of gaining access to Hitler—and this seems to have gone largely unnoticed—was a project that became an important tool for the German army's recovery from its Normandy debacle.

On the eve of these events, Army Group B had shifted some troops to the American sector, in particular Panzer Lehr, as it continued to defend Caen. On the night of July 5/6, when tide conditions similar to those of D-Day prevailed, and again during Goodwood, the Germans anticipated a second invasion. Its failure to materialize at last ended expectations of another Overlord landing. From this time on, the Germans initiated measures to improve capabilities for crossing the Seine, especially with barges and ferries, which increased supply flows in the near term but later proved critical to a withdrawal.

Meanwhile, the anti-Hitler plotters suffered setbacks even before their coup took place. The first was the disappearance from the scene of Army Group B commander Field Marshal Rommel, not as victim of Hitler's purge but from Allied military action. During the second week of July the British had finally made progress around Hill 112. After that Montgomery's front became ominously quiet as he consumed himself with arrangements for Goodwood. Rommel knew something was up. He told subordinates there would be a big attack around Caen on July 17 or 18—which proved exactly right—and visited the front there repeatedly. On the seventeenth Rommel motored to the area, a six-hour trip, successively visiting the 277th and 276th Infantry Divisions, the II SS Panzer Corps, and then I SS Panzer Corps headquarters, where he conferred with Sepp Dietrich. The corps commander summoned a few key officers, including SS Brigadier General Kurt Meyer, leader of the Hitlerjugend, then refitting near Falaise.

The dreaded jabos, the Allied fighter-bombers, were active through-out the area. The planes had a permanent patrol over the Falaise-Caen road. Panzer Meyer recalled that they "hunted" him during his drive to headquarters, delaying him over an hour. When Meyer arrived, Dietrich and Rommel were sitting under a tree. Field Marshal Rommel lauded the strenuous efforts of the Hitler Youth and all three went to lunch. Unex-pectedly, Meyer was asked to stay for the subsequent command briefing, where Rommel, again praising the 12th SS, asked Meyer's view. General Meyer replied: "A British offensive can be expected in the near future. The objective of the attack will be to smash the right wing . . . to enable them to advance into the heart of France. The units will fight . . . but they will not prevent the British tanks from rolling over their bodies and march-ing on Paris. The enemy's overwhelming . . . air supremacy makes tactical maneuver virtually impossible."[11] The only disagreement came on the last point, which Rommel somehow took as a criticism of him not making this clear to the high command.

In any case, the officers specifically discussed the Allied fighters, and Dietrich ended by begging Rommel to switch his big staff car for a non-descript auto and take back roads on his return trip. Rommel refused to change vehicles, and left Dietrich's headquarters in his staff car at four p.m. Sergeant Daniel, the driver, used back roads until Livarot, about twenty-five miles from Caen, where Rommel passed two hours later. They encountered frequent burning vehicles. Eight jabos were seen circling in the vicinity, attacking anything that moved. Rommel's car turned onto a covered road that entered the main highway a couple of miles outside Vimoutiers. At that point Rommel and Daniel decided to try a dash on the highway. A South African pilot with the RAF, Squadron Leader J. J. LeRoux, spotted Rommel. With his wingman LeRoux attacked quickly.

The official German report records what happened: "Suddenly, the air observer, Lance-Corporal Holke, reported two aircraft closing in right above the road . . . Sgt. Daniel drove at top speed . . . trying to reach a track and take cover there. Just as he reached it, the enemy aircraft, going flat out . . . opened fire. Field Marshal Rommel at that moment glanced backwards." Hit in the left shoulder and arm, Daniel lost control of the car, which ricocheted off a tree stump and ended up embedded against the embankment on the far side of the road. Rommel, sitting in the jump seat on the side away from the cannon fire, was nevertheless hit by shrapnel in the left temple and cheekbone. Lacerated by glass splinters from the windshield, he was thrown twenty yards from the car, with a triple fracture to his skull. "A second aircraft . . . flew back over the crash site firing at the wounded where they lay."[12] Only two of the four men with Rommel emerged unscathed. The field marshal was taken to a Luftwaffe hospital near Paris and eventually went home to recuperate with his family. Parenthetically, Rommel's attacker, RAF Squadron Leader LeRoux, never knew whom he had targeted. A veteran pilot with twenty-two confirmed victories, LeRoux was lost over the English Channel during a mission a month later.

Rommel's sure hand would be missing on July 20. More than that, the plotters, who had intended to make him their head of state, would be robbed of a key political chip in a high-stakes gamble.

The plot itself did not require direct action by officers in the West. They were to control their area and neutralize the Nazi apparatus and security forces. The conspirators relied on officers of the Replacement Army, headed by General Friedrich Fromm, Germany's recruitment and training establishment, who were to kill Hitler, take Berlin, wipe out the Nazis, and install a new government. The key actor was Colonel Count Nicolas "Claus" Schenk von Stauffenberg, Fromm's chief of staff. The troops to take down the Nazi apparat were to be deployed under a contingency plan called Operation Valkyrie, originally designed to counter any uprising among slave laborers, prisoners, or citizens. Valkyrie had been approved by Hitler himself, then, unknown to him, transformed into a cover for coup action.

No detailed recitation of the attempted coup is necessary. It miscarried due to a host of coincidental events, including the wounding of Rommel. Initial Valkyrie maneuvers were to be disguised as a rehearsal of the cover operation, but that became premature when the coup plan had to be changed. The cover op could not be repeated. Von Stauffenberg carried a briefcase bomb into Führer Headquarters at Rastenburg in East Prussia, as intended, for a July 20 meeting with Hitler, but the briefcase was moved aside by another participant annoyed by its location, and when the bomb went off it was not in optimal position. The meeting itself took place in a wooden building, which vented the bomb's blast effects, rather than a concrete bunker, which would have confined them. Von Stauffenberg remained out of contact during his three-hour flight from East Prussia, and the plot began to unravel even before he reached Berlin. Measures to cut communications from Rastenburg failed. A key guard battalion commander, Major Otto Remer, ordered to arrest propaganda minister Josef Goebbels, decided to check with Führer Headquarters first. He discovered that Hitler, though wounded, was very much alive. Hitler soon went on the radio to make that perfectly clear. Remer's unit became the vanguard of the Nazi counterstroke. Some officers who were aligned with the conspirators, worried about their own skins, began behaving like super-Nazis. Before the night was out Stauffenberg and several associates had been executed. Before his arrest he managed to telephone one of the conspirators in Paris to warn of the collapse of the plot. Early the next morning the Reich Foreign Ministry circulated a cable instructing diplomatic missions on how to minimize reports of an uprising.

In the West the conspirators were far more successful but quickly had to backtrack. The military governor of France issued orders to arrest all SS personnel, but delayed the move to avoid presenting Frenchmen with the spectacle of Germans fighting each other. During that interval the radio announced that Hitler was alive. Confusion ensued. Field Marshal von Kluge ended his flirtation with the plot, wavered, then changed sides a third time once convinced Hitler had survived.

Meanwhile, in Paris, army troops indeed took the SS and Gestapo into custody. Some Nazi intelligence (SD) officers escaped and warned Panzer Meyer, and the Hitlerjugend commander passed the news to Sepp Dietrich, who asked Berlin for instructions.[13] When Kriegsmarine officers threatened to use their troops to free the Nazi prisoners, the Paris plotters reversed course. General Günther Blumentritt, the OB West chief of staff and aligned with the conspirators, became the janitor who cleaned up the mess. Von Kluge told Blumentritt he would have taken measures had Hitler died, but at a late-night dinner von Kluge expressed horror to one of the conspirators that the SS had been apprehended—though even then the field marshal, rather than have the man arrested, advised him to shed his uniform and go into hiding.[14]

At the front there were questions. Waffen-SS general Sepp Dietrich, when first informed, was not certain whether the plotters came from the army or the SS. Fellow panzer leader Eberbach would be impressed. Later he told his son, "Even people like Sepp Dietrich, who really is a loyal disciple and who had just got the 'Diamonds' and 'Oak Leaves' [higher grades of the Knight's Cross medal] almost turned revolutionary. That means something."[15] On the army side, General von Lüttwitz is reported to have been ready to use his 2nd Panzer Division to further the plot, and doubts were expressed about the loyalty of the commander of the 116th, but the plot collapsed before they were called upon to do anything.

Though he survived, Hitler was wounded and spent time in a hospital, and weeks resting. His right arm partially paralyzed, leg and buttocks bruised and burned, an eardrum punctured, Hitler's injuries required treatment. With his altered regimen he had the chance to rethink his military approach, and came to accept one of the ideas floated during gestation of the plan for a major offensive in Normandy—the notion that risks should be accepted elsewhere to favor an offensive promising sufficient results. This contravened Hitler's standard demand to hold every inch of ground. The führer's new thinking is usually linked to the Battle of the Bulge, but it had more immediate consequences in the campaign for France. His distrust for army leaders also led Hitler increasingly to communicate directly with lower levels, which may have contributed to one of the biggest Allied intelligence coups of the campaign.

For weeks in the wake of July 20, German officers hovered on a knife's edge, uncertain who was implicated, which of their superiors or subordinates would be arrested next. "People's Courts" railroaded alleged participants to the gallows, after the Gestapo had tortured them for confessions identifying others. Hitler's purge of the generals, narrowly targeted before, became almost indiscriminate. Heinrich Himmler, the loyal SS chief—whom some suspected of harboring his own desires for a coup—became the head of the Replacement Army on top of his SS and Nazi Party roles. The führer fired the army chief of staff, a technician who had had nothing to do with the plot. His successor ordained that all General Staff officers must become political commissars, too, the "National Socialist Leadership Officers." These Nazi commissars would be attached down to divisional level in the Wehrmacht. "From then on until the end of the war," Blumentritt recalled, "many of us felt that we were under a cloud of suspicion."[16] Hitler's highest target would be Field Marshal Rommel, who killed himself rather than face a court. Next to Rommel stood von Kluge, who looked more and more worried in the days after the coup, and who told Blumentritt, "Events will take their course."[17] His demise took place at the height of the Normandy fighting. Dozens of senior officers took their own lives. More than twenty generals and thirty colonels were executed. Many others were forced into retirement.

Given all this it is remarkable that the German army fought on in Normandy, seemingly oblivious to the turmoil. Only steadfast dedication to the nation and tight unit cohesion made this possible. Waffen-SS and Wehrmacht officers continued standing shoulder to shoulder where they might have been at each other's throats. Colonel Hans von Luck records that younger *Landser* were angry at this stab in the back, but older soldiers had mixed feelings.[18] "It was treason and a great crime," observed Captain Hans Bernhard of the 1st SS Division. "The generals were too short-sighted. They were willing to lose the war in order to get rid of Hitler."[19] Apart from the implied judgment the war had not already been lost, Bernhard's view of the abortive coup was shared fairly widely among German soldiers.

Kurt Meyer writes, "The attempt had no influence on the relationship between the Army and Waffen-SS units. There was no difference of opinion among the combat units. The terrorist act was rejected equally by all."[20] Meyer had been home on leave as recently as two months earlier. He had marveled that in the face of strategic bombing, fierce privations, and constantly worsening war news, Hitler had succeeded in retaining the faith of the German people. Meyer called it *"utter madness"* that anyone—Nazi Party or military—would have thought that Germany could be changed with the führer still alive, or that the army might turn on the SS. "The simple soldier," Meyer said, "the majority of them have faith in the führer and are prepared to carry out any order he gives."[21] The SS panzers at Caen, alongside the Wehrmacht 21st Division and the infantry, fought Monty's Goodwood offensive to a standstill during these very hours. That solidarity became especially important now.

Of a certainty the Wehrmacht institution most crippled by July 20 was the Replacement Army. Besides its takeover by SS boss Himmler, the army's former chief General Fromm would be executed, his staff gutted, many subordinates imprisoned or retired. The military district (*Wehrkreis*) system would be shaken up with new leaders and close political supervision. Since this entity was responsible for the supply of fresh *Landser* to the field armies, its disarray should logically have led to the collapse of the German combat forces. Instead the opposite occurred. The Germans reconstituted units with astonishing rapidity even after tremendous losses both in Russia and the West. How could this happen?

Germany gained in one regard from the unfolding collapse of Army Group Center on the Eastern Front, which began late in June as the führer fixated on the West. The Russian emergency cued the Wehrmacht to the imminent need for a much-increased flow of fresh troops. This led to plans to create a series of so-called Volksgrenadier (People's Grenadier) divisions. These would have less training and heavy equipment than regular divisions but a greater weight of infantry firepower in the form of automatic weapons. The Volksgrenadiers are often portrayed as a stopgap, bottom-of-the-barrel measure by a German army desperate to put men into the field, but they were more than that. No less an adversary than General Dwight D. Eisenhower pictures the Volksgrenadiers as "equally fanatical" to the Waffen-SS. Indeed, he viewed them as interchangeable. The name, Eisenhower believed (incorrectly), "signified that these outfits were composed of elite fighters chosen for the defense of Germany in a mortal emergency."[22]

The reality of the Volksgrenadier program lay in the Replacement Army's creation of grenadier divisions to train new men, units then melded into the remnants of formations destroyed in battle. A hard kernel of experienced *Landser* thus joined a main body of nearly raw recruits to constitute a unit much better than either a burned-out infantry division or one of recent draftees. This program was set in motion by the crisis on the Russian front. It was a reality before the Normandy breakout, indeed before

July 20. In fact, the *reason* why Count von Stauffenberg's presence was required at Führer Headquarters that day was precisely to report on the evolving Volksgrenadier project. And von Stauffenberg's initial encounter with the führer had come on July 6, when Hitler approved the program. The first units were established the next day. Fifteen were in some stage of formation before July 20, and nineteen before the Allied breakout. Another wave of grenadiers began to be set up within days of that event.

The army also initiated a program to form new, stripped-down panzer brigades, also at this time, which again became vital to the post-Normandy recovery. Hitler sanctioned the creation of the first batch of these units on July 24, before Cobra began. Ten panzer brigades were established immediately, and several more, stronger ones, followed. The brigade program absorbed half of Germany's new tank production in August. Other than the panzer brigades, only a handful of all these formations fought as combat units at the front. The vast majority went to refurbish burned-out divisions then rechristened "Volksgrenadier."

The American official historian of Cobra underestimates the capacity of the Replacement Army and exaggerates the impact of new leadership when he writes, "Himmler took immediate steps to unify the military replacement system and eventually improved it."[23] The key decisions were made before July 20, and the system existed ahead of the Allied breakout. This timing would play a major role in enabling the Reich to reconstitute defenses in the West. And that capability was about to become a vital necessity.

CHAPTER 4

A HURRICANE OF STEEL

ield Marshal von Kluge may have upbraided Rommel while
assuming the mantle of command, but von Kluge was sensible
enough to realize his erstwhile subordinate had been right. Once
the new OB West visited the units, saw their leaders, and experienced
the dangers of getting around France, he had to agree the situation had
become dire in the extreme. Thus, Rommel's swan song, an appreciation
completed two days before his wound, reached the führer after all. Rommel's observations, a report from General Paul Hausser of the Seventh
Army, and von Kluge's accompanying letter painted a grim picture of the
battle for Normandy. They clearly anticipated a German collapse. Hitler,
confident of his own perceptions, smarting from July 20, and as distrustful
as ever, hewed to his fixed view, a fantasy.

Rommel's last weekly situation report covered the period to July 16.
In it he baldly stated, "The position on the Normandy front is becoming daily increasingly difficult, and it is rapidly approaching its crisis."[1]
Rommel presented figures on German losses, inadequate replacements
and inexperienced reinforcements, plus an analysis of curtailed road and
railroad transport capacity—which was expected to deteriorate further
as more vehicles were destroyed and the Allies stationed aircraft at con-
tinental bases. Equally disturbing was the continued buildup of Allied
armies. Rommel argued, "In these circumstances it must be expected that
the enemy will shortly be able to break through our thinly held front,

especially in the 7th Army sector, and push far into France." Army Group B included a comment from General Paul Hausser to the effect that local commanders could no longer guarantee they would hold against large-scale American attacks, citing plentiful enemy equipment and lavish artillery fire. Rommel fervidly warned there were no mobile reserves for the U.S. sector and concluded, "Our troops are fighting heroically, but even so the end of this unequal battle is in sight." He wrote of learning a "lesson" from this.[2] No advice to sue for peace appeared, but this was implicit in the analysis.

With Rommel's missive Field Marshal von Kluge included a situation report direct from Hausser, written just after the German retreat from Saint-Lô. Supplies were being disrupted, morale was weakening, and the last two divisions of reinforcements were completely inexperienced. General Hausser took credit for preventing any "operational breakthrough" but noted the cost: gradual withdrawal of the front and the isolation of small pockets cut off by the U.S. advance. The Seventh Army pointed to the vulnerability beckoning the Americans—"the left wing is considerably in advance of the rest" of the line. The hook in the German front began at Saint-Lô, swung to the north, and extended to Normandy's west coast. Hausser warned that "the enemy have sufficient forces . . . to launch another large-scale attack very soon," and pointed to signs of that very maneuver: "we have discovered that the enemy are regrouping," that the Americans were moving their artillery units, bringing up more divisions, and renewing their aerial assault on the transport network behind the Seventh Army. Hausser reported his entire army had but three infantry battalions in reserve. The Waffen-SS general, a hard-bitten experienced leader who had wrought veritable miracles on the Eastern Front, estimated his minimum needs at a full-strength panzer division, additional artillery, one or two *Nebelwerfer* brigades, and at least two fresh infantry battalions per division per month—the equivalent of several more divisions every few weeks. He also demanded increased Luftwaffe efforts to counter the American artillery.[3]

Field Marshal von Kluge added a letter of his own and a comment on Hausser's report. The fatalism is palpable, since the field marshal was well aware of Hitler's views, and von Kluge knew his own complicity in the July 20 Plot was a booby trap that could explode at any time. The OB West chief of staff, Blumentritt, advised Kluge to send the führer a letter affirming his loyalty. Instead, the field marshal's missive of July 21 raised the specter of the führer's *bête noire*, Rommel, and continued, "After long discussions with the responsible commanders on various fronts, especially the SS leaders, I have come to the conclusion that the Field Marshal was unfortunately right."

Von Kluge had spent part of the day on July 20 at Sepp Dietrich's command post, and his conversations with the I SS Panzer Corps leader, as the smoke cleared from the Goodwood offensive, confirmed his sense that "there is absolutely no way in which we could do battle with the all-powerful enemy air forces." The carpets of bombs "more or less annihilated" units, especially the infantry, and had pronounced psychological effects. "I came here with the fixed intention of making effective your order to make a stand *at any price*," von Kluge wrote. "But when one sees that this price must be paid by the slow but sure destruction of our troops . . . then the anxiety about the immediate future on this front is only too well justified." The bottom line: "The moment is fast approaching when this overtaxed front line is bound to break up. And when the enemy once reaches the open country a properly coordinated command will be almost impossible because of the insufficient mobility of our troops."[4]

The field marshal appended specific comments on Hausser's demands for his Seventh Army. The Panzer Lehr Division, von Kluge wrote, could be relieved by infantry reinforcements, but not for almost two weeks. The 2nd Panzer Division was becoming available, and officially rated as combat ready, but it had only forty Panther tanks (two-thirds under repair) and an unknown number of Panzer IVs.[5] OB West was torn between sending the unit to Caen or the Cotentin. On the air war, "we are attempting to engage the enemy, but . . . this has not yet been possible." As for the rest of Hausser's wish list, it was impossible to provide him the infantry, equipment, and supplies he needed; and the heavy artillery and *Nebelwerfers* were engaged on the British sector.

The question of Luftwaffe performance was certainly vital, and D-Day had revealed its virtual—but not complete—impotence. OKW had long had a contingency plan to send a thousand fighter planes to the West once the invasion came, a strong reinforcement for Field Marshal Hugo Sperrle's Third Air Fleet, which had had little more than 400 on D-Day. The Allies had 9,901 fighters and bombers, not counting their numerous transport aircraft. German redeployment did occur. Units were summoned from as far away as Hungary and Austria and funneled into eastern France and Belgium. A dozen fighter groups received their orders on D-Day, six more on June 8. By June 12 the Air Ministry put strength in the West at 1,615 warplanes. More aircraft joined at regular intervals.

But the Luftwaffe of 1944, while not a spent force, was no juggernaut. Before the invasion Allied intelligence calculated the Germans would be able to react with about 1,800 sorties (a sortie is one flight by one aircraft) on D-Day, declining to roughly 1,000 daily from D+5. In actuality there were 319 German sorties on D-Day. The Luftwaffe flew something more than 13,000 sorties in all of June, an average of 430 a day. "Large" bomber strikes typically involved forty to sixty aircraft—two or three bomber groups—not because Allied fighters hesitated to engage these formations but because they flew at night, and Third Air Fleet strength, though fluctuating, averaged about three bomber groups. Its peak effort on June 30 supported the "counteroffensive" at Hill 112 with 600 sorties. With Bradley's army, the U.S. Ninth Air Force alone made over 47,000 flights—nearly 1,600 sorties daily. That is without including the British Second Tactical Air Force or the American and British strategic bomber commands, each of which contributed plenty. The German generals rightly feared Allied airpower.

Many factors worked to diminish Luftwaffe effectiveness: Fuel remained a constant problem; new pilots had less training, experienced ones were few; spare parts were lacking; and poor communications hamstrung efforts. The aircraft groups in the Third Air Fleet typically reported serviceability rates of just 50 percent or a little higher, an important detriment. And Allied codebreakers were reading the air fleet's orders on a constant basis, as well as the redeployment instructions, enabling the Allies to counter Luftwaffe concentrations and attack the airfields critical to German operations. Source ULTRA became a key obstacle to German efforts, even before adding that Allied technology had caught and sur-passed the Luftwaffe in many areas, or that the Allies enjoyed a greater than nine-to-one advantage in raw strength. The Allies lacked little or nothing in quality and made their advantage decisive with quantity—and with intelligence.

The Luftwaffe tried to make essential tactical interventions and harass Allied operations. Its most sustained operation the Wehrmacht did not see—a night bomber campaign against the Allied invasion fleet, laying mines and dropping guided bombs—maintained at an average rate of 130 sorties daily through most of June. Some night raids on the beaches included up to fifty aircraft. By early August the Third Air Fleet had sewn between three thousand and four thousand mines off the Normandy beaches. Meanwhile, stung by the Allied jabos, the German army complained—and the Luftwaffe ceased converting its own aircraft to the fighter-bomber role, ordering them to concentrate on blunting Allied air missions.

The army complained of the Allied artillery, too—and a major Luftwaffe task became efforts to disrupt gun positions. The First U.S. Army would record 73 daylight raids (and 306 at night) in June, usually by two to four planes, and 52 daylight (273 night) raids during July. Antiaircraft units claimed to have destroyed 171 Luftwaffe planes with 130 "probables" during the weeks before the breakout. The journalist Ernie Pyle spent some time with a First Army antiaircraft unit. He records, "The Germans were as methodical in their night air attacks in Normandy as they were in every-thing else. We began to hear the faint, faraway drone of the first bomber around 11:30 every night. . . . It was the usual German pattern to have a lull from about 2 to 4 A.M. and then get in another good batch of bombing attempts in the last hour before dawn."[6] In mid-July, when Field Marshal Sperrle anticipated the British offensive around Hill 112, he ordered his guided-bomb units readied to strike Allied warships supporting the attack from the Bay of the Seine. Fighters put in a maximum effort against troop and tank concentrations—rest orders for two groups were canceled—and bombers made two night raids near the hill itself. ULTRA intercepts of Sperrle's orders specified attack times just the way Pyle noted them. A cou-ple of days later the commitment of the 12th SS Panzer Division to counter Goodwood would be protected by a special effort from German fighters.

Army officers nonetheless incessantly noted the Luftwaffe's absence. Of course, the *Landser* probably did not *see* the German night raids. Typically, General Heinrich von Lüttwitz, whose 2nd Panzer Division was being relieved from the front on July 20—a subject of the von Kluge letter to Hitler—recalled seeing the Luftwaffe over him just a half dozen times in two months. Instead, the Germans flung their limited capabilities at Allied installations, and in the dark of night their efforts—however effectual—could even amount to war crimes. Arnold Rodgaard, a medic with the U.S. Army's 5th Evacuation Hospital injured in his scramble for cover when Luftwaffe fighters strafed the Evac, rejected a proffered Purple Heart medal. The 5th Evac seemed destined for hot spots. It came ashore at Omaha Beach on June 9—its first location precisely where the U.S. cemetery stands today—when Nazi snipers were still shooting at GIs; now it had moved up to Saint-Lô for the Big Show, only to be bombed.

On the Luftwaffe's main task, countering Allied air missions, it strove mightily but was just not good enough. Allied aircraft were fast, agile, armored, and heavily armed. The old Luftwaffe mainstay, the Messerschmitt Bf 109 fighter, now in its umpteenth modification, had good armament but was otherwise outclassed. The Focke-Wulf Fw 190 was good but heavily outnumbered. In Normandy the Germans never employed the jet aircraft beginning to come off their assembly lines. Between air combat and attacks on the Luftwaffe's bases, losses were heavy. Fighter Group (JG, or Jagdgruppe) 26, based near Calais, averaged a loss of two pilots a day. At JG 54, close to Paris, Lieutenant Willi Heilmann recalled, "Wherever we appear we find an oppressive enemy superiority. . . . For eight days now I've been leading the [squadron]. During that time we have lost 50 percent of our aircraft and every fifth man is a casualty." As for pilot replacements, "All of them were mere boys, and their faces betrayed that they knew what lay ahead."[7] If they expected to succeed, the Germans simply could not afford an exchange ratio as low as one to one, as some sources record. June statistics from the U.S. 9th Air Force are somewhat better, conceding American losses of 259 aircraft while claiming the destruction of 127 Luftwaffe warplanes, with another 25 probably destroyed (an exchange ratio of 1.6 to 1 in German favor), but even at that rate the Luftwaffe would collapse long before the Allies could be defeated. As the Americans unleashed their Cobra offensive they knew from ULTRA that German fighters over the U.S. sector were controlled by a headquarters in Brittany that a few weeks earlier had had but a quarter of the available Luftwaffe fighters under its command.

A subject mentioned by both Field Marshal von Kluge and General Hausser was *Nebelwerfer* brigades. Understanding the Germans' employment of these *Nebelwerfer* rocket projectors—as well as the Tiger tanks—is crucial to appreciating Wehrmacht combat tactics in Normandy. In both cases the Germans created specialized units of these types and used them to stiffen key sectors by firepower (the *Nebelwerfers*) or by heavy tanks (the Tigers). In Russia the Germans had encountered Soviet rocket weapons, launched in massive numbers from projectors that became known as Stalin Organs. The Germans copied the technology and introduced their own system, using heavier rockets in smaller numbers. The unguided rockets traveled farther and had greater explosive power than the Soviet version. The Germans used 150mm, 210mm, and 300mm artillery rockets, grouped in *Nebelwerfer* brigades with fifty to sixty multitrack launchers. These they used as equalizers in important engagements. The *Nebelwerfers* were inaccurate and could hit a pinpoint target only by accident, but the sound of the rockets tearing through the atmosphere terrified enemies. All three German *Nebelwerfer* brigades were on the British sector, where they helped stop the Goodwood offensive, among others.

The Tiger battalions often formed the nucleus for a battle group, stiffened a key defense point, or were committed as reserves at a fancied tipping point in battle. The Waffen-SS equipped two of these heavy tank battalions, one for each of their panzer corps. The Wehrmacht fielded one unit. The Germans used the Tigers as intervention units. Although detachments went to the Cotentin, most Tigers served on the British sector. Facing Operation Goodwood, Battle Group von Luck had had the Wehrmacht Tiger unit, Heavy Tank Battalion 503, with him. When Hausser appealed for help, sending either Tigers or *Nebelwerfers* to the west side of Normandy would have meant stripping the east.

With regard to replacements (and reinforcements) the situation was a little bit better. Histories from all sources as well as German memoirs recall the heavy losses in Normandy and the paucity of replacements. This proposition, true for the campaign as a whole, masks the evolution of the situation. The creaking German replacement system was slow to respond to the invasion and began feeding fresh soldiers in numbers into Normandy only in the second week of July, but it got going. Calculations using Army Group B casualty and replacement reports plus other German records—balancing losses against reinforcements—indicate a more favorable picture. By early July the Germans had suffered 100,000 casualties (96,000 Wehrmacht and SS officers and men plus 4,000 *Osttruppen*), yet 266,000 soldiers had gone to Normandy. Then replacements began arriving, almost 9,000 the first week, and thereafter the same or more. There were more than 46,000 German losses in July before the onset of Cobra, but in that period there were 88,000 reinforcements and 33,000 replacements. By this data German field strength on July 27—two days into Cobra—stood at 296,000, where there had been 242,000 *Landser* on July 1.[8]

Not to put too fine a point on this, the Allies had been building up themselves, and at every stage outnumbered the Germans by a large margin. At the moment of Cobra there would be about 1.3 million Allied troops. But in certain respects the balance of forces was better for the Germans in late July 1944 than it had been previously, and their net field strength would *continue* to rise throughout the Cobra operation *as well as during the subsequent Falaise Pocket battle*. Indeed, as Cobra kicked off, a fresh German panzer division was arriving. But realities of location and geography dictated that this unit, the 116th Panzer Division, would enter behind the British front. A long road march would be required to reach the U.S. sector. To say that the German generals felt challenged would be an understatement.

THE FALSE START

For the first few weeks of July, Normandy's weather was atrocious. General Eisenhower's aide, Harry Butcher, a media-mogul-turned-naval-reserve-captain, commented in his diary on July 7 that "the weather has generally been bad."[9] At the 1st Infantry Division, the renowned "Big Red One," Captain Joe Dawson, had taken to heading his letters home, "Cold and Wet—Normandy."[10] War correspondents in the July 17 issue of *Time* magazine noted, "cold, drizzling rain had turned much of the Normandy front into bogland."[11] In *Time*'s next issue the journalists wrote of the "gray, windswept Norman front," and later commented on Saint Swithin's Day (July 15), which if it rained (like the groundhog seeing his shadow) was supposed to betoken forty more days of rain.[12] It rained. The skies cleared long enough for the big air attack to kick off Monty's Goodwood, but *Newsweek* reporters covering that operation duly noted, "The weather, which had started the attack off with a bang, closed in."[13]

Eisenhower would say in his own memoirs, "the weather, which had been bad, grew abominably worse and for the following week all of us went through a period of agonizing tenseness."[14] Captain Butcher, looking for a plane to carry him to the Continent, affirms the weathermen forecast poor conditions for July 19, "and not too good for tomorrow."[15] Eisenhower himself, bucking the forecasters, and desperate to reach the front, went to the airfield in hopes the clouds would break and he could take off. No such luck. Ike fussed that if he had ordered up a warship, he could have been in France in a few hours. Harry Butcher, whose real function, in part, was to serve as press spokesman, told the war correspondents that if he had to characterize Ike's mood it would be concern about the weather.

One man did hop the channel on July 19—Lord Alanbrooke. The threat to Montgomery's continuation in command had become so acute, Alanbrooke felt, that the British chief of staff absolutely *had* to reach Monty and speak to him privately. Their conversation will be dealt with elsewhere, but here the point is that fog at Northolt delayed Alanbrooke's flight for hours. Moreover, he arrived at Montgomery's headquarters as the British commander struggled with the dilemma of whether to abort his great Goodwood offensive due to rain—and if Alanbrooke had stayed only a few hours longer he would have been caught in the thunderstorm that finally compelled Montgomery to cancel.

On July 20, if the German troops in Normandy *had* turned out in connection with the anti-Hitler plot, they would have faced a tremendous thunderstorm that flooded streams and turned dirt roads into bottomless pits. Bad weather also hindered Allied bombing of German V-weapons sites, and on July 22 London felt the pain, suffering its worst-yet flying bomb attacks.

Eisenhower crossed the Channel in a B-25 the next day—the only plane that flew, General Bradley recalls. Brad saw Ike stare disconsolately at the sky. "When I die," Eisenhower told an aide, "they ought to hold my body for a rainy day and then bury me out in the middle of a storm. This damn weather is going to be the death of me yet."[16] That awfully foul afternoon—the end of the runway disappeared into the mist—officers worried over Ike's safe arrival in England. At the First Army, one day Brad threatened to court-martial his chaplain if it still rained on the morrow. The half jest showed his frustration. Staff for Bradley's tactical air baron Pete Quesada estimated that bad weather had forced the cancellation of 40 percent of all the missions planned since the invasion. Every third day, on average, had been too bad to fly.

The weather was critical because of the anticipated Cobra aerial bombardment. The heavy bombers needed a cloud ceiling of at least nine thousand feet for the mission. Weather forced Bradley into a postponement, then a second. Any chance of simultaneity between Cobra and Goodwood evaporated. Captain Harry Butcher recalls Ike saying that "if he had just twelve hours of good weather, meaning tomorrow particularly, we would get a fine dividend." Later Butcher heard Ike comment, "if he had three days of good weather, he would really make a statement."[17] The statement would be Cobra.

The Big Push. Even the journalists knew something was up. Ernie Pyle writes, "We correspondents could sense that a big drive was coming. There are many little ways you can tell without actually being told, if you are experienced in war."[18] After seeing Ike off and grabbing a little dinner, General Bradley went to brief the reporters. The First Army psychological warfare staff—the folks responsible for publicity as well as the care and feeding of correspondents—had been begging him to see the press for days. Now, in the wake of the small triumph of capturing Saint-Lô, he made the appearance. Ernie Pyle listened. Bradley declared, Pyle wrote, that the attack would start "on the first day we had three hours of good flying weather in the forenoon."[19] General Bradley previewed the plan and spoke of a "carpet" bombing—pointing to the rug on the floor to illustrate. Then he embargoed the information.

The First Army itself had to complete its groundwork. And because the Allies intended to table a new piece—Patton's Third Army—that, too, had to be prepared for its share of the effort. All this meant introducing a new higher headquarters to lead the armies, the 12th Army Group, of which General Bradley was already the ordained master. Thus, in addition to everything else, Bradley needed to be ready to hand over the First Army to a new boss in the midst of this offensive. Brad would step into the role of leading all the U.S. armies, while General Courtney Hodges moved up to command the First Army. The wholesale revision of the higher command was a key concern for Eisenhower. It was also a neuralgic point for General Montgomery, who could lose his authority as Overlord field commander once the American army group entered the lists. The intense behind-the-scenes maneuvers to preserve Monty's ground forces command need not detain us except to note that they sharpened differences among the Allied commanders—and *those* soon had a real effect.

Monday, July 24, dawned beautifully. Forecasters predicted a slight overcast might develop late in the morning, but that day and the next the weather should be suitable for ground action and moderately favorable for air missions. Cobra was on.

Much more than good weather was required to execute one of these huge air attacks. For one thing, distinct entities that could only be coordinated at Eisenhower's level had to cooperate. No wonder Ike talked about making a "statement," really a euphemism for a blow to shake the enemy. Using heavy bombers meant Doolittle's Eighth Air Force, which had all the strategic aircraft. In addition there was Brereton's Ninth Air Force, used to working with Bradley's First Army, and possessed of medium bombers as well as Quesada's IX TAC fighter-bombers, those jabos the Germans so hated.

There were technical requirements for the strategic air strike as well. Bradley and his ground commanders wanted blast effect, inflicted in the briefest possible interval. That required split-second timing from many units of the assorted Allied air commands in this show. Operations planners finally orchestrated a two-hour-twenty-five-minute score, leading with a strike by 350 fighter-bombers, rising to a crescendo with a carpet laid down by 1,800 heavy bombers, then a second wave of jabos, followed by 400 medium bombers as a final movement. Clearly the sheer scheduling of this operation, and its mounting, represented a monumental test for SHAEF leadership, as well as its air commanders.

The sky captains failed in a critical regard. Targeting and safety were the fatal flaws of the Cobra air plan. Considering that his army had spent weeks clawing its way forward a couple of hundred yards a day, Bradley had rejected the deep safety zone they preferred. The First Army would pull back just before the bombers came, fire its guns immediately afterward, then advance as the last planes swept the area and the artillery shifted to pinpoint targets.

This hurricane of steel was set to begin at one in the afternoon. That morning Sir Trafford Leigh-Mallory crossed to Normandy to be on the scene. General Bradley records the dawn as wet and cloudy. Air commander Leigh-Mallory found the ceiling low and cloud cover thick, not thin. He ordered a postponement—but the dispatch came through after most aircraft had already launched. Only the medium bombers could be stopped before they left. Frantic efforts to recall the other formations followed. Second-wave fighter-bombers got the notice and turned back. But three air groups of the first wave—as well as almost four hundred heavy bombers—attacked as planned. They flew in from the north, missed the markers designating U.S. positions and—safety zone or no—dropped their bombs on Americans.

Meanwhile, the cancellation of the air strike required the First Army to postpone the Cobra ground attack. General Bradley, with Leigh-Mallory and others were at headquarters in Pont-Hébert, a town east of the bomb zone, was frustrated at the continuing obstacles to mounting their blow. They realized something had gone very wrong when whole squadrons of P-47 fighter-bombers started to fly over them and pound the Cobra zone. Bradley's aide Major Charles Hansen, remembering a tragic friendly bombing incident from the North African campaign, got a queasy feeling. Then came news of an artillery unit hit at Hauts Vents, behind them and some miles from the strike area. Suddenly eight fighter planes peeled off and attacked Pont-Hébert itself. Everyone ran for cover. Bombs landed only a few hundred yards away. Five GIs were killed when one struck a nearby ammunition truck, igniting a massive explosion. Luckily the generals emerged unscathed.

First Army commander-designate Courtney Hodges and another crowd of senior officers gathered to watch elsewhere. Unaware of the cancellation, General Hodges went to an observation post in a wrecked house. Among his retinue were reporters, including Hanson Baldwin of the *New York Times*. They rubbernecked as the fighters attacked and later saw a squadron strike far from its target area. It seemed clear the aircraft were paying no attention to the army's identification panels and smoke markers. Then bombs began to fall on them. One witness left this account:

> We could see their rocket markers flare off, designating time to drop, and then a few seconds later their clusters of bombs. We were watching unconcernedly when we heard a shrieking whistle, and knew that some were coming our way. There was a wild scramble for cover, but few reached farther than the rear door of the house before the bombs hit, crunch, wham, thud, some 500 or 600 yards southwest of us.[20]

One officer cut his hand on glass. A general peed in his pants. The men's nervous laughter deflected their fear. General Lewis Brereton, the Ninth Air Force commander, had an aide note the time so he could determine the guilty bomb group. Among those who could have been killed were Hodges's deputy, General William Simpson, commander-designate of the Ninth U.S. Army, and General Matthew Ridgway of the paratroops. They were unhurt.

The bombs killed 24 GIs and wounded about 128 others from the 30th Division's 120th Infantry, only half a mile down the road. Another Old Hickory regiment had 5 killed and 28 wounded. With victims else where the casualties exceeded 200. More men went to the rear with post-traumatic stress. It was from GIs of the 120th, fleeing the bombs, that General Hodges first learned the air raid had been canceled.

Since the Americans had fallen back to create a safety zone before the bombing cancellation, they now had to attack to restore their field positions. That cost nearly 200 more casualties, including the death of Paddy Flint, the hard-driving commander of the 39th Infantry Regiment and a key in Panzer Lehr's defeat a fortnight earlier. Flint was also the godfather of George S. Patton's only son. Patton took the time to go through Colonel Flint's papers, had a special coffin made, and attended the funeral.

THE MONEY PLAY

General Bradley, furious about the messy recall of the bombers, went apoplectic at the incoming reports of American casualties. He demanded an explanation from Pete Quesada, who had no idea how any of this could happen. Air Marshal Leigh-Mallory promised to investigate and returned to his headquarters at Stanmore. Late that night he telephoned Bradley to say the aircraft had, in fact, been following their designated flight path when they hit the GIs. Discovering only now that the aircraft had flown in from the north, not along the Saint-Lô–Périers road as he had understood they would, Bradley went ballistic. But Leigh-Mallory had some good news, too—weather forecasts held out a promise of rescheduling the carpet bombing for the next day, but the orders had to be finalized immediately, and the sky captains refused to change their intended route. Bradley now had to decide, even as he learned of the dangerous navigational path, if he wanted to try again. He needed the air support. Delay increased the chance the Germans might divine U.S. intentions. Brad accepted the risk of more friendly casualties. J. Lawton Collins, the principal Cobra corps commander, and Elwood R. Quesada, the air-ground coordinator, were also upset about the catastrophe but agreed with the decision.

On the German side of the hill, during the night of July 24 Field Marshal von Kluge spoke to the Seventh Army commander, General Paul Hausser. OB West, of course, had no idea the Cobra bombing had miscarried, and wanted to know what the American action portended. Hausser related what he knew—patrol activity west of Saint-Lô, shelling of the Vire River bridges (undoubtedly a U.S. effort to isolate the Cobra battle zone), some carpet bombing, limited attacks, reorganization of the front. Hausser believed Bradley was preparing to insert a fresh army corps into the front. This last point is very interesting, for it suggests the Germans had some inkling of the huge exploitation force poised behind American lines, which Brad had worked so hard to disguise.[21] Von Kluge specifically asked about the sector west of the Vire and whether Hausser expected "increasingly severe" fighting there. Then the field marshal repeated his question: "I'd like to ask you again, do you get the impression that you're headed for heavy fighting?" Hausser answered that fighting had to be expected somewhere. Having demonstrated this concern, von Kluge, incredibly, continued to focus his attention on Caen.

The new day dawned to drizzle and light mist. The GIs in their assembly areas had no idea whether the attack was on until after breakfast. The strike, set to begin earlier than before, would be preceded by a weather reconnaissance plane to verify conditions, which were deemed adequate. They were not perfect (the 405th Fighter Group, assigned to armed reconnaissance in the vicinity of the battle area, could not fly its P-47s before midafternoon).

Shortly after nine thirty a.m., the initial wave of fighter-bombers attacked. First over the target was Colonel Harold Holt's 366th Fighter Group. Looking over the scene, the masses of American tanks and vehicles parked nearly bumper to bumper to the north of the safety zone stunned Holt. Nothing at all showed on the German side of the front line, where the tanks and guns were carefully camouflaged. Red smoke and orange or pink cloth panels identified U.S. units. The attack began with Colonel Holt's jabos.

After ninety minutes of harrying by the fighter-bombers, bombs began to drop from the bellies of the first of 1,507 Eighth Air Force B-17s and B-24s. As per the plan, they were followed by another wave of jabos, then the medium bombers. In all on July 25 there would be 380 medium bomber and 1,546 fighter sorties, including those flown for armed reconnaissance. Some 4,350 tons of munitions were loosed.

As on the previous day not all the ordnance fell within the bomb zone. The approach from the north, altitude changes, plus missed landmarks and identification markers all contributed to misaimed bombs. American lines

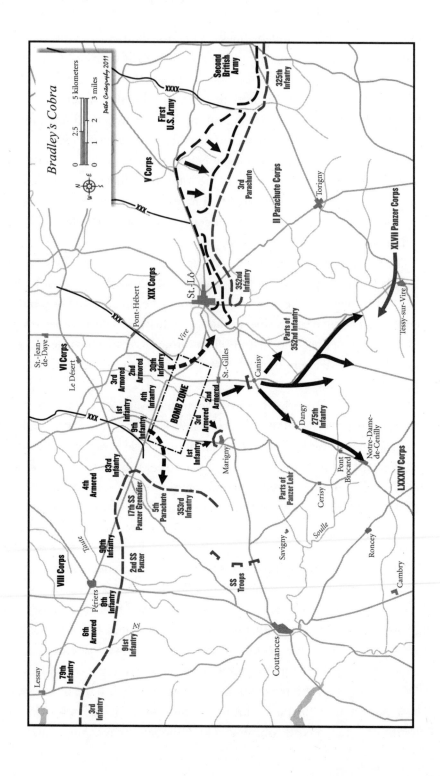

Bradley's Cobra

N
W — E
S

0   2.5   5 kilometers
0   1   2   3 miles

Pete Cartography 2011

Second British Army

First U.S. Army

325th Infantry

V Corps

3rd Parachute

II Parachute Corps

Torigny

352nd Infantry

St.-Lô

XLVII Panzer Corps

XIX Corps

Pont-Hébert

Tessy-sur-Vire

Vire

St.-Jean-de-Daye

VI Corps

Le Désert

Parts of 352nd Infantry

3rd Armored

2nd Armored

30th Infantry

St.-Gilles

Canisy

1st Infantry

4th Infantry

BOMB ZONE

3rd Armored

2nd Armored

Dangy

275th Infantry

9th Infantry

1st Infantry

Marigny

Parts of Panzer Lehr

Pont Brocard

Notre-Dame-de-Cenilly

LXXXIV Corps

4th Armored

83rd Infantry

17th SS Panzer Grenadier

5th Parachute

353rd Infantry

Cerisy

90th Infantry

2nd SS Panzer

Savigny

Soulle

Roncey

Taute

VIII Corps

8th Infantry

Périers

SS Troops

Cambry

6th Armored

91st Infantry

Ay

Coutances

79th Infantry

Lessay

3rd Infantry

were marked by long strips of colored cloth on the ground, plus matching colored smoke from generators, but it was not enough. Ernie Pyle, watching from a farmhouse about eight hundred yards behind the lines, wished for anything he had chosen a spot eight hundred yards behind that. He, along with officers of the 4th Infantry Division, scrambled madly for cover. Victims included a journalist—the photographer Bede Irvin—not Pyle, who wrote, "I've never known a storm, or a machine, or any resolve of man that had about it the aura of such a ghastly relentlessness."[22] At General Collins's VII Corps command post, Collins and Omar Bradley sat in the ruins of a café to observe. They did not discover the full extent of American casualties until communications disrupted by the attack had been restored. Altogether 111 Americans were killed and 490 wounded by their own aircraft.

Among the hardest-hit units was Old Hickory, including the same 120th Infantry that had suffered so much already. The 30th Division's assistant commander, Brigadier General William K. Harrison, on the line the day before, returned. Harrison wanted to show GIs he was with them, and he was—while scrambling for shelter. There were 64 killed, 374 wounded, 60 missing, and 164 GIs who succumbed to post-traumatic stress—then called combat fatigue—662 casualties in all. A chemical battalion was put out of action. Both initial assault groups suffered grievous losses. One rifle battalion's radios were rendered completely useless. Division commander Hobbs decided to avoid the confusion of a last-minute switch, keeping the unit in line. The 30th's history notes, "The bombing . . . caused the Division as many casualties as the most severe day of combat."[23] GIs of the 30th began calling General Quesada's IX Tactical Air Command the "Ninth Luftwaffe"—"We used to say the Air Force was good for only two things—destroying enemy buildings and killing friendly troops."[24]

Despite carnage and confusion Hobbs's lead battalion was off its line of departure just fourteen minutes behind schedule. Private Leo Temkin, to take one example, had been buried by bombs and, once he escaped, found himself without rifle or equipment. "My squad was just moving out," Temkin recalled. "I picked up the things I needed off some dead soldiers and caught up with them."[25] General Harrison got up after the bombing and discovered five GI survivors of the full squad that had been with him. Harrison personally led them off to capture a nearby hedgerow. Lieutenant Earnest Aas of Old Hickory's 743rd Tank Battalion advanced with his company, avoiding mines, wary of friendly aircraft, and creeping past bursts of German artillery for the rest of the day.

The most prominent victim would be Lieutenant General Lesley J. McNair, commander of U.S. Army Ground Forces. McNair had come to Europe to visit the troops and replace George S. Patton at the head of the fictive army group in the Fortitude deception. McNair insisted on going up to the very front, as he had done the previous day. Aides tried to convince him to hang back, but a junior officer told him how much the GIs valued his presence, and McNair went right back, to the 30th Division. He squatted in a foxhole not far from the Germans. Sticks of "short" bombs walked along the U.S. positions. Where McNair's foxhole had been was only a bomb crater. A rescue detail labored with picks and shovels but never found any trace of the general.[26] Other misguided bombs again fell near the higher-ups at their own viewing point, but at least there no one was hit.

For all that, devastation on the American side of the line seemed minor compared to that on the German. General Fritz Bayerlein and his Panzer Lehr Division were at ground zero. Just the day before Bayerlein had huddled with his operations chief, Major Kaufmann, trying to figure out what the Americans were up to. The abortive strike of the 24th had still caused considerable damage. Fighting that ensued as Bradley's forces strove to regain their initial positions convinced the Germans they had faced down a real attack. But Bayerlein had had to ask for extra troops to make up losses. They continued their conversation in the morning. Major Kaufmann thought attacks could resume at any time. "I think the weather is the only factor that's stopped [them] so far," he had said.[27] Moments later the phone rang from the 901st Panzergrenadier Regiment with news of bombing. Then, shortly after seven a.m., Colonel Guttmann's 902nd Regiment reported GIs falling back, news quickly confirmed all along the line. At nine forty, notices of heavy air attacks started flowing into Bayerlein's command post near Canisy, followed by word of the carpet bombing. German flak defended the troops as well as it could—Ernie Pyle was among those who saw American bombers shot down—but the attack was massive and the flak units themselves were wiped out. Within an hour headquarters had lost contact with every unit. Bayerlein sat mute as GIs began to advance. Panzer Lehr was in extremis.

Lieutenant General J. Lawton Collins of the VII Corps, radio call sign "Jayhawk," disposed of 88,300 troops exclusive of nondivisional units, according to the midnight strength return filed on July 24. With six divisions, his corps by itself was more than twice as powerful as all the Germans on the American front. Collins arrayed his forces carefully. The U.S. 30th and 9th Infantry Divisions massed at each end of the attack sector, to envelop the threads of the German line severed by the bombing. In the center Major General Raymond O. Barton's 4th Infantry Division would forge ahead and seize intermediate objectives. In the follow-on force Collins provided tanks of the 3rd Armored Division to accompany the advancing infantry, and also ordered that a regiment of Major General Clarence R. Huebner's 1st Infantry Division (the "Big Red One") be motorized and attached to Major General Edward H. Brooks's 2nd Armored. Collins expected to use Huebner, Brooks, and the rest of Major General Leroy H. Watson's 3rd Armored Division as integral units. Artillery included 20 corps and army battalions with 174 medium- and heavy-caliber guns, for which Collins had 140,000 rounds of ammunition.

As Cobra developed, Major General Troy H. Middleton's VIII Corps, on Lightning Joe's left, would apply pressure along Normandy's west coast. Middleton had five divisions (65,400 troops), supported by a dozen artillery battalions with 42,000 shells to expend. In all Normandy west of the Vire, Germans numbered perhaps 35,000 *Landser*.[28] To cap the Allied advantages, ULTRA revealed that the German artillery had used up so many shells the previous day that it had now run short.

Leland Hobbs's 30th Division's mission put it directly up against Bayerlein, as well as Meindl's parachute corps. The American rifle battalions were to skip past the heel of the gap opened by the bombers and push up to the left bank of the Vire, building a new flank for the American thrust. The redoubtable 120th Infantry, in a column of battalions, led the way. At a key road junction Colonel Birks's forward battalion bumped into a few Panther tanks and a "liberal assortment" of German infantry. The troops engaged. The divisional tank battalion covered the riflemen, firing on the Panthers. Over the radio came the plaintive exclamation of one of the Sherman gunners, "Good God, I fired three rounds and they all bounced off!"[29]

For a moment the advance hesitated. That afternoon General Collins faced the key decision of when to commit his exploitation force. Jayhawk sent Huebner's Big Red One on a thrust toward Coutances, adding enough trucks to motorize the infantry. Collins wanted to hold the 2nd and 3rd Armored until the assault divisions reached their initial goals, but disorganization from the bombs and pockets of Nazi resistance held up the advance. Thinking of the Germans, Collins wrote, "I sensed that their communications and command structure had been damaged more than our troops realized."[30] Jayhawk therefore unleashed most of the exploitation force, Collins withholding only part of Watson's armor. Ponderously the units began to edge forward. Huebner's slow progress bothered General Collins, but Brooks's armored division gained enough ground to disrupt the Germans. The pace quickened.

With every passing minute Fritz Bayerlein understood better the complete disintegration of the German front. Von Choltitz answered his appeals for reinforcement, committing his only reserve, two infantry regiments. One ran headlong into GIs and was sucked into a desperate defense. The other was obliterated. With no word from his Panzer Lehr troops, Bayerlein went to see for himself. Just as he jumped off his motorcycle at the command post of Colonel Scholze's 901st Panzergrenadier Regiment, a junior officer returned from scouting the front. It had been pummeled. "I did not find a single strongpoint that was intact," the lieutenant reported. "The main fighting line has vanished."[31]

Fortuitously the Germans avoided a complete U.S. breakthrough. In the center of the Panzer Lehr sector Ray Barton's 4th Infantry were not able to capture a key village until after nightfall. The town of Marigny, another Jayhawk objective, was held by determined paratroopers and graced by an American division commander's order to halt. The Germans held on. Watson's 2nd Armored Division rushed through Canisy, but stopped a little farther along where some German assault guns stood fast. General Hausser decided to release his army reserve, the 352nd Infantry Division, but it had barely moved when engaged. General Dietrich Kreiss's 352nd bought a day. Hausser also freed up a panzer battalion and a grenadier battalion of the 2nd SS Panzer Division, on Bayerlein's left, to send in from the flank. Waffen-SS tanks helped defend Marigny.

The public face Germany put on all this was opaque. Berlin's broadcast of the OKW war communiqué covering July 25 read, "A defensive struggle on a large scale . . . is raging. After fast enemy attacks, launched with the strongest artillery and air support, had been repelled the enemy succeeded in penetrating our front at a number of points and in crossing the Saint-Lô–Périers road in a southwesterly direction. Counterattacks are in progress."[32]

There is a bit of controversy over the extent of Panzer Lehr's losses—on July 23 it had reported thirty-one combat-ready tanks, and there were about five thousand infantry. Bayerlein claims extensive destruction, including all his tanks. But Helmut Ritgen, a battalion commander with the division's armored regiment, notes that on the night of the twenty-fourth the unit's Panzer IV battalion was sent to the rear, out of harm's way, and his account quotes enough tank exploits against the Americans to make clear some armor did survive.[33] In addition, Bayerlein's orders the night before Cobra anticipated more bombing, plus U.S. attacks, instructing his troops to sleep away from the roads and heavily dig in. The German units were coherent enough, in Ritgen's account, to carry out operations other than desperate defense. Allied intelligence recorded a July 28 message from the division's Luftwaffe observer noting Panzer Lehr had no battleworthy troops left. Ritgen's stories center primarily on the miscarriage of various counterattacks and how companies and battalions escaped the American onrush. Two days later ULTRA reported Panzer Lehr's remnants were leaving the front. But after a week of this hell, the division's strength return for August 1 credits it with eleven thousand men, sixty-seven tanks, and at least ten assault guns.[34] It is likely that the battle groups temporarily assigned to Panzer Lehr—Kampfgruppe Heinz of the 275th Division and the 14th Parachute Regiment, which had been slated to take over part of its line—suffered more from the bombing, which also inflicted losses on Bayerlein's division. Be that as it may, Panzer Lehr and the adjoining units of the II Parachute Corps were so damaged they were unable to defend effectively.

On July 26 the Jayhawk attackers chewed through the Germans and bypassed Marigny, which fell the next day. In a decoded intercept reported out before dawn, ULTRA thoughtfully supplied the entire order of battle of von Choltitz's corps from its situation report of the previous night. American spearheads reached into the German rear. Choltitz ordered his divisions on the west side of Normandy to fall back, screened by 2nd SS Panzer, re-forming to defend Coutances against Americans from the east. With the Germans suddenly disappearing before them, Troy Middleton's VIII Corps, radio call sign "Monarch," could advance. In two days Monarch captured fewer than three hundred *Landser*. It was Middleton's 4th Armored Division that actually took Coutances on July 28. Omar Bradley records that the war correspondents had challenged him during his pre-Cobra briefing to predict when Coutances would fall—and one later told Brad he had been off by just seven hours.

ONLY THE DEAD HOLD THE FRONT

It would not be quite accurate to say the Germans failed to appreciate the severity of developments, but it would not be far from the truth. The OKW communiqué that reported the kickoff of Cobra had the Caen front for its lead item. German accounts repeatedly cite OB West's reluctance to take the U.S. threat seriously. That night in his telephone report to Hitler, Field Marshal von Kluge stated, "As of this moment the front has . . . burst." But Kluge's response was to send his son, a General Staff officer, to order Panzer Lehr to stand fast. The officer had no answer when Bayerlein asked what troops he could use for that. During the night of July 25 the high command did order a change, relieving the XLVII Panzer Corps headquarters in the central sector of Normandy to send it into the fray. With the 2nd Panzer Division pulled out of the line near Caumont, and the arriving 116th Panzer Division, the corps at least gave the Germans a maneuver force. Von Kluge confronted Führer Headquarters on the realities, and the need for formations to oppose the Americans. He asked for a panzer division from southern France, plus infantry from the Pas de

Calais and Brittany. Hitler finally relented on maintaining the strength of the Fifteenth Army at Calais. Despite this von Kluge still fixated on the British. His initial idea was to use XLVII Panzer Corps at Caen, not against the Americans. At the Seventh Army, Hausser actually believed the greater danger lay on Normandy's west coast, at Coutances, not where Collins's GIs pressed their offensive.

Fritz Bayerlein knew better. He told von Kluge's emissary that the front looked like the surface of the moon. He had no troops. The officer referred to the 2nd SS battle group coming from the west. Bayerlein, overwhelmed, had a scathing answer. "Out in front everyone is holding out," he rasped, his voice tight. "My grenadiers and my engineers, and my tank crews—they're all holding their ground. Not a single man is leaving his post. Not one! They're lying in their foxholes mute and silent, for they are dead. . . . You may report to the field marshal that the Panzer Lehr Division is annihilated. Only the dead now hold the line."[35] Suddenly came the crash of a massive explosion—stockpiled munitions—as U.S. planes struck a nearby depot.

Forced to shift his command post on July 26, General Bayerlein selected a location at Cerisy just above the Soulles River, one of those water barriers that might have halted the U.S. advance. Soon after midnight, Brigadier General Isaac D. White's Combat Command B of the U.S. 2nd Armored Division, in a brilliant *coup de main*, seized a bridge over the Soulles at Pont Brocard. That afternoon the division's scout battalion happened upon Bayerlein's headquarters at a farm near the road the Americans were using. Armor began shooting at the house, where Bayerlein hunched over his situation maps. Abandoning vehicles, the Panzer Lehr staff had to escape by ones and twos. The general fled afoot. With a handful of others, Bayerlein would be out of contact for a critical day. Panzer Lehr lost its radios and records, not to mention the office equipment. For two days written orders could not be reproduced. Worse, the Americans overran Panzer Lehr's repair unit, forcing the Germans to blow up more than twenty newly refurbished tanks at a moment they were desperate for panzers. The mechanics barely slipped away with their precious tools. Battalion commander Ritgen believes the pressures of battle had finally gotten to Bayerlein and the general had momentarily lost his capacity to command.

However, Bayerlein was not alone in believing the front could not be held. A scene very much like the panzer leader's encounter with the emissary took place at the headquarters of the neighboring II Parachute Corps. Its chief, General Meindl, had just returned from the front, forced to hide from the jabos thirty times—a thirty-minute drive consumed four hours. Combat strength in Meindl's corps was down to 3,400 *Landser.* Ammunition was low, and OB West had just informed his staff that no howitzer shells were available. Meindl told the younger von Kluge, the emissary, "Kindly convey to your father exactly what I am going to say to you. The time has come when Normandy can no longer be held. . . . The enemy will break through to the west of us and outflank us. And what's going to happen then?"[36]

There are a couple of hypotheticals that go to the question of whether the Germans might have held the Cobra attack. Most prominently, von Lüttwitz of the 2nd Panzer Division argues that if his force, at that time joining the XLVII Panzer Corps and the 116th Panzer, perhaps in combination with Bayerlein's division, had actually been in reserve behind von Choltitz, they could have sealed off the U.S. penetration. This seems like wishful thinking. Without question the preponderance of force lay with Bradley and Collins, for every combination of conceivable possibility. With or without Panzer Lehr, the XLVII Corps amounted to little more than one of the U.S. armored divisions. Another of von Lüttwitz's alternatives—a greater proportion of German heavy tank (Tiger) and *Nebelwerfer* units allocated to the LXXXIV Corps front—represented capability at the margins, and would have been hampered by Nazi difficulties with ammunition supply. None of these options was capable of blunting the Cobra attack. The net impression is that Bradley's Cobra was overdetermined, so powerful that no combination would have enabled the Nazis to stop it.

All German accounts agree that July 27, hot and humid, offered ideal conditions for Allied aircraft. Quesada's air command flew 1,450 sorties that day. Only on the twenty-eighth, when a low pressure system took hold, did the Germans have any luck with the weather, but the sky cleared that afternoon. Allied air missions were fewer than the previous day, but not by much. During those two days the front collapsed. ULTRA revealed the

Luftwaffe's operations orders—in real time—for both fighters and bombers. Not until the night of July 27–28 did the Germans begin to concentrate on western Normandy. The average of 350 to 400 Luftwaffe sorties the first days had little impact. Within a week rates began falling as the Luftwaffe proved incapable of sustaining its effort. Meanwhile, Middleton's GIs started down the west coast, and Meindl's parachutists were directly challenged as fresh American troops began to attack *east* of the Vire.

The common themes in the recollections of *Landser* are chaos, disorganization, distress at the power of enemy artillery and air, plus wonder that the Americans had mastered the art of mobile warfare. Germans withdrawing down the west coast lost cohesion, abandoned equipment under the hammer blows of the jabos, became intermixed. Panzers that broke down or ran out of fuel were blown up, save for a few that other tanks attempted to tow. Throughout the area small parties of Germans made their way south as best they could, sometimes interspersed with advancing U.S. columns. German positions, like von Choltitz's hastily created defense line covering Coutances, might have looked strong on American situation maps but they were manned by fragments of shattered units.

The main body of the 2nd SS Panzer Division, for example, which had repulsed over a dozen attacks on the first day of Cobra, was ordered back to Coutances along the "Roman Road," as the Germans knew that north-south connection. On July 23 Colonel Christian Tychsen's 2nd SS had reported a strength of eighty-seven tanks and twenty-five assault guns, but some were with Battle Group Weidinger, on Panzer Lehr's sector; and a Panther battalion had been detached for a futile attack into the flank of the U.S. advance. Colonel Tychsen perished at the hand of an American patrol. He had lasted just two days. Shot-up vehicles lined the Roman Road, also used by Colonel Otto Baum for the retreat of his 17th SS Panzergrenadier Division. Only a fraction of the panzers reached Coutances. There they found Troy Middleton's tanks had arrived ahead of them. Instead of defending the town and screening an orderly withdrawal, the 17th SS fought desperately to slide past Coutances. The Luftwaffe contributed sixteen night raids, and even eight by daylight, but most with just a couple of planes. Subsequently the remnants of both Nazi divisions merged to form a single group under Baum with fewer than ninety armored vehicles of all sorts, including half-tracks. Even that consolidation was delayed by poor communications.

The officer soon to become chief of staff of the Seventh Army believes the strategic position had become untenable by the evening of the twenty-sixth. At Army Group B, Admiral Ruge similarly observed that "the American attack developed its fullest power" that day.[37] Paul Hausser puts the "ultimate breakthrough" on July 27.[38] This became the moment when the Germans developed the fixation that led directly to their Normandy catastrophe, the idea that an offensive launched from behind their relatively stable wing along the Vire River could reach the west coast, restore the front, and cut off the U.S. spearheads. The concept went through at least three iterations, each at a higher level of commitment. The first version, approved by Hitler at noon on July 27, was to use General Freiherr von Funck's two XLVII Panzer Corps divisions from Tessy and the town of Vire itself. The divisions, 2nd and 116th Panzer, were the same ones just regrouped below Caen, now sent to the American front. On the twenty-seventh, Field Marshal von Kluge again spent his day visiting the Caen sector, but at least he used the trip to personally coordinate the move of the panzers. The lead elements of the 2nd Panzer reached Tessy late that night. Two panzer divisions! Against Lightning Joe Collins's six and Troy Middleton's five divisions they did not count for much. General Meindl, busy managing his paratroopers' local retreats to preserve the front, had no time for this foolishness. "Tomorrow's tank attack is going to be a failure," he had told von Kluge's son, "because it is scheduled on too broad a front and because it isn't going to start until dawn. . . . Those tanks are destined to be smashed." Meindl saw clearly that against massive airpower the Wehrmacht could not fight and win the traditional way, declaring, "I can tell you already that these two divisions with their old methods won't get anywhere. It would have been far better to organize the tanks into a mobile armored defense force, instead of moving them against imaginary objectives as if this were a tactical exercise on a map!"[39]

Von Funck's panzer corps gathered as quickly as it could. Fuel shortage delayed some units. The movement orders for General Graf von Schwerin's 116th Panzer Division were not confirmed until the morning of July 28, following a phone conversation between von Kluge and OKW's

Warlimont. Most of the division delayed until late afternoon to minimize the danger of Allied air attacks—the fighter-bombers of the 9th Tactical Air Command flew 1,250 sorties that day. Losses were tolerable but the bulk of the unit arrived only the next morning, its final jump shielded by fog. Instead of leaping to attack, the 116th then needed to get its bearings. Source ULTRA warned Bradley within twenty-four hours of the concentration of a panzer corps on his sector. Meanwhile, GIs had already reached Tessy, and extended their penetration farther into the German rear. Von Lüttwitz's division, told to attack and reestablish contact with Panzer Lehr, advanced only a couple of miles. Then Panzer Lehr itself was crushed, moving the goalpost for the contemplated attack. Much as Meindl had foreseen, the new panzer corps merely shored up the German line along the east side of the American penetration. The planned offensive evaporated. On July 29 the Luftwaffe ordered—and ULTRA reported—a maximum effort to impede the American advance. GIs barely noticed. Admiral Ruge records that the Seventh Army "was apparently in a state of confusion."[40]

The withdrawal down Normandy's west coast now seemed more like a rout. Tank commander Ernst Barkmann of the 2nd SS had kept his head when the Nazis discovered GIs had beaten them to Coutances. He shot up an American column and used his damaged tank to tow other panzers that broke down or ran out of fuel. One after another Barkmann had to abandon them. He blew up his own panzer a few miles short of Avranches when its ammunition exploded after an air attack. Barkmann and the tank crews finally escaped by walking across the mud in the Gulf of Avranches at low tide.

Barkmann's nightmare was merely a microcosm of what befell many units. Lacking communication with the 2nd SS, von Choltitz had sent his chief of staff, Lieutenant Colonel von Criegern, to look for it. He discovered its remnants had merged with SS Colonel Baum's 17th SS Panzergrenadier Division. On the night of the twenty-eighth von Criegern instructed Baum to break out with the panzers and infantry troops converging down the west coast. An attack early the next morning proved a complete failure, and Baum planned a repeat effort that evening. But near Roncey in the afternoon of July 29 the retreating columns were caught in the open by the jabos. Allied air rampaged over them for half a day. In the "Roncey massacre," by some accounts, as many as 100 Nazi tanks and 250 other vehicles were destroyed. When the dust had cleared from this intense combat, American ordnance specialists went over the entire Cotentin battle area and tabulated German losses. They found 66 tanks or assault guns, 11 artillery pieces, and more than 200 vehicles destroyed. Among abandoned and captured equipment were another 56 tanks or assault guns, plus 55 other vehicles.

Colonel Baum's SS battle group, briefly encircled, found an unguarded road late in the night of the twenty-ninth and fought their way out. Baum saved his reconnaissance troops, perhaps half the *Panzergrenadiers,* and the equivalent of an artillery battalion. Portions of three infantry divisions and one of paratroops remained in the Roncey pocket, where Americans took eighty-three hundred prisoners. General von Choltitz lost touch with his entire right wing, as ULTRA reported on July 28, and two days later— again noted by Allied intelligence—the corps still had little contact with the SS panzers.

Many of the *Landser* were barefoot, with tattered uniforms, carrying only light weapons or none at all, stealing food from local farms to survive. Sergeant Helmut Günther, of the 17th SS Division's scout unit, had a typical experience. Sergeant Günther's party had to make its way cross-country furtively, repeatedly encountering Americans on the roads. By sheer coincidence they found some vehicles of their own unit on July 29. As they moved to take position, an officer who drove by called them crazy and warned that GIs already occupied the town they were headed for. Later they took over a farm, stole a pig, slaughtered and cooked it, then set a table to eat. Right then a paratrooper ran up, shouting, "The Americans are right behind me!" Günther's men gunned their car's engine just as the first Sherman tanks appeared behind them. "From then on, I could not distinguish the days," Günther recalled. "I had seen the first retreat from Moscow, which was terrible enough, but at least units were still intact. Here, we had become a cluster of individuals."[41] Such stories were legion.

Much of this the Germans only pieced together afterward. Early in August Hausser's headquarters forwarded the news: In addition to the SS troops at Roncey, four infantry divisions and battle groups of three others, plus the 5th Parachute Division, had been cut to shreds. Remnants eluded the Americans as best they could. Panzer Lehr had been clawed into pieces. Its main element had just eight tanks. German morale, needless to say, was badly shaken. Watching the disaster unfold, General Hausser ordered LXXXIV Corps east to link up with Meindl's paratroops and von Funck's panzers. Von Choltitz resisted. Hausser insisted. The latter lost his telephone connection to OB West, but von Choltitz got through, and he protested to von Kluge. The field marshal was furious. When contact with the Seventh Army was restored, Kluge countermanded Hausser, instructing him to send an officer to Choltitz to give the corps a new mission—to initiate a holding attack to cover the coastal withdrawal.

During the following days the field marshal repeatedly denounced General Hausser, in telephone conversations with Army Group B, OKW, and the Führer Headquarters, asserting that the order to escape eastward had led to the German collapse. Now von Kluge personally went to Baron von Funck's headquarters in an attempt to energize the panzer offensive. But Kluge's instructions for a holding attack did not reach Choltitz. Hausser could not get through on the phone. He finally got the message to the corps rear base, where the quartermaster went by bicycle to deliver it. General von Choltitz received this order about midnight. Given the late hour and lack of contact with his units, von Choltitz did nothing.

Next Field Marshal von Kluge woke up to the depredations of the U.S. VII Corps. At Bradley's behest Jayhawk had changed direction. Brad saw no point in directing Joe Collins's troops at the coast once Troy Middleton's divisions were advancing speedily along that same corridor. Collins now aimed south and southeast, initially to break the Sienne River line, accomplished when the town of Villedieu-les-Poêlles was taken, then toward the Sée River. Von Kluge recognized this as a bid to break out of Normandy, frantically trying to block it by assembling whatever scraps he could put his hands on. The 353rd Division reached Villedieu—only because it had followed Hausser's "mistaken" order to move eastward—and briefly blocked U.S. spearheads. Leading elements of Major General Dettling's arriving 363rd Division reached a point nearby on the morning of July 31, this time only because General von Funck used vehicles of his panzer units to carry the infantry. Source ULTRA intercepted Hausser's order assigning the division to Funck. Though it took codebreakers two days to recover the message, ULTRA reported it out just as the 363rd began to reach the front. But Dettling was unable to stop the American advance. Lightning Joe Collins himself drove along the Big Red One's route. He encountered a task force that, having passed Villedieu, was about to halt for the night. Collins quickly ordered Clarence Huebner's GIs to push on. As a result, on July 31 Jayhawk troops stood near the Sée east of Avranches. They would shortly seek a crossing.

The OKW communiqué for July 28, referring to the 2nd Panzer Division's "attack," claimed that "enemy assault groups were smashed in a counterattack." But even German propaganda acknowledged the developing disaster. The communiqué's recitation of developments noted, "In the western part of . . . Normandy the enemy's large-scale attack grew in extent. . . . The enemy, sending in fresh forces, succeeded in advancing farther southwestward after bitter fighting."[42]

The onus of defeat fell on the Seventh Army. Paul Hausser, an SS officer, was untouchable, but von Kluge fired the army chief of staff, General Max Pemsel, who had served loyally since D-Day. General von Choltitz was also relieved. Summoned to Führer Headquarters, without a doubt he was apprehensive. Von Choltitz would be amazed when Hitler, rather than cashiering him, treated the general to a forty-five-minute speech as though they were at a public meeting. Standing, Hitler spoke as if "reeling off a gramophone record" and "like a man stung by a tarantula." Later, in a British prisoner camp, Choltitz would tell fellow German senior officers that Hitler's hands seemed to "fester," and that the führer was fat and "broken-down," worn out more than wounded. "He gets drunk with his own speeches!" von Choltitz exclaimed.[43] The general had been able to get in only three comments during the entire conversation, and had had to bite hard on his own tongue to keep from retorting to some of Hitler's remarks. General von Choltitz got the acute sense that Hitler positively *hated* the German officer corps, yet the führer sent him on to Paris to organize its defense.

Von Choltitz's successor at LXXXIV Corps would be General Otto Elfeldt, an artillery specialist and staff officer, until then a division commander at the Pas de Calais. Elfeldt had a brief interview with Field

Marshal von Kluge at OB West, spent the night, and drove to the Seventh Army, which sent him on to his own command post, hidden in a woods and away from any village. Elfeldt discovered that there was no continuous front. His seven divisions were all battered, some with as few as three hundred men. The 353rd Division had eight hundred. Forty men remained to the redoubtable 6th Parachute Regiment, heavily engaged ever since D-Day. Estimates were that two-thirds of LXXXIV Corps's *Landser*— dead, wounded, or captured—never left Normandy.

General Elfeldt tried to muster troops for a defense of the Sée. "The first order I gave," he recalled, "was that all the troops south of the [river] . . . were to defend the south bank, while the troops from the east were to hang on where they were until the 116th Panzer Division arrived."[44] Elfeldt's choice of the Sée is highly significant. It meant giving up any hope of defending intermediate positions, the Sienne in particular, yielding the bocage to the Americans.

The instrument of Elfeldt's destruction would be Troy Middleton's corps. The VIII Corps had barreled down the west coast—it was Monarch GIs who repeatedly threatened German command posts and pocketed the Germans around Coutances and Roncey. Quiet, self-effacing, but supremely competent, Middleton represented George Patton's polar opposite. Perhaps for that reason the two worked well together. Like Courtney Hodges, Middleton was a "mustang," an officer promoted from the ranks, but Patton seemed to have none of the opprobrium for him that he reserved for his First Army colleague. Middleton moved his armor through the infantry for it to take the lead, as Patton preferred, and Monarch tanks beat the Germans to Coutances, then moved out smartly down Normandy's west coast.

The 4th Armored Division would come to be known as one of the best, perhaps inadvertently mirrored by its radio call sign, "Olympic." Nothing if not aggressive, its commander, Major General John S. Wood, had walked by himself into Coutances to discover the pattern of the German minefields, and had then ordered his troops in behind him, personally orchestrating the destruction of an 88mm gun that held up the tankers. Wood earned the Distinguished Service Cross for that exploit. Here was a man who, having played college football, graduated, and gone into teaching, went to West Point and did it all over again so he could play more football. Not one to wait for medals, Wood had part of his Combat Command B on the road south even before Coutances had been completely cleared of Nazis. So quick was the advance that artillery units supporting the armor had to leapfrog past each other to ensure that some guns were always available. The pace exposed artillerymen to direct combat. In fact, the 94th Armored Field Artillery Battalion at one point led the U.S. column. Some fierce firefights took place. There was also confusion among Americans highballing down the Norman roads. Once, Wood's troops came under fire from the 2nd Armored Division, a Jayhawk unit. Soon they approached the Sée River, which the German Elfeldt wanted so desperately to defend. GIs had just about battered their way out, for the Sée ran through Avranches, at Normandy's very foot. Great opportunity lay just ahead.

THE DECISION

"Monk" Dickson, Bradley's intelligence officer, had become distinctly upbeat. Only holding the Sée River line could save the Germans, but a defense by the broken units they had was distinctly dicey. Dickson's assessment read, "The destruction of LXXXIV Corps is believed at hand, and the destruction of II Parachute Corps is an immediate possibility."[45] In London, the Joint Intelligence Committee expected the collapse of German power. The Allies were at the brink of success. Both circumstance and opportunity made necessary certain command decisions that had not been anticipated or had previously been resisted. One set of choices was Montgomery's, made for his British Commonwealth forces. Their activities were important to the development of the U.S. front. Strategic options formed a second set of issues. During all the weeks of trudging through the hedgerows, no one had had to focus much on what the armies would do once they left Normandy. Overlord, along with Montgomery's ruminations, offered a concept, to be sure, but that planning had been generic. Generals gave some thought to the question, but the fighting before them naturally took precedence. The Normandy breakout, when it came, would be achieved by groups of forces in a specific configuration. A third issue lay in the timing and modalities for activating the U.S. Third Army, George S. Patton's army, and with it the ascendance of Omar Bradley to command the 12th Army Group. The prospect of two American armies would multiply U.S. possibilities.

When General Eisenhower braved the weather to go to Normandy, the SHAEF commander had been at the point of sending a dispatch to his ground forces commander, Bernard Montgomery. Ike's deputy Tedder wanted him to fire Monty, or at least put the British general on notice he stood to be dismissed if the Commonwealth forces did not get moving. More diplomatic than that, and with the British winding down Operation Goodwood, Ike's message simply reminded Montgomery of the need to press on, alluding to equally shared sacrifice. It would have been best, in Eisenhower's view, had Goodwood continued. The letter was the last of several along these lines. No doubt it stung.

General Eisenhower's frustration with Montgomery had been rising steadily. So had Prime Minister Churchill's anger at his field commander. Lord Alanbrooke had faced down one Churchill tantrum against Monty early in July with a diatribe of his own. Alanbrooke's private information was that Eisenhower had moved to the stage of denouncing Montgomery directly to Churchill. If those two ever joined forces, Monty would be done. The last straw for Churchill seemed to come when he planned a visit to the Continent at the time of Goodwood and Monty told him not to come. The prime minister, who was also minister of defense, was furious that Montgomery was denying him. Alanbrooke's purpose in risking his life to cross the channel on July 19 was the urgent mission of defusing this command crisis. His private conversations with Montgomery during that four-hour visit have gone unrecorded, but Lord Alanbrooke returned to London with a personal note from Monty to Churchill. No doubt worked out in close collaboration with Alanbrooke, the note delighted Churchill by providing a rationale for Monty's previous cancellation of his trip, and invited the prime minister to visit at any time.

The other side of the equation was the Americans, and Alanbrooke put Montgomery on notice, if any were needed, of SHAEF's dissatisfaction with his performance. Monty promised action there, too. But on July 26 Alanbrooke learned that Eisenhower and Churchill were again sharing their frustrations. He responded with diplomacy and by counterattack. The velvet glove was a dinner with Churchill and Eisenhower the next night. They sat to dinner on July 27, just as Cobra was breaking through. Alanbrooke exulted afterward. He saw the dinner as helping him get closer to Ike to facilitate "easy running between Ike and Monty." Alanbrooke recorded, "It did a lot of good. I have offered to go over with Ike if necessary to assist him in handling Monty. My God, what psychological complications war leads to!" Alanbrooke privately believed that Eisenhower knew nothing about strategy and was entirely unsuited to be supreme commander, though the British field marshal conceded that Ike "is all out" to preserve the best of relations between U.S. and British allies.[46] Yet he made no connection between that last observation and the fact that Ike had not actually made any demand that Montgomery be fired.

The situation between the Allies remained delicate. Now Alanbrooke struck with his sword. The attack came in a cable to the British staff mission in Washington, instructing Sir John Dill to tell U.S. chief of staff George Marshall that Eisenhower was guilty of blindsiding the Allies on his intentions, hinting that perhaps Ike had no plan at all. General Marshall, in turn, sent Eisenhower a dispatch on July 31 that recited the British complaints. While the text of Alanbrooke's order is not available, the timing of Marshall's message indicates it was sent *after* the dinner with Eisenhower had supposedly cleared the air. Marshall added that until he had received news from Eisenhower on the twenty-ninth, it could have been said that the U.S. High Command had been kept in ignorance also. Marshall suggested the SHAEF commander make a point of periodically informing the British. Eisenhower struggled a couple of days to craft his response. When he made it, as will be seen in the next chapter, Ike's answer would be breathtaking in scope and importance.

Meanwhile Montgomery, after further exchanges on both his private channel with Alanbrooke and his official chain of command to SHAEF, ordered a series of assaults on both sides of the Orne and promised another Goodwood-size offensive for early August. The first of these attacks would be Operation Spring, carried out below Caen by General Guy Simonds's

An aerial photo of an Orne River bridge west of Caen during a 9th Tactical Air Force strike on March 7, 1944. The width of the river and its steep, treelined banks—typical of many in Normandy—made the Orne a significant obstacle to any Allied advance.

American engineers work to restore railroad tracks onto the docks at Cherbourg, July 1944.

Infantrymen take cover in the ditch behind a hedgerow as they fire at Germans only a few yards away. During the big aerial bombardments for Operation Cobra, cover like this did not prevent GIs from suffering severe casualties due to friendly bombing.

A solution to the hedgerows was finally found with armored vehicles equipped with pitchforklike devices that could penetrate and carry away the brush. Here a Stuart tank of the 8th Infantry Division is equipped with one version of this device, thoughtfully made from steel reclaimed from the Germans' Atlantic Wall beach obstacles.

Part of Caen, north of the Orne River, which the British cleared during Operation Charnwood, seen here on July 11.

Sniper fire continued in this sector and fighting raged elsewhere in Caen as British troops attempted to clear rubble from the streets for their troops to advance, July 11. Even with bulldozers, restoring transit proved extraordinarily difficult.

Canada's 3rd Infantry Division held the important sector of Montgomery's line just above Caen, and would clear out the remainder of the city in Operation Goodwood, soon after this July 11 picture. Canadian soldiers here prepare for a sniper mission, with Lance Corporal Carmen Deshane smearing camouflage paint on the face of Corporal Allen Cameron.

Old Hickory GIs of the 30th Infantry Division fought the Panzer Lehr to a standstill on July 11 near St. Jean de Daye. This armored vehicle of the division's tank destroyer battalion had been hidden in the brush and now emerges to do battle. The Germans suffered heavy losses in their failed attack.

Taking position for Cobra, troops of Ray Barton's 4th Infantry Division move up behind Saint-Lô on July 23. These GIs are from the 3rd Battalion, 8th Infantry. They have less than twenty-four hours to reach their assigned attack sector. However, the road signs indicate they are not far from the scene of the victorious battle against Panzer Lehr two weeks earlier. This places them only a few miles from their final positions.

Saint-Lô in ruins on July 28, after American GIs had pressed beyond it to make their Cobra breakthrough.

Following the Cobra bombing American troops blitzed the Germans and quickly broke through. On the left flank of the attack front, the 30th Division advances through Hébécrevon, which had been in the bomb zone and was critical to plans for armored exploitation. Note the extensive damage and the bulldozer already clearing rubble. On July 27, the day after GIs of the 119th Infantry captured the village, soldiers of K Company, 3rd Battalion, 120th Infantry, move through.

Marigny, located about two miles below the Cobra bomb zone, became the locale for a fierce battle on July 27, as infantry of the Big Red One and tankers of the 3rd Armored Division blasted into the village. Marigny was so badly damaged that much of the armor had to bypass it. Here combat engineers blow up a wall to restore passage.

Cobra's breakout took American troops through a succession of ruined villages and towns. Here a Stuart tank and other armor passes a road control team on its way to find the Germans, July 27.

German commander von Choltitz ordered a determined defense of the important town of Coutances, but before his troops could prepare it, they were assailed by the Americans. The GIs of John S. Wood's 4th Armored Division mounted the key attacks. Here one of Wood's patrols enters Coutances. At the right the .30-cal. machine gun atop a half-track is trained on the upper floors of nearby buildings to respond to snipers.

The Luftwaffe fought to blunt the American advance with night air raids. Here photographers capture the illumination of tracers fired by flak against marauding German aircraft near Cerisy-la-Forêt on July 29.

Luftwaffe raids may not have impressed German ground troops, but they were terrifying enough to Americans that the command ordered special preparations. Here combat engineers inspect a just-completed underground bunker southwest of Marigny on July 30. Intended to protect the advanced staff of Monarch, the VIII Corps, the air-raid shelter was big enough for seventy-five people.

America's main weapon against the Luftwaffe night raids was the 90mm antiaircraft gun, the U.S. counterpart to the German 88mm. Taking his cue from the Germans, General Bradley also used the guns as antitank screens for his ground troops. In their flak role, guns posted in the Avranches-Pontaubault area inflicted heavy losses on the Luftwaffe.

Journalists posed a continuing headache for Allied commanders. One measure to keep track of them was to provide official transportation—and monitors. Robert Capa and Ernest Hemingway, representing *Life* and *Collier's* magazines, pose with their driver, Private Orin L. Tompkins (center), near Pont-Brocard on July 30.

Bradley's Americans drove full-tilt down the Cotentin, brushing aside German rear guards and pocketing some Nazi remnants. Here part of the U.S. second echelon, a mechanized column of the 6th Armored Division, drives past Coutances on July 31.

German troops tried to delay the advance by posting small bands of tanks and infantry at crossroads and in villages GIs would have to pass. Here, at Saint-Denis-le-Gast on July 31, two American tankers examine a German PzKw IV that had been knocked out by a 37mm shell.

Wrecked German half-tracks—along with a disabled Sherman tank—line the side of the road near Saint-Denis-le-Gast as GIs press their pursuit. This is equipment the Germans lost in the Roncey pocket.

Avranches on the brink: Frenchwomen and -men in Bréhal on July 31 watch the 6th Armored Division move through town on the final jump to the Normandy breakout. Also passing through were GIs of the 28th Infantry, 8th Division. These troops followed immediately behind Task Force Dager into Avranches.

A Frenchwoman celebrating the liberation of Avranches presents a bouquet of carnations to GIs as their half-track waits in the queue to pass through the town, August 3. The mademoiselle clearly considers this a formal occasion—she wears a jacket in the August summer heat of Normandy.

Germans captured in the fight for Avranches and loaded in a U.S. truck begin their journey into captivity, August 3. Note the French civilians making their way past the rubble at the side of the road.

French children lead their cows back into Avranches when it had become safe to return. Taken on August 6, this picture shows combat engineers had already put up additional bridges. Note the GI directing supply trucks onto one side of the bridge.

Vital to assisting the Normandy breakout, the French Resistance helped in all manner of ways. In Brittany especially, the Resistance had an important combat role. The Allied high command tried to strengthen French Resistance military potential by parachuting arms, supplies, and small groups of commandos. Central to this effort were the Jedburgh teams of advisers/coordinators. Here a Jedburgh team receives its final briefing in London before parachuting into France.

A Frenchman and his wife use their boat to ferry GIs of Task Force Weaver across the Mayenne River on August 6. The bridgehead the 90th Division established at Mayenne became the starting point for a deep thrust into the German rear.

A platoon of 2nd Armored Division tanks waits outside a village on August 10 for orders to resume the advance. These are the up-gunned 76mm versions of the Sherman tank, which remained in short supply in the U.S. Army.

In a Mortain suburb, Lieutenant Thomas Springfield's tank destroyer platoon took its toll on the panzers and barred their way. Much damage was inflicted by a single 57mm antitank gun and a tank destroyer. Mortain's railway station is in the distance. By August 12 the battle was essentially over. It had been nearly disastrous for the "Lost Battalion."

Old Hickory troops left Mortain and pushed into the German south flank. Here 30th Division armored elements also approach Domfront on August 16.

A GI patrol stops to look at the Cathedral of Argentan, along the edge of the battle area, as the Americans of the 2nd Battalion, 318th Infantry, 80th Infantry Division sought to close the trap on August 20.

Major Wladyslaw Klaptocz of the Polish 10th Dragoons meets with American Major Leonard C. Dull on August 20 in Chambois to plan efforts to block the German escape. Dull, from Denver, Colorado, led the 2nd Battalion, 359th Infantry of the "Tough 'Ombres."

The death of the German Seventh Army is encapsulated in this overhead shot of abandoned equipment southeast of Falaise. In this picture are a PzKw IV tank, an 88mm gun, an overturned cart, and several wrecked or deserted trucks and cars, plus one auto on the road likely still serviceable.

Another scene from the Falaise area shows the destruction even more poignantly. Dozens of wrecked or abandoned vehicles dot this landscape, showing not only how the Germans attempted to move off the roads, but also how the ground around many lost vehicles was strewn with supplies, baggage, and all manner of items left behind by the fleeing *Landser*.

General Eisenhower came to Chambois to see the destruction in the Corridor of Death for himself. He surveyed the field on September 3, almost two weeks after the fighting had ended. Wreckage and bodies still populated the battlefield. Behind Eisenhower, who is taking photos with a miniature camera, stands an abandoned German 100mm gun.

The main railroad yard at Le Mans on August 21. Formerly a logistics center for the German Seventh Army, for a time Le Mans became a forward supply head for U.S. troops. In this picture U.S. soldiers and Frenchmen unload ammunition and gasoline trained in from Cherbourg by American military railroad crews. In the intermediate distance in the yard, destruction from Allied bombing of the terminus is evident. Until that damage was repaired, the Le Mans yard could not itself function at full capacity.

II Canadian Corps. At the same time as Cobra, Simonds would try to seize Bourguébus Ridge and open the way to Falaise. With just a couple of days to get ready, and a concern to limit losses, Simonds produced a very tightly scheduled plan. In addition the Germans, always sensitive on this sector, brought back the 9th SS Panzer Division and happened to put it right on the Canadian attack front. On July 25 the Canadians fought hard and made some initial gains, but Spring foundered after just one day and fifteen hundred casualties. The second of Monty's proffered initiatives came on the right bank of the Orne—attacks south of Hill 112 on July 28, and Operation Bluecoat beginning two days later.

On the American side, it would be an understatement to say that "Georgie" Patton had champed at the bit to join the fight. Patton's letters home, to Ike and others, and various of his comments were only half joking when they expressed impatience. By his own account, this period was very unpleasant because "I was obsessed with the belief that the war would end before I got into it."[47] Patton bunked with Bradley during his first day in-country, and stayed on his best behavior, excited to take the field. On July 7 he visited Third Army headquarters, being installed in an apple orchard near Nehou, not far from Sainte-Mère-Église. Patton's advance staff, "Lucky Forward," was situated outside a château, which the new commander believed dated to Roman times. At their lunch with Monty that day, the latter tried to get Bradley to agree not to activate the Third Army until the Americans reached Avranches, something calculated to extend the British general's tenure as field commander. Patton, anxious to get in the saddle, was pleased that Bradley made no commitment. But Monty sent out an order on July 13 ordaining that very thing. Patton kept his counsel, using the day to visit the Roman château.

It was Omar Bradley, not Montgomery, who became the real obstacle to activating Patton. One worry concerned the Fortitude deception. The staff that would serve Bradley's army group were the same people pretending to plan another invasion in Operation Fortitude. Some feared moving the headquarters to France might expose the deception. By July there was not much life left in Fortitude, and this amounted to a minor objection.

More significant in Bradley's view was that leading a major offensive like Cobra was much simpler with a single army rather than three entities—two army commands plus an army group. And, of course, Bradley was comfortable with his First Army staff. Inevitable problems would occur in introducing a new command net, especially amid a major battle. And as the Cobra forces converged on Avranches there would be even more massive headaches. This would be easier to handle with a single army. On the other hand, the First Army's control over so many forces—including divisions and support units intended for the Third—challenged its ability to coordinate them. And there was the question of the prerogatives of the designated commander. For example, Bradley asked Patton whether it would be okay to commit the 4th Armored, a Third Army unit, early. Patton, anxious to make veterans of green GIs, happily agreed.

Eisenhower worried about the coordination problem but also saw the change as helping him deal with Monty. He pressed Bradley to complete the changeover. Conferring with Bradley on July 20, Eisenhower asked about preparations for activating the Third Army and 12th Army Group. Bradley laid out his arguments. Ike asked him to set a date anyway. Brad chose August 1. "That would give me at least a week of fingertip control immediately after the breakout," Bradley notes.[48] Satisfied for the moment, on July 25 Eisenhower issued a SHAEF directive authorizing the switchover. Remarkably, the battle moved to Avranches just as Brad's date came up. Montgomery could not complain, either.

In the interim George Patton fumed. It is recorded in a couple of places that before Bradley conceived Cobra, Patton came up with a similar concept, but with armored troops in the lead rather than infantry, though the evidence is not clear on whether he ever presented the idea to his superiors. "Please don't worry, George," Bradley told Patton on July 13, "I will get the Third Army in as soon as I can."[49] Commenting in his diary the next day, Patton wrote, "He could do it now with much benefit to himself, if he had any backbone."[50] Thereafter he supplied Bradley with a stream of suggestions for improving Cobra, while privately recording his opinion that Bradley and Hodges were "nothings."[51] On the seventeenth General Patton briefed his senior staff on the actual Cobra plan. But the briefing triggered another gaffe when his public relations officer went on to tell reporters of the impending operation. When war correspondents attached to the as-yet-dormant Third Army bragged to journalists with the First, who knew nothing, Bradley was furious and Patton had to make amends anew. Once Cobra finally began, it became clear at First Army that its command span really was inadequate. On the afternoon of July 27 Bradley asked Patton's chief of staff if his boss would be willing to "super vise" Middleton's VIII Corps, Monarch, as a "deputy group commander." Delighted, Patton swung into action the next morning. George Patton's nudging played a role in Middleton's armor arriving near Avranches as soon as it did. Monarch had two armored divisions, the 4th and the 6th, with the latter given the primary objective of capturing Avranches, the gateway to the French interior. The 4th Armored was supposed to guard the flank. But visiting the front on July 29, General Patton decided the 6th Armored Division was not being aggressive enough and had Middleton give the main mission to his other unit. Patton was in the saddle. Everything hinged on what happened at Avranches.

WHAT HAPPENED AT AVRANCHES

Brigadier General Holmes E. Dager, leading Combat Command B of the 4th Armored Division, became known for "crash-drives," of which Avranches would be the first (Dager later conducted a similar drive that put Patton's army on the bank of the Rhine). Dager was a natural competitor, from Asbury Park, New Jersey, who grew up boxing, swimming, hunting, and bicycle racing. He'd wanted to be a surgeon, had gone into the National Guard to serve in World War I, and won the Silver Star. Then he turned pro. Normandy was his first campaign in this war, but no one who saw him cut through Coutances would have thought that. General Wood had complete confidence in Dager. The Avranches dash began with a terse order from the division commander: "PRESENT MISSION CANCELLED— USING ANY ROADS . . . MOVE ON AVRANCHES . TO CAPTURE IT AND USE CROSSINGS EAST THEREOF."[52]

General Dager divided his troops into two columns. The right wing of Combat Command B had a preponderance of mechanized riflemen, most importantly Lieutenant Colonel Alfred Maybach's 51st Armored Infantry

Battalion. Dager went with the column that took the coast road behind the "Rolling Eight Balls"—Lieutenant Colonel Thomas Conley's 8th Tank Battalion. Troy Middleton backed the maneuver by lending trucks to the 8th Infantry Division, motorizing one of its regiments to catch up with Wood's 4th Armored and stiffen the tankers. Dager encountered a blown bridge below Coutances and could not restore it until German mines were cleared. Captain William F. Pieri took on the mines until one blew him up. Combat Command B got back on the road—or, better, roads—because the routes of Dager's columns diverged. Traffic slowed one of them—its route crossed into the sector of Joe Collins's VII Corps. The other column, spearheaded by Lieutenant Colonel Alexander Graham's 94th Armored Field Artillery Battalion, was harassed by German barrages and occasional parties of infantry. Corporal Albert O. Maranda of the 94th recalled that he survived on K rations and five hours' sleep and had not been able to shave in three days. Dager's columns made ten miles that first day, came up on the Sienne River, and sought places to cross it. They were within twenty miles of Avranches, hindered only by blown bridges. Dager bounded over the Sienne on July 30 on a new bridge erected by his engineers.

The Germans' only direct defense was a single company of the 341st Assault Gun Battalion, which had come up from Rennes to join Elfeldt's corps. Together with a few infantry remnants this company defended the road used by Dager's mechanized infantry. The Germans ambushed Dager's eastern column, destroying half a dozen of the 51st Battalion's half-tracks. Colonel Maybach unlimbered his towed antitank guns to neutralize the enemy. The Germans retreated but took position on a rise, which Maybach attacked with riflemen backed by fighter-bombers. The Germans pulled out toward dark and his GIs bedded down for the night.

Meanwhile, there were no obstacles confronting General Dager's own tank column. His element of Combat Command B advanced as if on motor tour. Avranches loomed.

Field Marshal von Kluge watched with horror. He arrived at the Seventh Army main headquarters at Le Mans in the evening of July 30. There were no ranking officers present. Paul Hausser was actually trapped behind American lines. Von Kluge had ordered the army's forward command post not to move without his personal approval. As a result Hausser stayed put even as General Dager's Americans passed by. Hausser even came under fire at one point. He and his staff, including newly minted chief of staff Colonel Rudolph-Christophe Freiherr von Gersdorff, who had replaced General Pemsel, finally escaped after midnight through a gap between U.S. road convoys. They were completely out of touch for six critical hours. Hausser set up a new command post at Mortain on the morning of July 31. Also out of play was General Elfeldt of LXXXIV Corps. His command post, too, was passed by the 4th Armored just as Hausser reached Mortain. Elfeldt's staff fought in the front line all day and slipped away after dark. Generals Hausser and Elfeldt were no doubt as concerned as von Kluge to find someone, anyone, to defend the Sée, but they were in no position to do so. The net result: On the crucial day of July 31 Field Marshal von Kluge had an unusual personal role in the German defense of the gateway town. On the eve of this crucial event, Colonel von Gersdorff notes, "the situation at Avranches remained obscure."[53]

Behind the gateway lay one last obstacle, the Sélune River, its most direct crossing at the town of Pontaubault. The question was whether von Kluge could rustle up troops to block the Americans here, for beyond Avranches and Pontaubault lay all of France. Staff officers at OKW spoke of the "Avranches defile" as if it were an opening in some mountain fastness. French citizens would have been puzzled to hear it—the town's highest point towered at most only a couple of hundred feet above the surrounding countryside. There were reports that Americans were already in Avranches, but others that German columns were moving east and southeast through the town or even bypassing it. A German engineer officer had been stationed there to coordinate activity in Avranches, but he could not be found.

General Dager's column of Combat Command B—the one that threatened Hausser's headquarters—used unobstructed roads and arrived at the Sée in the late afternoon, A Company of the 8th Tank Battalion leading. There was a brief shoot-out with some German armor. Dager found the bridges intact and sent troops across early in the evening. A scout detachment of a dozen armored cars, an antitank battery, and some jeep-borne

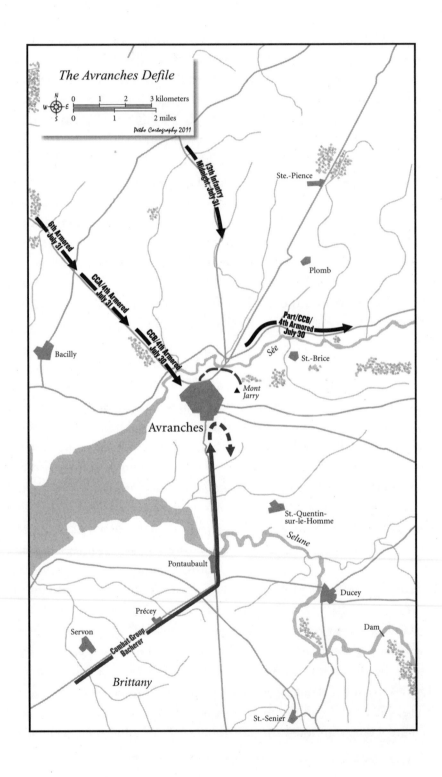

The Avranches Defile

0 — 1 — 2 — 3 kilometers
0 — 1 — 2 miles

Petho Cartography 2011

13th Infantry
Midnight, July 31

Ste.-Pience

6th Armored
July 31

CCA/4th Armored
July 31

CCB 4th Armored
July 30

Plomb

Part/CCB/
4th Armored
July 30

Sée

St.-Brice

Bacilly

Mont
Jarry

Avranches

St.-Quentin-
sur-le-Homme

Selune

Pontaubault

Ducey

Précey

Dam

Servon

Combat Group
Bacherer

Brittany

St.-Senier

infantry of the 25th Cavalry Reconnaissance Squadron were first over the Sée. French citizens cheered as the GIs passed them. Dager set up outposts in Avranches. At division headquarters, General Wood gave Dager command of all U.S. troops in the vicinity, and put Olympic's second echelon, Colonel Bruce C. Clarke's Combat Command A, under Dager's temporary control.

General Troy Middleton at VIII Corps knew from prisoners that the German units in this sector were completely out of touch with each other. Monarch was not certain of Olympic's location but learned of Wood's advance late in the evening. General Middleton promptly ordered him to push past Avranches to the Sélune at Pontaubault, and the 13th Infantry, the unit he had sent to reinforce Olympic, to hurry up. Though the infantry had not arrived by morning, the fat was in the fire.

The first Germans to reach Avranches were survivors of the Cotentin battles in a truck convoy down the coast road, directly into General Dager's command post area. Thinking this an ambulance unit because the lead vehicles were painted with red crosses, Colonel Conley's tankers let the first few across the Sée bridge, only to have German soldiers open fire. When U.S. tanks responded, several hundred *Landser* surrendered. Prisoners told the GIs that another, larger group was behind them. The second convoy arrived around midnight and its troops formed up for battle, whereupon a jittery American officer abandoned the bridge and his prisoners and retreated along the north bank. More Nazis appeared before dawn. While some German columns made off toward Mortain, other troops deployed in the town. Meanwhile, Dager had sent two companies of Conley's tanks to look for a rumored Sée crossing a few miles to the east. They ran into another German convoy, which they shot up, but had to assume defensive positions. By morning the situation inside Avranches remained unclear. Though some American infantry were posted there, the bridge remained under German fire; Dager's GIs had secured the north bank of the Sée and Colonel Clarke's combat command was coming up for an assault into the town.

Dominated by Mont Jarry, a hilltop that overlooked the Sée, Avranches had probably had its moment in the sun during the seventeenth century, when peasants revolted against a newly imposed salt tax. It was a sleepy coast town at the outlet of the river, best known as a gateway to the abbey of Mont Saint-Michel, prominently visible beyond an expanse that alternated as bay or mudflat. A town of about eight thousand in normal times, Avranches was swollen with several thousand more Frenchmen, refugees of the fighting in the Cotentin.

A pause at Avranches is worthwhile because the singular focus on the military campaign neglects the very real fears of civilians trapped by war. George Patton once said that Saint-Lô was the worst-destroyed place he'd ever seen until he became better educated. You can be sure that Caen, above all, stood in ruins. Yet at Avranches, where the war had just arrived, where there was no preliminary bombardment and no generated battle, fifteen hundred structures had already been shattered. No doubt this was a consequence of U.S. efforts to interdict the passage of German troops into Normandy. Though toppling houses and buildings, bombers left the town's castle intact. The square was just piled rubble. The day the Americans approached Avranches, one of its churches collapsed during services due to structural damage inflicted by the bombs—fortunately the faithful who had turned up for mass numbered only ten. At Val Saint Petré church, Père Duguépeyroux had the bell rung that Sunday. But the père had promised a First Communion ceremony, one the war had delayed for six weeks. Children who were refugees from Cherbourg sang for the choir, their parents considering the bell's toll an act of madness, attracting unwanted attention. Frightened townspeople crouched in the remains of their homes. The war could be heard already, though not yet seen. No one knew what might happen. Avranches was already a place of misery wrought by war.

Indeed, planes struck nearby during the Communion, and the first artillery shells began to pitch around the town. At the moment of the elevation of the Eucharist came a deep rumble. Instead of a procession from outside the church, twenty frightened children were hurriedly rushed up the aisle and given their Hosts. Then Père Duguépeyroux told everyone to go home. The fleeing parishioners encountered a tank on the road. After that, four more. They were American.

On July 31, 1944, Mont Jarry, at a height of about two hundred feet, offered a perfect position from which to dominate the Sée bridges. The arriving Germans set up several artillery guns there. There were short, sharp scraps in the town. *Landser* who moved through Avranches collided with GIs guarding the far side of it. An American private, William H. Whitson, won a posthumous Distinguished Service Cross, having used his .30-caliber machine gun to decimate a German infantry platoon, destroying a number of vehicles. At the Carmelite convent, a German squad with a machine gun occupied the refectory while Americans shot at the road from downstairs. The mother superior begged the Germans not to start a firefight. Not so lucky was the church Notre Dame des Champs, where Germans used the steeple for an observation post. It was destroyed. The contractor François Brière and several friends broke into the town hall and hung French, American, British, and Belgian flags. Only when they finished did they notice a panzer outside, aiming at them. They fled. The Germans did not pursue; they had more important things to do. General Dager learned of the fighting. Colonel Bruce Clarke's troops were arriving, engaged by the German guns as they appeared in the distance. Clarke's tanks took the hill under fire while GIs sprinted across the bridge and assaulted Mont Jarry. The battle raged for two hours until the surviving Germans fled. Five Luftwaffe fighters intervened but accomplished little. Counterattacks by scratch German units were beaten off.

But a different Nazi threat loomed. At one a.m. on July 31, Field Marshal von Kluge telephoned Hans Speidel at Army Group B and approved a new defense line from Villedieu to Avranches.[54] Forty-five minutes later he telephoned the commander in Brittany to demand whatever could be gotten from that quarter. That officer, General Wilhelm Fahrmacher, had only two companies of the 266th Infantry Division, plus a weak battalion cobbled together from the Parachute Infantry Training Regiment. They would have to march from Saint-Malo, about thirty-five miles away. Fahrmacher pointed out that there were many Luftwaffe and German navy personnel in the area over whom he had no authority.[55] Meanwhile, von Gersdorff was able to locate staffs of the 5th Parachute and 275th Infantry Divisions, which had retreated nearby. He set them to defend the river with stragglers plus any stray units they could scrape up.

One more formation could be called upon and was. The 77th Infantry Division had been pulled out of the line to lick its wounds from the bocage. It had camped west of Pontaubault. Since late June an experienced colonel named Rudolf Bacherer led the 77th. On the critical night of the thirtieth, OB West signaled the division headquarters, "Avranches is to be taken and held at all costs. It is the keystone of our defense. On it hinges the decision in the West."[56]

Colonel Bacherer called his men to arms and set out, at first to Pontaubault, then against Avranches from the south. Along the way he picked up a detachment of fourteen assault guns and some squads of the 5th Parachute Division. Battle Group Bacherer secured Pontaubault and disposed his *Landser* for combat. At first Bacherer made good progress. After dawn he mounted an attack that got into the town. But the battle group was engaged by "Hellcat" vehicles of Lieutenant Colonel Delk Oden's 704th Tank Destroyer Battalion in their first action of the campaign. Then low cloud and drizzle suddenly cleared and—in the words of the U.S. official history—the "providential appearance" of a flight of P-47 fighter-bombers made all the difference.[57] The Americans laid smoke to disguise their positions from the German armor. The warplanes set upon the enemy. Within an hour all Bacherer's assault guns were smashed. GIs ejected the grenadiers from the houses they had occupied. Hundreds of Germans surrendered; the rest retreated south and west.

Colonel Bacherer sent a demolition squad to blow up the Sélune bridge at Pontaubault. It was wiped out. He dispatched a second team—it succumbed to ambush. Meanwhile, General George Patton visited Monarch headquarters. Troy Middleton told Patton he had reached his objective, Avranches, and had no orders beyond that. His troops were at the Sélune but had not crossed. Middleton, who would come under Patton's command once the Third Army became operational, seemed to be looking for guidance. Patton—still eighteen hours away from having the authority—seized the moment. Wars had been lost throughout history, Patton told Middleton, by generals who failed to cross rivers when they had the chance to do it unopposed. Middleton took the hint and ordered an advance into Pontaubault. Patton felt he earned his pay that day. General Wood got his U.S. 4th Armored Division back in gear. They found the Pontaubault bridge undefended. Bruce Clarke's troops captured it. The

German corps in Brittany reported (falsely) that Pontaubault bridge had been destroyed. By nightfall GIs were outside Bacherer's command post. He and his men slunk away down a sunken path. The road into the French interior stood open.

Field Marshal von Kluge's frantic desperation is apparent from his telephone conversations. At nine twenty a.m., General Speidel told von Kluge that Americans were in Avranches; the blockade by assault guns north of it had obviously failed, and nothing was known of Battle Group Bacherer's intervention. American aircraft (Elwood Quesada's fighter-bombers flew more than a thousand sorties that day) were making movement almost impossible. Von Kluge demanded efforts to recapture Villedieu and block the roads leading out of Avranches and Villedieu. When he asked what reinforcements could be thrown in immediately, the field marshal was told an infantry division would arrive in about eight days. Von Kluge then telephoned Colonel von Gersdorff at Seventh Army. Aside from desultory talk of halting the Americans at Villedieu, where Lightning Joe Collins's men held the town but von Kluge professed its status unknown, the field marshal believed the Americans had only a spearhead at Avranches. At ten a.m. von Kluge spoke again to General Fahrmacher in Brittany, demanding the troops from Saint-Malo be sent immediately. That he had not ordered this in talking to Fahrmacher nine hours earlier suggests the field marshal's grasp of the situation remained shaky at best.

Von Kluge's exchange with Warlimont at OKW, which took place at ten forty-five, also attests to this ignorance. The two had known each other since before the war, and von Kluge customarily phoned Warlimont each morning to update OKW. Now the field marshal alluded to the "Miracle of the Marne" in 1914, when the French general Gallieni had mobilized Paris taxis to rush reinforcements to the front, stymieing a German offensive in an earlier war. Von Kluge wanted to use all possible means to get men into the battle. It was only now that he asked Hitler's approval for the use of navy and Luftwaffe ground personnel. Kluge knew as well as any senior German general that the führer's habit was to stay up late, then sleep late. He might have gotten a decision from OKW had he broached this issue when Fahrmacher raised it the previous night. All that Warlimont could do now was promise to ask once Hitler held his noontime staff conference. This was D-Day all over again.

But the most poignant exchange, one for which we have direct quotes, took place between Field Marshal von Kluge and his own chief of staff at OB West, Blumentritt, about twenty minutes before he spoke to Warlimont. "It's a madhouse here," the field marshal told Blumentritt. "You can't imagine what it's like. Commanders are completely out of contact with their troops."

Blumentritt was sympathetic. Kluge went on, "Jodl and Warlimont ought to come down and see what is going on."

Von Kluge repeated his denunciation of General Hausser and his belief that only an American advance guard so far held Avranches. "Unless I can get infantry and antitank weapons there," he continued, "the left wing cannot hold."

The OB West chief of staff now mentioned that OKW had asked for information on possible defense lines in France behind Normandy. What? "All you can do is laugh out loud," Field Marshal von Kluge retorted. "Don't they read our dispatches? Haven't they been oriented? Are they living on the moon?"

Field Marshal von Kluge ended on a despondent note. "Someone has to tell the führer that if the Americans get through at Avranches they will be out of the woods."[58]

For the next week the Luftwaffe would attack the Avranches and Pontaubault bridges every night, and even some days, with little success. Down to fewer than 300 flights a day for all of Normandy, the Germans put maximum effort into the breakout zone, with 291 sorties over Avranches during the first two days. The Luftwaffe typically sent an aircraft over at altitude to distract the American gunners while the real strike came in at low level, or they would have one plane fly past on a given heading as the rest attacked from another point of the compass. Attacks were recorded against Patton's headquarters—the Third Army went active twenty-four hours after the fight for Avranches—every day for a week. One fierce assault on the bridges and nearby dams went in with fifteen fighter-bombers loaded with rockets. A strike on the Sélune bridge at Pontaubault used radio-controlled bombs—early smart bombs—which the Germans had designed to attack ships. A few bombs damaged one bridge. American engineers built another just to be sure—and to speed the crossing of the troops.

Antiaircraft units packed into the area, including 90mm guns borrowed from the First Army. The 777th Antiaircraft Artillery Battalion, newly reassigned to Patton's army, defended the bridges and claimed the destruction of eighteen German aircraft over a forty-hour period, out of thirty-three shoot-downs through the battle. The 115th Battalion, reinforced by a battery of the 411th, brought down thirty-five more. The battalion fired more than four thousand rounds, enough to ensure chronic shortages. At one point a black quartermaster crew was just arriving with ammunition when the Germans struck, and the shells had to be rushed to the guns. The truckers cheered when several of the Luftwaffe planes were blown out of the sky. One of the battalion's guns got so hot its barrel had to be cooled for a time by pouring a jug of French hard cider over it. By August 5 the Luftwaffe was instructing aircraft to *avoid* the bridges. Avranches was just too heavily defended.

Two major roads from the north and one from the east converge on the Sée above Avranches, but only one crosses the Sélune, headed south at Pontaubault. That four-mile interval suddenly threatened to become a bottleneck. The Germans might still cork it if they could stop the "small spearheads" of GIs. George Patton and his corps and division commanders made sure that could not happen. Patton personally spent much of one day directing vehicles crossing the bridges. With generals and senior staff officers playing traffic cop among bumper-to-bumper troop convoys, the Americans squeezed four divisions through Avranches inside of twenty-four hours. Suddenly the Sée-Sélune bridgehead contained the 4th and 6th Armored Divisions and the 8th and 79th Infantry Divisions. These were not isolated vanguards. Von Kluge had no possibility of corking the bottle. The OKW communiqué for that day said nothing at all about Avranches.

War correspondents who for weeks had been as frustrated as the troops joined in the heady feeling of breaking out. Radio listeners heard Columbia Broadcasting System reporter Allen Jackson proclaim, at six a.m. on July 31, "In Normandy this morning, American troops have entered Avranches, one of the main objectives in their drive down the Cotentin peninsula." A little after nine that night Charles Collingwood broadcast from London:

An American tank column has lunged forward all the way to Avranches, the French town which lies at the hinge. . . . This means that any German line to keep us bottled up on the Cherbourg peninsula has already been turned. Ahead of us now lies the whole of France, spreading out in any direction General Montgomery decides to advance.[59]

The headline in the next day's *New York Times* read: "AMERICANS ROUT GERMANS IN WEST NORMANDY, SMASH PATH INTO BRITTANY."[60] France beckoned.

CHAPTER 5

ALL THE FÜHRER'S HORSES

General George Patton's Third Army rushed into the Avranches breach. His strenuous efforts to speed troops across the bridges made the breach unassailable. Thus began what Patton staffer Robert S. Allen recalls as a "wild and tumultuous" phase. On the very first day General John S. Wood's 4th Armored Division, busting out of Normandy, thrust into the adjacent Breton peninsula. Wood's spearheads reached to within ten miles of Rennes, an important security and communications center at the base of the peninsula. Major General Robert W. Grow's 6th Armored Division followed, driving into the center of Brittany and east for the port of Brest at the far tip. A scratch task force of Monarch troops headed toward Saint-Malo on Brittany's northern coast. Troy Middleton commanded all Breton operations. Middleton annoyed Patton by not immediately sending infantry to back up his armor, but soon enough Monarch made that right. The advance proceeded rapidly.

Working with his advance headquarters, Lucky Forward, George Patton put into practice the precepts of mobile warfare that had made him such a fearsome adversary in North Africa and Sicily. On August 1, for the first time, Omar Bradley met with Patton as his official superior, chief of the 12th Army Group, under which Patton led the Third Army. General Bradley showed maps that delineated boundaries between the Third Army and the First, now coming under Courtney Hodges. General Patton did not like the narrow section of Normandy given him for his egress but his mission, after all, lay in Brittany.

Under the Overlord plan it had always been the primary goal of the Third Army to capture Brittany. George Patton had thought about that. Since those days, the code name Chastity had referred to the capture of most Breton ports, and Swordhilt to a specific attack on Brest. Patton had been in Normandy since July 6, and it was he who was supposed to capture Brittany. While Bradley's GIs were still blocked in Normandy, Patton had dreamed up the idea of a *real* second invasion, a small one that might put a single army corps ashore on the north coast of Brittany, but that concept never left the sketch pad. On the day Cobra began, Patton was considering the objectives for his army once activated. It is clear from his diary and other source material that three-quarters of the Third Army would aim at Brittany, with a single corps sent into the French interior to guard the Allied right flank.

But as the moment of truth neared the urgency of the mission seemed to recede. What was the Third Army to do if not attack Brittany? General Bradley would make the decision. Yet Brad appeared reluctant to change the long-standing Overlord scheme. General Eisenhower seemed no more inclined to dictate orders to Bradley than to Montgomery, especially at this moment of intense fighting. When and how Brad changed his orders determined the campaign's outcome. Brittany became the anvil on which the role of Patton's Third Army was hammered out.

The Overlord strategy had been that Patton would guard the flank facing the French interior but use the bulk of his strength to seize Brittany. Demands for opening ports to Allied shipping were legion. Yet the Mulberry had been performing better than expected, and at the moment of the breakout Cherbourg was finally reaching full capacity, with an active rail line to forward depots. Though another Channel storm was shortly to crimp over-the-beach deliveries for a few days, the supply flow at the beginning of August looked better, making Breton ports less desirable and those across the Seine, with their greater capacities, more enticing.

German dispositions were another factor. The long hedgerow battle had progressively sucked Nazi troops into Normandy. Brittany had been a ready source of reinforcements and German strength there diminished commensurately. On D-Day there were eight German divisions in the peninsula, plus assorted smaller formations and detachments that were the equivalent of about two more, as well as security troops worth about another division, over 100,000 men without counting the Kriegsmarine or Luftwaffe. By the time of the breakout only two of those divisions and parts of two others remained. They had been augmented by the newly forming 2nd Parachute Division, but in all mustered only about 26,000 *Landser*. The strong Kriegsmarine presence remained, particularly at Brest, Saint-Nazaire, and Lorient, to support the U-boat campaign. But even with security troops, Luftwaffe ground crews, and ad hoc naval infantry, there were fewer than half the defenders the Nazis had had on June 6. Overlord plans, based on pre–D-Day expectations of the defenses, were obsolete.

In addition, the Allies had greater capabilities in Brittany than Overlord planners had anticipated. The French Resistance had been resilient and a strong contributor to intelligence and sabotage efforts. Formally known as the French Forces of the Interior (FFI), the Resistance permeated the countryside. The French provisional government had established a general staff in London to oversee the FFI. At Third Army, General Patton had a special group of Office of Strategic Services personnel headed by Lieutenant Colonel Robert I. Powell specifically to mesh Resistance activities with those of the U.S. Army.

Beginning with D-Day the SHAEF Special Forces Headquarters (SFHQ) initiated several programs to stiffen the Resistance. One was Jedburgh, under which small (three-man) teams of American, British, and French operatives parachuted into France to serve as advisers, supply coordinators, and sometimes leaders of Resistance groups. A dozen Jedburgh teams were active in Brittany at the moment of the breakout, and more were sent now. In addition, there was a similar but separate operation utilizing small contingents of the British Special Air Service or French paratroopers, performing the same functions but also furnishing the Resistance with a core of tough commandos. Bountiful shipments of Allied equipment even endowed the Resistance with armed jeeps for a miniature mechanized column. Resistance *maquisards* fought a pitched battle with German troops in Brittany as early as June 18. At the beginning of July SHAEF adopted—and SFHQ implemented—an initiative to mobilize as

many as thirty thousand armed fighters in the peninsula by August 5—
which happened to be exactly the moment they were needed.

The SFHQ did not quite attain its goal. By August there were somewhat fewer than twenty thousand armed Breton *maquisards*, and their
effectiveness was reduced by bickering among communist and conserva-
tive partisan groups. But the Resistance proved a force to be reckoned
with, and simplified Allied problems. Combined with weakened German
garrisons and Hitler's usual order to defend every inch of territory, which
made it impossible for Nazi commanders to create a defense line across
the peninsula, liberation could be accomplished by smaller forces than
Overlord had envisioned.

In their dispatches Eisenhower and Montgomery had both mentioned
the ports of Brittany as a key Allied objective. Monty had reiterated this in
directives to Allied ground forces on July 10 and 21, and Ike did so as well in
correspondence with American subordinates. But now the French Channel ports beckoned Ike and Monty. At the same time, the planned invasion of southern France to take place in mid-August—disputed between
SHAEF and Alanbrooke, and at an even higher level between the United
States and Britain, but now definitely on—promised access to the major
port of Marseilles. And the Allies knew from ULTRA that the Wehrmacht
had already sent most of its good troops from Brittany to Normandy. The
Breton peninsula suddenly seemed like small potatoes. There had been a
staff study at SHAEF called "Lucky Strike" that started with the assump-
tion that the Nazis had stripped most of their forces out of Brittany, and
the shape it took very much resembled what Allied armies actually did.

The progress of operations in Brittany lent weight to the Allies' incli-
nation to avoid a large force commitment there. Rennes fell on August 4,
but could have fallen sooner. The delay occurred because General Wood
halted his division's advance on the city in favor of circling around to attack
Rennes from the opposite side, while the arriving 8th Infantry Division
made a direct approach. At Bletchley Park codebreakers who had focused
so hard on Norman town names for their ULTRA reporting were mysti-
fied when Rennes turned up in the traffic. They had to look the place up
in an atlas. That became the moment when the codebreakers knew for
sure that the Allies had broken out of Normandy.

Resistance forces liberated a number of Breton towns, furnished guides to American columns and flank protection for their advance, and fought some stand-up combat actions, including against the German 2nd Parachute Division. *Maquisards* were key to the early capture of Rennes. At one point the FFI leader at Brest even hoped to take that city from the inside. Gathering German forces rendered that a futile hope—and also canceled the possibility that rapidly driving U.S. armor might take the city on the fly. Nevertheless, Grow's 6th Armored stood near Brest by August 7. In seven days, Third Army staff noted with approval, Middleton's corps cleared the enemy from an area of ten thousand square miles.

A week after that, when a 4th Armored Division combat command seized the city of Nantes, the German presence in Brittany had been reduced to perimeters around a handful of ports—Saint-Malo, Lorient, Saint-Nazaire, and Brest. The German colonel Bacherer, who had tried to stop the American advance through Avranches, made his last stand outside Saint-Malo. Germans there resisted fiercely, but succumbed in late August. Fighting for the fortresses became the new order of the day. That was infantry work, and Troy Middleton eventually exchanged most of his armor for rifle units. An extended siege of Brest followed, and it fell only in late September. But Brittany had become a sideshow.

Thus, by August the use of most of Patton's army in Brittany seemed a waste of resources. In one of their early conversations Bradley had told Patton—one indication of his looking ahead—that the Third Army might use one corps to seize the peninsula while the rest guarded the Allied flank in the advance toward Germany. With the immediate success of the advance into Brittany, this suddenly became practical. The changed strategy can be timed with precision because Omar Bradley, once he assumed command of the 12th Army Group, issued directives that defined the Third Army's role. Bradley's initial 12th Army Group order, drafted on July 29, in fact provided that the Third Army should flood into Brittany as planned. General Bradley repeated the Overlord formula when speaking to Patton on August 1. But two days later Bradley reversed Patton's priorities. The assault force would be cut back to a single corps, Middleton's VIII. The decision was cast in stone. Those seventy-two hours revolutionized the campaign.

THE TURNING

For all the months of careful Overlord planning, it is remarkable that once the dam broke and U.S. armies began to surge from the lodgment, the long-nurtured strategy would be tossed overboard. With astonishing rapidity the preinvasion strategy morphed; the new approach combined elements of the old plan with a sweep across France—and a chance to bag the German armies into the bargain. Transformation began with the generals but quickly involved everyone down to the lowliest rifleman. This became the decisive phase.

These calculations are worth exploring. Omar Bradley recounts that he made the decision to cut back the forces allotted to Brittany in consultation with Eisenhower, Patton, and Montgomery. In Bradley's first memoir he gives Eisenhower credit for realizing that an encirclement of the Germans in Normandy might be possible. Ike himself spares few words for this important design, simply writing, "With a clean and decisive breakout achieved, Bradley's immediate problem became that of inflicting on the enemy the greatest possible destruction. All else could wait upon his exploitation of this golden opportunity."[1] He effectively awards the credit to Bradley. The latter is more forthright in the memoir he published in 1983, reflecting that the German failure to "withdraw in textbook fashion began to suggest to us a fabulous opportunity," one never anticipated in the Overlord plan.[2] Over the next few days Bradley refined this concept, giving Patton the main role in an armor-led advance, with a supply buildup, an airborne landing to set a deep trap for any Germans fleeing through the Seine-Loire land bridge, and a swing around Paris and north to Dieppe. Bradley envisioned a grand strategic turning movement to isolate Paris, promising to eliminate the vast bulk of the German army in the West.

When Brad first unveiled this scheme before his operations and intelligence chiefs, he declared, "Let's talk big turkey. I'm ready to eat meat all the way."[3]

As with many grand concepts, Bradley's seems elegant but impractical. A halt to build up supplies along the Caen–Le Mans line would have given the Germans a chance to react after all. The Channel storm at the beginning of August retarded the supply accumulation. The gasoline and other supplies for such a vast maneuver would strain an Allied logistics effort already laboring at the edge of its envelope. The airborne force, recently reconstituted as the First Allied Airborne Army, was operationally assigned to Montgomery. Most problematical, the idea of a turning movement beyond Paris presumed that the German Fifteenth Army in the Pas de Calais stayed put and did not redeploy to defend the Seine or block the U.S. pincer. Even after recent reductions to reinforce the embattled Nazi armies, that force embodied almost a dozen divisions. The German army in the field also had to be weighed on the scales. Simpler to execute, a Normandy encirclement would be immediate and could be decisive. According to Bradley he presented the idea to Eisenhower, who in turn took it up with U.S. Army chief of staff General George Marshall.

Omar Bradley's intuition became the heart of Dwight Eisenhower's plan. At the end of July Marshall, prodded by the British at Lord Alanbrooke's behest, had asked Ike about his intentions. The SHAEF supremo immediately realized the potential inherent in Bradley's concept and made it the centerpiece of his answer to Marshall. This response to Marshall's query—triggered by Alanbrooke's machinations—would define Allied strategy for the last phase in Normandy. Harry Butcher saw Ike laboring on his dispatch late into the night, until breakfast, then through the morning of August 2. Eisenhower took direct aim at the Germans. He wrote that he expected that in a few days Bradley would "so manhandle the western flank of the enemy's forces;" their line would be left hanging. Bradley would then "devote the greater bulk of the forces to completing the destruction of the German Army . . . and exploiting beyond that."[4]

Eisenhower also apologized for not having kept Marshall—and the British, as they had complained—as well informed as he used to do in 1943, during the North African campaign. But that became a minor aspect in light of Eisenhower's ambitious strategic scheme. In any case, the British accusation was at some level bogus. After all, SHAEF headquarters and the British command staff were both located in London and talking to each other every day. The debate over the invasion of southern France had certainly involved SHAEF and the British directly and constantly. The Cobra offensive, Patton's unleashing, offers of U.S. reinforcements to Monty, an extension of the U.S. line to the east to enable the British to concentrate more powerfully for their attacks—all had been directly coordinated, often face-to-face, among Eisenhower, Montgomery, and Bradley. Ike's plans were the real issue.

After sending his dispatch, Eisenhower visited his war room and learned that Bradley had not only broken into Brittany but to the east from Avranches—as Butcher put it, "to slice the disorganized German forces." Ike was virtually skipping in the hallway when the aide encountered him again before lunch. The supremo even hinted at the ULTRA secret: "If the intercepts are right, we are to hell and gone in Brittany and slicing them up in Normandy!" Ike exclaimed.[5] Butcher uses the "slice" wording twice. This was the first time a key player expressly foresaw the chance to trap the Nazis before they could escape.

One of Eisenhower's boyhood heroes had been the Carthaginian general Hannibal, whose great victory at Cannae (216 BC) had come when he held back the wings of his army as a Roman juggernaut passed them, then pulled his troops in beyond the enemy flanks, effectively encircling and trapping a superior Roman army. Normandy offered the same possibility— Ike's "golden opportunity." The jaws of the Allied forces—Montgomery on one flank and Patton on the other—could close around von Kluge's hapless Germans in a similar fashion. What is striking about what happened at SHAEF on August 2 is that Eisenhower responded instantly to a suggestion for change, immediately grasped the opportunity to trap the German army, accepted with equanimity a huge reduction in the long-planned Brittany operation, and made that intention explicit in a cable to higher command. General Eisenhower's choice was strategic in its essence and aggressive in execution. That one decision refutes claims that Ike did not understand strategy. The fact that Bradley revised his own orders only the following day shows that he acted on the basis of Eisenhower's instructions.

Montgomery fans prefer to credit the British general, attributing the envelopment to a concept Monty had developed at the end of June, and refined in a series of orders during July. His July 21 strategy directive, for example, envisioned Bradley sending a "strong right wing in a wide sweep south of the Bocage country," first toward Laval and Mayenne, and later Le Mans and Alençon.[6] After the war Montgomery muddied the water with his standard claim to prescience. But Monty's plan, even in its most recent version, on July 27, retained the idea of concentrating Patton's weight in Brittany. Montgomery wanted the First U.S. Army to advance to Mayenne, on through Le Mans–Alençon, and toward Paris. Though this axis was near to Bradley's concept, it offered a weaker pincer and threatened the Nazis below the Loire, not those in Normandy, who would have been free to retreat across the Seine. There was no provision here for a junction of the Allied armies to pocket the Wehrmacht. The best that can be made of this—for Montgomery—is that the idea of advancing along the Mayenne–Le Mans axis represented Allied conventional wisdom. Bradley's scheme actually went further with its provision for a thrust beyond the Seine to the Channel, which might have created a different pocket if the Germans did not succeed in evading it. Only Eisenhower foresaw an immediate encirclement *in* Normandy.

At a July 28 meeting with British and Commonwealth senior officers, Montgomery reiterated—with Bradley's breakout already at midstride— that Brittany was the single Allied geographical objective. On August 4, the day *after* General Bradley's revised order, Monty would tell London that *he* had turned only one U.S. corps toward the Breton ports. Of course, Montgomery's authority over American troops had changed at noontime on August 1, when the 12th Army Group (as well as Monty's 21st) were activated. Henceforth—until SHAEF assumed direct command—he was to "coordinate" the Allied army groups. Yet more grist for the war between the generals. Some interpret Montgomery's role as embodying a continued directive function. Bradley saw it more as a matter of setting the boundaries between the army groups and ensuring their operations conformed to SHAEF intentions.

George Patton's partisans would like to attribute the Normandy encirclement to him. His admirer and biographer Ladislas Farago writes that Patton was the "major architect" of the Allied breakout and that "Ike could not visualize either the opportunities that began to open to Patton or Patton's ability to make the most of them."[7] Another of the general's biographers, Carlo D'Este, also the author of a noted study of the Normandy campaign *and* a biography of Eisenhower, similarly maintains that Patton was "the first to grasp the immense possibilities."[8] Colonel Robert S. Allen of Patton's staff writes that his chief "started setting the stage for the sweep across France," and did it on August 4, "keenly aware that certain potent personal and political factors topside did not mesh with . . . his underlying combativeness." Thus, Patton, "with his eyes always restlessly on the next operation," ordered the eastward advance—"he didn't wait for topside's nod to go ahead."[9]

This is heroic, but not history. The Third Army daily operations summary, compiled by the very staff that would have responded to a Patton order to exploit eastward, notes nothing of the sort. The summary *does* record orders from Patton on August 2 for his left flank formation, XV Corps, to *hold* positions along the Mayenne River.[10] That was consistent with the former intention of protecting the Allied flank. Patton's book *War as I Knew It*, compiled by another of his stalwarts, Colonel Paul D. Harkins (of later Vietnam fame), contains no claim Patton masterminded the envelopment, and Patton's diary for August 4 states that *Bradley* was the source of the order that XV Corps should push on to Le Mans, the initial step in what would become the sweep.[11]

Victory, it seems, has a hundred fathers. But as a matter of record we have General Bradley's 12th Army Group letters of instruction, his field directives. Issued on July 29, Letter of Instruction No. 1 allotted Third Army the Overlord mission of protecting the flank and conquering Brittany. Letter of Instruction No. 2, on August 3, ordered Patton to use minimum force in Brittany and to "secure crossings of the Mayenne River . . . prepared for further action with strong armored forces towards the east and southeast." That order revamped the Allied advance, without yet aiming it to trap Nazis. Three days later, Letter of Instruction No. 3 directed Patton to "advance east in [his designated army] zone," continue the reduction of Brittany, and be "prepared for further action with strong armored forces in the direction of the Orleans-Paris gap." That order, on August 6, still amounted to Bradley's grand plan, not the immediate envelopment of Germans.[12] This record indicates that Bradley had yet to fully accept Eisenhower's quest for a Cannae in Normandy. Thus, Omar Bradley was quite correct to attribute the Normandy encirclement to Dwight D. Eisenhower. But the turning would not finally aim at a trap until the Nazis themselves made that the obvious alternative.

THE FÜHRER COMMANDS

At OKW and at Führer Headquarters, disaster loomed on every front save, perhaps, Italy. On the Eastern Front the line had stabilized more or less along the Vistula River and the East Prussian and Baltic state borders, but fighting had broken out in Warsaw. In the West, General Warlimont records, by the end of July even Hitler had begun considering possible defenses in central France. Some preparations began. General Jodl also focused on the Volksgrenadier and Panzer brigade programs. It was on the evening of July 30 that OKW learned of the fight for the "Avranches defile," which led Jodl to concoct a draft order for withdrawal from Normandy. Hitler looked at the draft but rejected it. Instead, he ordered Warlimont to go west, see the field commanders, and assess the situation. Prior to the general's departure Hitler personally expounded the views that were to guide him. This became the only time in five years at Führer Headquarters that Hitler favored Warlimont in this manner.

"The object remains," Hitler declared, "to keep the enemy confined to his bridgehead and there to inflict losses upon him in order to wear him down and finally destroy him."[13]

Despite crisis in the West the German High Command remained distracted. Indeed, the führer functioned as an agent of this distraction, and the most important event at Rastenburg on July 31 would be this meeting, which Hitler convened just before midnight. Warlimont, Jodl, and an inner circle of staff officers attended. In a typical monologue, occasionally punctuated by Jodl's brief comments, Hitler ruminated on where to give battle. He could not do more than hold in the East; in Italy an offensive would be wasted. "In any case," Hitler observed, "it is still better if I lead a battle in a different country than if I bring it close to Germany. . . . In the West, in my view, there is actually one very decisive question. If we lose France as a war theater, we will lose our point of departure for the submarine war."

Here was cold calculation, no boasting about wonder weapons and little maundering over the glories of the past. Hitler recognized obstacles: The Reich might have to accept "a substantial reduction of the German living space," and the decision could be forced only if all resources of the homeland and occupied territories were brought to bear. The Luftwaffe would have to be built up—Hitler believed the crisis could be overcome if he could throw in two thousand fighters. But preparing that force would take time. Holding certain ports could gain months—Hitler referred to "6 or 8 or 10 weeks"—which would advantage both the submarine war and the requisite force building—and again he complained of the supposedly weak defense of Cherbourg. The führer no longer wished to leave the battle to OB West, overburdened by events, but Jodl's comments make clear the reference was to von Kluge personally, not the post of C in C. Jodl noted a feeling among senior officers that Field Marshal von Rundstedt should return to the command. Some of the discussion revolved around preparing a rearward defense, though Hitler repeated his standard complaint about generals looking over their shoulders. Bridges and streets should be prepared for demolition and a new level of antitank forces attained. A special staff should conduct this activity removed from the concerns of front commanders.

Most important, Hitler recognized the tactical disparities between German and Allied forces. "We can move with some of our troops, but only in a limited manner," the führer declared near the beginning of this exchange. "With the other ones we cannot move, not because we don't possess air superiority, but because we can't move the troops themselves: the units are not suited for mobile battle—neither their weapons nor in their other equipment." True strength, Hitler opined, should be measured in mobile formations, not overall numbers of divisions. With existing units barely capable of manning a front in Normandy, "we can see the complete hopelessness of holding [a line in the French interior] with the forces that are available to us."

In this late-night conversation is evident the genesis of the offensive about to be demanded in Normandy, as well as the evolution of Hitler's thinking on the great gamble that became the Battle of the Bulge. An immediate restoration of the Normandy front was necessary because the bulk of German forces were not mobile and because Hitler needed time to rebuild air and ground strength, plus prepare rearward defenses. Given the führer's proclivity for holding to fixed ideas, his weeks of harping on Cherbourg and the American sector, and the U.S. breakout at Avranches, an offensive to restore the Normandy front had to aim at that point. Though much has been written about Hitler's intent to trap Patton's army by means of this offensive, that subject was never mentioned. It was inherent in the tactical situation that success would have left Patton behind German lines, but this was not the primary goal seen at Rastenburg. For whatever reasons Warlimont did not appreciate from this exchange that orders for a Normandy attack would follow. Both Warlimont himself and other German accounts record that the OKW emissary was surprised when, during his visit to the West, the attack order came.

Meanwhile, it is clear that as of July 31 Hitler had become serious about a large-scale counteroffensive, one that might stabilize the West. Several things about that concept were also established: It would be unleashed only when every resource had been mustered, at a point when the Luftwaffe had been sufficiently rebuilt to intervene; and it would be conducted outside Germany, "to use [forces] where we can possibly create a change again." While the führer had declared, "I can't tell now where the last dice will fall," his analysis of the potential of the Italian and Eastern fronts left the West as the only reasonable possibility.[14] In a very real sense, a direct line connects the von Rundstedt–Rommel proposals at the forgotten Margival conference with the projects for such an attack in Normandy, and finally to the cosmic throw of the dice at the Bulge. These things were immanent at the moment of the Allied breakout.

The next morning General Warlimont had his usual telephone briefing from Field Marshal von Kluge and participated at the standard noontime staff meeting. The conversation left no doubt the Allied breakthrough had widened. Von Kluge wished to stop it by ruthlessly pulling troops from less threatened points. When Jodl requested instructions, Hitler responded "with every indication of ill-humor," Warlimont records. "You tell Field Marshal von Kluge to keep on looking to his front, to keep his eyes on the enemy and not to look over his shoulder."[15] Shortly afterward the emissary left by plane for Strasbourg, where he picked up a car for Paris on the first leg of his mission. While the OKW staff officer made his way forward, Hitler received an investigative file revealing von Kluge's sympathies with the July 20 conspirators, immediately suspecting Warlimont of collusion with the field marshal. General Jodl barely dissuaded the führer from recalling the OKW planner to accuse him of complicity. At Munich Warlimont would be called to the phone. Jodl came on the line to instruct him to be alert for evidence of the plotters. Yet another distraction from the emergency at hand. Meanwhile, the German scheme for a *Normandy* counteroffensive, because it meant advancing while holding the existing front, became the equivalent of putting their heads into the mouth of a lion.

TOUJOURS L'AUDACE

Warlimont the emissary reached Paris around noon on August 2. During the long drive from Strasbourg he noticed that little had been done to implement Hitler's week-old orders—reiterated during the late-night meeting— to protect transport in rear areas by concentrating antiaircraft guns at river crossings and along key roads. Warlimont speculated the inaction was due to loss of the weapons. As he'd been leaving Strasbourg, the general flashed back to 1914: That city had been Warlimont's first duty post as a young artillery officer, and thirty years earlier—to the day—he had first marched off to war. Field Marshal von Kluge also made comparisons to 1914, and Allied generals and journalists had worried privately and in print that the Normandy campaign was degenerating into trench warfare like the last war. It is remarkable in this summer of 1944, at the brink of a war of lightning movement, so many thoughts turned to World War I.

What the Germans were about to attempt would be to restore conditions of static warfare by means of an operation of such audacity that it, too, evoked 1914, when the French army professed a doctrine of *élan*, offensive spirit, in which the all-out offensive, the *offensive à outrance*, took pride of place. The phrase *"toujours l'audace,"* always audacity, which was actually used by Danton during the French revolutionary period and repeated by the marshals Foch and Joffre in World War I, perfectly suited the German course at this critical moment.

In the run-up to this operation, Warlimont arrived in Paris and quickly huddled with Blumentritt. Not much had changed save for what the Germans did not know—the rapidity with which General Patton poured troops of his Third Army through Avranches. OB West had taken some countermeasures: Forces which held the Biscay coast were to take up positions along the Loire River, while reinforcements from southern France, led by a corps headquarters summoned from Calais, assembled in the German rear in Normandy. Field Marshal von Kluge hoped in this way to block an American advance toward Paris while threatening the flank of any troops who thrust into the French interior. Germans in Brittany would be left to their own devices. The word Warlimont brought from Führer Headquarters was familiar—steadfast defense, no retreat, no looking back. No alternative.

Early the next morning von Kluge asked Warlimont to see him at Army Group B, where he continued to conduct operations personally. When General Warlimont arrived at the La Roche-Guyon headquarters, he learned that just before midnight von Kluge had received orders for a bold move using all the panzer formations to recapture Avranches. Apparently there was first a telephone conversation, then a written instruction. The core of the directive read:

> The enemy is not under any circumstances to be permitted to break out into the open. Army Group B will prepare a counterattack, using all panzer units, to push through as far as Avranches, cut off the enemy units that have broken through and destroy them. All available Panzer forces are to be withdrawn from their present front sectors, even if there are no divisions to relieve them, and are to be employed for this purpose. . . . The outcome of the campaign in France depends upon this counterattack.[16]

"There could be no doubt," Warlimont writes, "that once more Hitler had taken a snap decision without any preliminary study or form of preparation by his staff."[17] Warlimont believes that the führer's Berchtesgaden meeting with von Rundstedt and Rommel showed that already by late June no one put stock in an offensive anymore. Von Kluge told the OKW emissary that he had already considered and rejected this course. But now the führer insisted. Hitler, according to Warlimont, must have decided on the fly the previous night. But in fact Hitler's demand had been prefigured in his discussion before Warlimont's departure—and at Berchtesgaden the conversation about Luftwaffe formations concerned one of the leader's prerequisites for an attack. The führer had brooded about committing the mobile troops and Luftwaffe home defense forces. His strategic choice had been to build for a bigger offensive, but the immediate question remained: The Allies had to be stopped. Sometimes audacity did pay. Von Kluge and Warlimont agreed the scheme needed to be carried out immediately if it were to have any chance. Von Kluge made the first phone calls to gather the panzers while the OKW emissary sat in his office.

Omar Bradley understood the German situation well. In his first volume of memoirs Bradley sketches the broad strategic situation and notes the alternatives facing Berlin: retreat from Normandy, pulling German forces behind the Seine River; or mount the counteroffensive. Despite Allied airpower Bradley believed withdrawal would probably have worked. As for the attack option he remarks, "before gambling against the considerable risks . . . the enemy should first have calculated the odds that were arranged against him." Of Hitler's choice Bradley concludes, "That decision, more than any other, was to cost the enemy the Battle for France."[18]

At the front General Hausser of the Seventh Army believed, in common with other top leaders, that only an immediate operation had any chance. Von Kluge met with Hausser to coordinate the plans. Both they and their staffs were afflicted with doubts. Hausser favored a dawn attack on August 3 with whatever panzers the Germans could muster. Führer Headquarters rejected that possibility. There were arguments on both sides of the issue. Hausser was right that immediate responses, before the enemy became established, often had the best chance of success. On the other hand, this option had already been tried—and had failed—during Bradley's Cobra advance down the Cotentin. OKW probably had reason to dismiss it—and Hitler had been plumping ever since Margival for a fully generated offensive. To come full circle, however, Hausser was correct to anticipate that by August 8—the date for the projected attack—the Americans would have become quite strong. Some historians believe that Hitler actually wanted the later date in order to pull more GIs into the supposed trap.[19]

Tremendous energy would be required for any strike. But Admiral

Ruge, the OB West naval aide, found Field Marshal von Kluge exhausted. So too was General Baron Hans Freiherr von Funck, whose XLVII Panzer Corps would carry it out. Von Funck also stood aghast at the prospect of moving panzer divisions all around Normandy within five days to prepare this operation. "My God! What are they thinking of?" von Funck groused to his chief of staff. "The Jabos will smash every vehicle we possess! We can't group up because of those airborne devils and if we don't group, we can't attack!"[20] All were overruled by the führer, who demanded concentrated force.

General Warlimont visited the front. When he stopped at Panzer Group West its commander, General Hans Eberbach, pressed for an immediate retreat behind the Seine. Warlimont answered that Hitler would never agree. That night he returned to Army Group B. By then a certain optimism prevailed. The OKW emissary heard no more complaints. On August 4, again at the front, the emissary found field commanders hastening to ready the ambitious gambit, christened Operation Luettich (German for Liège). As for the situation this day, Admiral Ruge observed, "the Americans . . . pressed en masse into France. Their advance could now only be delayed, but not stopped."[21] Ruge felt relieved to be leaving Paris for a new assignment.

The German command was all in, betting against Ruge's view. In a meeting at OB West, Warlimont heard Field Marshal Hugo Sperrle promise to employ every Luftwaffe resource to ensure success. Hans Speidel, Army Group B staff chief, attended also. Von Kluge's war diary reports preparations and notes, "The first mission is to cut off the enemy units . . . from their rear communications and to reestablish our [line to] the coast."[22]

The Germans began quietly and progressed quickly, building on measures already taken to remedy the American breakout. The II SS Panzer Corps, pulled out of the line in front of the British, was to be inserted northeast of Vire, between Meindl's parachutists and the new corps from Calais. Its leading element, the reconnaissance battalion of the 10th SS Panzer, arrived to stiffen the infantry. General Hausser instructed Meindl to extend his line, using the mobile troops to shift farther south, where

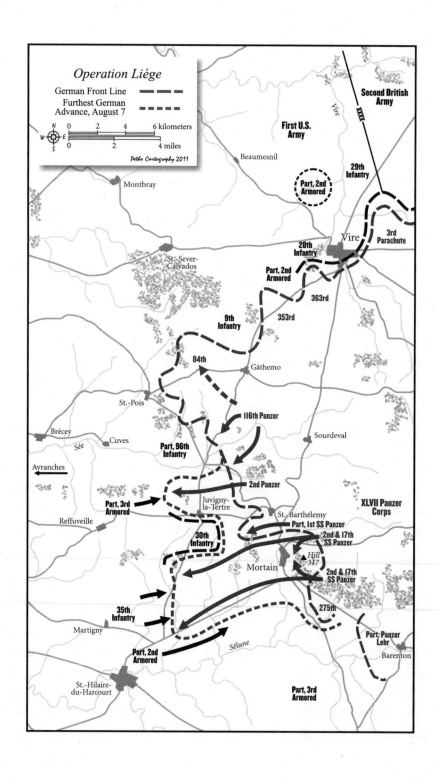

Operation Liége

German Front Line ━ ━ ━
Furthest German
Advance, August 7 ▪ ▪ ▪ ▪

0   2   4   6 kilometers
0   2   4 miles

Petho Cartography 2011

Second British Army

First U.S. Army

Beaumesnil

Montbray

Part, 2nd Armored

29th Infantry

Vire

3rd Parachute

28th Infantry

Part, 2nd Armored

363rd

St.-Sever-Calvados

9th Infantry

353rd

84th

Gâthemo

St.-Pois

116th Panzer

Sourdeval

Brécey

See

Cuves

Part, 96th Infantry

Avranches

2nd Panzer

Part, 3rd Armored

Juvigny-la-Tertre

St.-Barthélemy

Part, 1st SS Panzer

XLVII Panzer Corps

Reffuveille

30th Infantry

2nd & 17th SS Panzer

Hill 317

Mortain

2nd & 17th SS Panzer

35th Infantry

275th

Part, Panzer Lehr

Martigny

Sélune

Barenton

Part, 2nd Armored

St.-Hilaire-du-Harcourt

Part, 3rd Armored

a new, scratch defense would be assembled with von Funck's panzers. Both made certain withdrawals. Baron von Funck used this pullback to reassemble the 2nd Panzer Division for the attack. The 116th Panzer Division would also contribute. The OB West war diary on August 4 noted that the attack would employ "withdrawn and reorganized tank formations, while defending the right flank."[23] Until then the German flank was in the air, with only "alarm" units or odd detachments to hold key places. The town of Mortain, for example, was garrisoned only by the 87th Flak Regiment. Helmut Ritgen, leading a group with the remaining battleworthy troops of Panzer Lehr, held Villedieu. On August 4 the 1st and 12th SS Panzer Divisions began disengaging from the British sector prior to moving west.

But General Meindl proved correct—the German army could not simply operate as if on exercises. Normandy's roads again proved an encumbrance, this time for the Germans. Supplies for the front, medical convoys, and tactical redeployments all competed for the same limited road space. Motor transport created another bottleneck. More than one German commander carped that troops were ready and tanks available, but they lacked prime movers, trucks, and motorcars, especially Volkswagens. Fuel supplies were a key stumbling block, slowing movements, often restricting them to portions of units rather than entire formations. The Allied codebreakers would decrypt repeated messages from von Lüttwitz of 2nd Panzer complaining the fuel shortage hampered his preparations. Everything happened under threat from the dreaded Allied fighter-bombers, the jabos. Some German infantry and panzers expected to participate, or to help create the new flank force, were still en route from south of the Loire River, and on August 2 Field Marshal von Kluge also summoned from there the headquarters and support troops of the First Army. That day Pete Quesada's IX Tactical Air Command damaged two Loire bridges, ensuring delays. A few days later the IX Bomber Command attacked nine bridges over the Loire and Seine, virtually isolating Le Mans, long the Seventh Army's base. Most of all, the Germans were in a desperate race with Americans erupting from Normandy. The stakes included the assembly areas to mount the Nazi offensive, the front line that would shield the attackers, and the deep rear of the German army. The Allies reached for their own objectives. This race would go to the swiftest.

THE OFFENSIVE THAT NEVER WAS

Eisenhower and his lieutenants knew of Operation Liège, though when and how much remains obscure. "Bradley and I," Eisenhower writes, "aware that the German counterattack was under preparation, carefully surveyed the situation."[24] They were certainly alert to the possibility. On the first day of August—before Hitler had issued any orders at all—General Bradley expressed worry about a counterattack. That day he instructed Hodges and the First Army to change the direction of their advance from south to the southeast, putting more distance between the Germans and Avranches. Bradley records that ULTRA was of little or no value until just prior to the attack,[25] so American situational awareness must have flowed from other sources. General Hodges, in turn, gave Lightning Joe Collins the mission of maintaining contact with Patton as the Third Army gushed out of Normandy. Collins recounts that he also was concerned about an attack, and had that in mind when he issued his own orders on August 1.

George Patton wrote in his diary that day, "Bradley is worried about an attack west from Mortain," that is, an assault aimed at Avranches.[26] Patton doubted it but was happy to assuage Bradley's concern, moving the 90th Infantry Division up to guard the hinge of the breakout, using the threat to get more troops into forward positions. To push the 90th forward meant squeezing it through the same town and down the same road simultaneously being used by two other divisions. Patton reflected that at Fort Leavenworth, the army's Command and General Staff School, instructors would certainly have flunked the student who proposed such a maneuver. Meanwhile, on August 2, having missed a meeting with Patton, General Bradley bypassed the Third Army commander to order another of Patton's divisions to Fougères, also a flanking position but one that built inertia for what became the U.S. turning movement and the concentration of XV Corps, completed when Patton added the 5th Armored Division. Third Army's envelopment of the German flank began with these moves, initially taken simply to protect American troops surging into Brittany.

In reviewing the tactical dispositions to be assumed by the Big Red One of his corps, on August 3 General Collins instructed General Huebner to be sure to hold the town of Mortain and the overlooking Hill 317, which dominated the area. Huebner assured Collins that his GIs were already on the hill. The situation seemed well in hand.

On the German side, Field Marshal von Kluge continued his preparations. The line would be shortened in the Vire sector. Tessy-sur-Vire fell to the Americans. The Wehrmacht pulled the 2nd and 2nd SS Panzer Divisions off the line. How tight its situation actually was is illustrated by the fact that General Hausser had to recommit portions of the 2nd to stem the Allied tide. Regrouping of II SS Panzer Corps was delayed, too. The 116th Panzer Division, also slated for the attack, was so heavily embattled that at first it could release only its reconnaissance battalion. Troops to replace the panzers only arrived on August 4. By then von Kluge had given up on using the II SS Panzer Corps against Avranches, and pinned his hopes on bringing up the 1st SS Panzer Division from the British sector. That unit, too, was delayed by the late arrival of formations to replace it. The Germans had become so desperate they resorted to some daylight movement for the 1st SS—which meant additional losses. The entire maneuver would be further delayed when a British warplane, shot down, crashed right on top of the lead tank in the SS column at a place where the road was too narrow to pass the wreckage. All the vehicles had to back up a full mile to take a different road to the battle area.

Paul Hausser's judgment was that success depended entirely on reducing Allied air supremacy—which the Luftwaffe could hardly do—and he continued to believe in instantaneous attack, limiting the Allied opportunity to consolidate. Hitler himself put the kibosh on the timing, suddenly releasing replacement tanks from Wehrmacht stocks, and adding the 11th Panzer Division to the troop list to make the sum of 140 extra tanks. Integrating 60 replacement panzers pushed Operation Liège back another day. Now the soonest it could occur was August 7—and then it turned out there was no possibility the 11th Panzer could reach position by that time.

Hausser also pointed out that reinforcements were absolutely necessary to hold what ground the panzers gained. That, too, was an impossibility, a foreseeable one. There were a number of infantry divisions and one armored formation (9th Panzer Division) on the way to Normandy. A couple would do no more than replace panzers slated for the attack. The others were to create a new defense behind the German flank from the Loire River northeast. Otherwise there would be no front at all. That meant no fresh infantry for the offensive itself.

Meanwhile, Hitler's intervention caused yet more disruption. On August 5 he dispatched another emissary, General Walter Buhle, chief of the army staff at OKW, to keep an eye on von Kluge. Buhle brought word that Hitler had ordained the attack should be carried out by General Heinrich Eberbach, with an even larger force in which Baron von Funck's XLVII Panzer Corps would become just one element. Eberbach's former command on the British front, Panzer Group West, would be restyled the Fifth Panzer Army, while the general led a new Panzer Group Eberbach. His force should include the II SS Panzer Corps and the 9th Panzer Division, still outside the battle area. Those units could not be assembled immediately—August 10 was the latest estimate—and Hausser was still arguing for an instant attack. Von Kluge agreed, and issued orders on August 6 for Operation Liège to go ahead that night. The late arrival of the 1st SS Panzer Division relegated it to the second echelon, with the 2nd and 116th Panzers leading, along with remnants of the 2nd SS Panzer Division. The operations staff officer of the 116th complained that the 1st SS was supposed to be on hand to back them up, but Baron von Funck was furious at the supposed dilatoriness of the 116th's own commander. At least the night attack would minimize aerial interference, and went without artillery preparation to maximize surprise.

At the First U.S. Army, General Hodges felt the pressure. As Patton's troops advanced a gap yawned between the American armies. Hodges ordered General Collins to fill it, and Lightning Joe tapped the troops around Mortain. Clarence Huebner's Big Red One, which had captured the town on August 3, moved away to link Hodges's and Patton's armies. Hodges sent Major General Leland Hobbs's 30th Infantry Division to Mortain on August 5. Hobbs, under Collins, took up the positions Huebner's men left behind. On the sixth the GIs were on the road to the new positions. The Old Hickory division officially took over this front late that day. Thus, the Germans attacked a sector held by GIs who had arrived just hours before, were unfamiliar with the terrain, and had poor maps. The 30th Division men occupied works built to shield GIs temporarily, while they were on the offensive, not ones designed for defense. Telephone wire circuits left by Big Red One communications specialists increasingly developed problems and needed to be replaced. Hobbs's division was also short by roughly a thousand casualties who had not yet been replaced, and two infantry battalions sent on other missions; General Collins further thinned the defense by ordering the 30th to deploy one regiment to cover a wider frontage. Finally, General Hobbs had little information regarding U.S. troops around him, and VII Corps initially supplied him little intelligence about the Germans in his sector. A bad omen was that one of the battalions Hobbs had detached for a special mission—advancing ahead of his main force—was struck by Luftwaffe aircraft during the evening of August 6.

But in the end there would be no surprise. Commanders above the level of Old Hickory's leader were on the alert—and then the Luftwaffe gave away the game to Allied codebreakers. Withdrawals of the units of the II SS Panzer Corps, the intended shift of 1st SS Panzer Division, and the regrouping of Baron von Funck's panzers were all betrayed to ULTRA in the form of Luftwaffe notices. Later the actual movement of the 1st SS became known the same way. So did the assembly of the 2nd SS Panzers. ULTRA indicated specific German interest in the Mortain sector from August 5, when the Allies decrypted Luftwaffe orders to concentrate bomber missions there. On August 6 the Allies learned that 2nd SS Panzer had requested fighter cover over a zone that encompassed Mortain. That evening ULTRA could report that the four panzer divisions involved had all been subordinated to Baron von Funck for an attack toward the west. The crowning achievement—which ULTRA signaled at eleven minutes past midnight the day of Liège—derived again from the Luftwaffe, whose fighter command explicitly noted that the Seventh Army would attack westward from the Mortain area that night. Source ULTRA also recorded a message from von Funck's corps that mentioned Avranches as an objective.

Among American field commanders, Bradley and Collins both note they learned of the German offensive shortly after midnight. The 30th Division operations journal shows the warning to expect an attack within the next twelve hours reached it at 12:38 a.m. of August 7.

Two hours before the key ULTRA dispatch, Baron von Funck had telephoned the Seventh Army with an appeal for postponement. The troops were simply not yet in place. General Hausser, calling this madness, rejected von Funck's request out of hand. Panzers started to advance shortly after midnight. The battle of Mortain began a little after two a.m. Before dawn assault groups of the 2nd SS Panzer Division were inside the town and investing Hill 317. Nearby villages were overrun or threatened. To the west of Mortain, GIs of the 1st Battalion, 120th Infantry were engaged on Hill 285 before dawn. Lieutenant Murray S. Pulver's stand with his company gave them time to reorganize. His first sergeant, Reginald Maybee, handed Pulver a bazooka with which he knocked out a Panzer IV tank. Pulver's men stopped the first Nazi rush. But other Germans infiltrated past roadblocks into Mortain. Leland Hobbs sent his last reserve to the 120th even before dawn. "Custer" was the regiment's unfortunate radio call sign.

THE LOST BATTALION

Meanwhile atop Hill 317 (also known as Hill 314) the main body of the 2nd Battalion, surrounded and holding on by sheer will, became the "Lost Battalion" of Mortain. The Luftwaffe treated them to a fighter-bomber attack just as they climbed the slope, at midafternoon, carrying everything they could. The hill seemed better suited for a German assault than a U.S. defense, for it was open toward the sides the Germans approached but had sheer cliffs along its western face, where Americans might have to attempt a withdrawal. Lieutenant Colonel Eads Hardaway, leading the Lost Battalion, posted two and a half companies plus part of his weapons unit on the hill, and an attached rifle company from another battalion at its southern rim. Together there were about six hundred GIs defending Hill 317. Their worst problem was limited ammunition. The ordeal began at 1:25 a.m. on August 7, when GIs heard firing off to the east. Only a few moments later the first German tanks and infantry appeared. The fight went on for days.

Colonel Hardaway had broader responsibilities than Hill 317. Battalion headquarters was at a hotel in Mortain, garrisoned by a rifle company. They were quickly in trouble. Germans advanced into the town from the southeast with tanks and infantry, and they infiltrated from the north. Both thrusts came *behind* Hill 317. Regimental boss Colonel Hammond D. Birks had no reserves. Before three a.m. he had to pull an infantry company off another hill to send to Mortain. When Hardaway reported an hour later that Nazis were on Hill 317, Birks told him to use his own troops as reinforcements. The 2nd Battalion held on for dear life. By midmorning Hardaway was hard-pressed. In the town, a small place of perhaps sixteen hundred souls with only a few streets, his command post was overrun. Hardaway, call sign "Cuff," lost contact with Custer. He also lost his phone connection to Hill 317. A company of the 1st Battalion was driven out. Hardaway's command group hid for several days, but most were captured on August 9 as they tried to make their way up Hill 317.

Colonel Birks's own headquarters came under attack several miles to the rear. Custer had its hands full. That afternoon a telephone switchboard operator felt so threatened that he left his post to hunt tanks with a bazooka. Germans were all over the place. West of Mortain, on Hill 285, where Lieutenant Pulver had blunted the first German rush, an extended battle developed. North of Mortain, Custer's roadblocks and Old Hickory's 117th Infantry also fought hard. A 117th Regiment battalion commander was surrounded and had to fight his way out, using his pistol to shoot the commander of a Panther tank parked right outside. He and his staff escaped out a window. One of his rifle companies was smashed. Regiment commander Lieutenant Colonel Walter M. Johnson began calling the stone farmhouse that served as his command post "Château Nebelwerfer." His headquarters company and the remnants of a rifle battalion were all that was left. Frenchmen reported Nazi tanks just over a mile from division headquarters.

Through all this no concentrated attack occurred at Hill 317 itself. By not clearing the height before dawn the Nazis lost their moment of greatest advantage, and also left an immensely valuable observation post in American hands. Only minor patrol actions took place. When the Germans did attempt a significant probe it was by daylight, from the west, from Mortain town. "They came almost up to our foxholes," observed Private Grady

Deal of G Company, 2nd Battalion. "Then our artillery started to fall right on 'em. Their tanks turned right around and went back down the hill. I never understood it. . . . We couldn't have stopped them."[27]

Higher command lost no time responding. Leland Hobbs, a West Point classmate of Eisenhower and Bradley's, sent in his reserve to bolster the front north of Mortain where the Germans were infiltrating. Fortunately, when they set up position, they found the enemy spearheads had halted and were concealing their vehicles before dawn came and Allied aircraft arrived. At VII Corps, Lightning Joe Collins asked Bradley for armor, combat commands of which he attached to each of the threatened 30th and 4th Infantry Divisions. He lined up an arriving infantry division behind Mortain in case the Germans broke through. Jayhawk held a combat command of the 2nd Armored Division south of the attack zone and ready to intervene.

Equally helpful, once the morning fog burned off, August 7 turned into a beautiful day—and a splendid opportunity for Elwood Quesada's IX Tactical Air Command. Hitler had promised three hundred Luftwaffe aircraft to support Liège, but, disrupted by the Americans, few of them turned up over the battlefield. Not so for IX TAC. Quesada's planes were ready. Having suffered an all-time peak in mechanical failures on August 2, General Quesada had been standing down his groups two a day for maintenance. By August 7 IX TAC had returned to normal readiness rates. It flew just under five hundred sorties that day. Quesada also got British help, rocket-armed Royal Air Force Typhoon fighter-bombers with a deserved reputation as tank busters. Before the day ended the flyboys claimed the destruction of 109 German tanks, and on August 8 Quesada's airmen were credited with another 47 tanks and 122 motor vehicles—a likely exaggeration, given that Baron von Funck had only about 120 panzers in the offensive. A team of British operations research specialists later went over the battlefield and counted only 78 wrecked armored vehicles of all types, many of the losses attributable to artillery or antitank fire. Meanwhile, American troops recorded nearly a dozen friendly air attacks on themselves. There were 4,012 IX TAC sorties in this sector alone during the period from August 8 through 14. Delighted at its achievements, the RAF established 84 Group to combine its ground attack capabilities.

Meanwhile, at Reffuveille, maintenance specialists of the 3rd Armored Division were fixing its tanks when the word came to drop everything. Brigadier General Truman Boudinot's Combat Command B received orders to intervene, sending one force to stop the Germans on the north side of the attack sector and another detachment to Mortain to relieve the Lost Battalion. General Boudinot took the first assignment himself, playing a role in repulsing the 2nd Panzer Division.

Boudinot gave the Mortain relief mission to a task force under tank commander Colonel Dorrance S. Roysden. The latter had a personal reason to succeed. A month earlier, during the Panzer Lehr blitz above Saint-Lô, it had been Roysden's armor that had been saved from German attackers by the strong efforts of Old Hickory's 120th Infantry. Now their positions were reversed. This was to be the cavalry riding to rescue the wagon train.

Once on the road, the same good visibility that aided Allied aircraft benefited the German artillery observers and their panzer gunners. As Colonel Roysden drove toward his goal, the task force entered a valley where the Nazis let them have it. Ranging shots began to fall shortly before noon, and heavy fire continued for more than four hours. When Roysden tried to move his command post the vehicles came under fire. His radio half-track was knocked out. "Orchard," Roysden's radio call sign, went off the air. The colonel himself took cover beneath a tank. The valley floor became littered with the hulks of Roysden's 33rd Armored Regiment. His relief attempt failed. Over the next five days the unit's mechanics processed forty-one replacement vehicles and repaired more than sixty others.

Fights erupted north and south of Mortain. On the north flank von Funck's panzers collided with the U.S. 4th and 9th Infantry Divisions, themselves attacking, too. Here the assault formation was General von Schwerin's 116th Panzer Division. Its experience demonstrates the factors that doomed Operation Liège. Von Schwerin's panzers had been facing north, parrying American thrusts toward Vire. As the attack hour approached, various emergencies had to be faced. If the Americans smashed through past Vire, the 116th and another German division would have been surrounded. Most of Schwerin's tank strength had been detached to reinforce the 2nd Panzer. When von Schwerin finally pulled his men off the line, the defenses came under tremendous pressure. He had to leave behind his artillery. Then the Americans began to employ armor at Vire, forcing the 116th to send back its antitank unit and most of a regiment.

Hours before Liège was to begin, a different American penetration forced von Schwerin to deploy the ready elements of his battle group. Thus, the 116th's "division" attack came down to a couple of battalions from a single *Panzergrenadier* regiment. One of those made good progress, but the news did not reach XLVII Panzer Corps. Baron von Funck ordered a daylight jab during the afternoon, in rolling country in full view of the Americans. It was crushed. Meanwhile, the division's Panther battalion, at the tip of the 2nd Panzer Division's column, made the farthest advance of the offensive but was set upon by Allied air. The panzers recoiled with heavy losses, including two company officers killed and the battalion commander—awarded the Knight's Cross—wounded. Baron von Funck was furious at von Schwerin's alleged poor performance and, accusing him of not attacking at all, demanded his relief. Field Marshal von Kluge, at the front for the Big Day, complied.

In view of the stalled efforts, Baron von Funck called off the offensive. Operation Liège finally resolved itself into the scattered firefights around Mortain plus the German siege of Hill 317. Atop that height GIs improved their positions, and the several rifle companies linked up. They rejected a German offer to surrender and beat off a midnight attack. In the evening of August 9 another Nazi assault failed. American artillery support was critical. Food was a headache, too, though GIs were able to dig up cabbages and potatoes from a farm field within their lines, and they found a well just outside them. Augmented by a number of refugees from other units crumpled up in the fighting, the Lost Battalion battled Germans where they had to but mostly called in targets for the artillery.

The key difficulties were medical supplies and radio batteries. Colonel Birks tried to solve the deficit by organizing a relief attempt from Hill 285. Lieutenant Pulver's company was selected to carry it out. At Custer headquarters Pulver fell asleep while being briefed for the mission. With the men so exhausted, Birks now realized that an overland expedition was simply impossible. The 30th Division next tried to use its little artillery spotter planes to make a low-altitude supply drop, filling them with batteries and medicine. Two were shot up trying. One of the planes crashed. Then Division went to VII Corps for a major airdrop, but Jayhawk responded that procedures required thirty-six hours to arrange the flight plans. General Hobbs finally resorted to having his gunners adapt canister shells, designed to fire smoke. The artillerymen crammed them with medical supplies and batteries instead. The canisters were blasted into the Lost Battalion's perimeter to provide it with something, at least. Eventually, airdrops also sustained the GIs.

The siege became an artillery duel. It was not broken until August 11. That morning the GIs on Hill 317 woke up to see convoys of German vehicles disappearing into the distance. Naturally they called down barrages. Shortly before noon on August 12 scouts of the advancing U.S. 35th Infantry Division reached the Lost Battalion. Only 357 soldiers of the units atop the hill walked off it that day. About an equal number were casualties. Across the division as a whole, these six days of battle brought in a butcher's bill of 1,854 men, including 165 killed and 442 missing. But the fifty-two-year-old General Hobbs could be justly proud of Old Hickory—of ten Distinguished Unit Citations earned by the 30th Infantry Division in the last part of World War II, half would be awarded for its defense of Mortain. One of these went to the Lost Battalion, Colonel Hardaway's 2nd Battalion, 120th Infantry; another to the detached K Company of the 3rd Battalion, which had been on Hill 317 with it.

BACK TO THE DRAWING BOARD

The Germans had suffered considerable losses to no avail. There were many reasons for the failure. Not all have even been touched upon—reading tactical accounts reveals a host of instances where German assault groups lacked initiative, failed to press home advantages at moments where they had them, and halted at the first indication of resistance; above all, they were extremely cautious about the Allied aircraft.[28] The fractionation of the offensive due to supply shortages and combat emergencies elsewhere, exemplified by the experience of the 116th Panzer Division, greatly reduced its effectiveness. Allied airpower and intelligence advantages also figure in the mix. But the essential dilemma was and remained that the Americans had overwhelming superiority on the ground.

All this left only Adolf Hitler's Big Solution—the wallop utilizing multiple corps under Panzer Group Eberbach. OB West began preparing that while the Mortain battle still menaced the Lost Battalion. Hitler's distrust of the German generals—magnified in the wake of the July 20 Plot—led the führer to review these plans with extra care. OKW approved the overall framework and confirmed it on August 9. Urgency led Führer Headquarters to send the message by radio—a dispatch that ULTRA intercepted. The führer's dispatch said of the attack, "On its success depends the fate of the Battle of France."

Sent by teleprinter shortly before midnight, this order was promptly intercepted and decrypted at Bletchley Park. The intelligence analyst John Prestwich was on watch at Bletchley's Hut 3 when the decrypt came through: "I remember it. My goodness I remember it. I remember we queried it at the time. We said, 'It cannot be true.' It seemed to us inconceivable . . . and this opened up the whole possibility of wiping out the cream of the German armed forces. . . . But it was an order from Hitler. . . . The German generals might have thought it was lunatic . . . but they obeyed."[29]

In a circuitous way the anti-Hitler plot thus led to an Allied intelligence windfall. Hitler wondered how the Allies could be so well informed on German operations, yet remained blind to the possibility he was telling them himself.

At first Hans Eberbach had no idea what forces were even assigned to him, much less their status, yet he was expected to mount the offensive. Hitler reiterated his orders, specifying forces, naming Eberbach as commander, and making the execution date August 11. A fresh corps headquarters, General Walter Krueger's LVIII Panzer Corps, recently arrived and now quickly retrieved from Montgomery's sector, actually had no troops. Eberbach intended to assign him the divisions of the II SS Panzer Corps, stiffened by the Panther battalion of the 9th Panzer Division. But Field Marshal von Kluge, though approving Eberbach's plan, repeatedly delayed releasing the SS panzers. The plan had von Funck's corps repeating its Mortain attack, with a supporting thrust by Krueger to the east of him. It quickly became apparent that Eberbach's offensive could not be mounted within the time allotted. On the designated day, tank strength available totaled seventy-seven Panzer IVs and forty-seven Panther tanks. More seemed necessary. The continued presence of the SS panzers on the British sector forced repeated delays. The maneuvers of Patton's army created fresh dangers to the flank and rear. But even a strengthened offensive had little chance, while the weakening of German forces on the British front, required to carry it out, would have accelerated Montgomery's advance in such a way as to make encirclement a continuing threat. The only difference would have been the shape of the pocket.

Eberbach and von Kluge recast the maneuver plan to counter Patton, launching in a different direction, but that in itself robbed the operation of its avowed purpose of cutting off the Allied breakthrough. Each recasting of the German scheme increased the delay, and then would be overtaken by the swift advance of Patton's GIs. The net effect—due to source ULTRA—was that for a time the Allies *expected* a German blow that never materialized. In the end, all the führer's horses could accomplish had been an assault of local importance, one that they sustained around Mortain for little more than twelve hours. And this came at the price of giving George S. Patton freedom to roam at will through the German rear. How dangerous that could be soon became painfully evident.

NO FINGERS IN THE DIKE

A token of Eisenhower's confidence—and Allied daring in this transformed campaign—was that despite the prospect of the German counterattack SHAEF made no effort to rein in its own offensive. This quickly led to the siege of Brest in Brittany, but more important, Omar Bradley's grand scheme every day put the Germans in Normandy into greater peril. At the same time Hitler's fixation on the counterstroke prevented the Nazis from taking the measures that might yet have saved their armies. Eisenhower recounts that he was with Bradley when they made the crucial decision. Ike believed that U.S. strength was such that the Germans could not gain an inch—close to what happened. Holding back would "diminish the number of divisions we could hurl into the enemy's rear and so sacrifice our opportunity to achieve the complete destruction for which we hoped."[30] Given improved weather, Ike assured Bradley that even if the Germans did reach Avranches and temporarily cut U.S. forces off, Allied air transport would supply the trapped units long enough to regain contact. The advance should continue. American intelligence maps indicated a paucity of German formations to hold them back. While Ike was still at 12th Army Group headquarters, Bradley telephoned Montgomery to inform him of the decision. Monty expressed misgivings but went along. Brad, in turn, released Patton to add his XX Corps to the forces moving into the French interior.

The first American spearheads departed even before the Mortain battle. Leading the pack was Major General Raymond S. McLain's 90th Infantry Division, a bit ironic because the 90th had so far been considered a sad-sack outfit. Just prior to Cobra one of the 90th's battalions had been so badly handled that several hundred of its soldiers had surrendered to a German force a fraction of their size. In July the division took more than five thousand casualties. Since D-Day the 90th had lost half its men. Many GIs with it now were fresh-faced replacements. Bradley had fired its leaders for failure, repeatedly, and relieved at least two regimental officers as well. Even before the onset of Cobra, George Patton, who thought McLain had enough personality to turn the division around, had talked to the responsible corps commander, Troy Middleton, about elevating McLain. Once the Third Army became operational his appointment was one of Patton's first actions. General Bradley approved heartily.

Ray McLain was the third commander of the 90th Division in three weeks. The fifty-four-year-old McLain was not a professional soldier, but his appointment was no gamble. A long-service National Guardsman, Raymond McLain had been with Pershing on the Mexican border and in World War I. He was among the few National Guard officers who had gone through the army's Command and General Staff College at Fort Leavenworth. McLain went to war with Troy Middleton, leading the artillery in Middleton's division, and had won the Distinguished Service

Cross in the invasion of Sicily. At Anzio McLain's artillery helped smash one of the most threatening German counterattacks. He knew how to get the best from his men. An Oklahoma banker, he kept up with subordinates like account holders. McLain was ready to delegate, but he expected results, and he benefited from the efforts of his immediate predecessor, who, while not quite satisfying General Bradley, had cleared most of the deadwood out of the division.

On August 2, with McLain's division moving out from Avranches, Patton had caught up and marched for a few miles in one of its columns. He'd found poor discipline, apathetic officers, and filthy GIs with low morale. They reached Saint-Hilaire nonetheless, where Frenchmen took to the streets in impromptu celebration. The lead company of Lieutenant Colonel Christopher Clarke's battalion of the 358th Infantry, with some tanks, seized a nearby bridge over the Sélune River before the Germans could demolish it. In a night march Clarke captured another town, too. In common with other American accounts—and contrary to German—participants recall the Luftwaffe buzzing incessantly overhead.

Soldiers who had clawed toward the next hedgerow suddenly found themselves advancing at twenty miles an hour and beating Germans when they encountered them. Colonel George B. Barth, leading the 357th Infantry Regiment, commented, "an undercurrent of excitement seemed to go down the column and you could almost see the men's spirits rise."[31] On August 5 General Wade Haislip, commanding the XV Corps, ordered General McLain to press ahead and take Mayenne, still thirty-seven miles away. While the main body waited for the Big Red One at Saint-Hilaire, McLain created a combat team under his assistant commander for the Mayenne mission. Called Task Force Weaver, the column included Barth's regiment, the 712th Tank Battalion, the 345th Field Artillery Battalion, a company of engineers, and a troop of the division's 90th Reconnaissance Battalion. Brigadier General William G. Weaver had made his mark a few days earlier, personally leading an assault. Now he drove the American spearhead. As Pete Quesada had promised Bradley, a squadron of P-47 fighter-bombers on rotation over the vanguard provided continual air cover.

The tank battalion commander, Lieutenant Colonel George B. Randolph, led the advance guard, overcoming several German roadblocks, breaking up Nazi defenses in the woods outside Mayenne. By afternoon Weaver was deploying to take it, a town of fifty thousand, with a key bridge spanning the Mayenne River. To capture Mayenne, Weaver wanted troops across the river. Not waiting for rubber assault craft to arrive, Colonel Barth found a skiff and a leaky old boat along the shore. GIs knocked down a wooden fence to make oars. Infantrymen paddled quickly across the river and created a bridgehead on the opposite bank. It grew rapidly. At the bridge, battalion commander Major Edward Hamilton, with a few engineers, ran out and ripped the detonating wires off the German demolition charges. By nightfall Mayenne was in American hands.

The next morning General McLain ordered Weaver to divide his group, with a new task force under Colonel Barth. Both formations were to head southeast to capture the city of Le Mans. Task Force Weaver held back to await the arrival of the 1st Infantry Division, which took position at Mayenne. Barth got under way at midafternoon with most of his 357th Infantry, the artillery battalion, and some tanks, reinforced later by another tank company, plus a detachment of the 607th Tank Destroyer Battalion. The men marched for several hours before trucks caught up to them. By nightfall they had advanced a quarter of the way, brushing aside German resistance to reach Sainte-Suzanne. In the darkness a Nazi unit made a well-coordinated attack, trying to pass through Task Force Barth to get beyond the American spearheads. Major Hamilton's battalion, leading the column, had to send GIs back to rescue the main body. Hamilton was credited with preventing Colonel Barth's command group's being overrun. On August 7, as Barth was about to resume his advance, the Germans mounted an armored attack, which was beaten off with some difficulty. On August 8, as they neared Le Mans, a Nazi column of as many as fifty vehicles also approached. Hamilton ambushed them, taking over two hundred prisoners.

While Barth's combat group raced for Le Mans on one road, Task Force Weaver came up another, and Major General Ira T. Wyche's 78th Infantry Division neared the city, too. There was a nasty friendly fire incident in which Wyche's troops shot at Barth's, but the damage was not too great. Le Mans fell quickly. One 90th Division GI wrote home, "If this keeps up, we will be in Russia by Christmas."[32] The division nickname, "Tough 'Ombres," suddenly seemed justified.

To complete Wade Haislip's XV Corps, Major General Lunsford E. Oliver's 5th Armored Division soon arrived, then the Free French 2nd Armored Division. Two more divisions of Lieutenant General Walton H. Walker's XX Corps also exited Normandy to guard the flank. Counting another of Walker's divisions, which Bradley briefly held back, and the Big Red One of Hodges's army, eight American divisions were suddenly maneuvering in the German rear. For the moment they awaited orders.

The swift fall of Le Mans reflected German regrouping. Nothing much had been left in the city except supply dumps the Nazis had been unable to move. Hausser's Seventh Army headquarters withdrew. The general himself left in an armored car with a single aide and his driver. Meanwhile, Field Marshal von Kluge summoned General Kurt von der Chevallerie's First Army headquarters up to the Loire to take over this sector, previously deep in the rear. The handoff did not go smoothly. Still responsible for the French Atlantic coast to the south, the First Army had few forces, and most of those facing Patton were security troops or fragments of units en route to Normandy. The field command, General Adolf Kuntzen's LXXXI Corps, flung its units in piecemeal as they arrived, rather than marshaling the divisions before committing them. It was a desperate attempt to block the U.S. advance. The mobile troops who engaged McLain's Tough 'Ombres were most likely from the 9th Panzer Division. The 708th Infantry Division, a poor-quality unit—and a single formation—was the sole substantial force to confront Haislip. These two divisions plus a security unit were all Kuntzen had. Worse, Hitler ordered the corps assigned to Panzer Group Eberbach for the renewed Avranches attack. No Germans were left to plug the dike that leaked GIs out of Normandy.

SHAPING THE TRAP

The day the Tough 'Ombres fought for Le Mans, August 8, was the moment the Normandy battlefront began to assume its shape for the endgame. One huge consequence of the fall of that city would be that the German command lost the main telephone trunk lines serving the region, which forced them to rely on the radio, handing a tremendous advantage to the ULTRA codebreakers. With the Lost Battalion still under siege, the Germans trying to make something of their putative offensive, and British forces beginning to gain traction, Allied commanders made the decisions that put the Nazis into a bag.

At the height of the Mortain fighting Omar Bradley visited George Patton, approving the Le Mans thrust and explaining his grand scheme. "It occurred to me that night," Brad records, "that Hitler's Mortain offensive had set the stage for an Allied coup de main."[33] Later he told staff that the German attack was the greatest military blunder he could think of, a thousand-year event. The next morning the U.S. army group commander received a forecast of good weather—just what he needed to advance confidently—and spoke to General Hodges, who verified that the Germans remained stalled at Mortain.

Brad turned to his chief of staff. He exclaimed, "We'll shoot the works!"[34]

General Bradley then drove to Third Army headquarters once more, to see Patton and describe this new concept. He would hurl GIs east, then north, in a shorter turning movement that would meet Montgomery's Canadians, punching their way south from Caen, bagging the Germans. Bradley recounts that George Patton seemed reluctant, which he attributes to the more dramatic role given the Third Army in the previous "grand" scheme. Brad countered, fairly enough, that the shorter maneuver would be easier to supply. That cut no ice with Patton, who commented to his diary that he wanted to toss the long pitch but "Bradley won't let me."[35]

To tie up loose ends Bradley now contacted "Shellburst," the new SHAEF forward headquarters, just arrived in Normandy, to discover that Ike was touring the battle area around Coutances. Bradley rushed there, found Eisenhower's Packard automobile on the road, and collared the C in C, getting into his car to outline the plan. Ike was so taken with Bradley's idea, he insisted on driving with Brad to 12th Army Group headquarters to look at the maps. The SHAEF commander then sat while Bradley telephoned General Montgomery and cleared the concept with him. The

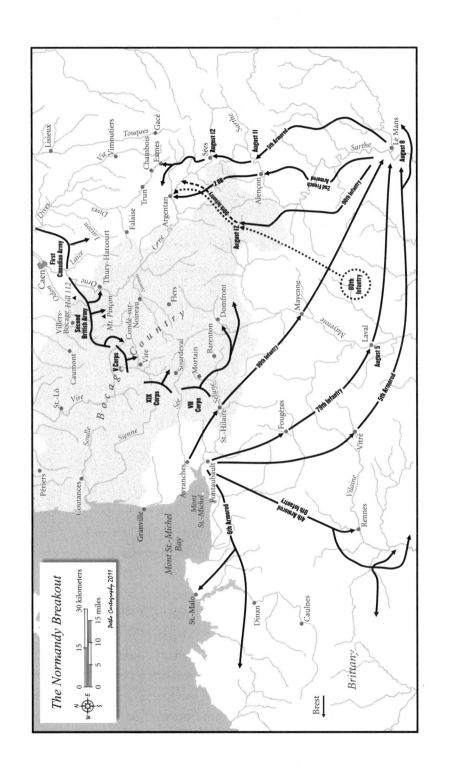

The Normandy Breakout

most sensitive element, which will figure again later, was setting the point at which the American and British Commonwealth forces should meet to close the trap. After dinner Eisenhower went on to Monty's command post to seal the deal. Bradley, meanwhile, entertained visiting U.S. treasury secretary Henry Morgenthau at 12th Army Group.

"This is an opportunity that comes to a commander not more than once in a century," Bradley told Morgenthau. "We're about to destroy an entire hostile army."[36]

Omar Bradley clarified his intentions in a letter of instruction on August 8, directing Patton to advance deep behind the enemy to the Alençon-Sées area, now the major supply hub for the Germans in Normandy, and to be prepared to head north to meet Monty's troops in the vicinity of the town of Argentan, quite close to the long-sought objective of Falaise. General Patton signed his own directive to XV Corps to carry out this scheme. Two staff officers who witnessed the act pronounced it "historic." Patton noted to his diary, "I hope so."[37] On August 9 General Hodges circulated complementary guidance to his First U.S. Army. In a postwar public report implying all this was his idea, General Bernard Montgomery wrote that on the afternoon of the eighth he had signaled that "Twelfth Army Group will attack with the least practicable delay in the direction of Argentan to isolate and destroy the German forces on our front."[38] But source material indicates that this goal, locating a potential junction point between American and Commonwealth forces in the Argentan vicinity, appears in a directive Montgomery issued on August 11—after Bradley's suggestion and Eisenhower's visit. Montgomery's previous orders, five days earlier, were predicated upon a German withdrawal beyond the Seine and set lines of advance toward that river. The origins of the trap seem clear.

The decision taken, events moved quite swiftly. General Wade Haislip used a cavalry group to screen as he forged ahead. At Third Army, Patton pushed forward his newest division, Major General Horace L. McBride's 80th Infantry, to guard his flank. Haislip took a day to assemble, during which the French armor arrived and Patton visited Haislip at Le Mans. Haislip's corps would lead with armor, Oliver's Americans on the outside of the wheel, the French with the interior track. The Tough 'Ombres of the 90th swung back to maintain contact with the First Army. Bradley would extend the U.S. line to build a new front behind the Germans. This operation jumped off late on August 10. There were a few skirmishes with Nazi troops, while enemy artillery that had the range laid down some barrage fire. Traffic congestion posed bigger headaches than the Nazis.

The troops dashed forward. McLain's 'Ombres moved the fastest at the start, gaining over ten miles on the first jump. On the eleventh, Combat Command R of the 5th Armor led the pack, romping twice that far. General Patton went in search of the French 2nd Armored Division, packing a bag of Bronze Stars to award deserving soldiers. But, like Patton himself, the French commander led from the front. Major General Jacques-Philippe Leclerc, soon to achieve fame as the liberator of Paris, spent the whole day with his spearheads. Patton never found him. After spending far too long on the chase, Patton gave up. The Great Cavalryman returned to army headquarters.

On August 12, as if on a Saturday tour, all Haislip's divisions made about twenty miles, despite a major foul-up between Oliver's 5th Armored Division and the French 2nd, which motored one column through an American corridor to get past a forest. The French division actually violated every unit boundary Haislip had set because Leclerc sent columns around both sides of the forest and through the middle, which was his own sector. But in Oliver's zone the French traffic delayed the 5th Armored's tankers six hours, long enough for the Germans to assemble a scratch defense of Sées, his objective. Fortunately, the only troops the Germans had for the purpose were a company of bakers from the 116th Panzer Division.

Eberbach was at the LXXXI Corps command post in the afternoon on August 11 when General Kuntzen reported U.S. armor on the move. The generals could hear American tanks firing, and soon enough machine guns, too. Eberbach ordered a flak regiment at Alençon to hold position, and sent the 116th to Sées. It never arrived. Elements were destroyed by the Americans on August 12, and the farthest the panzers could reach was the vicinity of Argentan. Kuntzen tried to stem Patton's tide with the arriving 9th Panzer, but that division had an effective strength of a single infantry battalion, half a dozen tanks, and an artillery battalion. Its scraps with Patton's spearheads had been costly. When nearby Americans forced Kuntzen to move once more, General von Funck took charge of the 9th Panzer's remnants.

The main line of communications for the German Seventh Army ran from Chartres through Le Mans. When Le Mans fell, the alternate supply route entered the battle area by way of Alençon. Sées lay just a few miles from there—Alençon was directly threatened. German supplies for a fresh offensive were already limited and now promised to become a major headache. Prior to relinquishing command of the Fifth Panzer Army, General Eberbach had to order its supply services to provide fuel and ammunition to Hausser's army, also. As the Germans were forced into a pocket, increasing density made transport much more difficult, even given the reduced distances within their lines. A corps headquarters needed six hours to move less than twenty miles on August 12. Once Alençon and Sées fell, only three roads were left to supply all the German troops in the developing pocket—and they could be used safely only at night.

Meanwhile Jacques Leclerc's 2ème Blindée (2nd DB), to give the division its French name, was accused of poor road discipline and high-handed tactics—and not just by 5th Armored Division tankers. Troops of the 3rd Armored, newly under the command of Brigadier General Maurice Rose and running at the far edge of Hodges's First Army, at Carrouges, also encountered a French detachment coming up. This was actually in the 90th Division sector and on the very junction between the Third and First armies. Arthur Rutshaw, a military police lieutenant, recalled, "I saw that French column hit a crossroads at 40 miles an hour. One vehicle went straight ahead, one to the right, and another to the left.—Nobody was directing traffic!"[39] Americans groused that the French did not bother with camouflage, rushed around at high speed, or bumper to bumper, or simply stopped to confer, blocking traffic all around them. But Leclerc's Frenchmen still made their twenty-mile advance. By the evening of August 12, as the Germans gave up trying to finish off the Lost Battalion at Mortain, the Allied spearheads were close to Argentan, forty miles behind them. The Nazi situation had become critical.

Courtney Hodges had his baptism of fire with the press that day, because SHAEF had decided to reveal George Patton's presence on the battlefront. It became necessary to introduce both the new American army commanders to the folks back home. A reporter asked General Hodges if the German army had decided to commit suicide. Not even Berlin was pretending anymore. The OKW communiqué for that day read, "North of Le Mans the enemy, after having been reinforced, is trying to push through toward the north in order to attack our main fighting lines from the rear."[40] To complete the nightmare, Montgomery's armies were surging, too. Nazi Germany hovered on the brink of a precipice.

CHAPTER 6

THE CAULDRON

Now it had all come down to this. Millions of men and tons of supplies; thousands of aircraft, tanks, and guns on both sides; hundreds of operations, large and small; the opinions and demands of leaders and generals; the sufferings of GIs, Tommies, *Landser*; all of it centered on a little patch of Norman countryside, where Nazi armies struggled to regain their balance while Allied ones hustled to burst from their confinement. The pent-up energy in those Allied armies was irresistible. They were on the march everywhere. Not just on Patton's front, or Bradley's, but on Montgomery's sector, where some of the key events would occur. For Dwight Eisenhower and his colleagues, the horizon had become almost infinite.

German dilemmas were different and rather more complex. Hitler and his OKW minions were the only ones who still dreamed of restoring the front. Field Marshal von Kluge also thought in terms of a front, though he at least recognized there was no going back to the convenient bottling up of the Allies. But von Kluge had a skeleton in his closet—complicity in the July 20 Plot—that threatened to break into the open at any moment. Von Kluge could not dispute any of Hitler's intentions. Other German commanders were intent on salvaging whatever they could. Even SS General Sepp Dietrich, called to Führer Headquarters to be invested with another medal and promoted, promised comrades he would confront Hitler with the realities. That conversation, if it took place, had no discernible impact.

Hitler's eyes remained fixed on a renewed Avranches offensive. German strategy, to the extent one can speak of a strategy under these conditions, would be an artifact of that fantasy.

THE LOST WEEKEND

Allied forces were pressing hard almost everywhere as Field Marshal von Kluge shuffled troops for the second shot at Avranches. Americans of Hodges's army pressured the extended German line from Vire to Sourdeval. Even some of the spearheads of the Mortain attackers had had to recoil. West of the Orne the British of Dempsey's army were inching toward Mont Pinçon. And most important, the Canadian First Army attacked south of Caen on August 7. Executing the Avranches gambit meant pulling the panzer troops out of defensive positions just as Allied forces lunged ahead. None of the German field commanders felt good about that.

The 21st Panzer Division remained on the British sector. Movement orders for the 9th and 12th SS Panzer Divisions were canceled, leaving at least some heavy forces to bolster the front, though Hans Eberbach valued the 9th SS as worth merely half a division, and the 12th SS and 21st Panzer Divisions only as "miserable handfuls of troops."[1] Already on the road, the 10th SS, its strength little more than that of a regiment, would not be recalled. In the German rear the 9th Panzer Division, already enveloped by Patton, had its hands full and would not be available. First its reconnaissance battalion, against orders, had gone off in a futile attempt to stop the Americans. Then the full division had been sent to forestall U.S. spearheads. The 116th Panzer, which was supposed to come off the line and regroup, remained engaged west of Sourdeval, reinforced by 2nd SS Panzer Division. The 2nd Panzer and 1st SS were in the Mortain area with assorted infantry. In short, the very troops intended as the backbone of von Kluge's punch were tied down while GIs erupted into their rear.

General Hans Eberbach grasped this as soon as he saw the Seventh Army map room. The field marshal telephoned the general and asked him to lead the attack, turning over his Fifth Panzer Army to Sepp Dietrich.

Eberbach was briefed on the crisis. No one volunteered to help. He found chaos, and was not relieved by Hausser's people, deeply suspicious of a new formation inserted between Seventh Army and the majority of its corps. Then there was the escalating supply crunch, not to mention the rapidly shifting situation, exacerbated by the repeated necessity for German command posts to move so as to avoid capture. Eberbach was further hampered by his inability to assemble a staff. He demanded and got von Kluge's son as his chief of staff, but had no other help save a few aides— and never more than three radios. "Panzer Group Eberbach" existed only in name. The incoherence of the command was manifest.

It was apparent to General Eberbach that he could not simply renew the Mortain assault. The troops had to redeploy. Eberbach wanted to attack through Saint-Hilaire; the Americans captured it. Supplies would have to be ensured, which meant the defense of Alençon. Patton's men were soon there, too. More troops were necessary. Replacing the armor with infantry, weak as the rifle units were, required shortening the line. That not only helped the Allies, it would consume time—Eberbach estimated five days—in which the enemy would progress farther. "It was unaccountable that OKW could not see this," Eberbach wrote later, offering comparisons to such disasters as Stalingrad, the loss of the Crimea, and the Tunisian campaign.[2] The panzer leader reported his views. Field Marshal von Kluge repeated them to General Jodl at OKW. Hitler was adamant. General Eberbach nevertheless forwarded his negative opinion to Paul Hausser of the Seventh Army, who concurred.

That day, August 10, proved disastrous for the Germans. General Hausser's chief of staff reported the army had discovered U.S. troops pivoting in a direction that threatened to encircle them. But the German command focused on its offensive, unaware source ULTRA had already tipped off the enemy. Eberbach briefed Army Group B chief of staff Hans Speidel that morning, and sat in on a later meeting where his written report was read to Field Marshal von Kluge in his presence. Eberbach felt the operation had no chance unless the 11th Panzer Division came up from southern France—as it stood, the designated units mustered less than the strength of a single combat-ready panzer division. Logistics would have to be guaranteed, ammunition provided for flak units and rocket launchers, and more. He now believed that no push could begin before August 20. Paul Hausser added an appreciation that enumerated additional requirements: reinforcements for the defensive front, protection of the supply bases, stockpiling, neutralization of Allied airpower. Additional infantry was still necessary to hold the restored line. On Hausser's behalf, Freiherr von Gersdorff, newly promoted to major general, put an elaborate plan for withdrawal from Normandy on the table.

At that point the alternatives were squarely posed. The Allied maneuver to pocket the German armies had become evident. There were three good east-west roads within the German perimeter. On August 10 all were available. The loss of Falaise would block one route, Alençon the second, Argentan the last. Without any one of those critical road junctions a German withdrawal became increasingly complicated; without all of them it would become a matter of trudging along country lanes with the hedgerows inhibiting dense traffic.

A withdrawal, if begun on August 10 or 11, might have saved the bulk of the German infantry, even the troops farthest from the escape point. The panzer units, with their greater mobility, would also have survived in vast majority, despite their optimal use in blocking Patton's spearheads. The U.S. forward elements were still weak and the panzers would have incurred losses, but they could have evaded the pocket. A withdrawal begun on August 13 would have exacted a greater toll on the infantry, though more might have escaped if bad weather grounded Allied airpower. Rear guards would be sacrificed, but many of the *Landser*, even so, would be arriving at the exit simultaneously with the Allies. Panzer forces still had brighter prospects, though their losses would increase, primarily because the German armor would have to stand and hold open the escape route. The German days of decision fell on the weekend between August 10 and 13. At later dates an escape became more problematical.

On August 10 Field Marshal von Kluge heard out his subordinates on the new Avranches offensive. Though the Allied advance on Montgomery's sector had halted temporarily, Patton's left hook was becoming painfully evident. That night OB West reported the latest developments. After talking to Eberbach on the telephone, von Kluge spoke again to Jodl during the early morning hours of August 11. There was no possibility of meeting Hitler's timetable for an offensive, the field marshal reported. He wanted to redirect the thrust toward the east, Alençon, in effect a sally toward the Normandy escape point, which von Kluge characterized as a preliminary to a renewed Avranches attack. Exchanges continued through the day, culminating in Hitler's approval of an attack into the flank of Patton's advancing XV Corps, still by Eberbach's panzer group. The German front was finally taken in to free up the requisite forces, with an attempt to defend another minor river, the Noireau, and a new line of resistance in the south beyond Domfront. On August 11 the 116th Panzer Division was ordered immediately to Alençon, while the 1st SS Leibstandarte and 2nd Panzer Divisions regrouped the next night.

The 430 Squadron of the Royal Canadian Air Force had a unique perspective on the situation. A photographic reconnaissance unit, 430 Squadron was one of SHAEF's major sources for concrete tactical intelligence. On August 10 the unit completed eleven missions over the battle area. Seven reported no German movement. The most significant displacements were recorded on the one mission over Mortain, and clearly related to the Nazi siege of Hill 317. The next day there were six successful sorties, and half of them detected nothing. For August 12, six of twelve recce missions found the Germans quiescent. The intelligence indicated the Germans were wasting precious time. On the U.S. side, Colonel Elliot Roosevelt, the president's son, who commanded the 7th Photo Reconnaissance Group, set a record on August 12 when his pilots completed fifty-six successful missions. The planes brought back so many good pictures that photo labs manufactured seventy-one thousand prints, more than 80 percent of them within a day. An important maneuver the Canadians detected on the twelfth was a shift of panzers to oppose GIs at Argentan. The shift was confirmed by ULTRA information on certain Nazi units. But the key discovery by aerial reconnaissance, that evening, was a column of German motor transport leaving the Sées area in the direction of the Seine. This would be the first sign of a withdrawal.

Thus, the Germans, in search of fresh offensive schemes, let pass the days of August 12–13. The Lost Weekend made all the difference. A withdrawal started as the weekend began would in all likelihood have succeeded, and one initiated during the weekend would have been largely successful. But by the end of that weekend the fat was in the fire: U.S. troops threatened Alençon and Sées, and British Commonwealth forces were on the road to Falaise. The only favorable element was that the 116th Panzer Division, helped by GI delays—caused by Free French monopolization of the roads—prevented the fall of Argentan. This setback momentarily obstructed the U.S. maneuver. Divisions following behind, the 2nd Panzer and the Leibstandarte, took up blocking positions. The panzers assembled with such difficulty were shoveled into battle merely to create a frontal crust in this new combat zone. The jaws were closing on a trap for the Germans.

CANNON TO THE LEFT OF THEM

The British sector, more properly that of the 21st Army Group, now belched fire. No longer the immovable obstacle to Commonwealth progress, the Germans, stripped of their panzers, were as hard-pressed as the *Landser*, who struggled vainly to stop the Americans. General Montgomery had ordered action, initially to supplement Cobra. The II Canadian Corps had managed to do that, attacking Bourguébus Ridge in Operation Spring. On July 27 Monty brought together his senior commanders and ordained an all-out effort *west* of the Orne and Hill 112, to capture Mount Pinçon and erupt in the German rear. Eisenhower encouraged this—and demanded speed—viewing an immediate assault by a few divisions as preferable to a later one by half a dozen. Montgomery canceled a planned probe so as to ready Dempsey's army. He advanced the offensive's timing from August 2 to July 30. Monty's directive observed that the Germans were so well entrenched below Caen that results there were not expected. Instead he aimed to gain ground, improve positions, and prevent the transfer of enemy forces—in short, that the Germans be "worried and shot up, and attacked, and raided, whenever and wherever possible."[3]

The offensive from which Montgomery expected results was Operation Bluecoat. That began as scheduled in the Caumont area and ground toward Mont Pinçon. Dempsey struck a sector in which the Nazis had no armor at that moment, but Wilhelm Bittrich's II SS Panzer Corps responded. By August 4, with the Americans breaking out and Bluecoat grinding ahead, Montgomery understood that the German army could possibly be made to disintegrate and began to plan accordingly. Dempsey kept up his attacks. Under Monty's original scheme, the Second Army was to hold a corps of two armored divisions in reserve to be employed in conjunction with the First Canadian Army, newly inserted in the front below Caen. The Canadians would advance on Falaise. But when Montgomery added impetus to Bluecoat, Dempsey committed the British reserve armor at the western end of his line.

Like the Germans scrambling to ready their Operation Liège, the British were slowed by congestion on those Norman roads. Some units got late instructions—the 11th Armored Division, for example, learned its objectives only as it moved. Pip Roberts had to instruct his brigades even as they drove ahead. This time Roberts got the infantry support he had been denied during Goodwood. The 3rd British Infantry Division was in reserve for the offensive, and its 185th Brigade was committed under Roberts a few days into the battle. There was tremendous confusion as the two forces meshed. At one point the brigade's 2nd King's South Lancashire Infantry, atop a hill, was shelled by Nazi tanks from both the front and rear.

The offensive made little headway at first, but it accelerated. On July 31 the British closed in on Vire and the Vire-Caen road—and used the position to ambush assorted German columns. Disarray grew along the boundary between the British and American armies, affecting attacks on Vire. On the other hand, this sector was also where two German formations linked (the LXXIV and II Parachute Corps), and some objectives fell because they were completely undefended—each corps thought the other responsible.

The British general G. C. Bucknall's XXX Corps originally took the vanguard position, with General Richard O'Connor's VIII Corps in support. Bucknall advanced slowly where O'Connor moved out smartly. His soon became the main body. Miles Dempsey fired Bucknall, bringing General Sir Brian Horrocks in to take over XXX Corps, which he led through the rest of the war. On the front there was hard fighting. Backed by the 8th Tank Brigade, the 43rd "Wessex" Division got into some tough fights. While General Horrocks thought them dashing, some in the Sherwood Rangers Yeomanry, an 8th Brigade unit, found the infantry scared. Lieutenant Stuart Hills of the Sherwood Rangers saw the Wessex riflemen work well with his tanks, but felt they liked the armor to put out smoke when they encountered opposition, hose down villages before they entered, and carry the Tommies on their backs.

The general commanding the Germans opposing them, the 326th Infantry Division, was killed while scraping together a counterattack. The Fifth Panzer Army, which had summoned its 21st Panzer Division to Caen, was forced to return it within forty-eight hours. Panzer counterattacks proved ineffective. Bluecoat's most important effect, apart from wearing out German defenses, was to suck almost the last panzers away from Caen. Nearby forests and hills critical to the Germans fell one by one. A battle group of SS armor arrived, followed by Bittrich's full corps. On August 4, Horrocks captured Mont Pinçon, the highest peak in Normandy, from which he surveyed the surrounding countryside. The biggest German counterattack came on August 6 in an attempt to clear the road, with units of the 9th SS and 3rd Parachute Divisions. They failed to restore the situation. But infantry tactics built around the Germans' very effective machine guns slowed the British advance to a crawl. Small bands of *Landser*, often in company strength with two or three tanks and some *Nebelwerfer* rocket launchers, got in between the British spearheads and obstructed them. The terrain afforded possibilities even to weak defenders.

There would be no Bluecoat breakthrough, though General Dempsey at one point considered jumping O'Connor ahead to Flers, which would have cut one of the main lateral roads left to the Germans. Instead, on August 8 Dempsey stood down some of his troops for rest. Lieutenant Hills of the Sherwood Rangers appreciated the move to a splendid orchard near Villers-Bocage. Horrocks visited the battalion the following day, radiating confidence, and using a large map of Normandy to describe the general situation and predict the Nazis were in for a drubbing. Soon after, in a different offensive action, Dempsey's other formation, XII Corps, finally reached the Orne River near Thury-Harcourt. That success offered a fresh line of advance toward Falaise.

CANADIAN GUNS

Meanwhile, General Henry Crerar of the First Canadian Army prepared his great stroke, Operation Totalize, which Montgomery had billed as a Goodwood-size attack. Starting with another grand-slam strategic bombing to paralyze the Nazis, to be followed by a full-blooded offensive on Falaise, Totalize had begun as a private project. Crerar wanted to have a plan ready, though Monty had not ordered this offensive. As of the evening of July 31 Montgomery anticipated no major Canadian operation for at least a week. The next day he still spoke to Crerar in terms of "prods." Verbally on August 3, and in writing on the fourth, Montgomery converted the hypothetical Canadian plan into a reality. Dempsey's Bluecoat had made an offensive with three or four armored divisions impossible—so this would not truly be a "Goodwood-size attack"—but it was much more than a prod. Only Crerar's own tank units, the 4th Canadian and 1st Polish Armored Divisions, were available. Montgomery hoped the Canadian attack would take place quickly, yet difficulties completing the alignment of forces delayed it until August 7. Guy Simonds, the tactical commander, drew on his experience in Operation Spring to plan the assault. He wanted to ensure the tank units would team with infantry as combined arms groups. On the Bluecoat front the British had had to resort to trial and error to come to the same sort of combined arms tactics that General Simonds had prescribed.

For their part the Germans could no longer offer a Goodwood-size defense. The Hitler Youth of the 12th SS would be the only mobile formation in the Canadian zone when Totalize struck. Previously, in addition to the 21st in reserve, there had been two panzer divisions on Bourguébus Ridge. But the 21st Panzer departed to fight Dempsey, and the Leibstandarte would leave for the Mortain attack, leaving only the Hitlerjugend below Caen. Sepp Dietrich put the fresh 89th Infantry Division on Bourguébus, reconstituting the 12th SS as a small reserve. During his visit the OKW's Warlimont had promised some Waffen-SS brigades from Denmark. Both Dietrich and Hans Eberbach objected that would take too long. Dietrich foresaw the inevitable: If the panzers left Caen the Allies would break through. His protests had no effect. The Leibstandarte began to shift out of the battle line during the night of August 4–5. That left only the 89th Infantry, a single rookie rifle unit in a sector formerly held by two panzer divisions.

General Crerar met with senior air commanders to arrange the carpet bombing on the same day Montgomery promulgated his instructions. Simonds issued formal orders at noon, August 5. For the Canadians and the 1st Polish Armored Division the major headache was, again, road congestion. There were also physical and mechanical difficulties modifying armored vehicles to carry infantry, which Simonds wanted for his combined arms groups. The week of training that Simonds counted on shrank to just one day. Monty ordered changes, putting Falaise in the British zone, less than twenty-four hours before the attack. The Canadians could capture the town but must then hand it over. Simonds revised the Totalize plans to provide that the armor should move up to the line of departure and enter the battle, rather than be held for a second phase.

General Simonds began the attack in the middle of the night, taking a page from the German playbook, something the British and Americans rarely dared to do. The initial bombing was set for eleven p.m., just half an hour ahead of the kickoff. Some 1,020 aircraft dropped 3,462 tons of bombs. The artillery, rather than firing a preparatory bombardment, engaged only with the advance under way, putting down a rolling barrage ahead of the attackers. In the lead the 2nd Canadian and British 51st "Highland" Divisions encountered a new problem: Dust raised by the bombing and vehicles, plus ground mist, cut visibility so much that units lost their way. Nevertheless, initial objectives were secured.

Simonds unleashed his armor just before two p.m., preceded by another aerial bombardment. This onslaught involved 678 bombers, which loosed 1,488 tons of munitions. Much as had happened with the Americans at Cobra, some aircraft sent to slam the Germans dropped their loads on friendly troops instead. The erroneous bombing mostly struck Vaucelles. The Polish and 3rd Canadian Divisions were hit hard moving through this Caen suburb, suffering several hundred casualties, including Canadian commander Rod Keller, wounded so badly he was evacuated. But bombs did nothing to retard Simonds's spearheads, which advanced steadily, unlike Goodwood, where British troops were mired in the moonscape the strike created.

More problematic would be German initiative. The Nazi mobile reserve was the fanatical Hitlerjugend. Until the Canadian attack the 12th SS had been preoccupied with the British, who had forced the Orne near Thury-Harcourt in the German rear. There were several places infantry could ford that river, but its banks were so steep the tanks and heavy weapons could only cross once new bridges were built. Dempsey had put several battalions of the 59th Division over the Orne in the XII Corps thrust. They completed a bridge and got a few tanks across. Captain David Jamieson of the Royal Norfolk Regiment won the Victoria Cross defending against fierce counterattacks, which were broken up by British artillery fire. Kurt "Panzer" Meyer of the Hitlerjugend sent one of his two battle groups to cooperate with infantry and reduce the bridgehead before the threat became overwhelming. Captain Michael Wittmann's Tiger tanks joined them. The Germans managed to contain the British attack.

That night the Canadian offensive began. Panzer Meyer argues that the Canadians lacked a dynamic tank commander in the style of a Rommel or a Patton, and that their units performed by rote, but this was characteristic of the British, too, and really simply a contrast to the initiative Germans often displayed, starting with Meyer himself. Returning from Thury-Harcourt, the SS officer immediately sensed the disruption on the main front. He succeeded in getting rescinded the orders that would have sent the 12th SS off for the renewed Avranches offensive. He also recalled his troops near Thury-Harcourt.

Though Meyer's detachment on the Orne was a dozen miles away, the bulk of his tank strength resided in the battle group behind the sector which the Canadians struck. The 12th SS had been augmented by a Panther battalion of the 1st SS Panzer Division, as well as most of the Tigers of the 101st Heavy Tank Battalion. In all Meyer had something like eighty tanks and assault guns, including twenty Tigers.[4] German infantry was raw but fresh, having had only a couple of days to settle in, and the 89th Division was one of their smaller formations.

Panzer Meyer heard the rumbling of the Allied bombers and saw the horizon lit by flashes. He rushed forward with a few dispatch riders. Meyer quickly realized the defenses had collapsed. He knew that unless the Canadians were blocked they could simply roll on into Falaise. Panzer

Meyer encountered stragglers and shattered remnants of fleeing units. He rallied a few men and summoned Battle Group Wuensche, his strongest unit. Meyer had learned a lot about Allied airpower since D-Day. Now he ordered the troops to hug the Canadians, thinking they could avoid Allied air by attacking. When more bombers came at noontime, Meyer proved correct. Meanwhile, a local commander posted a detachment of assault guns at a key point. There it ambushed a Canadian tank regiment, virtually wiping it out. And some 89th Division *Landser* also fought on, retarding the Allied second echelon.

In this battle the Germans lost their tank ace Michael Wittmann, who took eight Tigers to support the German blocking position at Cintheaux and participated in the hasty attack that so disrupted the Allies. Wittmann, who had scored 130 tank kills in this war, perished in his Tiger, destroyed by flanking shots from Fireflys, probably of the British Sherbrooke Fusiliers, 33rd Armored Brigade, paired with the 51st Highlanders. Several other Tigers fell victim, too. The loss of Wittmann affected German morale. Cintheaux fell to Major General George Kitching's 4th Canadian Armored Division late that afternoon.

Meanwhile, Simonds's assault troops suffered setbacks. The spearheads of Major General Stanislaw Maczek's 1st Polish Armored Division reported Tigers not very far east of Cintheaux and stopped to regroup. General Kitching also proved extremely cautious. One Canadian combat group became disoriented and wandered more than a mile east of its objective, Hill 195. They were nearly destroyed. Many soldiers fell and forty-seven tanks were wrecked. The real Hill 195 was captured by the Argyll and Sutherland Highlanders of Canada on August 9, and reinforced the next morning by the 22nd Armored Regiment. The Germans realized Hill 195 was a crucial position. It overlooked the town of Potigny, and its loss would open the road to Falaise. They made furious counterattacks using, among other weapons, remote-controlled "Goliath" explosive "tanks," actually a sort of robot bomb on tracks. Assisted by the arrival of the new 85th Infantry Division, the Germans fought the Canadians to a standstill. After his frustrating lack of progress, on August 10 General Simonds called a halt.

General Montgomery's last-minute assignment of the Falaise objective to his British forces raises the whole issue of Canadian performance in World War II. In 1914–1918 the Canadians had been considered shock troops. It is puzzling that now such a Commonwealth force should have been looked at askance, including by some Canadians. Bernard Law Montgomery, to judge from his decisions, agreed with that view. Since the war the Canadians have gotten bad press, starting with their own official historian, Charles P. Stacey. The British official history is standoffish toward their Commonwealth comrades, while such popular historians as Max Hastings, Anthony Beevor, and Robin Neillands are occasionally even dismissive. More sophisticated analysts like John English and Russell Hart have examined Canadian training, officer preparation, staff work, and tactics to argue the Canadians were ill-fitted for modern warfare. Typically Guy Simonds is rated as the only really capable general, while figures such as Crerar, Keller, and Kitching are presented as useless or worse.

Very recently a fresh group of investigators, led most prominently by Terry Copp, have begun to reframe the conventional wisdom on the Canadians in World War II. These historians include Marc Milner and Brian A. Reid, and their views furnish an important corrective. On the evidence of Totalize—and what will shortly be seen of Operation Tractable—the newer perspective seems more suitable. It was the Canadians of Keller's 3rd Division who made the deepest advance on D-Day—and by the following day had attained almost all their D-Day objectives. They were the only ones in Montgomery's army to do so. Then for several days, as Milner points out, the Canadians fended off the strongest panzer attacks the Hitlerjugend could throw at them. As for planning, the Canadians had had a cogent vision of that role and prepared for it quite capably. Earlier in the war Canadian troops had performed creditably in Italy and at Dieppe. In the latter case, the 1942 landing on the French coast that had gone down in flames, the Canadians had certainly been defeated, but no British unit would have done better. The reasons for failure were many and the actual fighting not among them.

Operation Totalize showed the Canadians' real quality. In Goodwood the British had blundered into German antitank defenses on Bourguébus Ridge, which intelligence had informed them of and which they ignored. With the Allied intelligence advantage there was no excuse for that. In Totalize the Canadians went in deliberately, eyes open. Simonds instructed his tank troops to engage only on the move. Tactically, some criticize the Canadians for putting too little weight in the tips of their spears, but this was a wider problem in the British army, not merely the Canadian one, exemplified by O'Connor's employment of his armor in Goodwood. As Brian Reid points out, Crerar's army in Totalize actually captured Bourguébus Ridge—which Dempsey had failed to do—and advanced deeper into the German defenses than had any British operation so far in the campaign. At the time that achievement was hailed, despite how it may have been regarded after the war. Yes, the Canadians fell short of their ultimate objective, Falaise, but so had the British—in numerous attempts. To the objection that the Germans were weaker when Crerar and Simonds launched Totalize, the answer is that the assault forces were weaker, too, by a third or more. One can argue the relative merits of generals like Henry Crerar or Guy Simonds, but the fact remains that the Canadians—with the Poles beside them—came close to shutting the trap on the Germans. In some ways Normandy was Canada's finest hour. The close race to shut the Nazis in a pocket was on, and it would be the Canadians and Poles who ran it.

Meanwhile, Guy Simonds prepared a fresh effort he code-named Tractable. The historian Alexander McKee reports the troops dubbed this gambit a "mad charge,"[5] and it happened despite the fact that by now Montgomery had reconfirmed his instructions relegating the First Canadian Army to the more peripheral role of passing eastward of Falaise to trap fleeing Nazis, moving on a town called Trun. Dempsey's British were to be accorded the glory of capturing Falaise. Tractable began the night of August 13–14 with another big air strike—811 bombers, 77 of which again dropped their loads on Canadian and Polish troops. This time 3,472 tons of bombs pounded the front. There were even more Allied bombing casualties than in Totalize. Still, both Canadian and Polish troops plowed ahead on schedule. Crerar's army accomplished a difficult opposed crossing of the Laizon River. Maczek's Polish armor cleared Potigny and exploited east and south toward Trun. The lay of the land and the need to get past German obstacles forced Canadian troops into the zone assigned to Dempsey. With Dempsey's slower progress, on August 14 Monty bowed to the inevitable and instructed Crerar to take Falaise after all.

The object on all sides of so many hopes, dreams, and fears, Falaise was a town of almost ten thousand souls. Its name traced to the Norman word for "rock," the feature on which a château was built that became the birthplace of William the Conqueror. The town lay in ruins from bombing a couple of nights earlier, and it was defended by Hitlerjugend troopers. A German antitank gun barred entrance to the Canadians who first arrived, men of Major General Charles Foulkes's 2nd Division. A battalion commander ran hundreds of yards up from the rear of his column to knock the gun out. Troops began moving. Before midnight Canadians were in the square, assailed from all sides. Lieutenant Colonel Freddie Clift of the South Saskatchewan Regiment ordered his men to mount up and make a dash for the other end of town. Falaise thus fell early on August 16. Canadians behind Clift's battalion mopped up the last German resistance. A small band of Nazis, about fifty men with an assault gun, never got the order to leave and holed up in the high school, where they held on another day. But Foulkes's Canadians were exhausted. Colonel Clift rejected instructions to continue the advance. His men, then the rest of the division, bedded down.

By then the tanks of Kitching's 4th Division were on the verge of capturing Trun, and Polish armored spearheads were beyond there to the southeast. In fact, the Poles were just a few miles away from the GIs of the U.S. Army. Once they linked up, the Germans in Normandy would be hard trapped. The Wehrmacht's fate hung by a thread.

CANNON TO THE RIGHT OF THEM

Effecting a junction between Canadian and American armies proved a matter of some delicacy. There were many aspects to this, not least a fateful Allied command decision. The key day was August 13. At that moment

Crerar's Canadians and Poles were still six miles north of Falaise, while Wade Haislip's U.S. XV Corps ranged from Argentan to Alençon. A gap of nineteen miles separated Haislip and Crerar. More important, they were divided by the army group boundary Montgomery had set, limiting U.S. troops to the area south of Carrouges and Sées. GIs around Argentan were already across that boundary. Americans thought they had the answer for the critical question of who should close that gap. Officers with Bradley felt the Canadians were advancing with all the speed of molasses. George Patton maintained that Haislip's corps could easily punch through. The decision rendered would be controversial the instant it was made.

The immediate catalyst came with Wade Haislip's dispatch of the evening of August 12, where he reported his troops about to take their last assigned objective, requesting new instructions. During the predawn hours Patton ordered Haislip to complete the capture of Argentan, then advance cautiously toward Falaise until he made contact with Crerar's army.

Telephone conversations between Patton and Bradley ensued, then meetings, then later that day General Montgomery convened the Allied senior commanders. Patton famously quipped, "We've got elements in Argentan. Let me go on to Falaise and we'll drive the British into the sea for another Dunkirk."[6] General Bradley knocked down that idea, hard. He immediately ordered Patton to hold Haislip's corps back. Later Bradley confirmed that instruction.

The choice here lies at the heart of controversy about Normandy. Observers concur that Omar Bradley insisted the Americans stand down. After the war he agreed, denying the responsibility of anyone else, including Montgomery. Bradley's reasoning was that the Germans were reinforcing the neck of the gap and beginning their withdrawal. "Already," he wrote in 1951, "the vanguard of panzers and SS troops were sluicing back through [the gap] toward the Seine."[7] Bradley amplified this recitation in the 1980s, now referring to Source ULTRA, commenting that General Sibert's intelligence briefing the morning of August 13 patched together various bits of data—no specific dispatches impressed Bradley— but enough to convey a sense that on Hitler's orders or in spite of them the

Germans "were already carrying out a substantial withdrawal to the east."[8] Inside the developing pocket, he notes, the Nazis were in chaos. It was no longer possible to define their order of battle. They might even stampede.

Bradley's version smacks of after-the-battle judgment. Aerial reconnaissance data has already been cited. No "sluicing" was in progress. Far from a stampede, ULTRA confirmed the German creation of a new defensive crust, with specific data on the destination of the 116th Panzer Division. Source ULTRA also noted a concentration of Luftwaffe effort to counter Patton, plus orders to funnel every tank or assault gun reaching Normandy, no matter to whom consigned, to the forces opposing Montgomery. These things suggest purposeful activity, not panic. Perhaps unknown at the time—but equally significant—the Germans were ramping up both replacement activity and reinforcements. More than 10,000 replacements joined units between August 6 and 13, nearly double the previous week, and almost that many were en route. The Germans also committed half a dozen fresh divisions, most from the Pas de Calais. Their estimated strength on August 13—378,000 troops—represents a peak for the entire campaign. Von Kluge's war diary would soon be captured. The entry for August 12 reads that "movements of withdrawal"—referring to the constitution of a new front against Patton—"were carried out according to plan." No panic there, either. Only two days later does the OB West war diary record that "the necessity to withdraw the Army in order to prevent a break-through of the enemy into the rear of our defensive front arises."[9] The Germans remained solidly within their operational envelope.

Omar Bradley raises other points that have more substance. He did not doubt Patton's ability to close the pocket, he writes, but he worried about keeping the door shut, and about the Hitler–von Kluge counteroffensive, now aimed at the flank of Haislip's corps. That force was in an exposed position. Bradley's secret knowledge of the German offensive plan— gained through Source ULTRA—influenced his impressions. Here is an instance where the German intention to attack had been sent on the radio, and the changes to the plan that redirected it and ultimately led to the scheme being overtaken by events were largely made face-to-face or on the telephone. *To the extent that Bradley's fear flowed from ULTRA information, that represents a negative impact of the Allied intelligence advantage.*

In the event, Bradley ordered Hodges and Patton each to put a corps in readiness to extend the line, connecting the spearhead XV Corps with the main U.S. force and protecting its inner flank. Bradley also fretted that putting Haislip across the army group boundary might subject GIs to Allied aircraft, now roaming freely over the German pocket; and that Allied ground forces could mistakenly shoot at each other. These were real concerns, but did they justify passing up a thousand-year opportunity?

Finally, Bradley notes that Falaise had long been a British objective and "a matter of immense prestige" to them; its seizure by the U.S. Army "would be an arrogant slap in the face."[10] Unspoken in that is another consideration: Given Montgomery's known sensitivity, and that general's desire to retain the overall command, barreling across the group boundary meant directly challenging Monty's residual authority as "coordinator" of the forces.

Raising the matter of the British brings the discussion to Bernard Montgomery. Issues here cut both ways. George Patton believed that the army group boundary, which Monty had set on August 11, was intended to reserve the glory for his Commonwealth troops. But Miles Dempsey's notes of the luncheon and command conference on August 13 reveal that Monty did not consider his boundary impermeable—he ordered Crerar to ensure troops paid attention to the proper recognition signals for meeting the Americans. Thus, Montgomery anticipated a U.S. "short hook" even if he did not exactly encourage it. Nevertheless, there is some truth to Patton's view. By August 10 Montgomery, aware Crerar had stalled above Falaise, had told Dempsey to shift weight from Bluecoat to take Falaise with the British XII Corps. The practical effect was that British troops *swept* the pocket, driving the Germans ahead of them—toward the exit. Much of Bradley's distress at Montgomery flowed from this. Monty's instructions to Crerar to pivot farther east through Trun actually lengthened the Commonwealth pincer of the envelopment and delayed its achievement. That was deliberate. The fact that XII Corps itself proved slow and that it was the Canadians who actually liberated Falaise does not change the effect of Montgomery's decision: to retard closure of the pocket while pushing Nazis out of it.

Bradley seems to have thought Montgomery's error lay in reposing too much trust in the untried Canadians and Poles, but if anything Monty's attitude toward them was the opposite, as his command decisions demonstrate. Yet, if Montgomery did doubt the Canadians, why did he not specifically ask the Americans to go the last few miles? Again Montgomery appears to have relied upon British troops as against American ones, this time with the Canadian-Polish longer hook as insurance. Since Montgomery revised this scheme *again,* on August 14, once more making Crerar's Canadians the main strike force, at that point it became incumbent on him to invite a U.S. advance, which he still did not do. Inaction wasted vital time.

General Bradley records his "shattering disappointment" with the meeting of August 13, a golden opportunity truly lost, noting that Eisenhower, also present, shared his misgivings. Not only did Bradley fear the longer hook would endanger the projected encirclement, but Montgomery spent much of that afternoon unveiling a plan for operations *after* Normandy, advocating that he be given all of SHAEF's logistics resources for a "rush right on into Berlin."[11] This moment, while the Normandy battle still raged, became the initial go-round of the strategic debate over a broad advance versus a narrow thrust that consumed the Allies for months afterward, as well as the first enunciation of the dream that the war could be ended in 1944 with the capture of Berlin by the western Allies. In the Normandy battle that vision was a distraction. Yet Monty acted in service of it. At the height of the encirclement he reassigned the 7th Armored Division from Dempsey to Crerar. But the Desert Rats were not to reinforce Crerar's siege ring, they were to exploit past the battle zone toward the Seine.

An odd aspect in all of this is the way the generals switched roles. None were consistent. Eisenhower had backed the short hook as soon as he heard of it and continued to do so. But now he sided with Montgomery on the inviolability of the army group boundary, which went against the principle of aggressive offensive action. Eisenhower also *refrained* from intervening when Bradley issued his stop order. This accorded with Ike's command method of not interfering with subordinates, but it prevented the hook— his Cannae—from being realized. Montgomery made opportunity shifts between favoring British or Canadian wings of his forces, but stuck to his general stance of according primacy to Commonwealth forces. When the

Americans stopped he could have asked them to resume the advance. He did not. Since GIs were already slightly across the group boundary, Monty was not protecting it by forgoing such a request. The U.S. official history, in fact, uses Monty's inaction at this point to help explain what Bradley did. Finally, in an August 16 conversation, Montgomery pushed Bradley to jump ahead after all. But in doing so he never reset the group boundary separating the Anglo-American forces.

Omar Bradley, on the other hand, initially espoused a grand encircle-ment, then conceived the short hook at the time of Mortain, yet now, on the verge of accomplishing that, stopped his troops. Instead of hav-ing XV Corps close the pocket, he would send Haislip on a longer run toward Dreux, nearer the Seine, and the corps could cross that great river. This was a sort of deeper hook—but a reversion to the grand plan. Brad left the 90th Division and the French 2nd DB in place, and they would be joined by a green unit, the 80th Infantry Division. That choice was made early—Patton ordered Haislip on August 14 to prepare for this, and the latter advanced the next day. Bradley also did not do all he could to close the trap. Even with the new maneuver, had Bradley turned Haislip northwestward from Dreux, this could have interposed a block between the Nazis and the Seine at a place where there was no danger of colliding with Canadians or Poles. Here again Bradley resisted violating the group boundary. He eventually decided to do something like that, but not until the very last days of the battle, too late to affect it.

As for the short hook itself, the British advance through the pocket gradually disengaged Courtney Hodges's First U.S. Army. By August 18 Bradley's daily situation map would show only four American divisions still engaged. It would have been easy for him to leapfrog U.S. corps along the southern edge of the Falaise Pocket to complete the seal beyond Argentan—and indeed he did come to that in part, redeploying General Leonard T. Gerow's V Corps headquarters to replace Haislip's XV, taking over from a provisional corps Patton set up that existed for only about forty-eight hours. This freed the Third Army. It also occasioned a monumental screwup. For a full night—a miserable, rainy one—Gerow drove around behind U.S. lines trying to locate his new command. During those hours, the general would complain, the V Corps consisted of himself and ten staff officers with their handful of vehicles. Once Gerow reached Alençon and set up his advanced command post at a hotel bar, he had trouble asserting control. Patton's chief of staff, Major General Hugh Gaffey, in charge of the provisional corps, claimed to command the same troops. Worse, Gaffey had had orders to advance while Gerow awaited instructions. Straightening out the muddle consumed the whole day, during which the two generals argued over who was in charge while their divisions stood immobile.

Bradley spent much of that afternoon closeted with Patton and Courtney Hodges ironing out their roles, no doubt partly sparked by the fracas between Generals Gerow and Gaffey. Afterward Brad issued a fresh directive that explicitly put the divisions at Argentan and to the east under Hodges and with Gerow. Consonant with the Bradley-Montgomery exchange of August 16, the instruction then gave First Army this specific objective: "Seize the area Chambois-Trun and continue the advance north until contact is gained with the British. Complete the destruction of the Germans caught in the pocket."[12] Had that goal been set on August 12—apparently the weekend had been lost on both sides—few Germans would have escaped.

At the First Army, Hodges's XIX Corps was also drawn into the wholesale exchange of units and missions Bradley effected. Led by General Charles H. Corlett, the corps annexed Gerow's former troops, added the 2nd Armored Division, and took Lightning Joe Collins's place in line. Many of Corlett's divisions, in turn, were left alone for a time, then sent to Brittany. Was this the moment to take crucial pieces off the board? Whatever may have been the merits of bringing back the fresh but blooded U.S. troops at Brest, that rotation came at a critical moment—and there was no way Troy Middleton's divisions, leaving Brittany, could affect the outcome. The 4th Armored Division is a case in point. General Wood's GIs actually reached a position behind what became the XIX Corps sector. They sat around Carrouges for a week, fixing worn-out equipment. On August 18 Corlett had only one division fighting Germans.

Then there was Collins's brilliant VII Corps. Bradley had previously regarded Jayhawk GIs as his best troops, and saw inserting them into the ring of steel being built around the Nazis as a powerful supplement to

Haislip's initial maneuver. Lightning Joe advanced boldly on August 13 and reached his last designated objectives three days later. Bradley and Hodges may have agreed that Jayhawk was worn out by Cobra and its exploitation, but Brad now permitted Hodges to leave VII Corps underemployed. Collins remained largely out of contact. Like the 4th Armored Division, GIs of the Big Red One spent a week resting and replenishing.

The postwar final report on Hodges's operations contains this comment for August 17: "Except on the extreme right, the First U.S. Army had finished its task and was now facing the Anglo-American boundary. It was time for a new plan and for readjustments."[13]

For his part Patton had plumped for the grand encirclement. Bradley had had to argue him around to the short hook. Now, in accusing Monty of responsibility for the stop order (which precluded Patton's sealing the trap), he clearly favored the short hook he had resisted. On Haislip's arrival in the Argentan area, Patton had ordered XV Corps to close the gap cautiously, which order he had renewed with Hugh Gaffey. But *then* he had gone along with the scheme to send Haislip on a farther advance—and had failed to instruct Gerow to seal the gap himself—a reversion to the grand scheme. Thus, *every* senior Allied general involved with the Falaise decisions wavered in some aspect. If there is blame for what happened, it can be shared widely.

Bradley's assignment of the Falaise Pocket mission to Hodges put Patton back in his cavalry role, on the high road as charging knight. He subsequently focused on pushing spearheads toward Paris and the Seine, and through the Paris-Orléans gap. Haislip's corps reached Dreux on August 17. The Third Army's XX Corps captured Chartres on the sixteenth, while Patton's XII Corps took Orléans the same day. No longer had SHAEF any need of an airdrop in the Paris-Orléans gap. Paratroop commander Matthew Ridgway attended some of Bradley's command conferences, but in vain. Instead, American troops now stood barely forty miles from Paris itself.

Meanwhile, Hodges's staff had already noted, on August 15, "stronger indications, now more than before, that the Boche have successfully extricated, and are extricating, far more of their force than was thought possible."[14] Bradley had the same information and made his decisions in the light of it. This evidence suggests that Omar Bradley had already discounted the Falaise battle as a trap. At SHAEF headquarters on August 17, Eisenhower told press aide Harry Butcher of his chagrin that the haul of prisoners from the pocket would be less than he had hoped. The following day the commander in chief put the same thought in a cable to General George C. Marshall. Ike, too, had begun to discount the outcome.

Despite everything, Allied strategy tightened the grip on the Germans, who faced cannon aimed at them from every direction. Bradley had swung his army group around, even if not enough. The shift that put Hodges in control of the whole southern face of the pocket had at least concentrated command with a single army. Orders to seal the pocket came late, but now they were on the books. The Nazis, meanwhile, remained inside the bag. Even before U.S. armies linked up with Montgomery's, the Germans were trapped. What Omar Bradley had thought a thousand-year chance had come to pass.

DESPERATE MEASURES

Richard Rohmer, a reconnaissance pilot with the 430 Squadron, had a ringside seat. "Strapped in our Mustangs flying at low level over the pocket," Rohmer would recall, "we would watch the Germans gather, form columns of vehicles in broad daylight and drive 'on towards the Seine ferries.'"[15] Rohmer, who retired as a major general in the Canadian air force, forever blamed George Patton for failing to seal the Falaise Pocket. But the Allies were not the only actors in this drama. Hitler's fixation with Avranches actually led to the beginnings of withdrawal, though for quite different reasons: regrouping the remaining panzers for his offensive. This is what Rohmer and fellow pilots had seen beginning on August 12, when the Germans abandoned the siege of Mortain. Once begun, the Normandy pullback became difficult to halt and easily transformed into a full-scale retreat. The threat along the southern face of the developing pocket demanded more of the mobile troops the Nazis wanted at its nose for the attack.

On the morning of August 13, Sepp Dietrich, temporarily leading the Fifth Panzer Army, for the first time broached the need for a withdrawal, in a telephone conversation with Hans Speidel at Army Group B. The next day the OB West war diary joins in commenting on the necessity of getting out of Normandy. Führer Headquarters agreed to retraction of the Mortain salient. On the fourteenth also, Field Marshal von Kluge held a meeting with the newly appointed commandant of Paris, General Dietrich von Choltitz, whose purpose was to discuss how to defend the city. Von Kluge's staff also pressed him to order withdrawals from southern France. At that very moment Allied invasion convoys were nearing the French Mediterranean coast for the true second invasion, Operation Anvil, on August 15.

This was a fateful day for the Nazis. OB West chief of staff General Günther Blumentritt warned OKW that the moment, in effect, was five minutes before midnight. The Germans had to shorten the line again to extend their southern front, and on the fifteenth they abandoned Flers and, with it, any chance of defending the Noireau River line. Field Marshal von Kluge began the day talking to Sepp Dietrich, listening to warnings that the Hitlerjugend were spent and Falaise about to fall. Dietrich begged von Kluge to return him the 21st Panzer Division—another formation lost to the hoped-for counteroffensive—though even with that expectations were slim that the Fifth Panzer Army could stem the tide. Von Kluge then motored to Nécy, only four miles from Falaise, to see Generals Hausser and Eberbach. He was stuck in traffic for hours until the airplanes hit. Kluge filed his last radio report at nine thirty a.m. Not far from Falaise the jabos shot up the field marshal's Horch car and accompanying radio van. Four men died. Von Kluge, his son, and an aide took cover, crouching for hours. After dark he became lost.

One of those von Kluge sought was Hans Eberbach, presently visiting the 116th Panzer Division. There Eberbach got the message to meet the field marshal at Nécy. He went, then waited several hours, but Kluge never showed. Others had similar experiences. At OB West, frantic that U.S. troops were closing in on nearby Chartres, requiring new decisions about the defense of Paris, there were repeated appeals for von Kluge's input. Late that day OB West notified OKW that the field marshal had gone missing. General Jodl burned up the telephone wires demanding news.

Blumentritt had no information. Hans Speidel at Army Group B knew no more than Jodl. Eberbach returned to his own headquarters that evening and received a fresh inquiry from Army Group B, followed by the identical text from Führer Headquarters. He reported complete ignorance. OKW wanted Eberbach to find von Kluge.

Hitler became hysterical, consumed with suspicion that von Kluge had held a secret meeting with the American general Patton, intending to surrender the German army in the West.[16] A few days earlier the führer had become convinced of von Kluge's foreknowledge of the July 20 Plot, and the afternoon before he had met privately on this subject with Heinrich Himmler. Even if Kluge had not participated, the field marshal had done nothing to stop the plot. At Hitler's audience that day one of his aides hinted darkly that the circle of guilt was wider than believed. Not awaiting explanations, at seven thirty p.m., Hitler put Paul Hausser in temporary charge of Army Group B. Next he summoned Field Marshal Walter Model, famous as the "Führer's Fireman," from the Eastern Front, and sent him to take up the reins in the West.

Hitler would credit anything. For hours there was no word on von Kluge's whereabouts. But the führer's fears were apparently not entirely misplaced. Rudolf von Gersdorff, the Seventh Army chief of staff, who had fought under von Kluge on the Eastern Front, had in fact tried to convince him to open a channel to Omar Bradley. Acting very much like a broken man, Field Marshal von Kluge had rejected all such entreaties. He resigned himself to what might happen and soldiered on. Ironically, von Kluge's absence had had nothing to do with any private surrender to the Allies. The mystery resolved itself: Near midnight the field marshal strode into Eberbach's command post. Explanations were sent but none satisfied the führer. Later Model arrived in Paris with instructions to take over OB West and the army group. Only in that written order, on August 17, did von Kluge learn he had been fired.

The day before, von Kluge's last in command, his two a.m. report to OKW finally came to the proposition that the troops were just too weak for a successful offensive. Now, forty-eight hours after OB West foresaw this necessity, von Kluge recommended withdrawal from Normandy—adding that hesitation was fraught with unforeseeable consequences. He and Jodl exchanged telephone calls into the afternoon. Shortly after one p.m. Army Group B staff chief Speidel informed the field marshal, based on different conversations with OKW, that a führer directive was expected. Field Marshal von Kluge issued the OB West withdrawal order at 2:39 p.m. Hitler's actual instructions arrived only a couple of hours later. The die had been cast.

Once again Source ULTRA put the Allies in the know. Codebreakers recall the lengthy dispatch with the retreat order. It was a ten-part message. Though only six sections were intercepted at first, German intentions seemed clear enough. Susan Wenham went on duty at Bletchley's Hut 6 that evening and remembers, "It was the most exciting night I had."[17] During her watch the listening posts intercepted a German retransmission of the full message, and it was clear from comparison that this was the same text but included the missing parts. The Germans had violated their own rule against sending identical messages. Wenham and her colleagues put all other work out of the way, alerted Hut 3 to ready its analysis, and recovered the whole text by morning. Eisenhower and his cohorts would not be taken by surprise. If the Germans escaped the Normandy trap it would not be due to any Allied intelligence failure.

The OB West war diary for August 16 records, "the withdrawal of the front line . . . was carried out generally according to plan." American inaction shows in the observation that "at the right and central sector no essential activities [occurred] except enemy artillery harassing fire." Yet the Anglo-American aims were plain: "The intention of the enemy to cut off the bulge of the army by attacking from the south and the north is by now clearly evident."[18] The Germans did not know they were inside the Allied decision loop—their retreat order came twenty-four hours ahead of Bradley's one to close the gap.

Just to finish out his piece of the story, Field Marshal von Kluge convened another parlay on defending Paris. Because of recent Allied bombings, this was held in an underground bunker. OB West intelligence indicated the Allies wished to avoid Paris. The field marshal directed General von Choltitz to evacuate German wounded and noncombatants and prepare to contest the approaches. Siding with Hitler, von Kluge made clear Paris would be a battlefield. "It will be defended," von Kluge declared, turning to Choltitz, referring to the city "and you will defend it."[19] The C in C argued that Paris would ensnare Allied armor under unfavorable conditions and impede enemy exploitation across France. Later he sent von Choltitz a dispatch that confirmed his orders for demolitions in Paris. But the field marshal would not be there to supervise his city commandant. Günther von Kluge was summoned to Rastenburg.

Before leaving on the long drive to Germany, von Kluge had one last encounter with Blumentritt. As his chief of staff entered, the field marshal stood over a map of the battlefront. Von Kluge pointed to the offending place and turned wistful.

"Avranches, Avranches!" von Kluge repeated. "This town has cost me my reputation as a soldier. I'll go down in history as the Benedek of the western front. I did my best but that's fate for you."

Benedek was the Austrian commander who had completely failed in the face of Prussia in the Austro-Prussian War of 1866. The reference was telling. At least, von Kluge ruminated, he could not be faulted in every way:

"Let nobody accuse me of sparing my son and heir."[20]

Von Kluge's son remained in the Falaise Pocket.

Hans Speidel has written that von Kluge "had lost his resiliency" since July 20 and "he seemed at times to face the prospect of the inevitable collapse with fatalistic resignation." The chief of staff, closer to the field marshal than almost anyone, saw von Kluge as "torturing himself with thoughts of trying to find a way out of the dilemma after having failed to act against Hitler."[21] On his drive to Germany, the field marshal was dead before reaching Metz. He left a letter to Hitler, delivered by Sepp Dietrich: "When you receive these lines . . . I shall be no more." Von Kluge rejected the notion of a different outcome. "The panzer formations were in themselves far too weak in striking power," he wrote. "Even if one assumes that Avranches could have been reached . . . the danger to the Army Group certainly would not have been averted." Von Kluge insisted he had done the impossible to comply with the führer's demands: "Everyone who knew the actual state of our own troops, particularly of the infantry divisions, would, without hesitation, agree that I am right. . . . Our own actual line of defense had already been so weakened that it was no longer to be expected that it could hold out for any length of time." The field marshal added, "I cannot bear the reproach that I have sealed the fate of the West through faulty strategy."[22] Von Kluge took potassium cyanide.

The field marshal might be gone but the *Landser* were still in the soup. One division had blown up its artillery because it could not be moved. Panzers were abandoned everywhere for lack of fuel. The Leibstandarte demolished some tanks rather than abandon them. Army commanders begged for the Luftwaffe to airlift gasoline and provided coordinates for a drop zone to parachute ammunition and supplies. On August 17–18 a formation of forty-five Luftwaffe bombers actually did make a night supply delivery. Food was a problem, too. The staff of Panzer Group Eberbach ate nothing for two days. Antiaircraft defense was weakened because Army Group B, on the night of August 14–15, ordered independent flak units to leave the pocket. Equally important, the capture of Le Mans and Alençon brought the loss of most telephone cables connecting the German commands, which meant communication would have to be by radio, more grist for ULTRA. And many of the radio posts were themselves affected by combat. At the critical moment of the Falaise battle, when the II SS Panzer Corps attacked to reopen the gap, its effort would be slowed because radio orders could not be sent: the sets had been destroyed. Another German corps, radioing the Seventh Army, experienced such confusion that its message took two hours to arrive. At the time the commands were physically located just three miles apart. The report could have been carried faster by hand.

Units had become shadows. General Erwin Jollasse's proud 9th Panzer Division, forced to detach its Panther and Reconnaissance battalions early, had been reduced to the equivalent of a battalion of infantry, one of guns, five tanks, and the scouting abilities of two eight-bicycle patrols. On August 16 the division was pulled out of the pocket. Panzer Lehr had the equivalent of a battalion along with eight tanks. The 2nd Panzer Division, which von Kluge's last testament cited as an example of one of the few powerful mobile units at the time of Mortain, was down to twenty-five battleworthy tanks on August 13 as it fought the Americans along the pocket's south face. Two days later it had seven tanks and five assault guns plus fewer than two thousand troops. On the fifteenth Eberbach reported the

Leibstandarte with thirty panzers, the 116th with fifteen. The latter had lost 40 percent of its panzer strength to Allied air attacks while moving to the new battle zone in daylight. The divisions of the II SS Panzer Corps joined Eberbach on August 15, each with about twenty tanks—but what was considered remarkable was they had fuel to cover twenty to fifty kilometers. The 276th and 326th Infantry Divisions were reduced to weak battle groups, the 89th Division to three hundred men. Replacement clearing units in some divisions were thrown into battle like combat formations.

Nevertheless, the Germans were beginning to take action to preserve the Wehrmacht for battles after Normandy. The latest arriving divisions went into the line outside the pocket, strengthening the front from the Channel inland. On August 17 General Wilhelm Bittrich's II SS Panzer Corps pulled into reserve at Vimoutiers, beyond the pocket. The 9th and 21st Panzer and Panzer Lehr Divisions were also brought out. And—most important—the rear services and repair units of many mobile divisions had already begun leaving. Vehicles lined up in double ranks, bumper to bumper, moving east on the roads still open. Allied aerial reconnaissance on August 17 reported a minimum of twenty-two hundred vehicles. Some road convoys were so densely packed they could not be counted. The escapees would form one basis for a new German army.

For the Germans these measures came just in time. The American paladin Patton was pressing close. On August 18 at La Roche-Guyon, Army Group B had to evacuate its headquarters—a Paris exurb had come under American artillery and mortar fire. Army Group B made the logical but ironic move of relocating to Margival, the site of Hitler's fateful meeting with his field commanders. That day Hitler dismissed Field Marshal Hugo Sperrle, his western theater Luftwaffe maestro, and replaced him with General Otto Dessloch. Versailles fell on the eighteenth also, and Fontainebleau on the twentieth, the day the first GIs crossed the Seine River.

Not many hours remained to the Germans. Field Marshal Model arrived in the evening on August 17. Speidel writes that Model came with "preconceived notions and accusations against his new staff and the army commanders." General Speidel did not think much of the Führer's Fireman, leaving a portrait of a man submissive to Hitler's ideology, disdainful of details, focused on tactics rather than strategy, erratic but ardent; some-one who overestimated his powers and "lacked an ability to judge what was possible." On the other hand, Speidel concedes that Model possessed enormous energy, hardly slept, and, skilled at improvisation, did not fear visiting the front even in the heat of battle.[23] The OB West operations chief, General Bodo Zimmerman, believes Model "did not immediately grasp the full gravity of the situation in France and hoped that he might yet restore it."[24] Other interpretations are possible. Model's biographer, Steven Newton, argues that he had become skilled at playing on Hitler's proclivities, typically "publicly issuing the orders that Hitler demanded while quietly suborning them."[25]

Field Marshal Model's first staff huddle took up the defense of Paris and the Seine. Hitler had approved repositioning three more infantry divisions from the Pas de Calais and thought this sufficient. At Army Group B Speidel judged Model's rejoinder ridiculous: The Seine could be held with thirty fresh divisions—200,000 men and several hundred tanks. Model, in Newton's view, promised what Hitler wanted—provided the führer met that impossible condition. The biographer writes, "Model capitalized on Hitler's mention of the Seine as de facto authority to save the troops in the Falaise pocket. . . . In reality Model had no intention of defending Paris."[26]

On August 18 Field Marshal Model traveled to Fifth Panzer Army headquarters, now in a farmhouse, to meet his senior commanders. Sepp Dietrich ordered the woman who owned the place into the kitchen while the generals conversed in the front room. Officers noticed Allied aircraft circling outside the house where they met. The target was worthwhile but the jabos could not know. General Eberbach attended personally. Hausser sent his chief of staff, von Gersdorff. The latter reported on the extremely weak Seventh Army. Eberbach, who had journeyed for eight hours to cover less than fifty miles to this encounter, seconded the view. "I had, as often as possible, visited the divisions subordinated to me," Eberbach recounts. "I could, therefore, give Model a true picture of the situation—strength, supply, morale—and did so." Sepp Dietrich reported the abject failure of an attempted counterattack on Trun, which the Canadians had just captured, by Bittrich's II SS Panzer Corps. Not even the transfer of several divisions from the Seventh Army to Dietrich improved his prospects much. Eberbach quotes Model's instructions, contrary to his stated order to hold to the last man: "'My intention is withdrawal behind the Seine. For this purpose, first we need a stiffening of the bottleneck at Trun and Argentan with panzer divisions, in order to enable Seventh Army's infantry divisions to retreat.'"[27]

The German commanders noted that the relaxation of American pressures against the south side of the pocket facilitated their pullout, for which two or three days were deemed necessary. Model ordered that the north side of the neck should be held open or restored. Eberbach would lead panzers into the gap on the south side. Model put Hausser in control. Afterward the Seventh Army issued a directive summarizing the plan. This set the stage for a very desperate sally.

NAILS IN THE COFFIN

The OKW war communiqué for August 18 asserted that "the salient jutting out far west of the Orne has been withdrawn to behind the river. Strong enemy forces attempted to thrust into these movements from the north in an area east and northeast of Falaise but were halted after bitter fighting."[28] This sparse language cloaked a hellish expanse of confusion, conflagration, and fierce competition for a series of villages and low hills, land that held the key to German escape from the pocket. Canadians and Poles—and finally Americans, too—battled the Nazis across this terrain in the climactic struggle of the Normandy campaign.

Sir Guy Simonds's Canadian corps had begun the maneuver that would break open the situation. On the sixteenth Simonds sent Canadian and Polish armor on a flank march, across the Dives River and toward Trun. The Polish division became the left-hand column, the rim of the wheel. The Canadian 4th Armored took the inner track to capture Trun. They were joined on August 18 by the 3rd Canadian Infantry, the heroes of D-Day, who would make the Dives a wall of the pocket. The Germans recognized the danger. Hausser's withdrawal order specifically called for holding the very point where the Allied armor broke through. Nazi defenses were simply too weak. Simonds now wanted his tanks to push ahead and meet the Americans. He ordered both armored divisions to make for Chambois, the same town named in Omar Bradley's directive to the First U.S. Army.

This became the moment of glory for the 1st Polish Armored Division. The Poles were propelled by pride and hope in equal parts. Pride, for many of them were veterans of Poland's futile defense against Nazi invasion in 1939; they were now determined to smite the hated foe. Hope, because at this very moment the Polish Resistance had risen, and Poles in the West hoped their efforts might inspire the British and Americans to help their brave countrymen fighting the Battle of Warsaw. General Stanislaw Maczek, commander of the 1st Armored, had led the only fully mechanized Polish army unit in 1939, organized refugees into a brigade in France the following year, and formed the armored division in England in 1942. His battles in Poland and France, like those of many compatriots, had been desperate ones. Now the Poles had scores to settle. They became the cutting edge of the encirclement.

Not that it was easy for the Poles. The division had shipped out for France late in July with slightly more than sixteen thousand officers and men, 4,050 vehicles, and 381 tanks. They landed at Juno Beach. Intended from the beginning for Crerar's Canadian army, which was activated on July 23, it was early August before Maczek's legion appeared on SHAEF situation maps, in reserve near Bayeux. Operation Totalize, its baptism of fire, put the division up against veteran Nazi units. Panzers of the Hitlerjugend wiped out three-quarters of one Polish armored column. There were also Canadian complaints that Maczek's tanks had come near one of their beleaguered spearheads, but then drove away after shooting up the Canadian armor. However, the Polish division did as well as the Canadians, and in Operation Tractable it repeated that performance, achieving a crossing of the Dives River at the village of Jort, the point of departure for the advance on Trun and Chambois. The worst mishap would be another friendly-fire incident near Jort in which Major Antoni Stefanowicz's 1st Armored Regiment fired on tanks of Major Wladyslaw Zgorzelski's 10th Dragoons. It was the Dives assault that the Germans knew had to be parried to effect their retreat. That the Nazis were unable to stop them is a testament both to Maczek's brave legion and the Canadian armor that joined it for the thrust to and past Trun.

The Poles felt the power of Allied bombers right away—Maczek's troops would be attacked by friendly aircraft in every one of their Normandy drives. In Totalize there were 44 casualties among the divisional antiaircraft regiment. In Tractable, 42 of Maczek's men died under Allied bombs, and more than 50 others could not be found afterward. But the worst excesses came in the advance beyond the Dives, when the jabos ranged freely, clobbering anything that moved. Units and brigade headquarters were struck repeatedly. Half the gasoline en route to the legion's 2nd Armored Regiment was blown up by fighter-bombers. Between August 16 and 18 some 72 Polish troopers were killed and 191 wounded by the Allies' own air strikes. Maczek's experience lent substance to the bitter jokes that made the rounds in Normandy about the destructiveness of friendly airplanes. The friendly air attacks were so demoralizing that General Crerar finally issued an order that cited air force claims for German tanks and vehicles destroyed and invited commanders to compare losses to see their advantage over the enemy.

Maczek's mission would be Chambois. For this he created two task forces. One was under Lieutenant Colonel Stanislaw Koszutski, with his 2nd Armored Regiment, plus the 8th Rifle Battalion. Under Zgorzelski, the other combat group comprised the 10th Dragoons, motorized cavalry of the 24th Lancers, plus antitank batteries. Kickoff was delayed through the morning as the Poles engaged a German convoy moving near their position. Koszutski's force took the lead when the Poles moved out at midafternoon on August 17. Initially they faced a German infantry division, now worth a reinforced battalion plus a couple of guns. Later a few hundred *Landser* stiffened by a few Hitlerjugend tanks and some 88mm weapons opposed Koszutski's combat group. One source notes four Tiger tanks as well. The Poles brushed them aside.

Pressing on into the night, Colonel Koszutski became lost. His French guide disappeared and his column took the wrong turn at a crossroads, finding the track so tight the tanks could not turn around. This land of rock outcroppings and narrow valleys where the rivers cut through was not suited to mechanized warfare. Presently the force happened upon another crossroads, where German troops flowed and an officer directed traffic. The German actually stopped convoys for the Poles to pass. Koszutski believed the enemy recognized them but pretended otherwise to avoid a firefight. In the morning the Poles happened on some vehicles of the 2nd Panzer Division at the village of Les Champeaux. Identification documents taken from bodies and prisoners showed some of the Germans had actually fought Maczek's unit in Poland in 1939, or had participated in that invasion elsewhere. It was retribution of a sort. Afterward Koszutski put his force in motion again toward the objective. Then came fuel shortages— anxious to get started, the column had left with only half a load, and now Koszutski was victimized by the jabos.

Chambois was in a valley. Holding it meant nothing if the enemy had the high ground. General Maczek wanted his troops to capture the village of Coudehard and nearby Mont-Ormel, a dominant feature that overlooked the German escape route, now just six miles wide. The Zgorzelski column had moved out a couple of hours after Koszutski's. Though not lost, the Poles halted at nightfall. So it was on August 18 that Zgorzelski skirted north of Trun, passed Chambois, and made for nearby Hill 262, a part of Mont-Ormel, which the Poles would call Maczuga (Mace) because the 262-meter-high peaks at either end of the ridge resembled a caveman's mace with two bulbous heads. Zgorzelski consolidated this position. Then he sent a detachment down toward Chambois. On the nineteenth Koszutski's combat group arrived to reinforce Maczuga. From the height the Poles could engage German columns retreating to either side. Only a narrow strip of land separated these positions from the Americans.

Across the gap from the Poles were the Tough 'Ombres of Ray McLain's 90th Infantry Division. The 90th had been in place since August 15, when it had relieved the 5th Armored, off for Bradley's deeper hook to Dreux. McLain's men followed orders, which meant they avoided crossing the army group boundary. Instead they saturated the gap with fire. Major Frank Norris, commanding the division's 345th Artillery Battalion, recalled those days as "a combat artilleryman's paradise," with great observation from hills the 'Ombres held along the southern shoulder of the gap, and good weather for spotter planes. But, like his comrades, Norris was impatient with the restraints that kept GIs from closing the gap. "The wisdom of Bradley's order can be debated endlessly," he recalled. "But those of us on the ground did not like it at all."[29]

Although the gloves came off with Bradley's new directive on August 17, General McLain could not respond immediately. First there was the matter of the transfer to General Gerow's V Corps. Gerow delayed the attack a day to bring up corps artillery. Meanwhile, the 90th Division found itself fending off furious German attacks. General Bradley watched with trepidation, at least for a day, as the 'Ombres pulled back a little, but Ray McLain rallied his GIs. Their positions in the Gouffern forest and the town of Le Bourg–Saint-Léonard lay astride the road from Argentan the Nazis needed for escape. Exmes, on McLain's right flank, was of special importance, since there lay one of the few bridges spanning the Dives, which the Germans had to cross. The Germans were desperate to open the way or, failing that, at least hold the 'Ombres in place, securing the gap. The situation was further complicated by spontaneous fights with Nazi columns, which, blocked on one road, tried another, only to bump into the Americans.

Gerow's V Corps assault began on August 18. The 80th Infantry Division tried to grab Argentan itself. Major General Horace L. McBride's men were novices, further hampered since Gerow had taken one of his regiments for corps reserve. McBride did not capture Argentan, but his troops cut the road east of it, adding another block on this German escape route. General Leclerc's 2nd DB, west of Argentan, held an anomalous position, being squeezed out of the line by the advance of Dempsey's Second British Army. Leclerc probed toward Argentan from the west until Pip Roberts's 11th Armored tanks passed his position. The French general also had a private agenda, preparing for a lightning march on Paris; it is not clear whether the corps commander knew anything about that. In any case, Gerow instructed Leclerc to shift troops from Argentan to the corps' outer flank, on McLain's right. Leclerc sent Colonel Paul de Langlade's combat command on this mission, while stockpiling gas and supplies for the rest of his division to make the Paris run, and preparing another unit to take the lead there. Langlade took until August 19 to come up behind the Tough 'Ombres.

All this made Ray McLain's 'Ombres the big boys in the push for Chambois. The division had come a long way since its days as the poor sisters of the U.S. Army. Now they fought like lions. At midafternoon of the eighteenth artillery expert Major Norris was giving McLain's assistant, General Weaver, a briefing on how U.S. guns were playing havoc with the enemy, when, about a half mile down the ridge, an intense firefight brewed up. "Wild Bill" Weaver ended the orientation. "It sounds like they can use me down there," he said, and rushed off. Norris marveled, "My God, what a fighter!"[30] Indeed they could. The battles for Le Bourg–Saint-Léonard were among the fiercest of the campaign. The town changed hands a half dozen times. Lieutenant Colonel Harold S. Sundt of the 607th Tank Destroyer Battalion won the Silver Star there. Even his headquarters clerks fought. The 773rd Tank Destroyer Battalion won a Presidential Unit Citation. Until main forces of the Tough 'Ombres arrived, the antitank units formed the core of the American defense.

Lieutenant George W. King's platoon of C Company, 773rd, scouted ahead to Chambois on the evening of August 19. General Weaver set up the main action that night, slotting a battalion of the 358th Infantry to block the roads east and north from Chambois, while the regiment's other elements aimed at the towns of Sainte-Eugénie and Bon Menil. The 3rd Battalion of the 357th Regiment attacked toward high ground overlooking Chambois. The 3rd Battalion of the 359th Infantry set out for the town itself. The GIs moved out from Le Bourg, where they had relieved another unit of the regiment, still fighting off Germans, the day before. With them were Lieutenant John J. Kelly's company of the 607th Tank Destroyer Battalion and the 712th Tank Battalion. A few Free French tanks also put in an appearance. There were twenty-one artillery battalions in support— eleven just for one attack column. The Americans approached from the south.

The thrust began at eight a.m. the next morning with the 2nd Battalion, 359th Infantry. German armor held up progress, but the advance resumed after K Company destroyed a Panzer IV and a pair of German half-tracks. By early afternoon GIs had reached the east road and added a command car, a radio truck, a tank, and two trucks to their bag. Then came a full-scale donnybrook—with a convoy of twenty to thirty trucks, half a dozen panzers, towed artillery, ambulances, and many *Landser*. At nightfall the battalion score had mounted to eleven tanks, eight assault guns, many more vehicles, over a hundred German dead, and about 320 prisoners.

The 3/359 began the advance on Chambois proper early in the afternoon. Privates Caldwell and Giebelstein of K Company, 3/359, stood their ground and knocked out four German tanks with their bazooka. At about six p.m., Captain Laughlin E. Waters of G Company, 3/359, was approaching Chambois, his men in skirmish order under intense fire. He went ahead to check his GIs' alignment and saw a man step out on the road in what appeared to be a British uniform. Waters identified him as Major Zgorzelski. Taken to meet an American staff officer, Zgorzelski gave up trying to teach the pronunciation of his name and finally wrote it down on a pad. Zgorzelski and Waters celebrated, toasting with Polish vodka that had been taken from a German *Kübelwagen*. Polish sources credit a patrol of the 10th Dragoons led by Lieutenant Jan Karcz with making the junction, but there is no doubt that Zgorzelski and Waters would defend Chambois in coordination with each other.

Meanwhile, determined to catch the Germans in the trap, General Guy Simonds ordered the advance on Trun on August 16. The Canadians muscled ahead against Panzer Meyer's troops and some infantry, reduced to shards, who tried to set up new defenses. Tough fighting took place at Trun, where the Lincoln and Welland Regiment and an independent machine-gun company repelled continuous German attacks. There they captured a German division commander. Later Bittrich's SS panzers intervened and failed also. The 4th Canadian Armored Division received orders to thrust past Trun to the town of Saint-Lambert. Personally supervised by the corps commander, the 4th was to close up with the Poles and Americans and seal the pocket. This degree of contact was typical of Simonds, whose biographer concludes that "his own experience . . . made him inclined to fight his divisional commanders' battles for them."[31] Simonds ordered the 3rd Canadian Infantry Division up in support. It was to drive down the east bank of the Dives and hold the river against crossing attempts. Major General D. C. Spry took over the 3rd after the wounding of Rod Keller. Once it regrouped following its capture of Falaise, Simonds added the 2nd Division to this blocking force.

The wounded General Keller was far from the only Canadian leadership loss. The 4th Armored Division's own 4th Brigade had lost three successive commanders, one of them killed. More than a dozen Canadian unit commanders fell in Normandy. Three leaders of the Governor General's Foot Guard, a unit of the 4th Brigade, went down in just one day. And the situation was complicated by Simonds's propensity to relieve officers he found wanting.

In any case, the 4th Armored Division formed the tip of the Canadian spear, and units of its 4th Brigade were the cutting edge. The South Alberta Regiment, among the brigade's tank battalions, rolled through Trun on August 18. That afternoon it received the order to capture Saint-Lambert. The assignment went to the squadron led by Major David Currie, supported by infantry of Lieutenant Colonel David Stewart's Argyll and Sutherland Highlanders of Canada. Currie and Stewart decided to advance at six p.m. Just as they got under way they were attacked by British aircraft, costing Currie two tanks. Then a pair of panzers blocked the approach. The force reached the edge of Saint-Lambert in darkness. They received orders to wait until dawn. In the morning Currie's troops attacked. The 4th Armored shot its way into Saint-Lambert. Tanks of the South Albertas and infantry of the Argylls captured more than twenty-five hundred Germans. Currie reported the town secure at midmorning, but new firefights kept erupting. At least he had the Dives River bridge under his guns. The Falaise trap had closed.

THE CORRIDOR OF DEATH

The Nazis may have been down but they were not out. For all their disadvantages they conducted this retreat quite systematically. General Eberbach's panzer group was abolished. He resumed command of the Fifth Panzer Army, its headquarters pulled outside the pocket to coordinate. General Hausser led the trapped forces. One corps was relieved of all combat responsibilities, given military police units, and put in charge of traffic control. Supply columns were escorted by officers with authority to claim priority on the roads. At the Orne, the critical river barrier before reaching the Dives, the Germans still held four crossings. One they reserved only for westbound traffic—the supply convoys. The others were for withdrawing troops, and formations were given specific crossing points. Hausser assigned two corps to delay the Allies while the Germans collapsed the pocket behind them. Meanwhile, other units, particularly panzer formations, fought hard on the shoulders to preserve the gap.

Incredible compression occurred as Wehrmacht and SS troops hastened toward safety. By August 19 the pocket had shrunk to an area perhaps six miles deep and a few wide, packed with desperate men, and covered by Allied fighter-bombers overhead. With fuel and supply problems, combat losses, and recovery and repair units already departed, huge amounts of German equipment were discarded. Inevitably the formations bunched up at the Dives. With the Canadians in Falaise, Trun, and Saint-Lambert, the Americans around Argentan and Chambois, and the Poles at Chambois and Mont-Ormel, the German predicament had become dire. The pocket contained only two roads that led to an escape point. One crossed the Dives at Chambois, the other at Saint-Lambert. A detour was possible below Chambois, but that route crossed the river at Exmes and led into country where Patton's spearheads were already at large. If the Germans could cross at Trun another exit route became possible. Using the lesser country roads added some partial alternatives, but all led back into the main roads—and to the same bridges. The Poles overlooked the entire area from their Maczuga.

Paul Hausser had no illusions. His command post departed Nécy under fire from approaching Canadian tanks. The staff became vagabonds. Eugen Meindl's staff shared that fate. Hausser kept the 116th Panzer Division up against the GIs on the southern shoulder, and it was they who contested Le Bourg–Saint-Léonard with the Tough 'Ombres. That town fell on August 18. The *Nebelwerfer* brigade supporting the panzers used up all its rockets. The division itself had little artillery ammunition left. Hausser ordered the 1st SS Panzer to reinforce them, but discovered that the Leibstandarte had already sent much of its strength out of the pocket.

General Hausser arrived at the 116th's command post around noon on August 19, just as a flurry of U.S. cannon shells rained around it. He agreed the situation was intolerable. Hausser had spent the previous night hunkering in a rock quarry, threatened by guns and planes. Only he had slept. At this meeting the general accepted a suggestion to try and break out in the dark, but then agreed to a larger plan. The conversation was dangerous—division headquarters lay in a cluster of houses near Tournai-sur-Dives, while GIs advanced only a few hundred yards away.

General Elfeldt of the LXXXIV Corps arrived to explain why the large-scale river assault Hausser wanted was impractical. Panzer leader Baron von Funck laid out his idea for a more focused breakout along the southern shoulder, with the 1st SS and 2nd Panzer in the lead and the 116th protecting the rear. Hausser had already spoken to the tough paratrooper Meindl and consulted the operations staff of Elfeldt's companion rearguard unit, the LXXIV Corps. The German generals expanded von Funck's concept into a design to break out by simultaneous assaults by battle groups comprising the remnants of whole divisions. General Meindl would take one force and attack between Trun and Saint-Lambert. General Hausser would accompany Meindl's 3rd Parachute Division. The army staff would go with him. A force on Meindl's right flank, between Saint-Lambert and Chambois, completed the disposition. The rearguard infantry would rush in behind to add power to the attacks. General Hausser attached his troops to Eugen Meindl's parachutists for the breakout. Baron von Funck would lead out his panzers toward morning, when better light might help them avoid the derelict wrecks dotting the land. From the outside Bittrich's SS Panzer Corps would attack the Polish rear to assist. The operation would start that night. If all went well the Germans would leap the Dives, barrel up the Maczuga, overwhelm the Poles, and leave the pocket behind.

Germans call the narrow neck the Corridor of Death. Somewhere between six and ten thousand men perished there. On August 18 and 19 the Allied air forces flew 5,592 sorties. "Maori" Coningham's 2nd Tactical Air Force claimed to have destroyed 176 tanks and damaged 188, with 1,741 vehicles destroyed and 2,705 damaged. Pete Quesada's IX TAC claims for the month of August as a whole include 466 tanks and armored vehicles, 4,058 trucks, and 598 wagons. Flight Lieutenant H. Ambrose, a

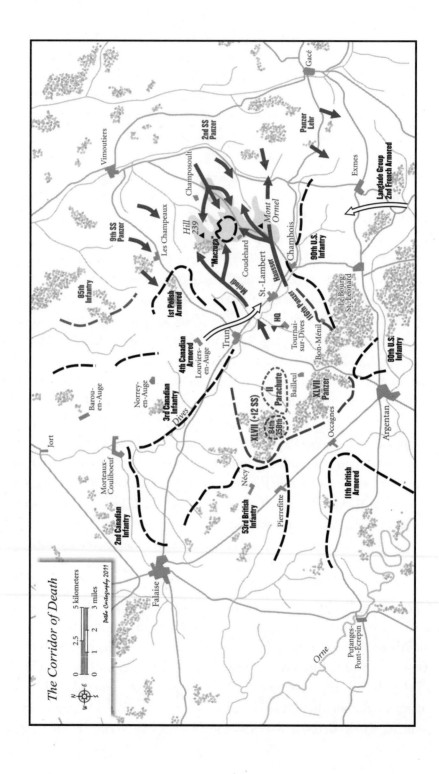

The Corridor of Death

N
W E
S

0   2.5   5 kilometers
0   1   2   3 miles

Dale Cartography 2011

Gacé

2nd SS
Panzer

Panzer
Lehr

Exmes

Langlade Group
2nd French Armored

Vimoutiers

Champosoult

Mont
Ormel

Chambois

9th SS
Panzer

Les Champeaux

Hill
239

"Maczuga"

Coudehard

Hausser

90th U.S.
Infantry

85th
Infantry

1st Polish
Armored

Méhali

St.-Lambert

116th Panzer

Le Bourg-
St.-Léonard

80th U.S.
Infantry

4th Canadian
Armored

Louviers-
en-Auge

Trun

HQ

Tournai-
sur-Dives

Bon-Ménil

Barou-
en-Auge

Norrey-
en-Auge

3rd Canadian
Infantry

Dives

II
Parachute

Bailleul

XLVII
Panzer

Occagnes

Argentan

Jort

XLVII (+12 SS)

84th/
358th

Morteaux-
Coulibœuf

Nécy

Pierrefitte

53rd British
Infantry

11th British
Armored

2nd Canadian
Infantry

Falaise

Orne

Putanges-
Pont-Ecrepin

Typhoon pilot with the 175 Squadron, RAF, was dismayed to discover he could smell the dead below, *inside* his cockpit at six thousand feet altitude. The Prince of Luxembourg, who flew an artillery spotter plane, had the same experience.

Had the Allies attacked strongly all along the front on August 19, the German units would have been so busy they could not have assembled for the assault. But the British only crept cautiously forward. Meanwhile, at Saint-Lambert Major D. V. Currie's force of the South Albertas were unable to control more than half of the town over many hours of pitched battle. They were reduced to just 60 men and a dozen tanks—with the tanks machine-gunning each other to knock off German riflemen climbing on top. Currie's combined force, including the infantry of the Argyll and Sutherland Highlanders, numbered no more than 120 men and five tanks. Their fight became a battle to hang on.

Saint-Lambert remained contested ground—and this made all the difference. The Canadians obstructed the river crossing only with tank or artillery fire. Here the remnants of the 2nd Panzer Division struggled to pass the Dives. Von Lüttwitz recalled the artillery bombardment as "a storm such as I had never before experienced." He had fifteen tanks remaining. "The crossing of the Dives bridge was particularly horrible," von Lüttwitz observed. "The bodies of the dead, horses and vehicles and other equipment having been hurled from the bridge into the river, formed a gruesome tangled mass."[32] Hans Braun, a senior noncom in the 2nd Panzer, was especially horrified at the screams of the horses and by the dead civilians lying at the side of the road. He saw broken baby carriages and discarded dolls. "We had been tempered, like the steel plating of our tanks," Braun remembered. "Inside us now there was hardly any human feeling left."[33] The Germans fought with courage born of desperation.

General von Lüttwitz set up his command post in the village church. When he moved on, the 10th SS and 21st Panzer Divisions would also cross at Saint-Lambert. An officer of the latter unit commented, "The closer we got to the breakout point the more ghastly was the scene that met our eyes."[34] Heinz Harmel, the operations staff officer of the 10th SS—who would soon succeed to division command—gathered every man he could around a house opposite the church. He battled five more hours that day. Major Currie's Canadians could hardly cope with the waves of rushing *Landser*. The war diary of the South Alberta Regiment recorded, "It could hardly be called an attack as there was no covering fire plan, simply a mass movement of riflemen."[35] On the other hand, Canadian officer Pierre Grandvallet recalled that the fight had been like "trying to stop a buffalo stampede. . . . They went around us, they went over us, and they went under us."[36]

Major Currie radioed for reinforcements four times during the night, at last warning he could be pushed out of Saint-Lambert if he did not get them. No one came, save a few remnants of nearby detachments, themselves recoiling from Nazi attacks. There were so many Germans throughout the area that Allied troops were simply tied to their positions. Every South Alberta Regiment officer except Currie was killed or wounded. He himself did not sleep for seventy-two hours. Major Currie would be awarded the Victoria Cross.

Paul Hausser's chief of staff, General von Gersdorff, joined a huge column of vehicles from mixed units that dashed across the Saint-Lambert bridge. The Canadians fired at every one. Von Gersdorff commandeered a pair of assault guns to distract the enemy while his column passed. On their wild ride the Nazis fired machine guns to suppress the Canadians and drove as fast as they could. They encountered automatic weapons and antitank fire, but the Allied artillery, without observation, stayed silent. Gersdorff records that hundreds of Canadian soldiers surrendered, but his column, unable to do anything with them, let them go. After dawn he organized an ad hoc battle group of a dozen or more tanks and assault guns, some self-propelled artillery, and about thirty half-tracks. There were perhaps fifteen hundred troops. Von Gersdorff formed them into scratch combat teams of about a hundred men each. Some leaders were paymasters or veterinarians. His troops edged along the Polish perimeter.

Chambois, also on the Dives, became another rock standing amid the German flood tide. A quiet little village among apple orchards and dairy farms, nothing distinguished Chambois save its Norman castle dating from the twelfth century. Suddenly its location made Chambois critical. The tough Poles and GIs there stuck to their guns. Three companies of the 359th Infantry held the town against all comers. There were probes, full-scale attacks, and chance encounters with Nazis, who, unaware of the situation, simply drove in. Like the Lost Battalion of Mortain, the GIs at Chambois spent most of the next few days completely surrounded. A German force drove a wedge into the town the morning of August 21, splitting two American companies apart and occupying a portion of the town with several hundred troops and half a dozen tanks. Within a few hours GIs destroyed the panzers and captured the riflemen. Machine gunner Sergeant John D. Hawk of 2/359 received the Congressional Medal of Honor for directing a couple of tank destroyers to shell a mass of Nazis into submission; despite wounds, he collected five hundred prisoners.

Captain Waters set up a prisoner cage in the center of town and soon filled it up. At a certain point in the battle the GIs were told the Poles would be bringing them fifteen hundred prisoners. A Polish officer later turned up with a much smaller number. His POW cage full, Captain Waters said he could not take them. The Pole insisted. When Waters asked why the number of prisoners was so much smaller than advertised, the Pole admitted the rest had been shot. These survived because he had no ammunition to kill them. The Americans accepted the prisoners after all.

Meanwhile, General Meindl's escape group moved off about eight thirty p.m. The tactical leader was Lieutenant General Richard Schimpf of the 3rd Parachute Division, who just two days earlier had been denouncing as false all reports that the army was trapped. It began badly. Schimpf suffered severe wounds in a scrap with a GI outpost. Meindl took personal command. They reached the Dives above Chambois about half an hour after midnight. Meindl found no easy way to ford. They swam. On the other side just twenty paratroopers were still with him. Deciding to strike a few hours later, he waited for more troops to appear. Meindl sent officers on bicycles to alert nearby units that he had an escape path. Anxious to keep to schedule, Meindl jogged in a circle to stay awake. The exhausted *Landser* around him fell asleep. When the arrival of soldiers slowed to a trickle, Meindl reckoned the time had come and woke up his men. They moved off, their way lit by Allied tracer bullets. Meindl's force worked its way toward Coudehard village, which bifurcated the twin peaks of Mont-Ormel. It began raining. Paratrooper Johann Bornert recalled, "The mist stank of death and gunpowder."[37]

Here the relief attack from the outside by II SS Panzer Corps made a difference. General Bittrich had difficulty organizing this. Delayed by a lack of fuel—a Luftwaffe airdrop was critical to getting the vehicles moving—Bittrich went in before his units had assembled completely. The 9th SS Panzer Division did not get its armor up in time, and so halted the grenadiers before they became too heavily engaged. The 2nd SS Panzer Division, Das Reich, committed two battle groups, but met Polish tanks counterattacking north of the Maczuga. The panzers encountered the Polish vanguard at a village northeast of the breakout area. It became a battle royal. With his unit's last Tiger, Will Fey had the experience of blowing up a Sherman tank that emerged suddenly between houses only two dozen feet away. The Poles were driven off. In this drastic situation Bittrich opened a narrow path of escape for a few hours. General Meindl responded. He found a few Das Reich tanks and some trucks, and with these created an impromptu ambulance convoy under the Red Cross. General Hausser, badly wounded in the face by a shell splinter, insisted on remaining with the combat group. He sat next to the turret of one of the panzers. Meindl gave up his last covering positions at five a.m. the next morning. Some four thousand troops escaped with him. Hausser was in contact with Bittrich by dawn on August 21.

A second assault group was led by Meindl's chief of staff, Colonel Ernst Blauensteiner. In the dark and confusion the two formations lost touch. Blauensteiner led his men up Mont-Ormel and hit the Poles. But the Maczuga proved too strong. Major Stephan, commanding the 9th Parachute Regiment, fell in the attempt. With daylight the Nazis took cover. They exchanged fire all day, then broke away in the night. The Germans skirted the Polish positions.

Panzer Meyer formed up the remnants of his Hitlerjugend at a farm. Bumping into General Schimpf, he sent two Tiger tanks to support the 3rd Parachute Division breakout. They moved off. General Elfeldt followed. Near Chambois Meyer joined a column of Leibstandarte troops who were about to attack. Suddenly they were struck by a welter of tank and artillery fire. Meyer, wounded, withdrew, leaving behind several hundred Allied prisoners, and assembled his party between Trun and Chambois, where from long garrison duty he knew every tree. Meyer's *Landser* climbed the ridgeline beneath Mont-Ormel and worked their way east.

About then General Otto Elfeldt arrived at Saint-Lambert, his crossing point. He had managed to maintain a continuous line and coordinate troops even while a Canadian barrage of a thousand shells fell around his command post. Elfeldt passed the Dives and came up on the Maczuga. His corps made up the last rear guard. The choice was logical in that LXXXIV Corps had had the farthest to go, but the selection is interesting in another way. After Elfeldt had spent a year on the Eastern Front, one of Germany's great panzer leaders, Hans Hube, had evaluated him as personally brave but rather pessimistic, not good material for a top commander. This time the general would be the only German senior officer not to escape the pocket.

Elfeldt could see Canadian tanks behind him, driving along the opposite bank of the Dives from Trun. He realized his separate line of retreat had been blocked. The troops bunched up hopelessly. General Elfeldt flung his last coherent formation, two hundred men and a couple of tanks, into a desperate attack on the Poles. The advance began well, but then the Germans behind him surrendered. Suddenly Elfeldt was trapped with his lead element, the crest of the Maczuga looming above. Captain Michael Gutkowski of the Polish 10th Mechanized Regiment used a loudspeaker to order the Germans to put their hands up. General Elfeldt surrendered with his staff. He was taken to Gutkowski, who gave the German his last cigarette. Elfeldt was surprised to have been captured by Poles, not Americans or British. For much of the day they conversed in French. Hans Hube's prediction had come true.

Late that afternoon another fierce German assault hit the Maczuga. "At the present moment I am your prisoner," General Elfeldt told Captain Gutkowski in French. "But you know how it is in war. Maybe in half an hour you will be my prisoner."

Gutkowski shot back, "*I do not surrender to Germans.*"[38]

Lieutenant General Erich Mueller of the 353rd Division crossed the Dives between Saint-Lambert and Chambois and sent assault teams of his 941st Grenadier Regiment with a few tanks against the Poles. They were beaten back with heavy losses and the tanks destroyed, but while that happened a river of Germans began flowing past Mont-Ormel. This became the safest escape route. Mueller's *Landser* went on to capture the other peak of Mont-Ormel, but they could not dislodge the Maczuga.

General Elfeldt never made the German rendezvous—he would dine the next evening with Courtney Hodges of the First U.S. Army.

Meanwhile, Baron von Funck formed up his panzer *Kessel*, the hedgehog disposition the German army favored for big mechanized movements. They drove through the night and reached the Saint-Lambert–Chambois area about nine a.m., with the 116th Panzer still in the rear. Von Funck's mobile troops suffered grievously from Allied artillery and air, but they surged across the Dives. Jupp Steinbuechel, in the lead echelon with Leibstandarte, remembers the roads packed and the air full of planes. Enemy fire was horrendous. At one point they came close enough to the Canadian artillery to see the gunners, wearing white gym shorts, cramming shells into their fieldpieces. Vehicles began driving straight across the fields. Had he not been in a tracked vehicle, Steinbuechel felt, he would have been lost. Then the *Kessel* stopped, its path blocked. Baron von Funck got in a shouting match with the 1st SS commander, SS Brigadier Theodor Wisch. "Everybody wanted to be right but no one knew what was going on," observed Captain Hans Bernard of the division staff.[39] Desperation showed on every face. Finally someone found another way forward. Wisch and Bernard started toward an old stone bridge, the captain just telling his boss this would be a good artillery target, when a shell exploded almost on top of them. Wisch's leg was blown off. Fortunately a half-track came by at that moment. Bernard knew its driver. They manhandled General Wisch into the track and made it to a barn near the next village, where Wisch received first aid. The retreat continued.

To the rear the 116th Panzer fought all day. Its crossing of the Dives at Saint-Lambert was as painful as that of other formations. That night the division broke out without serious loss, saving about fifty combat vehicles. Heinz Günther Guderian, like some other 116th Division soldiers, encountered no Allied troops at all. The unit still possessed fifteen tanks, three assault guns, and several pieces of self-propelled artillery.

Guderian's escape may not have been all luck. The Poles were mightily distracted on the night of August 20–21 by General Bittrich's efforts against the Maczuga. Bittrich's operation was not smooth but it did grab attention. This was the climax of the Polish battle of Normandy, hours of fierce defense of a key position assailed from all directions. Germans from Saint-Lambert had begun attacking Hill 262 on the nineteenth, and the Nazi breakout meant the Poles were surrounded. There were Canadian artillery observers on the Maczuga, so the Poles had good fire support, but by that evening they knew that neither American GIs nor Canadian troops were going to reach them, at least not yet. Before the German pressure became too great, Gerow's V Corps contrived to get a few supplies through to the Poles—a tanker truck with four thousand gallons of gasoline, 140,000 rounds of machine-gun ammunition, and 189 shells for the Sherman tank guns—but they were soon gone. Given their losses, on August 20 the Poles shortened their line, facing more panzer attacks. Poles called their Shermans "caskets." Sergeant Edward Bucko, a tank radioman, recounted, "The Sherman tank was just like butter."[40] But that also meant that an armor-piercing shell, if it did not hit something entering the tank, would go right out the other side. When this happened to him Bucko gained new appreciation.

By six p.m., the Poles were nearly out of ammunition. It was fortunate the SS troopers never reached their main lines. As evident, the Poles in their Maczuga were hard-pressed despite their dominant position. Their fight lasted more than seventy hours. Lieutenant Colonel Zygmunt Szydlowski, the senior officer present, commanded. There were actually two centers of resistance, the other held by the Koszutski group. It was Koszutski who saved the main position by engaging the 2nd SS Panzer Division outside the village of Les Champeaux. Other units were scattered across the area, from a low hill outside Chambois, to the 10th Dragoon elements in the town, to positions farther to the northwest. Assaults continued throughout August 20. An attempt by C-47 aircraft to parachute supplies on the morning of the twenty-first failed when the planes dropped in the wrong place.

Guy Simonds's Canadians held their ground, too, despite the reflexive power of the Germans' escape attacks. Simonds shifted troops, lending an infantry brigade to stiffen the 4th Armored Division and instructing its commander, Major General George Kitching, to cease the advance of others of his units upon Vimoutiers, outside the pocket. The reinforcements had barely dug in when they faced new blows. Another German divisional commander would be captured then. With morning the Canadians' terrible artillery resumed fire, but concentrated on supporting the Poles and their own positions. The Allies, observing such masses of Germans on the move, made little effort to block them. Guy Simonds, angry at Kitchings for allegedly poor performance, relieved him. Major General Harry Foster took over the 4th Armored and focused on strengthening the siege ring. British troops from the west finally reached Canadian positions this day. Now the Canadian infantry bounded forward from Saint-Lambert to Chambois, and armor drove ahead to link with the Poles. Their relief finally arrived in the form of the Canadian Grenadier Guards, which joined Polish troops just before eleven a.m. on August 21.

On the Maczuga the commander of the Polish 10th Motorized Rifle Regiment had been killed. At the end of the battle, there were only seventy men in fighting condition. Slightly over 1,000 Poles had been wounded, 325 killed, and 114 were missing. Many of their eighty-seven tanks were damaged or destroyed. On the other hand, the Germans left 55 panzers on the field (14 Panther, 6 Tiger), 152 armored fighting vehicles, 360 others of all types, and 44 guns. About two thousand German soldiers fell here. General Maczek contrived a novel way of replacing his losses: Captured enlisted men who were Poles impressed into the German army were handed new uniforms and became part of the division. Any Poles who had been German officers did not fare so well.

THE BOX SCORE

About midafternoon of August 20, recalls E. W. Beckman, sergeant major of the 359th Regiment, German soldiers began surrendering en masse. B Company of the 712th Tank Battalion, which fought in Chambois, collected 1,100 prisoners. The 607th Tank Destroyer Battalion took 516 POWs. A sergeant of the 358th Infantry captured 800 Germans by himself. The 90th Division as a whole took 5,000 Germans prisoner that day, and 5,500 more surrendered to it on August 21. The division claims 13,000 POWs in all. Gerow's V Corps as a whole listed 5,000 prisoners taken on August 19, after which the battle action was almost exclusively on the 90th Division sector. The Poles on the Maczuga are credited with capturing 5,000 more Nazis. The First Canadian Army processed 13,683 POWs for the last five days of the pocket battle, presumably including those taken by the Poles. The Second British Army recorded the capture of 7,500 prisoners. Altogether these figures amount to slightly more than 39,000.

In *Newsweek*, the British military theorist J. F. C. Fuller made an analogy between the Germans in Normandy and the Napoleonic age—to the defeated Russians after Austerlitz in 1805.[41] The war correspondent Drew Middleton, writing from SHAEF headquarters on August 24, also offered a Napoleonic comparison in the *New York Times*: "Throughout the battle area the Germans are reaching a state of disorganization surpassing anything that has happened to the German army since the Battle of Jena." Middleton's reference was to 1806, when the Prussian army completely disintegrated. A little further down in his piece Middleton recorded the prisoner claims: "Between 40,000 and 50,000 prisoners have now been taken from the Falaise Pocket."[42] That was the recap. The previous day the *Times*' lead story had carried the 40,000–50,000 figure as a partial one for overall German losses, and estimated the final number would come in at around 100,000. But who tabulated all this to give to the war correspondents? The simple explanation is that the numbers were invented, right across the board. Fifteen years after the fact the American official historian noted, "The Allies did not know how many prisoners they took." He estimates U.S. numbers for the days after August 17 and arbitrarily concludes Montgomery's forces captured an equal number of Germans, to arrive at a figure of 50,000 prisoners.[43] A couple of years later the British official historian would write, "What the total losses were in the six-day withdrawal, from the 16th to the 21st, is impossible to say."[44]

The same is true for German equipment losses. *Every* personal account of Normandy is replete with stories of how that person's unit wiped out huge quantities of tanks, trucks, whatever. After the battle the Allies had technicians survey the entire field and make a hand count of abandoned equipment for scientists and operations researchers to draw conclusions on what accounted for losses and, hence, weapons effectiveness. In the area of the Corridor of Death the searchers found 187 tanks, assault guns, or self-propelled guns; 157 other armored vehicles; 2,447 trucks and cars; and 252 guns. In the remainder of the former pocket there were another 121 armored fighting vehicles, 1,150 trucks, and 60 guns. British claims for destruction from the air on just two days of the battle amount to nearly the exact number of tanks left behind and 70 percent of the other vehicles. Add U.S. claims, German losses to artillery and antitank fire, losses in close combat, and vehicles abandoned because they ran out of fuel, and the conclusion must necessarily be that German losses were counted multiple times.

Observers widely noted the destruction of the Falaise Pocket. General Eisenhower, who visited the scene once the guns fell silent, remarked his horror at a field on which it was hard to walk in places without treading upon decaying human remains. Everyone, Ike included, recoiled at the stench of death. At Mortain, where the 5th Evacuation Field Hospital had moved after Cobra, the medic Arnold Rodgaard hated the smell, but what horrified him most was the carcasses of the horses, which littered the fields everywhere, in places—as Eisenhower found for human bodies in the Corridor of Death—so thick one could not walk without stepping on them. No question, the toll of this battle was appalling.

But whatever the actual losses in blood and matériel, there was a success of sorts for German arms in the midst of this disaster. German commanders, crippled by a dysfunctional high command and in the throes of a political purge, despite inferior mobility, fighting under difficult conditions against an adversary possessed of huge material advantages—one who also had intelligence dominance—managed to extricate a considerable portion of their force from a veritable trap. To put this differently, consider a more successful German withdrawal. The retreat could have been executed in good order had it begun around August 12—the Lost Weekend. When the decision was made four days later, its operational aspects had been enormously complicated by Allied progress toward and past Falaise. The sense is that, given material inferiority, mobility losses, and supply shortages—the German retreat could easily, and only, have been *less* successful than it was.

The Allies abetted the German withdrawal with command decisions that delayed the creation of the pocket until many Nazis had already escaped. That had enormous consequences in the campaign for Northwest Europe. There were tactical and doctrinal reasons that handicapped the advance, but these are secondary. The tensions within the Allied High Command, whether or not they reached the level of a war among the generals, have their real importance in influencing the conditions under which the German retreat took place. Omar Bradley's "stop order" preserving the artificial boundary becomes a primary factor here. Its impact is perhaps best viewed through the eyes of Major Frank W. Norris, the 90th Division artilleryman, who said this: "Our dislike of the order was later reinforced by our recognition that those same German units and senior commanders who escaped comprised much of the hard core of the units we were to confront later under much less favorable circumstances."[45]

CHAPTER 7

NORMANDY CRUCIBLE

While battle raged in the Falaise Pocket, in Paris the Resistance rose up against the Nazi occupiers. General von Choltitz suddenly discovered he had leapt from the Norman frying pan into an even more dangerous fire. On August 19, as desperate Germans in the Corridor of Death concocted their plan to break free, the many factions of the Resistance acted as one, coming into the open in Paris. Unlike elsewhere, particularly Brittany, the Resistance in the City of Light, though quite numerous, was not so well armed. On the other hand, von Choltitz had very weak forces to control the metropolis. Paris posed distinct problems to both sides. For the Nazis, battle in the city compromised the slim possibility of contesting the line of the Seine, for loss of the metropolis, which lay astride the river, would put the enemy squarely across it. For the Allies, this struggle for the French capital crystallized certain political, diplomatic, and strategic dilemmas that had carefully been avoided.

The battle for Paris itself is a story for another day. But the fact of that struggle, and the strategic and operational headaches it triggered, shine an important backlight on Normandy and Falaise. At the apex of the Allied command, General Dwight D. Eisenhower once more held the choice in his hands. And Ike's intention had been to avoid Paris—German intelligence was correct about that. Liberating the City of Light meant a major commitment, possibly of troops, but more directly to the health and well-being of a huge population within a French economy largely in ruins.

Capture of the City of Light would be a shining jewel for Allied propaganda, but it came at the cost of a king's ransom. Better, Eisenhower reasoned, to stand aside and avoid paying that price. Then the Resistance rose up. The jewel would be tarnished if Allied armies stood aside while Nazi occupiers crushed the Parisians. Eisenhower faced his dilemma anew.

There were also political considerations. Free French participation furnished a modicum of force, particularly in operations in southern France. But French efforts would be vital to restoring the nation, something that promised to so lift the burdens of emancipation, of supporting Paris, as to enable the Allies to focus on military operations. Naturally the French provisional government leader, Charles de Gaulle, had insisted upon returning to a liberated Paris at the earliest possible moment. Already he had begun pressing Allied authorities to permit him to land in France. In fact, de Gaulle left Algiers in an airplane on August 20. De Gaulle's price for supporting Allied efforts was the restoration of Paris.

Months earlier, when Operation Overlord had yet been a mote in the eye, the question of French rearmament and military cooperation in the Northwest Europe campaign had been raised and settled. Conversations at Algiers in December 1943 hammered out the final arrangement. General Eisenhower and his chief of staff, Walter Bedell Smith, both worked on the deal. The French had offered eleven divisions for southern France, and had also hoped for two armored plus an infantry division to participate in Overlord. At the time there had barely been two thousand Free French troops in England. Eisenhower had argued de Gaulle down to six divisions for southern France and a single armored division in the north. That became the origin of Philippe Leclerc's 2ème Blindée (2nd DB). De Gaulle had openly threatened that were these troops to be used in ways inimical to French interests they would be withdrawn from Allied command. SHAEF understood that from the beginning. De Gaulle also reserved the right to issue instructions to French forces by his own channels. There was no goal more central to the French than the liberation of Paris.

When the Leclerc division went into action in Normandy, de Gaulle immediately instructed his military representative in England, General Pierre Koenig, to update him constantly, no doubt with Paris in mind. General Leclerc, much like the Polish general Maczek, behaved in the field as both a unit commander and the senior leader of a national contingent, to whom Paris was as important as it was to de Gaulle. The French provisional government, conversant with Resistance plans for an uprising, also used its own channels to communicate with field commanders like Leclerc.

This led to a certain duality in Jacques-Philippe Leclerc's activities during the Falaise battle, because he anticipated the imminent arrival of orders to march on Paris. On August 14, still under Patton's command, Leclerc had implored Haislip, then his corps commander, to ask when the 2nd DB would be unleashed. Haislip rebuffed him. Two days later Leclerc wrote Patton directly, and he saw both Patton and Bradley, asking that his troops be taken off the line to prepare for the Paris maneuver. Both denied the request. Note that the French general made this appeal at the same moment when Bradley was permitting the First Army—about to assume control of Leclerc anyway—to stand down many of its own formations for rest and refit.

General Leclerc proceeded on his own—he set up a special vanguard unit ready to move off at a moment's notice and designated one of his combat commands to back it up. That meant extra maintenance, which minimized those units' role at Falaise. Commanders in the 2nd DB stopped reporting disabled vehicles in order to requisition fuel as if they were running—and thus stockpiled gas—and indeed the French resorted to every imaginable device to accumulate gasoline for a move on Paris. The Langlade group that Leclerc shifted to the V Corps right flank in the pocket battle had secret orders to proceed slowly and be ready to execute a Paris maneuver, and to desist and change direction upon instruction. This not quite covert operation ended with the Paris uprising. The next morning General Leclerc showed up at First U.S. Army headquarters, where he argued "incessantly" with Courtney Hodges to permit his division to move on Paris immediately, Allied plans notwithstanding. First Army diarists note that Leclerc "said he needed no maintenance, no more equipment, and that he was up to strength—and then, a few minutes later, admitted that he needed all three."[1] Not impressed, Hodges gruffly told Leclerc to hold position until directed otherwise.

These orders did not end the matter. General Eisenhower had previously agreed with the French provisional government that the Leclerc division would be sent to Paris at the appropriate time. Ike's way to resolve that contradiction was to avoid the metropolis altogether. The right moment could just as well be once the Allied front had progressed far beyond Paris. But within twenty-four hours of Leclerc's showdown at First Army headquarters it became impossible to ignore the issue. De Gaulle met with Eisenhower and asked that the 2nd DB be leapfrogged into the city. Ike backed him down. De Gaulle then sent Eisenhower a letter on August 21 saying, "Information received today from Paris leads me to believe that . . . serious trouble may shortly be expected in the capital."[2] On top of Eisenhower's refusal, the letter subtly hinted de Gaulle might resort to direct orders of his own. The same day Leclerc sent de Gaulle a letter, too: "I have been assured that my division's objective is Paris. But in face of the spirit of paralysis [of the Allied command] I have made the following decision: [an officer] has been sent with a light detachment—tanks, machine guns, and infantry—to Versailles with orders to make contact, to let me know, and to enter Paris if the enemy fall back."[3] The advance guard of the 2nd DB left at noon, an hour when the fighting at Falaise was at its peak. Leclerc had taken matters into his own hands.

De Gaulle approved Leclerc's maneuver at midnight that day. General Koenig appointed Leclerc as provisional military governor of Paris.

At this point General Gerow of V Corps, now the Frenchman's superior, received a complaint from the Third Army demanding to know what *his* troops—the Leclerc division—were doing in Patton's sector (which then included Paris). Steaming, Gerow sent a dispatch to the French general reminding him who was in command and demanding that Leclerc recall all 2nd DB troops. Meanwhile, Eisenhower, bowing to the political-diplomatic realities, recognized the *fait accompli* by setting new army boundaries that placed Paris within Gerow's V Corps zone. Ike summoned Omar Bradley that morning to make it official. General Bradley left SHAEF and flew directly to Hodges, where he told the First Army leader that "higher headquarters had decided that Paris could be ignored no longer, that entry of our forces was necessary in order to prevent possible heavy bloodshed among the civilian population, and he inquired what General Hodges could dispatch right away."[4]

Instead of disciplining Philippe Leclerc, the Americans sent the GIs of Ray Barton's 4th Infantry Division to reinforce him and follow up. Barton's GIs achieved the distinction of being at the cutting edge of the capture of Cherbourg, the Cobra breakthrough, and the liberation of Paris. Theirs was a remarkable performance.

The actual liberation of the City of Light is history. Rather than destroy it, von Choltitz negotiated a truce with the Resistance. Fighting continued sporadically until Leclerc's troops began entering Paris. Barton's Americans arrived a little later. At a certain point the German general surrendered his remaining men. Soon enough there were victory parades that GIs enjoyed as much as Frenchmen. Eisenhower happily appeared alongside de Gaulle.

All this shows just how delicate managing a multinational alliance could be. At the extreme, as at Paris, dispute could lead to insubordination. The possibility remained after the liberation as well as before, and concern about the French was not the worst problem. Eisenhower—and SHAEF—inevitably had responsibilities other than the military ones. Political-military relations with the British were by far the most sensitive issue. The debates with Montgomery had meaning beyond mere strategic substance. So did Eisenhower's decisions. Perhaps Lord Alanbrooke did not understand that so well—though his high-level deliberations in concert with the U.S. chiefs of staff ought to have educated him to that dimension. Normandy added to a bill of particulars for generals who already eyed each other with suspicion. The war among the generals was real. Normandy became a melting pot for their goodwill, because there the Allies faced an enemy who long frustrated every move, permitting real and imagined slights to fester.

In the analysis he published immediately after Falaise, J. F. C. Fuller, in addition to his Napoleonic analogy, compared the German situation with that of Robert E. Lee after the Battle of Five Forks in April 1865— the penultimate engagement of the Confederacy's main army before the South went down to defeat in the American Civil War.[5] This exemplified the sense that Nazi Germany was on the ropes and that victory was for the taking. These feelings now infected many on the Allied side. As in other places and other wars there was talk of Berlin before Christmas, home before the leaves fall. George Patton wrote in his diary on August 21, "We have, at this time, the greatest chance to win the war ever presented . . . we can be in Germany in ten days."[6] Similarly, many years later Omar Bradley would reflect, "There was wild jubilation in the Allied camp. Nothing of consequence lay between us and Germany. Hitler's vaunted military machine had been irretrievably smashed. . . . The war, many thought, would surely be over by the end of September."[7] Even the intelligence experts were affected: On the eve of Cobra, the British Joint Intelligence Committee, it will be recalled, was already predicting a German collapse before Christmas. Allied arms were triumphant.

That was victory disease. Normandy was its crucible. Visceral impression now held sway. The brilliance of Falaise and the easy advance over the following weeks seemed to confirm that illusion, but it was built on sand. In truth the Allies were neither so invincible nor as unchallenged as they imagined. The central problem was to convert the considerable advantage obtained in Normandy into an unassailable strategic superiority. That endeavor failed, in part, due to the difficulties of inter-allied cooperation just related. Again the French posed an exemplary case. Bradley records that "within a week we would be rooting Leclerc's Shermans out of every back alley in Paris, even threatening his division with dissolution to get it on the road."[8] The 2nd DB never again fought under Gerow. Instead, Bradley sent Leclerc back to Patton, who eventually passed the division off to the First French Army once the Allies coming out of Normandy had joined up with those from southern France. But more critical than the French problem, the American and British differences persisted, and grievance lists were freighted with new episodes. The British antipathy for the Canadians also remained. General Eisenhower announced that with SHAEF now solidly on the Continent—soon its headquarters would be located outside Paris—he would assume direct command on September 1, ending Montgomery's reign. Very likely—and hardly recognized by historians—the Leclerc episode had been Ike's last straw in deciding to assert his authority. He would still handle Montgomery with kid gloves. But only in the depths of the Ardennes battle crisis—coincidentally or not, around Christmas—would Eisenhower ever again endow Monty with anything more than command over his own army group.

Yet the precise fact of losing supreme command weighed on Montgomery. Prime Minister Churchill sought to mollify Monty by promoting him to field marshal exactly when the command change occurred—but even that act disrupted personal relationships, because it suddenly made Montgomery senior in rank to his own supreme commander, Eisenhower, and to every other U.S. general. And this took place with Montgomery already sensitive about the diminishing British Commonwealth share of the Allied effort. By August 31 the British had landed 829,640 Commonwealth and minor allied troops, while 1,222,659 Americans were ashore. The British had reached their limit, but the number of GIs continued to swell. Since roughly 250,000 of Monty's troops were Canadian, Polish, Czech, Belgian, or Dutch, the disparity compared to U.S. forces was even greater, and it would increase. Monty, who had rejected an American armored division during the Caen battles, would eventually have an entire U.S. army fleshing out his group. Command relationships remained delicate through the remainder of the war.

Equally important as impedimenta to attaining absolute superiority were three other factors: differences over a proper strategic approach; the continuing weaknesses in Allied logistics; and a misappreciation of the actual power of the German adversary. Every one of those issues emerged during the Cotentin-Falaise phase of the Normandy campaign.

Accounts of the Northwest Europe fighting are replete with discussions of the debate over Allied strategy after Normandy. Montgomery espoused the so-called Narrow Thrust, under which all Allied resources would be mustered under one command for a focused, concentrated assault to reach into Germany and conquer Berlin. American generals favored a "Broad Front" strategy, under which the armies would advance everywhere and take advantage of German weakness wherever it appeared.

That debate began at Montgomery's headquarters before the battle of Falaise was even fought, when the British commander presented his outline plan for the sequel. On August 17, with Falaise at its height, Monty briefed Bradley in greater detail on the concept, by then further refined, for all the armies to advance as a mass along his preferred axis. Six days later, when Eisenhower lunched with him just as the liberation of Paris had begun, Monty pressed his plan on Ike, too. That day George Patton wrote, "I cannot understand why Monty keeps on asking for all four armies in the Calais area and then through Belgium, where the tanks are practically useless now and will be wholly useless this winter."[9] None of the Americans favored Monty's scheme. The dispute was in full flower as the fighting ended in the Corridor of Death.

This is not the place to replay that debate, only to record that Normandy served as its incubator, as well as to condition the logistical factors that made it necessary for Eisenhower, the supreme commander, to choose. It is worth noting that Operation Market-Garden, the ill-fated application of Monty's Narrow Thrust approach—which led to the disaster at Arnhem—owed its approval in significant part to Eisenhower's appreciation of Montgomery's sensitivity and disappointment. That brought to a boil the brew stirred up in Normandy.

Considerations of supply were fundamental to strategic choice, and there, too, Normandy acted as crucible. The limitations of Norman ports and the Mulberry, still a significant constraint, promised to diminish with the capture of Toulon and Marseilles, the great Mediterranean harbor. But the logistics headaches of getting the supplies to the troops only grew—and they mushroomed as the velocity of the Allied advance increased. The Normandy breakout created a supply crisis almost automatically. General Clifford H. Lee and his Communications Zone experts labored to solve the puzzle. Railheads were left far behind. They would not catch up until the front became static—a moment as yet months into the future. And the pace of rail reconstruction would slow as the engineers entered the zone formerly behind the German lines, where Allied airpower had done its best to destroy the rail system.

Trucks were the alternative. General Lee's famed "Red Ball Express" delivery system began at Saint-Lô on August 25, the day the liberation of Paris was completed. There had been previous ad hoc trucking operations, especially during the breakout, as on August 6, when trucks sped ahead to deliver gasoline to Patton's forces exploiting from Avranches. Forward depots were built at Chartres (for the Third U.S. Army) and Dreux (for the First U.S. Army). The British initiated a similar operation. The Express opened with 67 truck companies and 3,358 vehicles, almost doubling (to 132 companies and 5,598 trucks) within days. But Overlord planners had calculated that 240 truck companies were needed. Supplementing Com Z trucks by pulling in companies organic to the combat divisions was an improvisation repeatedly required. That increased the tension between supply haul and combat support. American practice was to divert truck companies to transport infantry units whenever tactically desirable. Trucks that belonged to the divisions were insufficient to fully motorize them. During the breakout, the rapid advance of the 90th Division to Mayenne, for example, had been rendered possible by taking trucks away from supply duty. At Third Army, Patton's continuing practice was to ensure the availability of one motorized infantry regiment per armored division, at worst a regiment per corps. Each such formation represented the equivalent capacity for half or more of the daily supply requirement of a division. In the case of Com Z vehicle utilization, Normandy did not incubate the problem so much as serve as an oven for developing expedients attempted in its solution.

The logistics headache was, however, fundamentally insoluble. During the Normandy breakout the emergency delivery of gasoline to Patton had required forty-eight hours to transport the amount of fuel the Third Army typically consumed in two days. Air transport of gasoline helped Patton—but also grounded the Allied airborne forces and wore out the cargo planes. On August 24, with Bradley's units reaching for Paris, the Seine, and the deeper hook past Dreux, the First Army consumed 782,000 gallons of gas. The First and Third Armies on average burned 400,000 gallons a day. On August 26 each of them was short 100,000 gallons.

Forward depots received 5,000 tons of supplies per day on average. The peak performance of the Red Ball Express—an operation that continued through November—actually came on August 29, when the truck companies delivered 12,392 tons of supplies to the depots. Another 2,000 tons could in theory be delivered by aircraft (actual aerial deliveries during the full month ending with Market-Garden were 20,000 tons, hence 666 tons per day). In contrast, by the end of June, American forces alone were already consuming close to 14,000 tons daily, and many new divisions had deployed since, including the entire Third Army. With thirty-six divisions in the field, the requirement averaged 20,000 tons a day. This logistics crunch would not be solved until the railroads attained full capacity. In short, the realities of supply *demanded* an Allied strategic choice. Normandy had been the crucible for expedient solutions, but these were not capable of solving the underlying problem.

General Bernard L. Montgomery issued a special communiqué on August 21. In it he called the victory definite, complete, and decisive. Part of the text read: "The German armies in northwest France have suffered a decisive defeat. The destruction of enemy personnel and equipment in and about the so-called 'Normandy pocket' has been terrific. And it is still going on. Any enemy units that manage to get away will not be in fit condition to fight again for months."[10] Monty's manifesto is seconded in retrospect by Omar Bradley, who wrote of Allied jubilation and the feeling the Wehrmacht had been "irretrievably smashed." The OKW communiqué printed the same day had stated, "In Normandy our divisions north of Argentan, after an embittered struggle, have broken through the enemy barrier toward the northeast and established contact with a counterattacking German tank group."[11]

In a way, Berlin's propaganda seems more accurate than the declarations from the Allied camp, infected as they were by victory disease. Though enormous, the Allied achievement in Normandy had been less than advertised. And dysfunctional though it was, the Nazi High Command had laid the basis for a defense of the German frontier that put paid to all those illusions of ending the war by September. The reasons why are several.

The first goes to the box score from the Falaise Pocket. The Nazis salvaged more of the Wehrmacht than Allied officers believed. Even in the euphoria of victory there were indications this might be the case. *Newsweek* printed a war correspondent's coverage of the battle in its August 28 issue that specified a number of troops caught in the pocket: "estimates of the troops inside then varied from 100,000 to 350,000."[12] The figures for

German prisoners and losses were what they were, somewhere between 45,000 and 60,000. If the Nazi disposition in Normandy was anywhere close to the higher figure, then the proportion of their forces that escaped became much higher.

Martin Blumenson, the American official historian, who went on to write repeatedly on this subject, attempted a more systematic answer to this question in the 1990s.[13] There were 350,000 Germans in France west of the Seine, Blumenson found, and half of them had been in the Falaise Pocket. The 50,000 Nazis in Brittany were trapped and out of the equation. By his calculation, 125,000 German troops were outside the trap altogether, and some 240,000 Germans escaped across the Seine River. My arithmetic leads to the proposition that 115,000 Wehrmacht personnel escaped the Corridor of Death. Blumenson finds "well over 100,000," even accepting the highest estimates for German casualties. He also correctly notes that only one of five corps commanders was captured (Elfeldt), and just three of fifteen division leaders. One might add that all German army-level commanders also escaped.

Given the evidence of destruction around Chambois in the breakout battle, the most reasonable explanation is that a substantial number of German forces succeeded in making their way out of the developing pocket *before* the gap closed. This in turn lends credence to the assertion that the support and service elements of the German divisions, in particular the mobile formations, escaped in good time.

It is astonishing that a defense of the German frontier could have been reconstituted so swiftly after the Normandy debacle. Less than a month separates the huge Allied victory at Falaise and the bloody nose they suffered at Arnhem. Both the number of troops who escaped and the fact that German generals, staffs, and division service forces got out contributed to that development.

By *Montgomery's* standard—the number of months elapsed between the end of the Normandy campaign and the moment German formations were again battleworthy—the Wehrmacht performed excellently. The Fifth Panzer Army strength return for August 28 credits its seven panzer divisions with a combined strength of 1,300 combat troops, twenty-four tanks, and sixty guns. Yet many of the German divisions were back in action within days. The figures were misleading. The 9th Panzer Division alone reported a combat strength of 2,200 on August 22, but is estimated at about 11,000 troops at the beginning of September. As of that date the eleven panzer and mobile divisions in the West mustered 98,000 troops out of a starting strength of over 160,000 men. And the Germans had almost four times as many tanks in those units than noted in the oft-quoted Fifth Panzer Army return. Another forty-odd tanks and assault guns were in nondivisional formations. This was still not a lot of strength, but it was far more than the Allies believed existed, and indicated many fewer losses in Normandy.

A good number of the divisions recouped their combat power even while almost continuously engaged. This was true despite a smaller encirclement Montgomery achieved around Arras after crossing the Seine. Probably the key element that made possible this recovery was Hitler's approval of an initiative to establish panzer brigades, which had occurred in a timely fashion and quickly began to produce results. For the panzer divisions, incorporating brigades plus replacement tanks into the structures of the escaped units, which possessed a hard kernel of surviving cadre, was much easier than rebuilding formations from scratch. In addition, the Germans preserved the critical technical specialists—recovery teams, mechanics, ordnance experts, field hospitals, supply personnel, radiomen—that made their units effective. On August 18, with the Normandy battle still under way, OB West asked for the new panzer brigades, plus nine artillery battalions, 270 tanks, motor transport, and as many heavy guns as could be found. During the month of August, despite Allied strategic bombing, German factories turned out some 869 tanks and 744 assault guns. The bulk of them were sent to the West.

Reconstruction of the infantry force followed similarly from the German program to create Volksgrenadier divisions, which decision Hitler made not long after D-Day and was well under way by the time of Falaise. Melding the Volksgrenadiers with the remnants of the OB West infantry accelerated the recovery. While only a few of the nineteen Volksgrenadier divisions created in the initial wave went to the West, most subsequent units did so, and the system for setting up the Volksgrenadiers had become well established. The western command had already asked for at least twenty battalions of infantry replacements as well.

These initiatives make the swift German recovery more understandable. It would be crucial in the end, however, that the re-formed German divisions would be more brittle than their forebears—not as experienced, less well trained and equipped, and held to a rigid Nazi standard of political loyalty that reduced their operational flexibility. The new German army would not be the Wehrmacht even of D-Day, much less that of 1940 or 1941.

One additional element needs mention. Adolf Hitler, despite his often exhibited predilection for stand-fast orders and offensive action regardless of the situation, not to mention his exhortations to the generals not to look over their shoulders, now adopted timely measures to improve rearward defenses. Hitler's instructions toward the end of the campaign to create defenses along French roads have been noted. Not much seems to have been done about that, but the Nazi leader took the initiative to a higher level. Beginning as early as mid-July Führer Headquarters began issuing a series of decrees designed to put Germany in a state of readiness to repel direct invasion. Separate führer orders covered the Reich in general, the German Bight, and northern Italy. In a further directive he issued on August 24—as the defense of Paris collapsed—Hitler turned to the West. The führer not only ordered the preparation of the defenses, he mandated call-ups of the civilian population to help in construction, designated military authorities and party officials to take charge, and foresaw the use of portions of the old French defenses known as the Maginot Line. The directive included explicit instructions on the character of the fortifications to be prepared. Hitler had OKW issue a modification on September 7 to specify more precisely the authorities to be responsible in Holland. Apart from any of its other effects, the Normandy crucible had shaken Adolf Hitler out of his complacency.

The German rally came as a surprise to the Allies at the time, except perhaps insofar as the last element is concerned—aerial reconnaissance mounted an extensive effort deep behind the front to map the defenses and determine the status of fortifications along the German frontier. But the overall surprise is perplexing given that Allied intelligence advantages gave them such a unique window into German administrative service activities, unit strength returns, and the movement of replacement equipment. These particular kinds of Nazi activity were clearly central to the recovery. In particular, on September 5, the Japanese ambassador in Berlin reported, in a dispatch that was intercepted and decoded, that Germany was mobilizing more than a million more persons for its armed forces. There is no evidence of Allied commanders disputing the accuracy of Source ULTRA reporting. But staffs must have discounted the implications of the data. Officers simply found it difficult to believe the German army had reconstituted itself before their eyes. Victory disease had practical consequences. This became an obstacle to converting the Normandy victory into an absolute superiority.

There is another respect in which Normandy formed a crucible: *German strategy.* In a very real sense the Ardennes offensive of December 1944, the famous Battle of the Bulge, was born less than two weeks after D-Day. That conference at Margival on June 17, which is passed over so lightly in virtually every account, actually marked the inception of the idea of the Bulge. The proposal for a multi-corps counteroffensive—Rommel's proposal—was accepted by Hitler as the basis for German action. Thereafter Hitler's strategy aimed at creating conditions under which a maneuver of this dimension would be possible. The successive schemes for the German offensive—against the British, into the rear of the Americans attacking Cherbourg, against the Americans at Avranches, at Avranches again, into the American flank to gain a position to attack Avranches—were all the offspring of that concept. Each time one failed Hitler decided that execution had been imperfect. He demanded new efforts, done right.

German experience gradually added another element that became a fixture: The offensive must incorporate an active and operationally effective Luftwaffe. That meant time to generate requisite air strength. And the lack of sufficient mobile units created the necessity for a stable line from which to project an offensive. As early as July 31, at the conference immediately preceding the Warlimont mission and the first Argentan attack,

Hitler explicitly recognized these factors. After the destruction wrought at Falaise, of course, even more time became necessary to regenerate ground forces.

A last element that appears to have entered the calculation was a fixation on the Americans. Although Hitler remarked on July 31 that he could not yet say where he might decide to roll the dice, except for the Margival concept for an attack on the British above Caen, *every* subsequent offensive scheme centered on hitting the Americans. The battle at Avranches, where GIs finally broke Hitler's lockbox in Normandy, may have made the United States the führer's permanent quarry. From the standpoint of smart German strategy in late 1944, this was a mistake: We know now that British Commonwealth forces were near the end of their tether, a fact Montgomery specifically used to justify his brand of combat tactics. A massive offensive aimed at the British might actually have had a strategic impact. The Americans, though short of replacements and cutting back their intended creation of divisions, had more margin left than the Brits. Hitler defended the German frontier for months while accepting risks in battle, with the aim of creating conditions for the massive counteroffensive eventually made that December. Again the Allied codebreakers had a contribution to make: As early as August a pair of intercepted messages from the Japanese ambassador in Berlin implied a German intention to attack in the West, while the September 5 cable mentioned above cited Hitler's explicit declaration that that was what he would do. The Norman oven cooked many things, and in the end the Allies were lucky with this one, which emerged half-baked, for the Bulge attack frittered away the last reserves of strength with which Germany might otherwise have prolonged the war.

Normandy became a crucible, too, for men in battle and for combat tactics and techniques. Dwight D. Eisenhower, experienced with an interallied high command, would become the first commander in chief of the similar structure established for the cold war by the North Atlantic Treaty Organization (NATO), on his way to becoming president of the United States. Bernard L. Montgomery would hold a slightly less exalted position as joint commander of a NATO predecessor. Omar N. Bradley and J. Lawton Collins both followed Eisenhower as chiefs of staff of the postwar United States Army or chairmen of the Joint Chiefs of Staff, and both held those jobs during the Korean War. America's commanders in the Vietnam War were all in Normandy—Paul D. Harkins and Creighton V. Abrams fought under Patton, while William C. Westmoreland served in the 9th Infantry Division under Bradley. On the French side, Jacques-Philippe Leclerc became a marshal of France and helped restore French Indochina, though he made efforts to avoid the French war in Vietnam.

While the Normandy crucible exacerbated differences among the generals, it created bands of brothers, also. Here we will mention only two, one of GIs, one of Frenchmen. On the American side, the sad-sack 90th Infantry Division, which transformed itself into the Tough 'Ombres, had a significant legacy in the cold war Central Intelligence Agency (CIA). The resourceful battalion commander Edward S. Hamilton, his regimental operations chief William E. Depuy, and the division operations staffer Richard G. Stilwell, along with a number of other members of the 90th tribe, became a clique of CIA operations officers. Hamilton would command CIA efforts to infiltrate Red China in the early 1950s; Stilwell and Depuy both led divisions of the CIA clandestine service. Both returned to the army and rose to flag rank, Stilwell with a command position in Vietnam, Depuy leading the "Big Red One," the 1st Infantry Division, in that war. General Depuy later played a seminal role in the elaboration of the U.S. military doctrine called Air-Land Battle, which drew some of its proclivity for maneuver from the Normandy breakout, and which formed the basis for U.S. combat action in the Persian Gulf War of 1991.

On the French side the band of brothers were officers of the Leclerc division, the 2nd DB. Many of them followed General Leclerc to Indochina with the Corps Expéditionnaire Français d'Extrême Orient, the army that would fight the Franco-Vietnamese War. Paul de Langlade became a principal in returning French control to Cambodia. Jacques Massu, the leader of the column that first scouted into Paris, gained distinction as a commando and paratroop leader, and rose in the ranks until he led the 10th Paratroop Division in the Algerian war. Massu, now in his own right at the head of a division, earned a certain infamy—different

from Leclerc's—in the notorious Battle of Algiers. French professional soldiers, including Massu, were burned by public controversy that arose from
the use of torture in Algeria, a phenomenon the American military and
CIA officers caught up in today's war on terror would appreciate.

Finally, the Normandy crucible produced new evolutions in military
tactics and combat techniques. The Wehrmacht, forced to operate at night
for fear of Allied airplanes, began to rely on night operations to an unprec-
edented extent. Its Ardennes offensive would begin with night attacks in
some sectors. The Americans and British had resorted to night fighting
occasionally in North Africa, Sicily, and Italy, but this was considered a
novelty adopted in exigencies. In Normandy they absorbed the lesson.
Some of the offensives around Caen began at night, and lesser firefights at
night became a norm.

The use of strategic bombing in a tactical role, as on D-Day, at Cherbourg, at Caen, or in Cobra, was a technique that reached its apogee in
Normandy. The repeated instances of casualties and damage to friendly
forces from carpet bombing were painful and disturbing—and the most
careful planning did not prevent them. After one of these attacks, a winc-
ing General Eisenhower turned to his naval aide, Harry Butcher, and
said, essentially, "Never again." Following the death of General McNair at
Cobra, the military commentator Hanson W. Baldwin published a piece
subtitled "QUESTION OF SUCH USE OF 'HEAVIES' RAISED BY
OBSERVER IN REACTION TO McNAIR'S DEATH." In the article
Baldwin wrote, "The bombing of front line enemy positions still leaves
something to be desired."[14] The piece appeared just days before new strategic bombings preceded the Canadian offensives below Caen, inflicting
yet more friendly losses. The strikes also rendered Allied troop movements
more difficult, and their impact on the adversary may have been significant but was indeterminate. At Cobra results were clearly consequential,
but bombing effects could not be predicted with confidence. With the
exception of air bombardments against certain Channel ports, after Normandy there would be no more "grand slam" strikes in tactical actions.

The Normandy campaign naturally had a major strategic impact.
Allied forces completed the task conferred upon them at D-Day, breaking out of the peninsula where the Nazis had attempted to confine them,

restoring a war of movement hardly seen in the West since the early days of the Italian campaign. The fighting bled the Nazi armies, robbing them of the fruits of the long period of preparations for battle in the West. German losses from D-Day to September 1 totaled as many as 393,689, including almost 55,000 dead. Even excluding those Germans who never returned from southern France, perhaps 70,000 in all, the toll was still enormous. These results did not come cheaply. The American armies lost 20,838 dead, 94,881 wounded, and 10,128 missing in action. British, Canadian, and Polish casualties included 16,138 dead, 58,594 wounded, and 9,093 missing—a weighty butcher's bill.

So Normandy incubated many things, both favorable to the Allied enterprise and not. It inflamed delicate relations between the Allies, infected them with an overconfidence that led to error, taught lessons on tactics and doctrine, formed new bands of brothers, and failed to solve the supply problems that hampered subsequent efforts. The Germans were able to reconstitute their shattered forces with amazing rapidity, but did so on a diminished base of capability. Most pernicious on the German side would be the fixation on a major offensive against American armies, one that Hitler pursued at his peril. In many ways the Normandy crucible is a key to explaining what happened in the last phase of the war in the West, and with it the outcome of World War II.

APPENDIX

WAR-GAMING THE NORMANDY CAMPAIGN

I n setting out on this project, the Normandy campaign seemed an ideal subject on which to employ war-gaming techniques, leading to simulations analysis that might illuminate important aspects of the real historical events. The use of a board wargame as a research tool is something that fans of the genre have long speculated about. Historians, on the other hand, have long looked askance at such novelties and continue to do so. Perhaps it is in my training as a political scientist, but I have been less wedded to that common wisdom. Also, in my practical experience as a game designer, I have long relied on historical data as a foundation for simulation work, and thus am less resistant to the basic idea of creating what is, in effect, a laboratory for historical research. In addition, it would advance the methodology of historical inquiry to possess such a technique. Anyway, there is no harm in trying.

There are two sides to the proposition that a simulation can be used as a research tool. Both readers and historians already know—and accept— the conventional point of view. The sources are what they are, and they are the basis for any historical inquiry. The historian would be right to object that simulation cannot yield true "data," that the output of any simulation exercise is synthetic. But the question of utility resides in the uses to which data is put. To rely upon simulation-generated data as historical "fact" is wrong, and inadmissible. But to use a war game to aid in understanding the parameters and limitations on the real actors, or to visualize the impact of given hypotheticals, is in fact an aid to insight. Historians themselves have embarked increasingly on a similar path in recent years, postulating "counterfactuals" as a technique of analysis. War-gamers were dealing with "what if" problems—regarding history—decades before this historical method gained respectability. Hence the notion of a historical laboratory.

Research material is inherently limited by its nature, scope, and content. Historians typically contribute by uncovering fresh material or by reframing the data to derive new insights. In the case of Normandy in World War II, the historical data are well established. The main area for further advances must be in terms of insight. And it is in that regard that war-gaming can be especially useful. It is impossible to experiment with data. But to take that data as a set of stipulations, create a framework in which the given forces and capabilities interact, and observe the resulting interactions is eminently feasible. The war game makes possible an exploration of the potential of major—and some minor—alternative strategies and tactics that could have been used in the actual campaign. This creates an environment far more methodologically coherent for the treatment of counterfactuals than the rudimentary analysis typically applied.

The major drawback is a perennial argument that exists about simulation fidelity versus reality—that war games are not war and models cannot be crafted so perfectly as to replicate the reality. This is true, but again, value resides upon the uses to which simulation is put. No effort was made here to generate *actual* data. The simulation process aimed at obtaining *dynamic* impressions. By these I mean identifying trends, ranking the relative importance of the variables that bear on a situation, and projecting the utility of alternative strategies against each other.

This appendix describes in greater detail how a war game was used, as well as some of the results. Readers who are not interested in the specifics of the simulation device should skip the next section. The one beyond that covers some of the insights achieved by this technique.

The first step in operationalizing this project was to obtain the right simulation platform. My aim was to adapt an existing war game rather than design a model from whole cloth. As a professional in this field I am aware of many war games that cover this subject at varying levels of detail. The game I selected is called Cobra. It was designed by Brad E. Hessel and published by Simulations Publications, Incorporated, in 1977.

This game requires approximately ten hours per iteration and models the Normandy campaign at a regiment/division level. The game board overlays a map of Normandy with a hexagonal grid that regulates movement. Its scale is slightly less than two miles to the hex. It covers the area from Lisieux—outside the eventual Falaise Pocket—to the Cotentin coast on the east-west axis, and from Bayeux in the north to the area below Alençon in the south. Allied infantry units appear as divisions, along with some German infantry formations, while armored divisions and independent tank brigades are portrayed as regiments or brigades (an equivalently sized unit). The appearance of German units at the regimental level was especially important due to their practice of cross-attaching formations to create battle groups. In the war-game field this is called an "operational level" design.

Cobra was a good choice because Hessel pitched the design at a moderate level of complexity, which means the player does not have to keep track of too many things while working through the simulation.

Next, it was necessary to adapt Cobra for the specific purposes here. There have been many developments since Brad Hessel's game appeared, both in simulation design technique and in historical knowledge. For example, in 1977 the secret of code breaking had just recently become known, and the impact of Source ULTRA on combat was poorly understood. It was not included in that design. Similarly, knowledge of the rate at which new forces (reinforcements) arrived in Normandy, and the places from whence they came, has improved since Hessel crafted his simulation. Documents also now afford us precise knowledge of the rate at which German replacement troops arrived for Army Group B. An example from the modeling side is that Cobra required a calculation of mathematical odds between the forces involved on both sides in order to resolve each combat situation, of which there might be many during a game turn. With units valued up to twelve combat strength points and, again, many units potentially involved in each battle, odds ratio calculation becomes cumbersome. The odds ratios feed into what is termed a "combat results table," with columns for each possible ratio. For each battle a random number, generated by a die roll, determines the combat result. Various situational aspects, such as terrain, supply status, and command control, are reflected either by modifying basic unit values or the odds column on which the battle is finally resolved.

I streamlined Hessel's basic design to reflect the new information and ensure the game generated appropriate results. This modification—or "game development"—process required about eight plays of Cobra before I was satisfied with the result. There were several major changes. Orders of arrival for new forces and replacements in the game were altered to reflect today's more precise knowledge of the Normandy campaign. The mechanics for executing the "grand slam" or Cobra-style air attack were changed to better reflect the geographical extent of efforts of this type. The time scale for a turn was reduced from three days real time to two, because the game as designed rarely reached the "pocket" stage before ending (typically, German forces simply disintegrated and Allied ones ran for the edge of the map board). The odds-ratio combat results table was replaced by one based on the simple difference between total strengths involved on each side, both because this is a much easier mathematical calculation and because in the original, given the huge disparities in Allied versus German strength, virtually every battle was resolved on just a few of the odds columns, robbing the model of its ability to generate discriminating outcomes.

The Hessel design had used column shifts on the combat results table to model several elements. I capitalized on this and expanded their range of application, substituting column shifts for multiplication/division of unit strengths in accounting for more terrain elements, and for special effects, such as German *Nebelwerfer* and heavy tank units. I widened command control—also a column shift—to encompass Allied leaders, in addition to German corps headquarters. I then inserted an ULTRA/Intelligence system that enabled the player to *negate* the capability of adversary headquarters/leaders depending on intelligence success. "Combat Intelligence," representing the effect of aerial reconnaissance and prisoner interrogation, afforded the same ability, but was derived based on losses inflicted on the adversary during the preceding turn.

Finally, I modified the way the game conveys advantage to divisions for "unit integrity" and the range of Allied units considered to be mechanized. The details of these design changes are not so crucial as the point that Cobra was adapted in specifically useful ways. At the end of this process, however, the game reliably reproduced a campaign that mimicked the actual course of the one in Normandy.

To use the war game as a laboratory, it was important to adopt scientific principles in the successive plays, or "iterations," of the game. Parameters were set for each iteration and followed consistently throughout (for example, there could be a decision rule that the German player would retreat after combat whenever possible—mobile defense—versus accept losses rather than retreat—stand fast). To maintain consistent implementation—another parameter—I myself took the German side in each iteration. Record keeping was important to accumulate results that could then be compared. The conditions recorded for each turn of play included weather status, available Allied airpower, the level of Allied ULTRA success, and the status of other intelligence. Brief notes then described the main game events that occurred in the turn, losses for both sides, and, given the focus on consequences of the Falaise Pocket battle, German units that successfully escaped.

Each iteration focused on a specific hypothetical. Among scenarios employed were the historical one, an Allied focus on Montgomery's front, one on getting Patton's army into the open quickly, a German deployment on the "Cobra" sector consonant with one German generals argued might have given them a better chance, a German strategy of immediate withdrawal from Normandy as a whole, plus variants on the timing of a German withdrawal order from the pocket; variants on the Mortain attack, including Hitler's idea for an increased/improved Mortain attack, and the improved Mortain attack launched from south of the Domfront area; and variants on the timing of the Allied move to close the gap and seal the Falaise Pocket. Ideally each scenario would be played three or more times to preclude anomalous results.

In short, the simulation laboratory tested a relevant range of historical possibilities within a defined framework (the simulation) that aimed to examine the relative advantages of different courses. In *Normandy*

Crucible simulation data provides insights about the merits of combat in various regions of the battle area, the adequacy of alternate German deployments in the face of the "Cobra" attack, the impracticality of the German offensive against Avranches, and the potential of a German withdrawal from the Falaise Pocket started sooner than was the historical case. These are important findings.

A drawback of the simulation laboratory technique concerns the sheer difficulty of accumulating sufficient iterations of play. Had I come to this idea sooner or had enough time to devote to this aspect of research, or had I been able to organize multiple simultaneous plays to generate data more rapidly, results could have been more concrete. For example, a statement might have been possible that compared expected survival rates from mobile defense, in contrast to Hitler's stand-fast orders. My data is not sufficient to support findings of that order, though it could have been. Iterations of Cobra compiled under the research program were adequate to cover the waterfront of scenarios but not to generate comparative results.

For this reason, and because this simulation methodology is not well accepted in the historical community, I have confined this discussion to an appendix. Results drawn from the simulation exercises support arguments that are advanced in the narrative, but in all cases those assertions are based primarily on source materials and historical analysis, not on the simulation. The game helped the author visualize the Normandy battlefront at each successive stage in the campaign, provided a way to generalize from micro observations, and furnished a dynamic platform to test historical alternatives. The simulation opened fresh perspectives on the historical events. On balance it served successfully. Some of the results derived are detailed below.

Omar Bradley, as explained in the narrative, selected his axis of advance after map study in which he chose to try and avoid rivers. The simulation laboratory powerfully illuminates the geographic features of Normandy. The Orne River on the British sector and the Vire on Bradley's channelized the Allied advance. In Montgomery's sector specifically—and this is not mentioned in the main text due to the novelty of the use of a war game as explained here—the British had a special problem of their own, since the Orne bifurcated Monty's front and forced choices between offensive action on the left bank, around Caen, or the right, near Hill 112. Offensives could not easily be shifted from one sector to the other.

Smaller rivers, such as the Odon above Hill 112, or the Laize, Loison, and Dives below Caen, also posed difficulties. Simulation analysis showed that very small German forces could use these positions, in combination with reserves, to effectively block attack formations. This helps explain the stall of the British operation Epsom, the Canadian offensive Tractable, and other events in Montgomery's sector.

The war game also demonstrated the impact of the bocage, which effectively functioned as a huge fortress region. Allied advances in open country were typically two or three times faster—and more successful— than fighting in the bocage. Even the smaller rivers on Bradley's front, in combination with the bocage, made extremely powerful defensive positions. Had the Germans possessed sufficient troop units to set up river defenses, Bradley's attacks might have been blunted. In effect, the attrition inflicted upon the Germans during the battle for Saint-Lô and in the initial attacks of Cobra were especially important in securing the breakout.

In connection with the Cobra attack itself, the narrative cited the German general von Lüttwitz, who observed that with a panzer corps in reserve and/or with additional *Nebelwerfer* and Tiger tank assets, Bradley might have been stopped. Simulation analysis showed that the concentration of panzers necessary to hold a corps in reserve, including withdrawing two divisions from the front (Lehr, 2nd Panzer), would have weakened the defense lines enough that the general rate of U.S. advance accelerated, while in the Cobra strike itself the panzer corps could have held only some American spearheads. A Bradley breakthrough remained highly likely either from Saint-Lô southwestward or from Coutances southward. Splitting the panzer forces to oppose both lines of advance made each wing too weak to halt the GIs. The presence of Tigers and *Nebelwerfers* would have had no more than marginal impact on this general situation.

An argument often applied by the German generals against Hitler was that the führer tied their hands by demanding a stand-fast defense and that, had they been able to maneuver, they could have fought more effectively. Simulation analysis shows that this view cuts two ways. On the one hand, the generals were correct that mobile defense would have preserved a greater quantity of their forces in Normandy's bocage fighting. However, the retreats necessary to implement a maneuver defense would have brought the U.S. armies into open country sooner, and once that happened German losses would have been magnified, because their infantry simply could not march fast enough to escape the more mobile U.S. forces. At the same time there were some positions—the Caen front being the most prominent, since its loss would have resulted in a Montgomery breakthrough *behind* the bulk of the German army—that simply had to be held. Thus, a German mobile defense would nevertheless have been obliged to accept a certain amount of attrition. Simulation analysis shows German losses using mobile defense tactics still running at three-quarters or more of the average. Since, in addition, the mobile defense solution concedes an Allied breakout into the interior of France, the net result would have been a slightly larger German force confronted with the problem of defending a huge theater of combat.

Hitler's preference for staging the multi-corps counteroffensive proposed at Margival against the Americans in the Cotentin rather than against the British around Caen was also studied. The analysis indicated four main problems with this course. Most obviously, that strategy presupposed stripping the Caen sector of its reserves, and thus an increased risk of a British breakthrough. Second, given Allied aerial superiority, the panzer forces would have incurred significant attrition in concentrating in the U.S. sector, and an offensive there would have had extremely tenuous logistics, with a large proportion of the heaviest consuming German divisions at the very end of a lengthy supply line, again dominated by U.S. airpower. Third, in such an attack the protective advantage of the bocage would have been given to numerically superior U.S. forces. Finally, the limited road net behind the U.S. front, plus the bocage itself, would have greatly restrained the maneuverability of the German armor. Given the paucity of significant geographical objectives in Bradley's sector (the Allied supply base—the Mulberry at Arromanches—lay behind Montgomery's front), this scenario degenerated into a fight for what effectively became a U.S. fortress at Saint-Lô. The single benefit of this strategy from the

German perspective was that it placed the most maneuverable German formations in the sector that would have the longest path to safety in the event of an Allied breakthrough. The Nazi infantry would have had the shortest retreat route across the Seine into the Pas de Calais—*if* it had not been pocketed by a British advance on the left and an American one in the center.

Simulation analysis naturally focused on the Mortain attack and the variants thereof. This effort confirmed the historical outcome. Under no scenario—including that of the generated, multi-corps attack Hitler demanded for the second go-round—could German forces have successfully reached Avranches and cut off the American breakout. The best outcomes were that major German forces rather than scratch units faced Patton's exploitation forces, and that the Germans would have been much better situated to build a southern flank for what became the Falaise Pocket. While that conveyed a certain advantage, it was gained at the expense—as in others of these alternatives—of improving Montgomery's possibilities for a breakthrough on his sector.

The most interesting insight that flowed from the simulation analysis concerns the potential for German withdrawal from the developing Falaise Pocket. The majority of German forces, including the infantry, even those farthest from the escape point, survived in iterations of the war game in which withdrawal began by August 10. Due to their greater mobility and optimal employment in blocking Patton's spearheads, the panzer forces would have incurred losses, but the bulk of them survive also. This suggests that, had the initial failure of Operation Liège been immediately followed by orders for withdrawal from Normandy, the German escape would have been completed in good order and with forces intact. This result occurred in all scenarios and under all weather conditions.

In a withdrawal begun on August 13 the expected survivability of infantry units shrank to a third or less, with half possible if bad weather grounded the Allied air forces. Rear guards would be sacrificed, but much of the infantry, even so, would be arriving at the escape point at the same time as the Allied armies. Panzer forces had somewhat brighter prospects, with a survival rate of half or more in bad weather and of about 40 percent if Allied airpower could operate against them. German armor losses in some proportion were inevitable because the panzers had to hold open the escape route. When the war-game iteration featured a withdrawal begun after August 13—as in the historical events—Allied forces had the opportunity to arrive at the escape point ahead of the German rear echelons, compelling a fight, such as took place in the Corridor of Death. This result, too, occurred in all scenarios. In short, this analysis indicates that the days of decision for a German withdrawal fell between August 10 and 13, confirming the proposition advanced in the narrative of this book.

In connection with the simulation laboratory, I wish to acknowledge the assistance of William Kominers, who helped me find a copy of Cobra, a simulation game long out of print; and for participating in one or more iterations of the game, Kevin Zucker, David C. Isby, Paul Dobbins, Natasha Prados, and Danielle Prados.

ENDNOTES

PROLOGUE: THE DECISION

1   Martin Blumenson, ed., *The Patton Papers, 1940–1945*. Boston: Houghton Mifflin, 1974, p. 479.
2   Ibid.
3   Omar N. Bradley and Clay Blair, *A General's Life: An Autobiography by General of the Army Omar N. Bradley*. New York: Simon & Schuster, 1983, p. 272.
4   Thomas A. Hughes, *Overlord: General Pete Quesada and the Triumph of Tactical Airpower in World War II*. New York: Free Press, 1995, quoted p. 197.
5   Ibid.
6   Omar N. Bradley, *A Soldier's Story*. New York: Henry Holt, 1951, p. 330.
7   Bradley and Blair, *A General's Life*, quoted p. 273.
8   Nigel Hamilton, *Monty: Master of the Battlefield, 1942–1944*. London: Hamish Hamilton, 1983, pp. 697–701, quoted p. 700.
9   J. Lawton Collins, *Lightning Joe: An Autobiography*. Novato, Calif.: Presidio Press, 1994, p. 239.

1. GERMAN NIGHTMARES

1   Bradley, *A Soldier's Story*, quoted p. 241.
2   Bernard L. Montgomery, *The Memoirs of Field Marshal Montgomery of Alamein*. New York: New American Library, 1959, p. 202. The first set of italics are mine, the second Montgomery's.

3　Carlo D'Este, *Decision in Normandy*. New York: E. P. Dutton, 1983, p. 74.

4　Ibid., pp. 201–11.

5　Paul Carell, *Invasion—They're Coming!* New York: Bantam Books, 1964, quoted p. 106.

6　Walter Warlimont, *Inside Hitler's Headquarters, 1939–1945*, trans. R. H. Barry. New York: Praeger, 1964, p. 428.

7　Ibid., p. 431.

8　Nicolaus von Below, *At Hitler's Side: Memoirs of Hitler's Luftwaffe Adjutant, 1937–1945*, trans. Geoffrey Brooks. London: Greenhill Books, 2001, p. 203.

9　Some 9,251 V-1s were launched against Britain in what became a new "Blitz" like the 1940 Battle of Britain. Of them, 2,419 reached London (more than 4,000 were destroyed en route). The missiles were demoralizing for the target populations, who called them "buzz bombs," "doodlebugs," or "flying bombs," and they destroyed or damaged almost as many homes and other structures as did the Blitz (though causing only about a fourth as many casualties). But the V-1s were a terror weapon that had only incidental military effectiveness. The imprecision of the gyrocompasses of the day, relatively gross manufacturing tolerances, and the high stall speed of the V-1 made it difficult to rely on. Allied countermeasures also took advantage of the poor guidance system by broadcasting false messages in place of the brief indicators the V-1s sent out when beginning their final descent. The Germans used these to correct settings on the craft's gyrocompass, so the deception led to the V-1s being given false heading vectors. The Allies also bombed German rocket development and test facilities, manufacturing plants, and the ski ramps; and their armies progressively reduced the available launch sites by capturing France and the Low Countries. The V-2 rocket was not stoppable and had a longer range, but its use against England did not begin until after the Normandy campaign. For a brief, accessible account, see Stephen Zaloga, *V-1 Flying Bomb*. London: Osprey Publishing, 2005.

10　Hans Speidel, *Invasion 1944*, trans. Theo R. Crevenna. New York: Paperback Library, 1968, p. 89.

11　Von Below, *At Hitler's Side*, p. 204.

12　David Irving, *Hitler's War*. New York: Avon Books, 1990, quoted p. 640.

13　Speidel, *Invasion 1944*, p. 92.

14　Warlimont, *Inside Hitler's Headquarters*, p. 433.

15　Speidel, *Invasion 1944*, quoted p. 93.

16　Friedrich Ruge, *Rommel in Normandy: Reminiscences*. San Rafael, Calif.: Presidio, 1979, quoted p. 100.

17   Warlimont, *Inside Hitler's Headquarters*, p. 433.

18   Ruge, *Rommel in Normandy*, quoted p. 196.

19   Speidel, *Invasion 1944*, quoted p. 102.

20   Fifth Panzer Army War Diary, Appendix 33a. Quoted in L. F. Ellis et al., *Victory in the West, Vol. I: The Battle of Normandy* (History of the Second World War Series). London: Imperial War Museum, 1962, p. 321.

21   Ralf Georg Reuth, *Rommel: The End of a Legend*, trans. Debra S. Marmor and Herbert A. Danner. London: Haus Books, 2005, pp. 176–81; and Speidel, *Invasion 1944*, pp. 67–68.

22   Tim Saunders, *Normandy: Hill 112; Battles of the Odon—1944* (Battleground Europe Series). Barnsley, U.K.: Leo Cooper, 2002, quoted p. 30.

23   Will Fey, *Armor Battles of the Waffen SS, 1943–1945*, trans. Henri Henschler. Mechanicsburg, Penn.: Stackpole Books, 2003, p. 106.

24   Hamilton, *Monty: Master of the Battlefield*, quoted p. 768.

2. ALLIED ANXIETIES

1   Robert S. Allen, *Lucky Forward: The History of General George Patton's Third U.S. Army*. New York: McFadden-Bartell, 1965, p. 28.

2   Bradley, *A Soldier's Story*, p. 226.

3   Dwight D. Eisenhower, *Crusade in Europe*. Garden City, N.Y.: Doubleday, 1948, p. 286.

4   For the original revelation of ULTRA, see F. W. Winterbotham, *The Ultra Secret*. New York: Harper & Row, 1974. An early history of the role of the codebreakers in Europe is Ronald Lewin, *Ultra Goes to War*. New York: McGraw-Hill, 1978. For a more recent account, see Hugh Sebag-Montefiore, *Enigma: The Battle for the Code*. London: Cassell, 2004.

5   Ralph Bennett, *Ultra in the West: The Normandy Campaign, 1944–1945*. New York: Charles Scribner's Sons, 1979. Despite his title, Bennett's book is not about Normandy per se but takes in all the fighting from D-Day until the end of the war. Incidentally, Bennett has also contributed a similar account of ULTRA in the Mediterranean. For the British official history, see F. H. Hinsley et al., *British Intelligence in the Second World War: Its Influence on Strategy and Operations, Vol. 3, Part II* (History of the Second World War Series). London: Her Majesty's Stationery Office, 1988.

6   National Security Agency, Historical Monograph SRH-006, "Synthesis of Experiences in the Use of ULTRA Intelligence by U.S. Army Field

Commands in the European Theater of Operations." National Archives: Records Group 457, Records of the National Security Agency.

7   Alistair Horne, *Monty: The Lonely Leader, 1944–1945*. New York: Harper-Collins, 1994, p. 136.

8   Bradley and Blair, *A General's Life*, pp. 258–59.

9   For a fine account of the Oradour massacre, see Max Hastings, *Das Reich*. New York: Warner Books, 1983.

10   Eisenhower, *Crusade in Europe*, p. 234.

11   These theoretical calculations illustrate trends and should not be taken too literally. However, they do suggest the actual situation. For example, it is reported that the British 2nd Army had seven days' rations in stock at the outset of Operation Epsom, with fuel sufficient to cover 150 miles. On the other hand, ammunition was being rationed throughout the 2nd Army, with only one day's reserves of some kinds of shells, while British troop arrivals had slowed to such a degree that Montgomery was short by three divisions compared to Overlord schedules, whereas before the Channel storm arrivals had been only two brigades behind schedule (Ellis et al., *Victory in the West*, pp. 264–65, 274).

12   J. F. C. Fuller, "The Fall of Cherbourg and the Fate of Europe," *Newsweek*, July 3, 1944, p. 23.

13   Butcher Diary, June 27, 1944. Harry C. Butcher, *My Three Years with Eisenhower: The Personal Diary of Captain Harry C. Butcher, USNR, Naval Aide to General Eisenhower, 1942–1945*. New York: Simon & Shuster, 1946, p. 594.

14   A. Harding Ganz, "Questionable Objective: The Brittany Ports, 1944," *Journal of Military History* 59, no. 1 (January 1995), pp. 80–81. Ganz argues that even had the Brittany ports been captured they could not have been developed in time to alleviate Allied supply difficulties.

15   Butcher Diary, July 1, 1944, p. 601.

16   Ganz, "Questionable Objective."

17   Department of the Army, Field Manual FM 101-10, *Staff Officers' Field Manual: Organization, Technical, and Logistical Data*. Department of the Army, August 1949, pp. 298–302, 306–30.

18   First United States Army, *Report of Operations, 20 October 1943–1 August 1944, Vol. I*, pp. 93–94. United States Army, July 1945.

19   Bradley, *A Soldier's Story*, quoted pp. 322–23.

20   Culin received the Legion of Merit for this feat. Before the end of the year, having lost a leg at the battle of the Huertgen Forest, he would be invalided home.

21   Bradley, *A Soldier's Story*, quoted p. 342.

3. THE BEGINNING OF DISASTER

1   Collins, *Lightning Joe*, p. 231.
2   Compare Bayerlein's account in his August 1945 interrogation by U.S.
     intelligence officers (ETHINT 66—[ML-1079]) with that in Martin
     Blumenson, *Breakout and Pursuit* (United States Army in World War II:
     European Theater of Operations Series), Washington: Office of the Chief
     of Military History, 1961, pp. 135–39. American historical monographs,
     such as "Counterattack at St. Jean de Daye," report the same date as Blu-
     menson—that the attack occurred on July 11. General Bayerlein recounts
     these events as occurring on July 8. He was specifically asked about Panzer
     Lehr's attack of July 11 but remembered it as not any different from many
     local counterattacks carried out by his troops, and continued to maintain
     the July 8 operation was the only generated attack launched by the division
     during this period. Bayerlein repeats the date in other contexts, such as dis-
     cussing the relative merits of German and American tanks in other inter-
     views or in documents. On the other hand, Panzer Lehr veteran Helmut
     Ritgen agrees with the American dating (Ritgen, *The Western Front 1944:
     Memoirs of a Panzer Lehr Officer*, trans. Joseph Welsh, Winnipeg: Fedoro-
     wicz Publishing, 1995, pp. 85–89), as does Paul Carrell (Carrell, *Inva-
     sion—They're Coming!* trans. E. Osers, New York: Bantam Books, 1964, pp.
     241–42). Rommel's naval aide, Vice-Admiral Friedrich Ruge, also records
     Panzer Lehr's attack northwest of Saint-Lô on that day, and mentions none
     on the eighth (Ruge, *Rommel in Normandy*, pp. 210, 213, 217). These dif-
     ferences cannot be reconciled from the available material. I have chosen
     to record these events on July 11 because of the weight of the evidence,
     and because in 1945 Bayerlein, exhausted by months of hard fighting and
     all that had befallen his division, may not have had these events clear in
     his mind. However, the reader should be aware that Bayerlein may, in fact,
     have presented the sequence correctly. An example of the Fog of War.
3   The vaunted success of Allied codebreakers in providing high-grade
     SIGINT to field commanders in the form of ULTRA intelligence suffered
     a setback here, as a string of decrypted German messages over a period of
     several days yielded different conclusions as to the location and use of the
     21st Panzer Division. The whereabouts of the 1st SS Panzer Division were
     also uncertain until at least July 11. Hinsley et al., *British Intelligence in the
     Second World War*, pp. 205–08.
4   Kurt Meyer, *Grenadiers: The Story of Waffen SS General Kurt "Panzer"
     Meyer*, trans. Michael Mende and Robert J. Edwards. Mechanicsburg,
     Penn.: Stackpole Books, 2005, p. 266.

5 Robin Neillands, *The Battle of Normandy, 1944.* London: Cassell, 2003, quoted p. 208.

6 Alexander McKee, *Caen: Anvil of Victory.* New York: Dorset Press, 1984, quoted p. 220.

7 Army Group B Weekly Report, July 3–9, 1944, in James A. Wood, ed., *Army of the West: The Weekly Reports of German Army Group B from Normandy to the West Wall.* Mechanicsburg, Penn.: Stackpole Books, 2007, pp. 99–112, quoted p. 101.

8 Hinsley et al., *British Intelligence in the Second World War,* quoted p. 216.

9 Hans von Luck, *Panzer Commander: The Memoirs of Colonel Hans von Luck.* New York: Dell, 1989, quoted p. 201.

10 Neillands, *The Battle of Normandy,* quoted p. 263.

11 Meyer, *Grenadiers,* quoted p. 270.

12 "Official Report—The Wounding of Rommel," in John Pimlott, ed., *Rommel in His Own Words.* London: Greenhill, 1994, p. 183.

13 Peter Hoffmann, *The History of the German Resistance, 1933–1945,* trans. Richard Barry. Cambridge, Mass.: MIT Press, 1977, p. 475. Kurt Meyer rejects this version, recording that both he and Dietrich first learned of the plot when they heard radio news reports insisting the Nazis were in full control (Meyer, *Grenadiers,* p. 273). Colonel Hans von Luck records SS General Sepp Dietrich as having said, when first learning of the putsch, "Who was it, the SS or the Army?" (Von Luck, *Panzer Commander,* quoted p. 202).

14 B. H. Liddell-Hart, *The German Generals Talk.* New York: Berkley Books, 1958, pp. 218–20.

15 From a secret British tape recording of Eberbach conversing with his son in a British prisoner of war camp. Sonke Neitzel, ed., *Tapping Hitler's Generals: Transcriptions of Secret Conversations, 1942–45.* St. Paul, Minn.: Frontline Books, 2007, reprinted p. 103.

16 Liddell-Hart, *The German Generals Talk,* quoted p. 225.

17 Ibid., quoted p. 222.

18 Von Luck, *Panzer Commander,* pp. 201–02.

19 Anthony Tucker-Jones, *Falaise: The Flawed Victory: The Destruction of Panzer Group West, August 1944.* Barnsley, U.K.: Pen & Sword, 2008, quoted pp. 110–11.

20 Meyer, *Grenadiers,* quoted p. 273.

21 Neitzel, ed., *Tapping Hitler's Generals,* reprinted p. 120.

22 Eisenhower, *Crusade in Europe,* p. 517.

23 Blumenson, *Breakout and Pursuit,* p. 212.

4. A HURRICANE OF STEEL

1   Army Group B, "Analysis of the Situation," July 15, 1944, in James A. Wood, ed., *Army of the West: The Weekly Reports of German Army Group B from Normandy to the West Wall.* Mechanicsburg, Penn.: Stackpole Books, 2007, p. 137.

2   Ibid., p. 139.

3   Seventh Army, "Review of the Situation," July 19, 1944, in ibid., pp. 141–43.

4   OB West, Letter, Field Marshal Günther von Kluge to Adolf Hitler, July 21, 1944, in ibid., pp. 143–45.

5   Although these figures are drawn from von Kluge's correspondence, the 2nd Panzer Division's strength return for July 1 records tank strength at twenty one battleworthy Panthers (twenty-nine more in repair), eighty-five PzKw IVs (eleven more repairing), and twelve Jagdpanzer IVs (five more under repair). Niklas Zetterling, *Normandy 1944: German Military Organization, Combat Power and Organizational Effectiveness.* Winnipeg: Fedorowicz, 2000, p. 315. While 2nd Panzer undoubtedly incurred losses prior to July 21, contemporaneous German documents as well as postwar reflections of senior commanders repeatedly speak of the division as if it was at or near full strength.

6   Ernie Pyle, *Brave Men.* Lincoln: University of Nebraska Press, 2001, pp. 413, 414–15.

7   Richard Hargreaves, *The Germans in Normandy: Death Reaped in a Terrible Harvest.* Barnsley, U.K.: Pen & Sword Press, 2006, quoted p. 129.

8   These calculations are based on tabulations of German losses and replacements culled from the weekly reports of Army Group B, compared to strength data for individual German units and the order in which they were sent to Normandy, compiled from Zetterling, *Normandy 1944.* The net strengths I derive from taking the overall figure for the previous week, adding such reinforcements and replacements as arrive, then subtracting recorded losses. In other places in this narrative where current net strengths are given, the figures are based on this same set of calculations.

9   Harry Butcher, *My Three Years with Eisenhower: The Personal Diary of Captain Harry C. Butcher, USNR, Naval Aide to General Eisenhower, 1942 to 1945.* New York: Simon & Schuster, 1946, p. 604.

10 James S. Wheeler, *The Big Red One. America's Legendary 1st Infantry Division from World War I to Desert Storm.* Lawrence: University Press of Kansas, 2007, quoted p. 294.

11 "Heavy Going," *Time,* July 17, 1944, p. 26.

12 "Battle of France: War and Weather," *Time,* July 24, 1944, p. 25.

13 "Unrelenting Allied Attacks Keep Weary Foe Off Balance," *Newsweek*, July 31, 1944, p. 36.

14 Eisenhower, *Crusade in Europe*, p. 272.

15 Butcher Diary, July 19, 1944, in Butcher, *My Three Years with Eisenhower*, p. 616.

16 Bradley, *A Soldier's Story*, quoted p. 343.

17 Butcher Diary, July 22, 1944, in Butcher, *My Three Years with Eisenhower*, quoted p. 620.

18 Pyle, *Brave Men*, p. 456.

19 Ibid.

20 William C. Sylvan and Francis G. Smith, Jr., *Normandy to Victory: The War Diary of General Courtney H. Hodges and the First U.S. Army*, John T. Greenwood, ed. Lexington: University Press of Kentucky, 2008, p. 63.

21 In his codebreaking study, Ralph Bennett also notes a report that the 17th SS Panzergrenadier Division had detected the presence of Patton's thus far hidden Third Army (Bennett, *Ultra in the West*, p. 101). While the specific ULTRA message is not identified, it dates between July 18 and 21.

22 Pyle, *Brave Men*, p. 464.

23 Robert L. Hewitt, *Work Horse of the Western Front: The Story of the 30th Infantry Division*. Washington, D.C.: Infantry Journal Press, 1946, p. 37.

24 Alwyn Featherston, *Battle for Mortain: The 30th Infantry Division Saves the Breakout, August 7–12, 1944*. Novato, Calif.: Presidio Press, 1993, quoted p. 33.

25 Hewitt, *Workhorse of the Western Front*, p. 37.

26 The U.S. official history maintains that General McNair was buried secretly in order to avoid compromise of the Fortitude secret (Blumenson, *Breakout and Pursuit*, p. 236), but the eyewitness account of the keepers of Courtney Hodges's war diary is clear that no body was ever found (Sylvan and Smith, *Normandy to Victory*, pp. 67–69). On the other hand, other eyewitness accounts from GIs of the 30th Division recall seeing a mangled body with stars on the uniform, or even one they could identify (Featherston, *Battle for Mortain*, pp. 33–35). The latter account has McNair and an air liaison officer sheltering in a cottage, not a foxhole, and his body blown sixty feet away. This is another of those mysteries of the war.

27 Carrell, *Invasion*, quoted p. 257.

28 Despite the Allies' huge intelligence advantage, according to the historian Martin Blumenson they underestimated German field strength on this front, assessing it at about fifteen thousand troops rather than the larger figure used here (Blumenson, *The Duel for France, 1944*, p. 85).

29 Hewitt, *Work Horse of the Western Front*, quoted p. 37.

30   Collins, *Lightning Joe*, p. 242.
31   Carrell, *Invasion*, quoted p. 261.
32   The OKW communiqué typically described events of the previous day. This report was recorded by the United Press in London on July 26 (*New York Times*, July 27, 1944, p. 3). Subsequent references to the OKW communiqués will simply cite the day of the events. The two-day lag in this information becoming available should be kept in mind, however.
33   Ritgen, *The Western Front 1944*, pp. 98–103.
34   Zetterling, *Normandy 1944*, p. 43.
35   Carrell, *Invasion*, quoted p. 262.
36   Ibid., quoted p. 265.
37   Ruge, *Rommel in Normandy*, p. 236.
38   Paul Hausser, "27–31 July," U.S. Army Historical Monograph B-179, in David C. Isby, ed., *Fighting the Breakthrough: The German Army in Normandy from "Cobra" to the Falaise Gap*. London: Greenhill Books, 2004, p. 94.
39   Carrell, *Invasion*, quoted pp. 265–66.
40   Ruge, *Rommel in Normandy*, p. 238.
41   Tucker-Jones, *Falaise: The Flawed Victory*, quoted p. 80.
42   OKW Communiqué, July 29, 1944, *New York Times*, July 30, 1944, Pt. 2, p. 2.
43   Neitzel, ed., *Tapping Hitler's Generals*, reprinted p. 94.
44   Liddell-Hart, *The German Generals Talk*, quoted p. 211.
45   Blumenson, *The Duel for France, 1944*, quoted p. 127.
46   Alex Danchev and Daniel Todman, *War Diaries, 1939–1945: Field Marshal Lord Alanbrooke*. Berkeley: University of California Press, 2001, p. 575.
47   Patton, *War as I Knew It*, p. 93.
48   Bradley, *A Soldier's Story*, p. 351.
49   Ladislas Farago, *Patton: Ordeal and Triumph*. New York: Dell Books, 1965, quoted p. 422.
50   Blumenson, ed., *The Patton Papers*, p. 481.
51   Ibid., p. 482.
52   Don M. Fox, *Patton's Vanguard: The United States Army Fourth Armored Division*. Jefferson, N.C.: McFarland, 2003, quoted p. 49.
53   Rudolf-Christophe Freiherr von Gersdorff, "The American Breakthrough," U.S. Army Historical Monograph B-723, in Isby, ed., *Fighting the Breakout*, p. 59.
54   Details of this and other telephone conversations of July 31, except where otherwise specified, are drawn from contemporaneous notes appended to the war diary of OB West and included in the First U.S. Army's *Report of Operations, 20 October 1943–1 August 1944, Vol. I*, pp. 114–16.

55   This important conversation for some reason is omitted from the First Army final report, but it is reprinted with a set of the same material in Butcher, *My Three Years with Eisenhower*, pp. 665–66.

56   Carrell, *Invasion*, quoted p. 270.

57   Blumenson, *Breakout and Pursuit*, p. 319.

58   Ibid., quoted p. 323.

59   *From D-Day Through Victory in Europe*, quoted pp. 89, 93.

60   *New York Times*, August 1, 1944, p. 1.

5. ALL THE FÜHRER'S HORSES

1   Eisenhower, *Crusade in Europe*, p. 275.

2   Bradley and Blair, *A General's Life*, quoted pp. 290–91.

3   Ibid.

4   Blumenson, *Breakout and Pursuit*, quoted p. 431.

5   Butcher, *My Three Years with Eisenhower*, quoted pp. 630–31.

6   C. P. Stacey, *The Victory Campaign: The Operations in Northwest Europe, 1944–1945* (Official History of the Canadian Army in the Second World War, Vol. III). Ottawa: Queen's Printer and Controller of Stationery, 1960, quoted p. 182.

7   Farago, *Patton*, p. 454.

8   D'Este, *Eisenhower*, p. 562.

9   Allen, *Lucky Forward*, p. 79.

10   Third U.S. Army, *After Action Report, 1 August 1944–9 May 1945, Vol. I: Operations*, pp. 18–19.

11   Patton, *War as I Knew It*, pp. 96–98; and Blumenson, ed., *The Patton Papers*, p. 499.

12   All Bradley's directives are reprinted in 12th U.S. Army Group, *Final After Action Report, July 31, 1945, G-3 Section Report of Operations*, pp. 64–75.

13   Warlimont, *Inside Hitler's Headquarters*, quoted p. 445.

14   Conference Transcript, Hitler-Jodl and Others, July 31, 1944; reprinted in Helmut Heiber & David M. Glantz, eds., *Hitler and His Generals: Military Conferences 1942–1945: The First Complete Stenographic Record of the Military Situation Conferences from Stalingrad to Berlin*, trans. Roland Winter, Krista Smith, and Mary Beth Friedrich. New York: Enigma Books, 2003, pp. 444–63, quoted pp. 445, 450, 452, 445, 446.

15   Warlimont, *Inside Hitler's Headquarters*, quoted p. 446.

16 Speidel, *Invasion 1944*, quoted p. 122.

17 Warlimont, *Inside Hitler's Headquarters*, p. 448.

18 Bradley, *A Soldier's Story*, quoted pp. 370, 371.

19 Samuel W. Mitcham, Jr., *Defenders of Fortress Europe: The Untold Story of the German Officers During the Allied Invasion.* Washington, D.C.: Potomac Books, 2009, p. 131.

20 Samuel A. Mitcham, Jr., *Panzer Commanders of the Western Front: German Tank Generals in World War II.* Mechanicsburg, Penn.: Stackpole, 2008, quoted p. 41.

21 Ruge, *Rommel in Normandy*, p. 242.

22 OB West War Diary, August 4, 1944, in First U.S. Army, *Report of Operations, August 1, 1944–February 22, 1945, Vol. I* (hereafter cited as First Army Final Report). U.S. Army, no date (1945), excerpted, p. 5.

23 Ibid.

24 Eisenhower, *Crusade in Europe*, p. 275.

25 Bradley and Blair, *A General's Life*, quoted p. 291.

26 Blumenson, ed., *The Patton Papers*, p. 494.

27 Featherston, *Battle for Mortain*, quoted p. 85; and 12th Army Group Final Report, p. 494.

28 Many illustrations of this point exist in the two best monographs on the battle. See Featherston, *Battle for Mortain*; and Mark J. Reardon, *Victory at Mortain: Stopping Hitler's Panzer Counteroffensive.* Lawrence: University of Kansas Press, 2002.

29 Michael Smith, *Station X: The Codebreakers of Bletchley Park.* London: Pan Books, 2004, quoted pp. 182–83.

30 Eisenhower, *Crusade in Europe*, p. 275.

31 John Colby, *War from the Ground Up: The 90th Division in World War II.* Austin, Texas: Nortex Press, 1991, p. 176.

32 Ibid., quoted p. 213.

33 Bradley and Blair, *A General's Life*, quoted p. 294.

34 Bradley, *A Soldier's Story*, quoted p. 374.

35 Blumenson, ed., *The Patton Papers*, p. 504. Patton's ghostwritten *War as I Knew It* is completely silent on this episode. Confusion also exists as to the sequence of events on August 8, with some accounts written as though Bradley met first with Eisenhower and then saw Patton. I have relied upon Bradley's account (note 30) because he has details (catching Ike on the road, the presence of Kay Summersby, a picnic lunch, the return to 12th Army Group headquarters) that make clear Bradley was already traveling when he met Eisenhower, and ended at his own command post. Eisenhower aide Harry Butcher confirms that Ike met Bradley, "ate his lunch

alongside the road," and visited 12th Army Group headquarters, in that order (Butcher, *My Three Years with Eisenhower*, p. 636).

36 Bradley, *A Soldier's Story*, quoted p. 375.

37 Blumenson, *The Patton Papers*, p. 504.

38 Field-Marshal Viscount Montgomery of Alamein, "Operations in North-west Europe from 6th June 1944 to 5th May 1945," Dispatch of June 1st 1946, Supplement to *London Gazette*, September 3, 1946, as cited in Chester Wilmott, *The Struggle for Europe*. New York: Harper Collophon, 1963, quoted p. 415.

39 Third Armored Division Official History, *Spearhead in the West: The Third Armored Division, 1941–1945*. Frankfurt-am-Main: Kunst und Wer-bedrunck, n.d. [c. 1946], p. 76.

40 OKW War Communiqué, August 12, 1944, *New York Times*, August 13, 1944, p. 2.

6. THE CAULDRON

1   Mitcham, Jr., *Panzers in Normandy*, quoted p. 98.

2   Ibid., quoted p. 144.

3   Commander in Chief, SHAEF Ground Forces, Directive M515, July 27, 1944, in Stacey, *Victory Campaign*, quoted p. 199.

4   On August 4, the division had reported thirty-nine combat-ready Panzer IVs, fifty-nine Panthers, and ten assault guns; and the Schwere SS Panzer Abteilung 101 had twenty-two Tigers. As of August 7, the Canadian history puts its strength at thirty-seven Panzer IVs and nine Panthers, with twenty-one Tigers in the heavy battalion (Stacey, *Victory Campaign*, p. 221), but without listing assault guns or, apparently, accounting for the armor attached from 1st SS Panzer. The above is my estimate. The battle group returning from the Thury-Harcourt area, we are told, possessed seven Panther tanks on August 7 (Zetterling, *Normandy 1944*, pp. 356–57, 360–61).

5   McKee, *Caen*, pp. 331, 335.

6   Bradley, *A Soldier's Story*, quoted p. 376.

7   Ibid., pp. 376–77.

8   Bradley and Blair, *A General's Life*, p. 299.

9   OB West War Diary, August 12, 1944, First Army Final Report, reprinted p. 14.

10 Bradley and Blair, *A General's Life*, p. 298.

11   Ibid., p. 299; and Butcher, *My Three Years with Eisenhower*, p. 642.

12   12th Army Group, Letter of Instructions No. 5, August 17, 1944, in 12th U.S. Army Group, *Final After Action Report*, Annex D. In the original the names of the towns are printed in capital letters. The quotation also excludes the map coordinates of the towns given in the original.

13   OB West War Diary, August 16, 1944, in First Army Final Report, p. 16.

14   Sylvan and Smith, Jr., *Normandy to Victory*, p. 96.

15   Rohmer, *Patton's Gap*, p. 171.

16   This oddity apparently stems from a rumor at the time, reported by OB West operations chief General Bodo Zimmerman, that the OKW radio interception service had recorded some sort of transmission between OB West and the Americans (Bodo Zimmerman, "France, 1944," in Seymour Freidin and William Richardson, eds., *The Fatal Decisions*. New York: Berkley Medallion, 1958, p. 207).

17   Smith, *Station X*, quoted p. 183.

18   OB West War Diary, August 16, 1944, in First Army Final Report, quoted p. 16.

19   Larry Collins and Dominique Lapierre, *Is Paris Burning?* New York: Pocket Books, 1965, quoted p. 49.

20   Irving, *Hitler's War*, quoted p. 677.

21   Speidel, *Invasion 1944*, p. 125.

22   Milton Shulman, *Defeat in the West*. New York: Ballantine Books, 1968, quoted pp. 202–03.

23   Speidel, *Invasion 1944*, pp. 130–31.

24   Zimmerman, "France 1944," p. 210.

25   Steven H. Newton, *Hitler's Commander: Field Marshal Walther Model—Hitler's Favorite General*. New York: Da Capo, 2006, p. 308.

26   Ibid., p. 309.

27   Hans Eberbach, "Panzer Group Eberbach," U.S. Army Combat Narrative A-922, trans. A. Rosenwald, in Isby, ed., *Fighting the Breakout*, pp. 192–93.

28   OKW War Communiqué, August 18, 1944, *New York Times*, August 19, 1944, p. 2.

29   Colby, *War from the Ground Up*, quoted p. 219.

30   Ibid.

31   Dominick Graham, *The Price of Command: A Biography of General Guy Simonds*. Toronto: Stoddart, 1993, p. 283.

32   Tucker-Jones, *Falaise*, quoted p. 168.

33   Ibid., quoted p. 166.

34   Hargreaves, *The Germans in Normandy*, quoted p. 210.

35   Stacey, *The Victory Campaign*, quoted p. 262.

36 Denis Whitaker and Shelagh Whitaker with Terry Copp, *Normandy: The Real Story; How Ordinary Allied Soldiers Defeated Hitler*. New York: Ballantine Books, 2004, quoted p. 276.
37 Hargreaves, *The Germans in Normandy*, quoted p. 209.
38 Whitaker and Whitaker, *Normandy: The Real Story*, quoted p. 294.
39 Tucker-Jones, *Falaise*, quoted p. 163.
40 Kenneth K. Koskodan, *No Greater Ally: The Untold Story of Poland's Forces in World War II*. London: Osprey, 2009, quoted p. 146.
41 J. F. C. Fuller, "The Perfect Pursuit: The Allied Opportunity in France," *Newsweek*, August 28, 1944, p. 26.
42 Drew Middleton, "Enemy Flees 'Kill' by Allies at Seine," *New York Times*, August 24, 1944, pp. 1, 4, quoted from p. 4.
43 Blumenson, *Breakout and Pursuit*, pp. 557–58.
44 Ellis et al., *Victory in the West*, p. 447.
45 Colby, *War from the Ground Up*, quoted p. 219.

7. NORMANDY CRUCIBLE

1 First Army War Diary, August 20, 1944, in Sylvan and Smith, Jr., *Normandy to Victory*, p. 102.
2 Letter, Charles de Gaulle–Dwight D. Eisenhower, August 21, 1944, in Charles de Gaulle, *War Memoirs: Unity, 1942–1944; Documents*, trans. Joyce Murchie and Hamish Erskine. London: Weidenfeld & Nicolson, 1959, p. 403.
3 Letter, Jacques Leclerc–Charles de Gaulle, August 21, 1944, in ibid., pp. 404–05.
4 First Army War Diary, August 22, 1944, in Sylvan and Smith, Jr., *Normandy to Victory*, p. 105.
5 Fuller, "The Perfect Pursuit," *Newsweek*, p. 26
6 George S. Patton Diary, August 21, 1944, in Blumenson, ed., *The Patton Papers*, p. 523.
7 Bradley with Blair, *A General's Life*, p. 305.
8 Bradley, *A Soldier's Story*, p. 392.
9 Patton Diary, August 23, 1944, in Blumenson, ed., *The Patton Papers*, p. 527.
10 21st Army Group Communiqué, August 21, 1944, "Text of His Message," *New York Times*, August 22, 1944, p. 5.

11 OKW Communiqué, August 21, 1944, *New York Times*, August 22, 1944, p. 2.

12 "Victory in the West: Patton's Made in America Blitz Traps the Germans at the Seine," *Newsweek*, August 28, 1944, p. 24.

13 Martin Blumenson, *The Battle of the Generals: The Untold Story of the Falaise Pocket—The Campaign that Should Have Won World War II.* New York: William Morrow, 1993, p. 21.

14 Hanson W. Baldwin, "Front Line Bombing: Question of Such Use of 'Heavies' Raised by Observer in Reaction to McNair's Death," *New York Times*, August 3, 1944, p. 3.

BIBLIOGRAPHY

OFFICIAL SOURCES

Army of the West: The Weekly Reports of German Army Group B from Normandy to the West Wall, ed. James A. Wood. Mechanicsburg, Penn.: Stackpole, 2007.

Charles de Gaulle, *War Memoirs: Unity, 1942–1944: Documents*, trans. Joyce Murchie and Hamish Erskine. London: Weidenfeld and Nicolson, 1959.

Helmut Heiber and David M. Glantz, eds., *Hitler and His Generals: Military Conferences, 1942–1945*, trans. Roland Winter, Krista Smith, and Mary Beth Friedrich. New York: Enigma Books, 2003.

Roger Hesketh, *Fortitude: The D-Day Deception Campaign*. Woodstock, N.Y.: Overlook, 2000.

David W. Hogan, Jr., *A Command Post at War: First Army Headquarters in Europe, 1943–1945*. Washington, D.C.: Center of Military History, 2000.

Kriegstagebuch des Oberkommandos der Wehrmacht, v. 4: January 1, 1944–May 22, 1945. Frankfurt: Bernard & Graefe Verlag, 1961.

Sonke Neitzel, ed., *Tapping Hitler's Generals: Transcripts of Secret Conversations, 1942–45*. St. Paul, Minn.: Frontline Books, 2007.

OKW Daily Communiqués (as recorded by United Press International).

C. P. Stacey, *The Victory Campaign: The Operations in Northwest Europe, 1944–1945* (Official History of the Canadian Army in the Second World War, vol. III). Ottawa: The Queen's Printer and Controller of Stationery, 1960.

Supreme Headquarters Allied Expeditionary Forces, Report by the Supreme Commander to the Combined Chiefs of Staff on the Operations in Europe of the Allied Expeditionary Force. London: Her Majesty's Stationery Office, 1946.

UNITED KINGDOM

L. F. Ellis et al., *Victory in the West, Vol. I: The Battle of Normandy* (History of the Second World War Series). London: Imperial War Museum, 1962.

F. H. Hinsley et al., *British Intelligence in the Second World War, Vol. III, Part 2: Its Influence on Strategy and Operations* (History of the Second World War Series). London: Her Majesty's Stationery Office, 1988.

Ministry of Defense, *Second World War 60th Anniversary, No. 4: The Drive on Caen, Northern France, 7 June–9 July 1944.* London: Her Majesty's Stationery Office, 2004.

UNITED STATES

Department of the Army Field Manual FM 101-10, *Staff Officer's Field Manual.* Department of the Army, August 1949.

Martin Blumenson, *Breakout and Pursuit* (United States Army in World War II: The European Theater of Operations Series). Washington, D.C.: Office of the Chief of Military History, 1961.

Gordon A. Harrison, *Cross-Channel Attack* (United States Army in World War II: The European Theater of Operations Series). Washington, D.C.: Office of the Chief of Military History, 1951.

Forrest C. Pogue, *The Supreme Command* (United States Army in World War II: The European Theater of Operations Series). Washington, D.C.: Office of the Chief of Military History, 1954.

Roland G. Ruppenthal, *Logistical Support of the Armies, Vol. I: May 1941–September 1944* (United States Army in World War II: The European Theater of Operations Series). Washington, D.C.: Office of the Chief of Military History, 1953; *Vol. II: September 1944–May 1945* (United States Army in World War II: The European Theater of Operations Series). Washington, D.C.: Office of the Chief of Military History, 1959.

Kent Roberts Greenfield, ed., *Command Decisions.* Washington, D.C.: Office of the Chief of Military History, 1960.

First U.S. Army, *Report of Operations, 20 October 1943–1 August 1944.* Department of the Army, c. 1945; *Report of Operations, 1 August 1944–22 February 1945.* Department of the Army, c. 1945.

19th Tactical Air Command, "Twelve Thousand Fighter-Bomber Sorties: XIX Tactical Air Command's First Month of Operations in Support of Third U.S. Army in France," Interim Summary Report, September 30, 1944.

Third U.S. Army, *Final Report, 1 August 1944–9 May 1945.* Department of the Army, c. 1945.

12th Army Group "Eagle," *Final After-Action Report.* Department of the Army, July 31, 1945.

National Security Agency, File SRH-006, "Synthesis of Experiences in the Use of ULTRA Intelligence by U.S. Army Field Commands in the European Theater of Operations," no date. National Archives: Record Group 457, file SRH-006.

HISTORIES AND MEMOIRS

Patrick Agte, *Michael Wittmann and the Waffen SS Tiger Commanders of the Leibstandarte in WWII, Vol. II.* Mechanicsburg, Penn.: Stackpole, 2006.

Robert S. Allen, *Lucky Forward: The History of General George Patton's Third U.S. Army.* New York: McFadden-Bartell, 1965.

Mary Kathryn Barbier, *D-Day Deception: Operation Fortitude and the Normandy Invasion.* Mechanicsburg, Penn.: Stackpole, 2009.

Nicolaus von Below, *At Hitler's Side: The Memoirs of Hitler's Luftwaffe Adjutant, 1937–1945,* trans. Geoffrey Brooks. London: Greenhill Books, 2001.

Ralph Bennett, *Behind the Battle: Intelligence in the War with Germany, 1939–1945.* London: Sinclair-Stevenson, 1994.

——. *Ultra in the West: The Normandy Campaign of 1944–45.* New York: Charles Scribner's Sons, 1979.

Edmund Blandford, *Two Sides of the Beach: The Invasion and Defense of Europe in 1944.* Edison, N.J.: Castle Books, 2001.

Martin Blumenson, *The Battle of the Generals: The Untold Story of the Falaise Pocket—The Campaign That Should Have Won World War II.* New York: William Morrow, 1993.

——. *The Duel for France, 1944.* New York: Da Capo Press, 2000.

——. *Heroes Never Die: Warriors and Warfare in World War II.* New York: Cooper Square Press, 2001.

Martin Blumenson, ed., *The Patton Papers, 1940–1945.* Boston: Houghton Mifflin, 1974.

Omar N. Bradley, *A Soldier's Story.* New York: Henry Holt, 1951.

Omar N. Bradley and Clay Blair, *A General's Life: An Autobiography by General of the Army Omar N. Bradley.* New York: Simon & Schuster, 1983.

Terry Brighton, *Patton, Montgomery, Rommel: Masters of War.* New York: Crown Publishers, 2008.

Dino Brugioni, *Eyes in the Sky: Eisenhower, the CIA, and Cold War Aerial Espionage*. Annapolis: Naval Institute Press, 2010.

Arthur Bryant, *Triumph in the West: A History of the War Years Based on the Diaries of Field-Marshal Lord Alanbrooke, Chief of the Imperial General Staff*. Garden City, N.Y.: Doubleday, 1959.

Harry C. Butcher, *My Three Years with Eisenhower: The Personal Diary of Captain Harry C. Butcher, USNR, Naval Aide to General Eisenhower, 1942 to 1945*. New York: Simon & Schuster, 1946.

Raymond Callahan, *Churchill and His Generals*. Lawrence: University Press of Kansas, 2007.

James J. Carafano, *After D-Day: Operation Cobra and the Normandy Breakout*. Mechanicsburg, Penn.: Stackpole, 2008.

Paul Carrell, *Invasion—They're Coming!* New York: Bantam Books, 1964.

William J. Casey, *The Secret War Against Hitler*. Washington: Regnery, 1988.

Winston S. Churchill, *The Second World War, Vol. 6: Triumph and Tragedy*. New York: Bantam Books, 1963.

Aileen Clayton, *The Enemy Is Listening*. New York: Ballantine Books, 1980.

Elbridge Colby, *The First Army in Europe, 1943–1945*. Nashville, Tenn.: Battery Press, 1969.

John Colby, *War From the Ground Up: The 90th Division in WWII*. Austin, Texas: Nortex Press, 1991.

David P. Colley, *The Road to Victory: The Untold Story of the Red Ball Express*. New York: Warner Books, 2000.

J. Lawton Collins, *Lightning Joe: An Autobiography*. Novato, Calif.: Presidio Press, 1994.

Larry Collins and Dominique Lapierre, *Is Paris Burning?* New York: Pocket Books, 1965.

Belton Y. Cooper, *Death Traps: The Survival of an American Armored Division in World War II*. New York: Ballantine Books, 2003.

Terry Copp, *The Brigade: The Fifth Canadian Infantry Brigade in WWII*. Mechanicsburg, Penn.: Stackpole, 2007.

——. *Cinderella Army: The Canadians in Northwest Europe, 1944–1945*. Toronto: University of Toronto Press, 2006.

——. *Fields of Fire: The Canadians in Normandy*. Toronto: University of Toronto Press, 2004.

Ian Daglish, *Battleground Europe: Normandy: Operation Bluecoat: British 3rd Infantry Division/27th Armored Brigade*. London: Leo Cooper, 2003.

——. *Battleground Europe: Normandy: Operation Goodwood*. Barnsley, U.K.: Pen & Sword, 2004.

Alex Danchev and Daniel Todman, eds., *War Diaries, 1939–1945: Field Marshal Lord Alanbrooke.* Berkeley: University of California Press, 2001.

Patrick Delaforce, *Churchill's Desert Rats: From Normandy to Berlin with the 7th Armored Division.* Gloucestershire, U.K.: Sutton, 2003.

———. *Monty's Highlanders: 51st Highland Division in the Second World War.* Barnsley, U.K.: Pen & Sword, 2007.

———. *Monty's Iron Sides: From the Normandy Beaches to Bremen with the 3rd [British] Division.* Stroud, U.K.: Sutton, 2002.

———. *Monty's Marauders.* London: Chancellor Press, 2000.

———. *Smashing the Atlantic Wall: The Destruction of Hitler's Coastal Fortresses.* London: Cassell, 2001.

———. *Taming the Panzers: Monty's Tank Battalions, 3rd RTR at War.* Stroud, U.K.: Sutton, 2003.

Carlo D'Este, *Decision in Normandy.* New York: E. P. Dutton, 1983.

———. *Eisenhower: A Soldier's Life.* New York: Henry Holt, 2002.

———. *Patton: A Genius for War.* New York: Harper Perennial, 1996.

Michael D. Doubler, *Closing with the Enemy: How GIs Fought the War in Europe, 1944–1945.* Lawrence: University Press of Kansas, 1994.

Dwight D. Eisenhower, *Crusade for Europe.* Garden City, N.Y.: Doubleday, 1948.

John A. English, *The Canadian Army and the Normandy Campaign.* Westport, Conn.: Greenwood Press, 1991.

Ladislas Farago, *Patton: Ordeal and Triumph.* New York: Dell Books, 1965.

Alwyn Featherston, *Battle for Mortain: The 30th Infantry Division Saves the Breakout, August 7–12, 1944.* Novato, Calif.: Presidio, 1993.

Will Fey, *Armor Battles of the Waffen SS, 1943–45,* trans. Henri Henschler. Mechanicsburg, Penn.: Stackpole, 2003.

Constantine FitzGibbon, *20 July.* New York: Berkley Medallion, 1968.

Eddy Florentin, *The Battle of the Falaise Gap,* trans. Mervyn Savill. New York: Hawthorne Books, 1967.

Ken Ford, *Falaise 1944: Death of an Army.* London: Osprey, 2005.

Don M. Fox, *Patton's Vanguard: The United States Army Fourth Armored Division.* Jefferson, N.C.: McFarland & Company, 2003.

Seymour Freidin and William Richardson, eds. *The Fatal Decisions,* trans. Constantine FitzGibbon. New York: Berkley Books, 1958.

From D-Day Through Victory in Europe: The Eye-Witness Story as Told by War Correspondents on the Air. New York: Columbia Broadcasting System, 1945.

Adolf Galland, *The First and the Last.* New York: Ballantine Books, 1965.

Paul Gannon, *Colossus: Bletchley Park's Greatest Secret.* London: Atlantic Books, 2007.

Henry G. Gole, *General William E. Depuy: Preparing the Army for Modern War*. Lexington: University Press of Kentucky, 2008.

Norman Gelb, *Ike and Monty: Generals at War*. New York: William Morrow, 1994.

Dominick Graham, *The Price of Command: A Biography of General Guy Simonds*. Toronto: Stoddart, 1993.

Philip Graves, *A Record of the War: The Twentieth Quarter, July 1, 1944–September 30, 1944*. London: Hutchison & Coy, no date (c. 1944).

Heinz Guderian, *Panzer Leader*, trans. Constantine FitzGibbon. New York: Ballantine Books, 1961.

Heinz Günther Guderian, *From Normandy to the Ruhr: With the 116th Panzer Division in World War II*, trans. Ulrich Abele, Esther Abele, and Keith E. Bonn. Bedford, Penn.: Aegis Press, 2001.

Nigel Hamilton, *Monty: Master of the Battlefield, 1942–1944*. London: Hamish Hamilton, 1983.

Richard Hargreaves, *The Germans in Normandy: Death Reaped a Terrible Harvest*. Barnsley, U.K.: Pen & Sword Press, 2006.

B. H. Liddell Hart, *The German Generals Talk*. New York: Berkley Books, 1958.

—— et al., eds., *The Rommel Papers*. New York: Harcourt Brace, 1953.

Russell A. Hart, *Clash of Arms: How the Allies Won in Normandy*. Norman: University of Oklahoma Press, 2001.

Stephen A. Hart, *Colossal Cracks: Montgomery's 21st Army Group in Northwest Europe, 1944–45*. Mechanicsburg, Penn.: Stackpole, 2007.

Guy Hartcup, *Codename Mulberry: The Planning, Building and Operation of the Normandy Harbours*. New York: Hippocrene, 1977.

Max Hastings, *Overlord: D-Day and the Battle for Normandy*. New York: Vintage, 2006.

Robert L. Hewitt, *Workhorse of the Western Front: The Story of the 30th Infantry Division*. Washington: Infantry Journal Press, 1946.

Stewart Hills, *By Tank into Normandy: A Memoir of the Campaign in North-West Europe from D-Day to VE Day*. London: Cassell, 2003.

F. H. Hinsley and Alan Stripp, *Codebreakers: The Inside Story of Bletchley Park*. Oxford: Oxford University Press, 1994.

Peter Hoffmann, *The History of the German Resistance, 1933–1945*, trans. Richard Barry. Cambridge, Mass.: MIT Press, 1977.

Alistair Horne with David Montgomery, *Monty: The Lonely Leader, 1944–1945*. New York: HarperCollins, 1994.

Sir Brian Horrocks with Eversley Belfield and H. Essame, *Corps Commander*. New York: Charles Scribner's Sons, 1977.

Donald E. Houston, *Hell on Wheels: The 2nd Armored Division*. Novato, Calif.: Presidio, 1977.

Thomas Alexander Hughes, *Overlord: General Pete Quesada and the Triumph of Tactical Air Power in World War II*. New York: Free Press, 1995.

David Irving, *Hitler's War*. New York: Avon Books, 1990.

———. *The Trail of the Fox: The Life of Field-Marshal Erwin Rommel*. London: Weidenfeld & Nicolson, 1977.

———. *The War Between the Generals*. New York: Penguin Books, 1982.

David C. Isby, ed., *Fighting the Breakout: The German Army in Normandy from "Cobra" to the Falaise Gap*. London: Greenhill Books, 2004.

John Keegan, *Six Armies in Normandy: From D-Day to the Liberation of Paris*. New York: Penguin Books, 1994.

Kenneth K. Koskodan, *No Greater Ally: The Untold Story of Poland's Forces in World War II*. Oxford: Osprey, 2009.

Franz Kurowski, *Panzer Aces*. New York: Ballantine Books, 2002.

Paul Latawski, *Battle Zone Normandy: Falaise Pocket*. Gloucestershire, U.K.: Sutton Publishing, 2004.

Ronald Lewin, *Montgomery as Military Commander*. Conshohocken, Penn.: Combined Publishing, 1998.

———. *ULTRA Goes to War: The First Account of World War II's Greatest Secret Based on Official Documents*. New York: McGraw-Hill, 1978.

Bernd Freytag von Loringhoven with Francois d'Alencon. *In the Bunker with Hitler: The Last Witness Speaks*. London: Phoenix Books, 2007.

James Lucas, *Das Reich: The Military Role of the 2nd SS Panzer Division*. London: Arms & Armor Press, 1991.

——— and James Barker, *The Killing Ground: The Battle of the Falaise Gap, August 1944*. London: Book Club Associates, 1978.

Hans von Luck, *Panzer Commander: The Memoirs of Colonel Hans von Luck*. New York: Dell Books, 1991.

Geoffrey P. McGargee, *Inside Hitler's High Command*. Lawrence: University Press of Kansas, 2000.

Alexander McKee, *Caen: Anvil of Victory*. New York: Dorset Press, 2001.

John C. McManus, *The Americans at Normandy: The Summer of 1944—The American War from the Normandy Beaches to Falaise*. New York: Tom Doherty Associates, 2004.

Peter Mansoor, *The GI Offensive in Europe: The Triumph of American Infantry Divisions, 1941–1945*. Lawrence: University of Kansas Press, 1999.

Gregory L. Mattson, *SS Das Reich: The History of the 2nd SS Panzer Division, 1941–45*. St. Paul, Minn.: MBI Publishing Company, 2002.

Richard Mead, *Churchill's Lions: A Biographical Guide to the Key British Generals of World War II*. Stroud, U.K.: Spellmount Limited, 2007.

Robert E. Merriam, *The Battle of the Bulge*. New York: Ballantine Books, 1989.

Hubert Meyer, *The 12th SS: The History of the Hitler Youth Panzer Division* (two volumes). Mechanicsburg, Penn.: Stackpole, 2005.

Kurt Meyer, *Grenadiers: The Story of Waffen SS General Kurt "Panzer" Meyer.* Mechanicsburg, Penn.: Stackpole, 2005.

Robert A. Miller, *August 1944: The Campaign for France.* Novato, Calif.: Presidio Press, 1996.

Samuel W. Mitcham, Jr., *Defenders of Fortress Europe: The Untold Story of the German Officers During the Allied Invasion.* Washington, D.C.: Potomac Books, 2009.

———. *Panzer Commanders of the Western Front: German Tank Generals of World War II.* Mechanicsburg, Penn.: Stackpole, 2008.

———. *Panzers in Normandy: General Hans Eberbach and the German Defense of France, 1944.* Mechanicsburg, Penn.: Stackpole, 2009.

———. *Retreat to the Reich: The German Defeat in France, 1944.* Mechanicsburg, Penn.: Stackpole, 2007.

———. *Rommel's Last Battle: The Desert Fox and the Normandy Campaign.* New York: Stein & Day, 1983.

Bernard L. Montgomery (Viscount Montgomery of Alamein), *The Memoirs of Field Marshal Montgomery.* New York: New American Library, 1958.

———. *Normandy to the Baltic.* Boston: Houghton Mifflin, 1948.

Lord Moran, *Churchill at War, 1940–1945.* New York: Carroll & Graf, 2002.

Robin Neillands, *The Battle of Normandy, 1944.* London: Cassell, 2003.

Newsweek

Steven H. Newton, *Hitler's Commander: Field Marshal Walter Model—Hitler's Favorite General.* New York: Da Capo Press, 2006.

New York Herald-Tribune

New York Times

Ninetieth (U.S.) Infantry Division, *A History of the 90th Division in World War II, 6 June 1944 to 9 May 1945.* Nashville, Tenn.: Battery Press Reprint, 1999.

George S. Patton, Jr., *War as I Knew It.* New York: Bantam Books, 1980.

Geoffrey Perret, *There's a War to Be Won: The United States Army in World War II.* New York: Random House, 1991.

Mark Perry, *Partners in Command: George Marshall and Dwight Eisenhower in War and Peace.* New York: Penguin Press, 2007.

John Pimlott, ed., *Rommel in His Own Words.* London: Greenhill, 1994.

Forrest C. Pogue, ed., *The Papers of George Catlett Marshall, Vol. IV: Aggressive and Determined Leadership, January 1, 1943–December 31, 1944.* Baltimore: Johns Hopkins University Press, 1996.

Christopher Pugsley, *Battle Zone Normandy: Operation Cobra*. Gloucester-shire, U.K.: Sutton, 2004.

Ernie Pyle, *Brave Men*. Lincoln: University of Nebraska Press, 2001.

Andrew Rawson, *Battleground Europe: Normandy: Cherbourg*. Barnsley, U.K.: Pen & Sword Press, 2004.

Mark J. Reardon, *Victory at Mortain: Stopping Hitler's Panzer Counteroffensive*. Lawrence: University of Kansas Press, 2002.

Brian A. Reid, *No Holding Back: Operation Totalize, Normandy, August 1944*. Mechanicsburg, Penn.: Stackpole, 2009.

Michael Reynolds, *Steel Inferno: 1st SS Panzer Corps in Normandy*. New York: Dell Books, 1998.

Tim Ripley, *Patton Unleashed: Patton's Third Army and the Breakout from Nor-mandy, August–September 1944*. St. Paul, Minn.: MBI Publishing, 2003.

Helmut Ritgen, *The Western Front 1944: Memoirs of a Panzer Lehr Officer*, trans. Joseph Welsh. Winnipeg: J. J. Federowicz, 1995.

Richard Rohmer, *Patton's Gap: Mustangs Over Normandy*, 2nd ed. Toronto: Stoddart Publishing, 1998.

Ralf Georg Reuth, *Rommel: The End of a Legend*, trans. Debra S. Marmor and Herbert A. Danner. London: Haus Books, 2005.

Friedrich Ruge, *Rommel in Normandy: Reminiscences*. San Rafael, Calif.: Pre-sidio, 1979.

Kenn C. Rust et al., *The 9th Air Force in World War II*. Fallbrook, Calif.: Aero Books, 1970.

Cornelius Ryan, *A Bridge Too Far*. New York: Popular Library, 1974.

Tim Saunders, *Normandy: Hill 112; Battles of the Odon—1944* (Battleground Europe Series). Barnsley, U.K.: Leo Cooper, 2001.

———. *Battleground Europe: Normandy Operation Epsom: VIII British Corps v 1st SS Panzerkorps*. Barnsley, U.K.: Leo Cooper, 2003.

Franz W. Seidler and Dieter Zeigert, *Hitler's Secret Headquarters: The Führer's Wartime Bases from the Invasion of France to the Berlin Bunker*, trans. Geof-frey Brooks. London: Greenhill Press, 2004.

Milton Shulman, *Defeat in the West*. New York: Ballantine Books, 1968.

Michael Smith, *Station X: The Codebreakers of Bletchley Park*. London: Pan Books, 2004.

Steven Smith, *2nd Armored Division, "Hell on Wheels."* No place [USA]: Com-pendium Publishing for The Military Books Club, 2003.

P. A. Spayd, *Bayerlein: From Afrikakorps to Panzer Lehr*. Altglen, Penn.: Schiffer, 2003.

Hans Speidel, *Invasion 1944*, trans. Theo R. Crevenna. New York: Popular Library, 1968.

Frederick P. Stenhardt, ed. and trans., *Hellion WWII German Military Studies, Vol. I: Panzer Lehr Division, 1944–1945.* Solihull, U.K.: Hellion Books, 2008.

William C. Sylvan and Francis G. Smith, Jr., *Normandy to Victory: The War Diary of General Courtney H. Hodges and the First U.S. Army,* ed. John T. Greenwood. Lexington: University Press of Kentucky, 2008.

Third (U.S.) Armored Division, *Spearhead in the West: The Third Armored Division, 1941–45.* Nashville, Tenn.: Battery Press Reprint, 1980.

R. W. Thompson, *Montgomery, The Field Marshal: The Campaign in Northwest Europe, 1944–1945.* New York: Charles Scribner's Sons, 1969.

Time magazine

H. R. Trevor-Roper, ed., *Hitler's War Directives, 1939–1945.* London: Pan Books, 1964.

Simon Trew and Stephen Badsey, *Battle Zone Normandy: Battle for Caen.* Gloucestershire, U.K.: Sutton, 2004.

Anthony Tucker-Jones, *Falaise: The Flawed Victory; The Destruction of Panzergruppe West, August 1944.* Barnsley, U.K.: Pen & Sword, 2008.

Walter Warlimont, *Inside Hitler's Headquarters, 1939–1945.* New York: Praeger, 1964.

Russell F. Weigley, *Eisenhower's Lieutenants: The Campaign for France and Germany, 1944–1945.* Bloomington: Indiana University Press, 1981.

James S. Wheeler, *The Big Red One: America's Legendary 1st Infantry Division from World War I to Desert Storm.* Lawrence: University Press of Kansas, 2007.

Denis Whitaker and Shelagh Whitaker with Terry Copp, *Normandy: The Real Story.* New York: Ballantine Books, 2004.

Charles Whiting, *Bradley.* New York: Ballantine Books, 1971.

———. *Patton.* New York: Ballantine Books, 1970.

Olivier Wieviorka, *Normandy: The Landings to the Liberation of Paris,* trans. M. B. DeBevoise. Cambridge, Mass.: Harvard University Press, 2008.

Chester Wilmot, *The Struggle for Europe.* New York: Harper Colophon, 1963.

Alan F. Wilt, *The Atlantic Wall, 1941–1944: Hitler's Defenses for D-Day.* New York: Enigma Books, 2004.

Peter Yates, *Battle Zone Normandy: Battle for St-Lô.* Gloucestershire, U.K.: Sutton, 2004.

Steven J. Zaloga, *US Armored Divisions: The European Theater of Operations, 1944–45.* London: Osprey, 2004.

Niklas Zetterling, *Normandy 1944: German Military Organization, Combat Power and Organizational Effectiveness.* Winnipeg: J. J. Fedorowicz, 2000.

ARTICLES

Alexander S. Cochran, Jr., "Protecting the Ultimate Advantage," *Military History* (June 1985).

David P. Colley, "On the Road to Victory: The Red Ball Express," *World War II* (March 1997).

A. Harding Ganz, "Questionable Objective: The Brittany Ports, 1944," *Journal of Military History* 59, no. 1 (Spring 1995).

William I. Hitchcock, "The Price of Liberation," *MHQ: The Quarterly Journal of Military History* 21, no. 3 (Spring 2009).

Paul Johnston, "D+20,000: Still Fighting the Normandy Campaign," *Army Doctrine and Training Bulletin* (Canadian Ministry of Defense) 3, no. 1 (Spring 2000).

David Kahn, "German Comint Organization in World War II," *NSA Cryptologic Spectrum* 8, no. 2 (Spring 1978).

Marc Milner, "Stopping the Panzers: Reassessing the Role of the 3rd Canadian Infantry Division in Normandy, 7–10 June 1944," *Journal of Military History* 74, no. 2 (June 2010).

John Prados, "COBRA: Patton's 1944 Summer Offensive in France," *Strategy & Tactics* 65 (November–December 1977).

Michael Reynolds, "The Poles in the West," *World War II History* (May 2008).

Edward A. Shils and Morris Janowitz, "Cohesion and Disintegration in the Wehrmacht in World War II," *Public Opinion Quarterly* (Summer 1948).

INDEX